STUDY GUIDE TO ACCOMPANY

Introduction to Psychology
EXPLORATION AND APPLICATION

EIGHTH EDITION

Dennis Coon

Brooks/Cole Publishing Company

I(T)P® *An International Thomson Publishing Company*

Pacific Grove • Albany • Belmont • Bonn • Boston • Cincinnati • Detroit • Johannesburg • London
Madrid • Melbourne • Mexico City • New York • Paris • Singapore • Tokyo • Toronto • Washington

Sponsoring Editor: Faith B. Stoddard
Editorial Assistant: Stephanie M. Andersen
Production: Dorothy Bell

Cover Design: Laurie Albrecht
Cover Illustration: Jim Alford
Printing and Binding: Patterson Printing

For more information, contact:

BROOKS/COLE PUBLISHING COMPANY
511 Forest Lodge Road
Pacific Grove, CA 93950
USA

International Thomson Publishing Europe
Berkshire House 168-173
High Holborn
London WC1V 7AA
England

Thomas Nelson Australia
102 Dodds Street
South Melbourne, 3205
Victoria, Australia

Nelson Canada
1120 Birchmount Road
Scarborough, Ontario
Canada M1K 5G4

International Thomson Editores
Seneca 53
Col. Polanco
11560 México, D. F., México

International Thomson Publishing GmbH
Königswinterer Strasse 418
53227 Bonn
Germany

International Thomson Publishing Asia
221 Henderson Road
#05-10 Henderson Building
Singapore 0315

International Thomson Publishing Japan
Hirakawacho Kyowa Building, 3F
2-2-1 Hirakawacho
Chiyoda-ku, Tokyo 102
Japan

Printed in the United States of America

10   9   8   7   6   5   4   3   2   1

ISBN 0-534-35402-5

CONTENTS

Introduction

How to Use this Study Guide

This *Study Guide* for *Introduction to Psychology: Exploration and Application* is designed to help you learn more, study efficiently, and get better grades. The exercises in this guide are closely coordinated with text chapters so that you can practice and review what you have read.

Each *Study Guide* chapter contains the following sections:

- **Chapter Overview**
- **Recite and Review**
- **Relate**
- **Check Your Memory**
- **Final Survey and Review**
- **Mastery Test**
- **Answers**

A brief description of each section follows, along with suggestions for using them.

Chapter Overview

The Chapter Overview is a highly focused summary of major ideas in the text. By boiling chapters down to their essence, the Chapter Overview will give you a framework to build on as you learn additional ideas, concepts, and facts. Before you work on any other sections of this guide, read the Chapter Overview. In fact, it would be a good idea to re-read the Chapter Overview each time you use the *Study Guide*.

Recite and Review

After you have read a chapter in the textbook, this section will give you a chance to review major terms and concepts. Recite and Review is organized with the same Survey Questions found in the textbook chapters. This exercise will help you actively process information from the textbook so that it becomes more meaningful. Recite and Review also gives you a chance to practice recalling ideas from your reading, after you've closed the book.

As you work through Recite and Review, don't worry if you can't fill in all of the blanks. All of the answers are listed at the end of each *Study Guide* chapter. Filling in missing terms with the help of the answer key will focus your attention on gaps in your knowledge. That way, you can add new information to what you *were* able to remember. Page numbers are provided for each section of Recite and Review so that you can return to the text to clarify any points that you missed.

Relate

This section contains matching-type items. It will help you build associations between related terms, facts, concepts, and ideas. Where appropriate, art is reproduced from the text so that you can match to images, rather than to words. This is a good way to add links to your memory networks. Again, answers are listed at the end of the chapter.

Check Your Memory

The true-false statements in Check Your Memory highlight facts and details that you may have overlooked when you read the text. It's easy to fool yourself about how much you are remembering as you read. If you answered wrong for any of the items in Check Your Memory, you should return to the textbook to find out why. Page numbers listed for each group of items will make it easy for you to locate the relevant information in the textbook.

Final Survey and Review

This exercise might seem like a repeat of the Recite and Review section, but it's not. This time, you must supply a different set of more difficult terms and concepts to complete the review. The Final Survey and Review challenges you to consolidate your earlier learning and to master key concepts from the text. The Final Survey and Review is not a test. Don't be upset if you can't fill in some of the blanks. But do give missing ideas extra attention when you check your answers. Indeed, try to learn more each time you complete a *Study Guide* exercise, check your answers, or return to the text for review and clarification.

Mastery Test

The multiple-choice items of the Mastery Test are at least as difficult as those found on typical in-class tests. If you do well on the Mastery Test, you can be confident that you are prepared for in-class tests. On the other hand, a low score is a clear signal that further study and review are needed. However, don't expect to always get perfect scores on the Mastery Tests. In some cases the questions cover information that was not reviewed in any of the preceding *Study Guide* sections. The Mastery Tests are designed to continue the learning process, as well as to give you feedback about your progress.

Answers

Answers for all of the preceding exercises are listed at the end of each *Study Guide* chapter. Answers for the Mastery Test include page numbers so you can locate the source of the question in the textbook.

A FIVE-DAY STUDY PLAN

There is no single "best" way to use this guide. Getting the most out of the *Study Guide* depends greatly on your personal learning style and study habits. Nevertheless, as a starting point, you might want to give the following plan a try.

Days 1 and 2 Read the assigned chapter in the textbook. As you do, be sure to make use of the Learning Checks and all of the steps of the SQ3R method described on pages 21 and 22 of the textbook.

Day 3 Review the textbook chapter and any notes you made as you read it. Read the Chapter Overview in the *Study Guide* and do the Recite and Review section.

Day 4 Read the margin definitions in the textbook and the Chapter Overview in the *Study Guide*. Do the Relate and Check Your Memory sections of the *Study Guide*. Return to the textbook and make sure you understand why any items you missed were wrong.

Day 5 Review the textbook chapter and any notes you made as you read it. Read the Chapter Overview in the *Study Guide*. Then do the Final Survey and Review section, and check your answers. Return to the textbook and clarify any items you missed. Now take the Mastery Test. If you miss any questions, review appropriate sections of the textbook again.

Summary

The close ties between *Introduction to Psychology* and the *Study Guide* make it possible for the *Study Guide* to be used in a variety of ways. You may prefer to turn to the *Study Guide* for practice and review after you have completed a reading assignment, as suggested in the Five-Day Plan. Or, you might find it more helpful treat the *Study Guide* as a reading companion. In that case, you would complete appropriate *Study Guide* sections from each type of exercise as you progress through the text. In any event, it is nearly certain that if you use the *Study Guide* conscientiously, you will retain more, learn more efficiently, and perform better on tests. Good luck.

Chapter 1

Psychology: The Search for Understanding

CHAPTER OVERVIEW

Psychology is the science of human and animal behavior. Psychology's goals are to describe, understand, predict, and control behavior. Psychologists seek to answer questions about behavior by applying the scientific method and gathering empirical evidence.

Psychology developed from philosophy. The first psychological laboratory was established by Wilhelm Wundt, who studied conscious experience. The first school of thought in psychology was structuralism, a kind of "mental chemistry." Structuralism was followed by the rise of functionalism, behaviorism, Gestalt psychology, psychoanalytic psychology, and humanistic psychology. Five main streams of thought in modern psychology are behaviorism, humanism, the psychodynamic approach, biopsychology, and cognitive psychology.

The training of psychologists differs from that of psychiatrists, psychoanalysts, counselors, and social workers. Clinical and counseling psychologists specialize in doing psychotherapy. Other representative specialties are industrial-organizational, educational, consumer, school, developmental, engineering, medical, environmental, forensic, psychometric, and experimental psychology. Some common research specialties are comparative, learning, sensation, perception, personality, biopsychology, motivation and emotion, social, cognitive, developmental, and cultural psychology.

Critical thinking can be used to evaluate claims made about human behavior, especially the false claims often found in pop psychology. A key element of critical thinking is an ability to weigh the evidence bearing on a claim and to evaluate the quality of that evidence. Belief in various pseudo-psychologies is based in part on uncritical acceptance, the fallacy of positive instances, and the Barnum effect.

RECITE AND REVIEW

● *What is psychology?*

Recite and Review: Pages 1-4

1. Psychology is both a science and a _____.

2. Psychology is defined as the scientific study of _____.
3. Psychologists study overt and covert _____.
4. Psychologists seek empirical _____ based on scientific observation.
5. Scientific observation is _____ and systematic.
6. Answering psychological questions requires a valid, practical, and ethical research _____.
7. Other species are used as _____ models in psychological research to discover principles that apply to human behavior.

● *What do psychologists hope to achieve?*

Recite and Review: Pages 4-7

8. Developmental psychologists study the course of human _____.
9. Learning theorists study how and why _____ occurs.
10. Personality _____ study personality traits and dynamics.
11. Sensation and perception psychologists study the _____ organs and perception.
12. Comparative psychologists study different species, especially _____.
13. Biopsychologists study the connection between biological processes and _____.
14. Gender psychologists study _____ differences.
15. Social psychologists study _____ behavior.
16. Cultural psychologists study the ways that culture affects _____.
17. Psychology's goals are to describe, _____, predict, and control behavior.

● *How did psychology emerge as a field of knowledge?*

Recite and Review: Pages 8-14

18. Historically, psychology is an outgrowth of philosophy, the study of _____, reality, and human nature.
19. The first psychological _____ was established in Germany by Wilhelm Wundt.
20. Wundt tried to apply scientific methods to the study of conscious _____ .
21. The first school of thought in psychology was structuralism, a kind of "_____" chemistry.
22. Wundt and the structuralists used a combination of introspection and _____ measurement.
23. Functionalism was concerned with how the mind helps us _____ to our environments.
24. Functionalism promoted the growth of _____ and industrial-organizational psychology.
25. Behaviorism was launched by John B. _____.
26. Behaviorists objectively study the relationship between stimuli and _____.
27. The modern behaviorist B. F. Skinner believed that most behavior is controlled by _____ reinforcers.
28. Cognitive behaviorism combines _____, reinforcement, and environmental influences to explain behavior.
29. Gestalt psychology emphasizes the study of _____ units, not pieces.
30. According to the Gestalt view, in psychology the whole is often _____ than the sum of its parts.
31. The psychodynamic approach emphasizes the _____ origins of behavior.
32. Psychoanalytic psychology, developed by Austrian physician Sigmund _____, is an early psychodynamic approach.

33. Humanistic psychology emphasizes free will, subjective experience, human potentials, and personal _____.

34. Psychologically, humanists believe that self-_____ and self-evaluation are important elements of personal adjustment.

● *What are the major perspectives in psychology?*

Recite and Review: Pages 14-16

35. Five main streams of thought in modern psychology are behaviorism, _____, the psychodynamic approach, biopsychology, and cognitive psychology.
36. Computer models of _____ have been important to cognitive psychology.
37. Much of contemporary psychology is an eclectic _____ of the best features of various viewpoints.
38. To fully understand behavior, psychologists must be aware of human _____ as well as human universals.

● *What roles and specialties are found in psychology and related fields?*

Recite and Review: Pages 17-20

39. Psychologists who treat emotional problems specialize in _____ or counseling psychology.
40. Psychiatrists typically use both _____ and psychotherapy to treat emotional problems.
41. Freudian _____ is a specific type of psychotherapy.
42. Both counselors and psychiatric social workers have _____ degrees.
43. Some major _____ in psychology are clinical, counseling, industrial-organizational, educational, consumer, school, developmental, engineering, medical, environmental, forensic, psychometric, and experimental psychology.
44. Scientific research in psychology may be either _____ or applied.
45. Some research specialties in _____ psychology are comparative, learning, sensation, perception, personality, biopsychology, motivation and emotion, social, and cognitive psychology.

● *What is critical thinking?*

Recite and Review: APPLICATIONS

46. Critical thinking is the ability to _____, compare, analyze, critique, and synthesize information.
47. In psychology, _____ thinking skills help evaluate claims about human behavior.
48. Critical thinking involves evaluating the _____ of the evidence used to support various claims.
49. Scientific observations usually provide the highest quality _____ about various claims.

● *How does psychology differ from false explanations of behavior?*

Recite and Review: EXPLORATION

50. Palmistry, phrenology, graphology, and astrology are _____ systems or pseudo-psychologies.

51. Belief in pseudo-psychologies is encouraged by uncritical acceptance, the fallacy of positive instances, and the _____ effect, named after a famous showman who had "something for everyone."

RELATE

1. _____	biopsychology	a. hidden from view
2. _____	psychology	b. brain waves
3. _____	personality theorist	c. systematic observation
4. _____	empirical evidence	d. animal behavior
5. _____	covert behavior	e. detailed record
6. _____	scientific observation	f. human and animal behavior
7. _____	EEG	g. "why" questions
8. _____	comparative psychology	h. brain and behavior
9. _____	description	i. direct observation
10. _____	understanding	j. traits, dynamics, individual differences

11. _____	psychometrics	a. father of psychology
12. _____	control	b. natural selection
13. _____	Wundt	c. behaviorism
14. _____	Titchener	d. mental measurement
15. _____	James	e. functionalism
16. _____	Darwin	f. conditioned responses
17. _____	Skinner	g. Gestalt
18. _____	Pavlov	h. color vision
19. _____	Wertheimer	i. introspection
20. _____	Ladd-Franklin	j. influencing behavior

21. _____	Freud	a. self-actualization
22. _____	Adler	b. environmental forces
23. _____	Maslow	c. self-image
24. _____	psychodynamic view	d. psychoanalysis
25. _____	behavioristic view	e. information processing
26. _____	humanistic view	f. Ph.D., Psy.D., Ed.D.
27. _____	biopsychology	g. M.D.
28. _____	cognitive view	h. internal forces
29. _____	psychologist	i. physiological processes
30. _____	psychiatrist	j. neo-Freudian

CHECK YOUR MEMORY

Check Your Memory: Pages 1-4

1. Psychologists may be scientists or practitioners, but they are rarely both. T or F?
2. Psychology can be defined as the scientific study of human behavior. T or F?
3. Although it is a covert activity, dreaming is a behavior. T or F?
4. It is more difficult to compare mental images that are similar in size. T or F?
5. The term *empirical evidence* refers to the opinion of an acknowledged authority. T or F?
6. When hypnotized, witnesses to crimes can be made to have perfect memories of what they saw. T or F?
7. Psychology applies the scientific method to questions about behavior. T or F?
8. The term *data* refers to a systematic procedure for answering scientific questions. T or F?
9. Developmental psychologists study how and why learning occurs in humans and animals. T or F?
10. In psychology there is often no substitute for ethically done animal research. T or F?
11. Naming and classifying are the heart of psychology's second goal, understanding behavior. T or F?
12. The field of psychometrics is especially concerned with predicting behavior. T or F?

Check Your Memory: Pages 4-7

13. In 1879, Wundt established a lab to study the philosophy of behavior. T or F?
14. Wundt called his approach experimental self-observation. T or F?
15. Wundt's method replaced introspection with objective measurement. T or F?
16. Edward Titchener is best known for promoting functionalism in America. T or F?
17. The functionalists were influenced by the ideas of Charles Darwin. T or F?
18. Behaviorists define psychology as the study of conscious experience. T or F?
19. Watson used Pavlov's concept of conditioned responses to explain most behavior. T or F?
20. The "Skinner Box" is used primarily to study learning in animals. T or F?
21. Skinner emphasized the use of punishment to encourage desired behavior. T or F?
22. In behavior modification, Gestalt principles are used to change human behavior. T or F?
23. Max Wertheimer urged psychologists to analyze experiences into their basic building blocks. T or F?
24. Margaret Washburn was the first woman in America to be awarded a Ph.D. T or F?
25. Mary Calkins did early research on memory. T or F?
26. According to Freud, repressed thoughts are actively held out of awareness, in the unconscious. T or F?
27. All of the following are regarded as neo-Freudians, Alfred Adler, Karen Horney, Carl Rogers, and Carl Jung. T or F?
28. Humanists generally reject the determinism of behavioristic and psychodynamic approaches. T or F?
29. Maslow characterized self-actualization as the process of fully developing one's potentials. T or F?

Check Your Memory: Pages 8-14

30. The five major perspectives in psychology today are behaviorism, humanism, functionalism, biopsychology, and cognitive psychology. T of F?
31. Humanism offers a positive, philosophical view of human nature. T or F?
32. The cognitive view explains behavior in terms of information processing. T or F?
33. To understand behavior, psychologists must be aware of how people differ, as well as how we are all alike. T or F?

Check Your Memory: Pages 14-16

34. Most psychologists work in private practice. T or F?
35. The differences between clinical and counseling psychology are beginning to fade. T or F?
36. To enter the profession of psychology today you would need to earn a doctorate degree. T or F?
37. The Psy.D. degree emphasizes scientific research skills. T or F?
38. Psychiatrists are medical doctors who do psychotherapy but cannot prescribe drugs. T or F?
39. Developmental psychologists study the ways in which organizations change and develop over time. T or F?
40. Forensic psychologists are interested in crime and crime prevention. T or F?
41. In order to become a psychoanalyst, a person must first be trained as a psychiatrist. T or F?
42. More than half of all psychologists specialize in clinical or counseling psychology. T or F?
43. Clinical psychologists must be licensed to practice legally. T or F?
44. Over 40 percent of all psychologists are employed by the military. T or F?
45. Studying ways to improve the memories of eyewitnesses to crimes would be an example of applied research. T or F?
46. Comparative psychologists study people in group settings. T or F?
47. Forensic psychologists study problems of crime and crime prevention. T or F?

Check Your Memory: APPLICATIONS

48. Critical thinking is the ability to make good use of intuition and mental imagery. T or F?
49. Critical thinkers actively evaluate claims, ideas, and propositions. T or F?
50. A key element of critical thinking is evaluating the quality of evidence related to a claim. T of F?
51. Both open-mindedness and skepticism are elements of critical thinking. T or F?
52. Critical thinkers recognize that the opinions of experts and authorities should be respected without question. T or F?
53. Stating claims clearly is a valuable first step in critical thinking. T or F?
54. In general, anecdotal evidence provides the best basis for evaluating claims. T or F?
55. Unless you can make observations yourself, a claim cannot be evaluated because published evidence is unreliable. T or F?

Check Your Memory: EXPLORATION

56. Pseudo-scientists test their concepts by gathering data. T or F?
57. Phrenologists believe that lines on the hands reveal personality traits. T or F?
58. Graphology is only valid if a large enough sample of handwriting is analyzed. T or F?
59. The zodiac has shifted by one full constellation since astrology was first set up. T or F?
60. Astrological charts consisting of positive traits tend to be perceived as "accurate" or true, even if they are not. T or F?
61. The Barnum effect refers to our tendency to remember things that confirm our expectations. T or F?

FINAL SURVEY AND REVIEW

● *What is psychology?*

1. Psychology is both a _____ and a _____.

2. Psychology is defined as the scientific study of _____ and _____
_____.

3. Psychologists study both _____ and overt behavior.

4. Psychologists seek _____ evidence based on scientific observation. They settle disputes by collecting _____.

5. _____ observation is structured and systematic.

6. Answering psychological questions requires a valid, practical, and ethical _____
_____.

7. An animal _____ may be used to discover principles that apply to _____ behavior.

● *What do psychologists hope to achieve?*

8. _____ psychologists study the course of human development.

9. Learning _____ study how and why learning occurs.

10. _____ theorists study personality traits and dynamics.

11. _____ and perception psychologists study the sense organs and perception.

12. _____ psychologists study different species, especially animals.

13. _____ study biological processes and behavior.

14. _____ psychologists study male-female differences.

15. Social psychologists study _____ _____.

16. _____ psychologists study the ways that culture affects behavior.

17. Psychology's goals are to describe, understand, _____ and _____ behavior.

● *How did psychology emerge as a field of knowledge?*

18. Historically, psychology is an outgrowth of _____.

19. The first psychological laboratory was established in Germany by _____
_____.

20. His goal was to apply scientific methods to the study of _____
_____.

21. _____ self-observation combined trained _____ with objective measurement.

22. The first school of thought in psychology was _____, a kind of "mental chemistry."

23. _____ was concerned with how the mind helps us adapt to our environments. William _____ was one of its proponents.

24. Charles Darwin's concept of _____ _____ greatly influenced the functionalists.

25. Functionalism promoted the growth of _____ and _____ psychology.

26. _____ was launched by John B. Watson, who wanted to study the relationship between _____ and responses.

27. Watson used Ivan _____ concept of _____ responses to explain most behavior.

28. The modern behaviorist B. F. _____ believed that most behavior is controlled by positive _____.

29. _____ behaviorism combines thinking and environmental influences to explain behavior.

30. _____ psychology emphasizes the study of whole experiences, not elements or pieces.

31. According to Max _____, in psychology the whole is often greater than the _____ of its _____.

32. Three prominent early psychologists are _____ Ladd-Franklin, Margaret _____, and Mary _____.

33. The _____ approach emphasizes the unconscious origins of behavior.

34. The Austrian physician, Sigmund _____, developed a psychodynamic system called _____.

35. _____ psychology emphasizes free will, subjective experience, human _____, and personal growth.

36. Psychologically, humanists believe that _____, self-evaluation, and one's _____ of reference are important elements of personal adjustment.

37. Two prominent humanistic psychologists were Carl _____ and Abraham _____.

● *What are the major perspectives in psychology?*

38. Five main streams of thought in modern psychology are _____, _____, the psychodynamic approach, _____, and cognitive psychology.

39. _____ means "thinking"; _____ models of thinking and problem solving have been important to cognitive psychology.

40. Much of contemporary psychology is an _____ blend of the best features of various viewpoints.

41. To fully understand behavior, psychologists must be aware of human _____, as reflected in personal and _____ differences.

● *What roles and specialties are found in psychology and related fields?*

42. Psychologists who treat emotional problems specialize in _____ or _____ psychology.

43. Most clinicians follow a scientist-_____ model.

44. _____ are medical doctors who typically use both drugs and _____ to treat emotional problems.

45. Both psychiatrists and _____ may learn to do Freudian _____.

46. Both counselors and _____ _____ workers have master's degrees.

47. _____ psychologists specialize in the growth of children; _____ psychologists help design machinery; _____ psychologists study classroom dynamics.

48. Scientific research in psychology may be either basic or _____.

49. _____ psychologists do research in areas such as learning, sensation, perception, motivation, social, or cognitive psychology.

● *What is critical thinking?*

50. Critical thinking is the ability to evaluate, compare, analyze, _____, and _____ information.

51. In psychology, critical thinking skills help _____ claims about human behavior.

52. Critical thinking involves evaluating the quality of the _____ used to support various claims.

53. _____ observations usually provide the highest quality evidence about various claims.

● *How does psychology differ from false explanations of behavior?*

54. Palmistry, _____, graphology, and astrology are _____-psychologies.

55. Belief in false psychologies is encouraged by _____ acceptance, the fallacy of _____ instances, and the _____ effect.

MASTERY TEST

1. Data in psychology are typically gathered to answer questions about
   a. clinical problems   b. human groups   c. human cognition   d. overt or covert behavior

2. Dreaming, problem solving, and remembering are
   a. overt behaviors   b. empirical responses   c. covert behaviors   d. the focus of comparative psychology

3. To be scientific, observations must be
   a. carefully planned and recorded   b. anecdotal   c. made by a trained practitioner
   d. based on objective introspection

4. Which of the following types of psychologists would most likely be a practitioner?
   a. clinical   b. functional   c. gender   d. social

5. Who among the following would most likely study the behavior of gorillas?
   a. developmental psychologist   b. comparative psychologist   c. environmental psychologist
   d. forensic psychologist

6. An engineering psychologist helps redesign an airplane to make it safer to fly. The psychologist's work reflects which of psychology's goals?
   a. understanding   b. control   c. prediction   d. description

7. Who developed the method of experimental self-observation?
   a. Watson   b. Wertheimer   c. Washburn   d. Wundt

8. Which of the following pairs of persons are most closely associated?
   a. Titchener--Skinner   b. James--Darwin   c. Watson--Rogers   d. Wertheimer--Maslow

9. The behaviorist definition of psychology clearly places great emphasis on
   a. overt behavior   b. conscious experience   c. psychodynamic responses   d. introspective analysis

10. Which of the following did B. F. Skinner reject?
    a. study of the mind   b. conditioned responses   c. positive reinforcement   d. designed cultures

11. As a profession, psychology is fully open to men and women, a fact that began with the success of
    a. O'Sullivan-Calkins   b. Tyler-James   c. Ladd-Franklin   d. Neal-Collins

12. The idea that threatening thoughts are sometimes repressed would be of most interest to a
    a. structuralist   b. psychoanalyst   c. humanist   d. Gestaltist

13. "A neutral, reductionistic, mechanistic view of human nature." This best describes which viewpoint?
    a. psychodynamic   b. cognitive   c. psychoanalytic   d. biopsychological

14. "Marcia's depression is the result of threats to her self-image." This statement would most likely be made by a
    a. structuralist   b. behaviorist   c. humanist   d. functionalist

15. Which of the following professional titles usually requires a doctorate degree?
    a. psychologist   b. psychiatric social worker   c. counselor   d. all of the preceding

16. Who among the following is most likely to treat the physical causes of psychological problems?
    a. scientist-practitioner   b. psychoanalyst   c. forensic psychologist   d. psychiatrist

17. Which of the following titles does not require licensing and certification?
    a. therapist   b. psychologist   c. psychiatrist   d. counselor

18. More than half of all psychologists specialize in what branches of psychology?
    a. counseling and comparative   b. applied and counseling   c. psychodynamic and clinical
    d. counseling and clinical

19. The largest percentage of psychologists work
    a. for non-profit organizations   b. at colleges and universities   c. in hospitals and clinics
    d. in independent practice

20. Which of the following is usually most valuable for evaluating claims about behavior?
    a. formal evidence   b. authority   c. anecdotal evidence   d. casual observation

21. When critically evaluating claims about behavior it is important to also evaluate
    a. the source of anecdotal evidence   b. the credentials of an authority   c. the quality of the evidence
    d. the strength of one's intuition

22. Consuming excessive amounts of refined sugar has the greatest effect on what dimension of children's behavior?
    a. aggression   b. mood   c. cognitive skills   d. none of the preceding

23. Which of the following pairs is most different?
    a. pseudo-psychology--critical thinking   b. graphology--pseudo-psychology   c. palmistry--phrenology
    d. psychology--empirical evidence

24. The German anatomy teacher Franz Gall popularized
    a. palmistry   b. phrenology   c. graphology   d. astrology

25. A tendency to believe flattering descriptions of oneself is called
   a. the Barnum effect   b. the astrologer's dilemma   c. the fallacy of positive instances
   d. uncritical acceptance

26. Descriptions of personality that contain both sides of several personal dimensions tend to create
   a. an illusion of accuracy   b. disbelief and rejection   c. the astrologer's dilemma
   d. a system similar to phrenology

27. The best antidote for pseudo-psychologies is critical thinking, skepticism, and
   a. new theories   b. expert opinion   c. empirical testing   d. astrological guidance

ANSWERS

Recite and Review

1. profession
2. behavior
3. behavior
4. evidence
5. planned or structured
6. method
7. animal
8. development
9. learning
10. theorists
11. sense (or sensory)
12. animals
13. behavior
14. male-female
15. social
16. behavior
17. understand
18. knowledge
19. laboratory
20. experience
21. mental
22. objective
23. adapt
24. educational
25. Watson
26. responses
27. positive
28. thinking
29. whole
30. greater
31. unconscious
32. Freud
33. growth
34. image
35. humanism
36. thinking
37. blend
38. diversity (or differences)
39. clinical
40. drugs
41. psychoanalysis
42. master's
43. specialties
44. basic
45. experimental
46. evaluate
47. critical
48. quality
49. evidence
50. false
51. Barnum

Relate

1. h
2. f
3. j
4. i
5. a
6. c
7. b
8. d
9. e
10. g
11. d
12. j
13. a
14. i
15. e
16. b
17. c
18. f
19. g
20. h
21. d
22. j
23. a
24. h
25. b
26. c
27. i
28. e
29. f
30. g

Check Your Memory

1. F
2. F
3. T
4. T
5. F
6. F
7. T
8. F
9. F
10. T
11. F

12. T
13. F
14. T
15. F
16. F
17. T
18. F
19. T
20. T
21. F
22. F
23. F
24. T
25. T
26. T
27. F
28. T
29. T
30. F
31. T
32. T
33. T
34. F
35. T
36. F
37. F
38. F
39. F
40. T
41. F
42. T
43. T
44. F
45. T
46. F
47. T
48. F
49. T
50. T
51. T
52. F
53. T
54. F
55. F
56. F
57. F
58. F
59. T
60. T
61. F

Final Survey and Review

1. science, profession
2. human, animal, behavior
3. covert
4. empirical, data
5. scientific
6. research method
7. model, human
8. Developmental
9. theorists
10. Personality
11. Sensation
12. Comparative
13. Biopsychologists
14. Gender
15. social behavior
16. Cultural
17. predict, control
18. philosophy
19. Wilhelm Wundt
20. conscious experience
21. Experimental, introspection
22. structuralism
23. Functionalism, James
24. natural selection
25. educational, industrial
26. Behaviorism, stimuli
27. Pavlov's, conditioned
28. Skinner, reinforcers
29. Cognitive
30. Gestalt
31. Wertheimer, sum, parts
32. Christine, Washburn, Calkins
33. psychodynamic
34. Freud, psychoanalysis
35. Humanistic, potentials
36. self-image, frame
37. Rogers, Maslow
38. behaviorism, humanism, biopsychology
39. Cognition, computer
40. eclectic
41. diversity, cultural
42. clinical, counseling
43. practitioner
44. Psychiatrists, psychotherapy
45. psychologists, psychoanalysis
46. psychiatric social
47. Developmental, engineering, educational
48. applied
49. Experimental
50. critique, synthesize
51. evaluate
52. evidence
53. Scientific
54 phrenology, pseudo
55. uncritical, positive, Barnum

Mastery Test

1. d (p. 3)
2. c (p. 2)
3. a (p. 4)
4. a (p.18)
5. b (p. 6)
6. b (p. 7)
7. d (p. 8)
8. b (p. 9)
9. a (p. 9)
10. a (p. 10)
11. c (p. 12)
12. b (p. 13)
13. d (p. 15)
14. c (p. 16)
15. a (p. 17)
16. d (p. 18)
17. a (p. 18)
18. d (p. 19-20)
19. b (p. 19-20)
20. a (p. 21)
21. c (p. 22)
22. d (p. 22)
23. a (p. 23)
24. b (p. 23)
25. d (p. 24)
26. a (p. 25)
27. c (p. 23-25)

Chapter 2

Research Methods and Critical Thinking

CHAPTER OVERVIEW

In psychology, critical thinking and the scientific method are used to advance knowledge and avoid the pitfalls of informal observation. Important elements in a scientific investigation include observing, defining a problem, proposing a hypothesis, gathering evidence/testing the hypothesis, publishing results, and forming a theory.

Many psychological investigations begin with naturalistic observation. Four problems with this approach are the effects of the observer on the observed, observer bias, the anthropomorphic error (in animal studies), and an inability to explain behavior. In the correlational method, the strength of the relationship between two measures is investigated. Correlations allow predictions, but they do not demonstrate cause-and-effect connections. Cause-and-effect relationships are best identified by controlled experiments.

In an experiment, experimental and control groups are formed. These groups differ only with regard to the independent variable. Effects of the independent variable on the dependent variable are then measured. All other extraneous variables are held constant.

The clinical method employs detailed case studies of single individuals. In the survey method, people in a representative sample are asked a series of questions. This provides information on the behavior of large groups of people.

Information in the popular media varies greatly in quality and accuracy. It is wise to approach such information with skepticism regarding the source of information, uncontrolled observation, correlation and causation, inferences, over-simplification, and single examples.

Three ethical issues of importance in psychological studies of humans are deception, invasion of privacy, and lasting harm. Animal research also poses ethical dilemmas. The American Psychological Association strongly endorses the humane treatment of research animals.

RECITE AND REVIEW

● *Why is the scientific method important to psychologists?*

Recite and Review: Pages 27-30

1. The scientific method is used to improve upon _____ sense and avoid the pitfalls of informal observation.

2. Scientific investigation in psychology is based on reliable evidence, accurate description and _____, precise definition, controlled observation, and repeatable results.

3. The scientific method involves observing, defining a _____, proposing a hypothesis, gathering evidence/testing the hypothesis, publishing _____, and forming a theory.

4. Observation refers to carefully recording _____ or events.

5. To be scientifically _____ a hypothesis must be testable.

6. Psychological concepts are given operational _____ so that they can be observed.

7. A _____ is a system of ideas that interrelates facts and concepts.

8. In general, good theories summarize existing data, predict new _____, and guide further research.

9. Good theories must be falsifiable; that is, it must be possible to _____ them by collecting observable evidence.

10. The _____ of scientific studies are published in professional journals so they will be publicly _____.

● *How do psychologists collect information?*

Recite and Review: Pages 30-34

11. The tools of psychological research include naturalistic observation, the correlational method, the experimental method, the _____ method, and the survey method.

12. Naturalistic observation refers to actively observing behavior in _____ settings.

13. Two problems with naturalistic observation are the effects of the observer on the observed and _____ bias.

14. The observer effect refers to changes in behavior caused by an awareness of being _____.

15. Observer bias is the tendency for observers to _____ perceptions of events.

16. Problems with naturalistic observation can be minimized by keeping careful observational _____.

17. The anthropomorphic fallacy is the error of attributing human qualities to _____.

18. In the correlational method, the _____ between two traits, responses, or events is measured.

19. Correlation coefficients range from +1.00 to −1.00. A correlation of _____ indicates that there is no relationship between two measures.

20. Correlations of +1.00 and −1.00 reveal that _____ relationships exist between two measures.

21. The closer a correlation coefficient is to plus or _____ 1, the stronger the measured relationship is.

22. A positive correlation or relationship shows that _____ in one measure correspond to increases in a second measure.

23. In a negative relationship _____ in one measure correspond to decreases in a second measure.

24. Correlations allow _____, but correlation does not demonstrate causation.

25. Cause-and-effect relationships in psychology are best identified by doing a controlled _____.

26. Graphing a linear relationship between two measures forms a straight line. When curvilinear relationships are graphed, a _____ line results.

● *How is an experiment performed?*

Recite and Review: Pages 36-38

27. Psychologists carefully control conditions in an experiment to identify _____-and-effect relationships.
28. In an experiment, conditions that might affect behavior are intentionally _____. Then, changes in behavior are observed and recorded.
29. In an experiment, a variable is any condition that can _____, and that might affect the outcome of the experiment (the behavior of subjects).
30. Experimental conditions that are intentionally varied are called _____ variables.
31. _____ variables measure the results of the experiment.
32. Extraneous variables are conditions that a researcher wishes to _____ from affecting the outcome of the experiment.
33. Extraneous variables are controlled by making sure that they are the same for all _____ in an experiment.
34. Subjects exposed to the independent variable are in the experimental _____. Those not exposed to the independent variable form the control _____.
35. Extraneous variables that involve personal _____, such as age or intelligence, can be controlled by randomly assigning subjects to the experimental and control groups.
36. If all extraneous variables are _____ for the experimental group and the control group, any differences in behavior must be caused by differences in the independent variable
37. The results of an experiment are statistically significant when they would occur very rarely by _____ alone.
38. _____ experiments are studies that take place in the "real world."
39. A key element in any science is the ability to replicate or _____ observations or experiments.
40. Experiments involving drugs must control for the placebo _____.
41. In a single-_____ study, subjects don't know if they are getting a drug or a placebo. In a double-_____ study, neither experimenters nor subjects know who is receiving a real drug.
42. Researchers must minimize the experimenter effect (the tendency for people to do what is _____ of them).
43. In many situations, the experimenter effect leads to self-fulfilling _____.

● *What other research methods do psychologists use?*

Recite and Review: Pages 38-42

44. Clinical psychologists frequently gain information from _____ studies.
45. A case study is an in-depth focus on all aspects of a single _____.
46. Case studies may be thought of as _____ clinical tests.
47. In the survey method, information about large populations is gained by asking people in a representative _____ a series of carefully worded questions.
48. The value of surveys is lowered when the sample is biased and when replies to questions are inaccurate or _____.

● *How dependable is psychological information found in the popular press?*

Recite and Review: APPLICATIONS

49. _____ and critical thinking are called for when evaluating claims in the popular media.
50. You should be on guard for _____ or biased sources of information in the media.
51. Many claims in the media are based on unscientific observations that lack control _____.
52. In the popular media, a failure to distinguish between correlation and _____ is common.
53. Inferences and opinions may be reported as if they were _____ observations.
54. Single cases, unusual _____, and testimonials are frequently reported as if they were valid generalizations.

● *What ethical questions does psychological research raise?*

Recite and Review: EXPLORATION

55. Psychological researchers must be cautious and responsible with respect to moral or _____ issues.
56. Three ethical issues in research are _____, invasion of privacy, and lasting harm.
57. Deception may be necessary in psychological research, but its use should be _____ and subjects should be debriefed after participating.
58. The _____ and confidentiality of human subjects must be respected.
59. Ethical researchers treat participants with dignity and respect and ensure that they are not _____.
60. In addition to human subjects, _____ used in behavioral studies must be treated humanely.

RELATE

1. _____	common sense	a. tentative explanation
2. _____	scientific method	b. hypothesized relationship
3. _____	hypothesis	c. animal tool use
4. _____	operational definition	d. concrete procedures
5. _____	Clever Hans	e. controlled observation
6. _____	conceptual level	f. formal log
7. _____	Jane Goodall	g. related traits, behaviors
8. _____	observational record	h. math error
9. _____	correlational study	i. head signals
10. _____	correlation of +3.5	j. unscientific knowledge

11. _____	causes of behavior	a. effect on behavior
12. _____	correlation coefficient	b. reference for comparison
13. _____	independent variable	c. statistically significant
14. _____	dependent variable	d. pyramid power and dowsing
15. _____	extraneous variables	e. experimental method
16. _____	control group	f. linear relationship
17. _____	random assignment	g. Phineas Gage
18. _____	rarely by chance alone	h. using chance
19. _____	parascience	i. varied by experimenter
20. _____	lobotomy	j. excluded by experimenter

21.	_____	placebos	a. clinical method
22.	_____	endorphins	b. biased sample
23.	_____	case studies	c. biased answers
24.	_____	Eve White	d. voluntary participation
25.	_____	random samples	e. incomplete evidence
26.	_____	gender bias	f. animal research
27.	_____	courtesy bias	g. multiple personality
28.	_____	my-side bias	h. opiate-like
29.	_____	ethical research	i. sugar pills
30.	_____	medical vaccines	j. survey method

CHECK YOUR MEMORY

Check Your Memory: Pages 27-30

1. Commonsense statements tend to be vague but consistent. T or F?
2. The scientific method involves testing a proposition by systematic observation. T or F?
3. An operational definition states the exact hypothesis used to represent a concept. T or F?
4. Clever Hans couldn't do math problems when his owner left the room. T or F?
5. Operational definitions link concepts with concrete observations. T or F?
6. A theory that is falsifiable has no value. T or F?
7. Most research reports begin with an abstract. T or F?

Check Your Memory: Pages 30-34

8. Jane Goodall's study of chimpanzees made use of the clinical method. T or F?
9. Concealing the observer helps reduce the observer effect. T or F?
10. Correlational studies can be done either in the laboratory or in the natural environment. T or F?
11. A correlation coefficient of +.100 indicates a perfect positive relationship. T or F?
12. Strong relationships produce positive correlation coefficients; weak relationships produce negative correlations. T or F?
13. A perfect correlation produces a straight line when graphed. T or F?
14. Perfect correlations demonstrate that a causal relationship exists. T or F?
15. The relationship between air temperature and the amount of coffee consumed per day is probably positive. T or F?
16. The best way to identify cause-and-effect relationships is to perform a case study. T or F?

Check Your Memory: Pages 34-38

17. An experiment is a formal trial done to test a fact or principle. T or F?
18. Extraneous variables are those that are varied by the experimenter. T or F?
19. Independent variables are suspected causes for differences in behavior. T or F?
20. In an experiment to test whether hunger affects memory, hunger is the dependent variable. T or F?
21. Independent variables are randomly assigned to the experimental and control groups. T or F?

22. An experiment conducted at the side of the road would be a field experiment. T or F?

23. To be statistically significant, an experimental result must be one that would occur very rarely by chance alone. T or F?

24. The term parascience means "above or superior to ordinary science." T or F?

25. Unrepeatable results occur in parascience, but not in psychological research. T or F?

26. A person who takes a drug may be influenced by his or her expectations about the drug's effects. T or F?

27. Placebos appear to reduce pain because they cause a release of endogenous Dexedrine. T or F?

28. In a single-blind experiment, the experimenter remains blind as to whether she or he is administering a drug. T or F?

29. Subjects in psychology experiments can be very sensitive to hints about what is expected of them. T or F?

Check Your Memory: Pages 38-42

30. Phineas Gage is remembered as the first psychologist to do a case study. T or F?

31. Case studies may be inconclusive because they lack formal control groups. T or F?

32. The case of Eve White provided information on the after effects of a frontal lobotomy. T or F?

33. Representative samples are often obtained by randomly selecting people to study. T or F?

34. Ninety-three percent of participants in psychology experiments come from prisons and mental institutions. T or F?

35. Male subjects are more common in psychology experiments than female subjects are. T or F?

36. The famous Literary Digest poll erred because most people lied about how they would vote. T or F?

37. The term *my-side bias* refers to the tendency to give socially acceptable answers to survey questions. T or F?

38. A disadvantage of experiments is that they may be somewhat artificial. T or F?

Check Your Memory: APPLICATIONS

39. The existence of dermo-optical perception was confirmed by recent experiments. T or F?

40. Psychological courses and services offered for profit may be misrepresented, just as some products are. T or F?

41. At least some psychic ability is necessary to perform as a stage mentalist. T or F?

42. Successful firewalking requires neurolinguistic programming. T or F?

43. Violent crime rises and falls with lunar cycles. T or F?

44. If you see a person crying, you must infer that he or she is sad. T or F?

45. Individual cases and specific examples tell us nothing about what is true in general. T or F?

Check Your Memory: EXPLORATION

46. The Stanford prison experiment raised questions about the mistreatment of animals. T or F?

47. Deception is necessary to create realistic conditions in some psychology experiments. T or F?

48. Most of the subjects in Milgram's study of obedience to authority felt positive about their participation. T or F?

49. As a subject in a psychological study you have the right to expect that research results will be made available to you. T or F?

50. Ethical researchers accurately describe risks to potential subjects. T or F?

FINAL SURVEY AND REVIEW

● *Why is the scientific method important to psychologists?*

 1. The scientific method is used to improve upon _____ _____ and avoid the pitfalls of informal _____.
 2. Scientific investigation in psychology is based on reliable _____, accurate description and _____, precise definition, controlled observation, and repeatable results.
 3. The scientific method involves observing, defining a problem, proposing a _____, gathering evidence/testing the hypothesis, publishing results, and forming a _____.
 4. Observation refers to carefully _____ facts or _____.
 5. A hypothesis is a proposed explanation. To be _____ valid a hypothesis must be

_____.
 6. Psychological concepts are given _____ definitions so that they can be observed. Such definitions state the exact _____ used to represent a concept.
 7. A _____ is a system of ideas that interrelates facts and concepts. In general, good _____ summarize existing data, predict new _____, and guide further research.
 8. Good theories must be _____; that is, it must be possible to disconfirm them by collecting observable evidence.
 9. The results of scientific studies are _____ in professional _____ so they will be publicly available.

● *How do psychologists collect information?*

10. The tools of psychological research include naturalistic observation, the correlational method, the _____ method, the clinical method, and the _____ method.
11. Naturalistic observation refers to actively observing behavior in _____ _____, which are the typical _____ in which people and animals live.
12. Two problems with naturalistic observation are the effects of the observer on the _____ and observer _____. Also, naturalistic observation may not allow us to _____ observed behavior.
13. The _____ _____ refers to changes in behavior caused by an awareness of being observed.
14. _____ _____ is the tendency for observers to distort perceptions of events.
15. Problems with naturalistic observation can be minimized by keeping careful _____

_____.
16. The _____ fallacy is the error of attributing human qualities to animals.
17. In the correlational method, the _____ between two traits, responses, or events is measured.
18. Correlation _____, which range from +1.00 to −1.00, measure the _____ of relationships.

19. A correlation of _____ indicates that there is no relationship between two measures. Correlations of +1.00 and −1.00 reveal that _____ relationships exist between two measures.
20. The _____ a correlation coefficient is to plus or minus 1.00, the stronger the measured relationship is.
21. A _____ correlation or relationship shows that increases in one measure correspond to increases in a second measure.
22. In a negative relationship _____ in one measure correspond to _____ in a second measure.
23. Correlations allow prediction, but correlation does not demonstrate _____.
24. Cause-and-effect relationships in psychology are best identified by doing a _____

_____.
25. Graphing a _____ relationship between two measures forms a straight line. When _____ relationships are graphed, a curved line results.

● *How is an experiment performed?*

26. Psychologists carefully control conditions in an experiment to identify _____ relationships.
27. In an experiment, conditions that might affect behavior are intentionally varied. Then, changes in behavior are _____ and _____.
28. In an experiment a _____ is any condition that can change, and that might affect the outcome of the experiment.
29. Experimental conditions that are intentionally varied are called _____ variables; they are potential _____ of changes in behavior.
30. _____ variables measure the results of the experiment; they reveal any _____ on behavior.
31. _____ variables are conditions that a researcher wishes to prevent from affecting the _____ of the experiment.
32. Extraneous variables are _____ by making sure that they are the same for all subjects in an experiment.
33. Subjects exposed to the independent variable are in the _____ group. Those not exposed to the independent variable form the _____ group.
34. Extraneous variables that involve _____ characteristics, such as age or intelligence, can be controlled by _____ assigning subjects to the experimental and control groups.
35. If all extraneous variables are identical for the experimental group and the control group, any differences in behavior must be caused by differences in the _____ variable
36. The results of an experiment are _____ significant when they would occur very rarely by chance alone.
37. _____ experiments are studies that take place in the "real world."
38. A key element in any science is the ability to _____ (repeat) observations or experiments.
39. Experiments involving drugs must control for the _____ effect.
40. In a _____ study, subjects don't know if they are getting a drug or a placebo. In a _____ study, neither experimenters nor subjects know who is receiving a real drug.
41. Researchers must also minimize the _____ _____ (the tendency for people to do what is expected of them).

42. In many situations, the experimenter effect leads to _____ prophecies.

● *What other research methods do psychologists use?*

43. Clinical psychologists frequently gain information from _____ _____, which focus on all aspects of a single _____ .

44. Case studies may be thought of as natural _____ _____ of the effects of brain tumors, accidental poisonings, and other unusual conditions.

45. In the survey method, information about large _____ is gained by asking people in a _____ sample a series of carefully worded questions.

46. The value of surveys is lowered when the sample is _____ and when replies to questions are _____ or untruthful.

● *How dependable is psychological information found in the popular press?*

47. _____ and _____ thinking are called for when evaluating claims in the popular media.

48. You should be on guard for unreliable or _____ sources of information in the media.

49. Many claims in the media are based on unscientific observations that lack _____ groups.

50. _____ does not demonstrate causation. In the popular media, a failure to distinguish between _____ and causation is common.

51. Inferences and opinions may be reported as if they were objective _____ .

52. Single _____, unusual examples, and testimonials are frequently reported as if they were valid _____ .

● *What ethical questions does psychological research raise?*

53. Three _____ issues in psychological research are deception, invasion of privacy, and lasting _____ .

54. Deception may be necessary in psychological research, but its use should be minimized and subjects should be _____ after participating.

55. The privacy of human subjects and _____ of results must be respected.

56. Ethical researchers treat participants with dignity and respect and ensure that they are not _____ .

57. Animals used in behavioral studies must be treated _____ .

MASTERY TEST

1. If an entire population is surveyed, it becomes unnecessary to obtain a
    a. control group b. random comparison c. random sample d. control variable

2. Which of the following represents a mismatch?
    a. experiment--causes and effects b. parascience--replication c. clinical method--case study
    d. survey method--samples

3. Control groups are most often used in
   a. naturalistic observation   b. the clinical method   c. parascience   d. experiments

4. Concealing the observer can be used to minimize the
   a. observer bias effect   b. double-blind effect   c. observer effect   d. effects of extraneous correlations

5. A psychologist studying lowland gorillas should be careful to avoid the
   a. anthropomorphic fallacy   b. Gestalt fallacy   c. psychodynamic fallacy
   d. fallacy of positive instances

6. One thing that most commonsense statements have in common is that they are
   a. very consistent   b. always wrong   c. based on informal observation   d. completely worthless

7. Theories in psychology tend to lead to new
   a. observations   b. problems   c. hypotheses   d. all of the preceding

8. Testing the hypothesis that frustration encourages aggression would require
   a. a field experiment   b. operational definitions   c. adult subjects   d. perfect correlations

9. A graph of a perfect negative relationship would form a
   a. straight line   b. circle   c. horizontal line   d. U-shaped line

10. Results of an experiment that could occur by chance 25 times out of 100 are regarded as
   a. hypothetical   b. insignificant   c. extraneous   d. correlated at the .25 level

11. In experiments involving drugs, experimenters remain unaware of who received placebos in a
   _____ arrangement
   a. zero-blind   b. single-blind   c. double-blind   d. control-blind

12. The idea that Clever Hans' owner might be signaling him was an informal
   a. research hypothesis   b. self-fulfilling prophecy   c. operational definition   d. dependent variable

13. Useful scientific theories must be
   a. falsifiable   b. factual   c. statistically proven   d. all of the preceding

14. In psychology, the _____ variable is a suspected cause of differences in
   _____.
   a. independent, the control group   b. dependent, the experimenter effect   c. independent, behavior
   d. dependent, correlations

15. A person who is observed crying may not be sad. This suggests that it is important to distinguish between
   a. individual cases and generalizations   b. correlation and causation   c. control groups and experimental
   groups   d. observation and inference

16. In an experiment on the effects of hunger on the reading scores of elementary school children, reading scores are the
    a. control variable b. independent variable c. dependent variable d. reference variable

17. Which of the following correlation coefficients indicates a perfect relationship?
    a. 1.00 b. 100.0 c. −1 d. both a and c

18. Jane Goodall's studies of chimpanzees in Tanzania are good examples of
    a. field experiments b. experimental control c. correlational studies d. naturalistic observation

19. To equalize the intelligence of members of the experimental group and the control group in an experiment, you could use
    a. extraneous control b. random assignment c. independent control d. subject replication

20. Which pair of concepts is most closely related?
    a. placebo effect--experimenter effect b. my-side bias--courtesy bias c. experimenter effect--gender bias d. causal variables--correlation coefficient

21. Which method would most likely be used to study the effects of tumors in the frontal lobes of the brain?
    a. sampling method b. correlational method c. clinical method d. experimental method

22. Milgram's obedience experiment raised questions about which ethical issue?
    a. invasion of privacy b. excessive debriefing c. lasting harm d. maintaining confidentiality

23. Which of the following correlations demonstrates a cause-effect relationship?
    a. .980 b. 1.00 c. .50 d. none of the preceding

24. The release of endorphins by the pituitary gland helps explain the
    a. experimenter effect b. placebo effect c. multiple-personality effect d. gender-bias effect

25. Which type of research would most likely report its results as a relationship between two variables having a strength of .74?
    a. correlational study b. controlled experiment c. case study d. survey

26. Cause is to effect as _____ variable is to _____ variable.
    a. extraneous, dependent b. dependent, independent c. independent, extraneous
    d. independent, dependent

27. The specific procedures used to gather data are described in which section of a research report?
    a. introduction b. abstract c. method d. discussion

ANSWERS

Recite and Review

1. common
2. measurement
3. problem, results
4. facts
5. valid
6. definitions
7. theory
8. observations
9. disconfirm
10. results, available
11. clinical
12. natural
13. observer
14. observed
15. distort
16. records
17. animals
18. relationship
19. zero
20. perfect
21. minus
22. increases
23. increases
24. prediction
25. experiment
26. curved
27. cause
28. varied
29. change
30. independent
31. Dependent
32. prevent
33. subjects
34. group, group
35. characteristics
36. identical
37. chance
38. Field
39. repeat
40. effect
41. blind, blind
42. expected
43. prophecies
44. case
45. subject
46. natural
47. sample
48. untruthful
49. Skepticism
50. unreliable
51. groups
52. causation
53. objective
54. examples
55. ethical
56. deception
57. minimized
58. privacy
59. harmed
60. animals

Relate

1. j
2. e
3. a
4. d
5. i
6. b
7. c
8. f
9. g
10. h
11. e
12. f
13. i
14. a
15. j
16. b
17. h
18. c
19. d
20. g
21. i
22. h
23. a
24. g
25. j
26. b
27. c
28. e
29. d
30. f

Check Your Memory

1. F
2. T
3. F
4. F
5. T
6. F
7. T
8. F
9. F
10. T
11. F
12. F
13. T
14. F
15. F
16. F
17. T
18. F
19. T
20. F
21. F
22. T
23. T
24. F
25. F
26. T
27. F
28. F
29. T
30. F
31. T
32. F
33. T
34. F
35. T
36. F
37. F
38. T
39. F
40. T
41. F

42. F
43. F
44. F
45. T
46. F
47. T
48. T
49. T
50. T

Final Survey and Review

1. common sense, observation
2. evidence, measurement
3. hypothesis, theory
4. recording, events
5. scientifically, testable
6. operational, procedures
7. theory, theories, observations
8. falsifiable
9. published, journals
10. experimental, survey
11. natural settings, environments
12. observed, bias, explain
13. observer effect
14. Observer bias
15. observational records
16. anthropomorphic
17. relationship
18. coefficients, strength
19. zero, perfect
20. closer
21. positive
22. increases, decreases
23. causation
24. controlled experiment
25. linear, curvilinear
26. cause-and-effect
27. observed, recorded
28. variable
29. independent, causes
30. Dependent, effects
31. Extraneous, outcome
32. controlled
33. experimental, control
34. personal, randomly
35. independent
36. statistically

37. Field
38. replicate
39. placebo
40. single-blind, double-blind
41. experimenter effect
42. self-fulfilling
43. case studies, subject
44. clinical tests
45. populations, representative
46. biased, inaccurate
47. Skepticism, critical
48. biased
49. control
50. Correlation, correlation
51. observations
52. cases, generalizations
53. ethical, harm
54. debriefed
55. confidentiality
56. harmed
57. humanely

Mastery Test

1. c (p. 40)
2. b (p. 36)
3. d (p. 35)
4. c (p. 31)
5. a (p. 31)
6. c (p. 27)
7. d (p. 29)
8. b (p. 29)
9. a (p. 33)
10. b (p. 36)
11. c (p. 37)
12. a (p. 29)
13. a (p. 30)
14. c (p. 34-36)
15. d (p. 44)
16. c (p. 35)
17. d (p. 32)
18. d (p. 30-31)
19. b (p. 35)
20. a (p. 37)
21. c (p. 38)
22. c (p. 46)
23. d (p. 32)
24. b (p. 37)
25. a (p. 32)
26. d (p. 34-36)
27. c (p. 30)

Chapter 3

The Brain, Biology, and Behavior

CHAPTER OVERVIEW

The brain and nervous system are made up of networks of neurons. Nerve impulses are basically electrical. Communication between neurons is chemical in that neurons release neurotransmitters which affect other neurons. Rather than merely carrying messages, neuropeptides regulate the activity of neurons in the brain.

The nervous system includes the central nervous system (CNS), consisting of the brain and spinal cord, and the peripheral nervous system (PNS). The PNS includes the somatic system and the autonomic system, with its sympathetic and parasympathetic branches.

The basic functions of the lobes of the brain are as follows: occipital lobes--vision; parietal lobes--bodily sensation; temporal lobes--hearing and language; frontal lobes--motor control, speech, and abstract thought. Association areas of the cortex are related to complex abilities such as language, memory, and problem solving. The left and right cerebral hemispheres have different specialized abilities.

The brain is subdivided into the forebrain, midbrain, and hindbrain. The subcortex includes important brain structures at all three levels. These are: the medulla ("vegetative" functions), the cerebellum (coordination), the reticular formation (sensory and motor messages and arousal), the thalamus (sensory information), and the hypothalamus (basic motives). The limbic system is related to emotion.

The endocrine system provides chemical communication in the body through the release of hormones into the bloodstream.

Hand dominance ranges from strongly left- to strongly right-handed, with mixed handedness and ambidexterity in between. In general, the left-handed are less strongly lateralized in brain function than are right-handed persons.

Conventional brain research relies on dissection, staining, ablation, deep lesioning, electrical recording, electrical stimulation, micro-electrode recording, EEG recording, and clinical studies. Newer methods make use of computer-enhanced images of the brain and its activities.

RECITE AND REVIEW

● *How do nerve cells operate and communicate?*

Recite and Review: Pages 51-57

1. Biopsychology is the study of how _____ processes relate to _____.
2. The _____ and nervous system are made up of linked nerve cells called _____, which pass information from one to another through synapses.
3. The basic conducting fibers of neurons are _____, but dendrites (a receiving area), the soma (the cell body and also a receiving area), and _____ terminals (the branching ends of a neuron) are also involved in communication.
4. The firing of an action potential (_____ _____) is basically electrical, whereas communication between neurons is generally chemical.
5. An action potential occurs when the _____ potential is altered enough to reach the threshold for firing. At that point, sodium _____ flow into the axon, through _____ channels.
6. After each action potential, the neuron has a brief _____ after-potential. Next, potassium ions flow out of the _____, restoring the resting potential.
7. Chemical synapses are most numerous in nature, but some _____ synapses exist.
8. In chemical synapses, neurons release neurotransmitters. These cross to _____ sites on the receiving cell, causing it to be excited or inhibited. For example, the transmitter chemical acetylcholine activates _____.
9. Transmitters called neuropeptides appear to _____ activity in other neurons, thereby affecting activity in the brain. Through volume conduction, the effects of _____ can be widespread.
10. Nerves are made of _____ and associated tissues. Neurons and nerves in the peripheral nervous system can often regenerate; damage in the central nervous system is _____, unless a repair is attempted by grafting or implanting healthy tissue.

● *What are the functions of major parts of the nervous system?*

Recite and Review: Pages 57-59

11. The nervous system can be divided into the _____ nervous system (the _____ and spinal cord) and the peripheral nervous system.
12. The CNS includes the somatic (_____) and autonomic (_____) nervous systems.
13. The autonomic system has two divisions: the sympathetic (emergency, activating) _____ and the parasympathetic (sustaining, conserving) _____.
14. Thirty one pairs of spinal _____ leave the spinal cord. Twelve pairs of cranial _____ leave the brain directly. Together, they carry sensory and motor messages between the brain and the body.
15. The simplest _____ is a reflex arc, which involves a sensory neuron, an interneuron, and a _____ neuron.

● *How is the brain organized and what do its higher structures do?*

Recite and Review: Pages 60-65

16. The human _____ is marked by advanced corticalization, or enlargement of the cerebral _____, which covers the outside surface of the cerebrum.
17. The _____ cerebral hemisphere contains speech or language "centers" in most people. It also specializes in _____, calculating, judging time and rhythm, and ordering complex movements.
18. The _____ hemisphere is largely non-verbal. It excels at spatial and perceptual skills, visualization, and recognition of _____, faces, and melodies.
19. "Split brains" have been created by _____ the corpus callosum. The split-brain individual shows a remarkable degree of independence between the right and left _____.
20. The most basic functions of the lobes of the cerebral cortex are as follows: occipital lobes-- _____; parietal lobes--bodily sensation; temporal lobes--_____and language; frontal lobes--motor control, speech, and abstract thought.

● *Why are the brain's association areas important? What happens when they are injured?*

Recite and Review: Pages 65-67

21. Association areas on the cortex are neither _____ nor _____ in function. They are related to more complex skills such as language, memory, recognition, and problem solving.
22. Damage to either Broca's area or Wernicke's area causes _____ and language problems known as aphasias.
23. Damage to Broca's area causes problems with _____ and pronunciation. Damage to Wernicke's area causes problems with the _____ of words.
24. Damage in other association areas may cause agnosia, the inability to _____ objects by sight. A special form of such "mindblindness" is facial agnosia, an inability to recognize _____ persons.

● *What kinds of behaviors are controlled by the subcortex?*

Recite and Review: Pages 68-70

25. The brain as a whole can be subdivided into the forebrain, _____, and hindbrain. The subcortex includes several crucial brain structures found at all three levels, below the _____.
26. The medulla contains centers essential for reflex control of _____ _____, breathing, and other "vegetative" functions.
27. The cerebellum maintains _____, posture, and muscle tone.
28. The reticular formation directs sensory and motor messages, and part of it, known as the RAS, acts as an _____ system for the cerebral cortex.
29. The thalamus carries _____ information to the cortex. The hypothalamus exerts powerful control over eating, drinking, sleep cycles, body temperature, and other basic _____ and behaviors.
30. The limbic system is strongly related to _____. It also contains distinct reward and punishment areas and an area known as the hippocampus that is important for forming _____.
31. Electrical stimulation of the brain (ESB) has been used to study the functions of various areas. ESB holds promise as a medical treatment. It is unlikely that it could be used to forcibly _____ behavior.

32. There is tremendous redundancy, or _____ of function, in many brain structures, so there are few brain "centers" for various functions.
33. The brains of young children show greater plasticity of organization, allowing better recovery from _____ _____.

● *Does the glandular system affect behavior?*

Recite and Review: Pages 71-74

34. The endocrine system provides _____ communication in the body through the release of _____ into the bloodstream. Endocrine glands influence moods, behavior, and even personality.
35. Many of the endocrine glands are influenced by the pituitary (the "_____ gland"), which is in turn influenced by the hypothalamus.
36. The pituitary supplies _____ hormone. Too little GH causes _____; too much causes giantism or acromegaly.
37. Body rhythms and _____ cycles are influenced by melatonin, secreted by the pineal gland.
38. The thyroid gland regulates _____. Hyperthyroidism refers to an overactive thyroid gland; hypothyroidism to an underactive thyroid.
39. The adrenal glands supply _____ and noradrenaline to activate the body. They also regulate salt balance, responses to stress, and they are a secondary source of _____ hormones.

● *In what ways do right- and left-handed individuals differ?*

Recite and Review: APPLICATIONS

40. Hand dominance ranges from strongly left- to strongly right-handed, with _____ handedness and ambidexterity in between.
41. Ninety percent of the population is basically _____, 10 percent _____.
42. The vast majority of people are right-handed and therefore _____ brain dominant for motor skills. Ninety-seven percent of right-handed persons and 68 percent of the left-handed also produce _____ from the left hemisphere.
43. In general, the _____ are less strongly lateralized in brain function than are _____ persons.

● *How do biopsychologists study the brain?*

Recite and Review: EXPLORATION

44. Conventional brain research relies on dissection, staining, ablation, deep lesioning, electrical recording, _____ stimulation, micro-electrode recording, EEG recording, and _____ studies.
45. Computer-enhanced techniques are providing three-dimensional _____ of the living human brain and its _____. Examples of such techniques are CT and MRI scans, the MANSCAN technique, PET scans and MEG.

RELATE

1. _____ soma
2. _____ neurilemma
3. _____ axon collateral
4. _____ myelin
5. _____ dendrites
6. _____ axon terminals
7. _____ axon

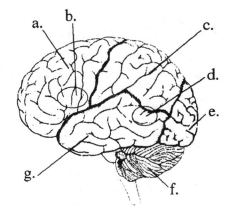

8. _____ spinal cord
9. _____ autonomic system
10. _____ parasympathetic branch
11. _____ peripheral nervous system
12. _____ sympathetic branch
13. _____ brain
14. _____ somatic system

15. _____ Wernicke's area
16. _____ temporal lobe
17. _____ cerebellum
18. _____ Broca's area
19. _____ parietal lobe
20. _____ frontal lobe
21. _____ occipital lobe

22. _____	midbrain
23. _____	reticular formation
24. _____	cerebrum
25. _____	medulla
26. _____	hypothalamus
27. _____	corpus callosum
28. _____	pituitary
29. _____	spinal cord
30. _____	thalamus

31. _____	pituitary	a.	brain waves
32. _____	pineal gland	b.	radioactive glucose
33. _____	thyroid gland	c.	testosterone
34. _____	adrenal glands	d.	surgery
35. _____	testes	e.	metabolism
36. _____	CT scan	f.	electrode
37. _____	EEG	g.	growth hormone
38. _____	ablation	h.	adrenaline
39. _____	deep lesioning	i.	computerized X-rays
40. _____	PET scan	j.	melatonin

CHECK YOUR MEMORY

Check Your Memory: Pages 51-57

1. The dendrites receive incoming information from the neurilemma. T or F?
2. Human axons may be up to 3 feet long. T or F?
3. The resting potential is about plus 70 millivolts. T or F?
4. The interior of the axon becomes positive during an action potential.   T or F?
5. The action potential is an all-or-nothing event. T or F?
6. The negative after-potential is due to an inward flow of potassium ions. T or F?
7. Nerve impulses travel faster in axons surrounded by myelin. T or F?
8. Neurotransmitters activate other neurons, neuropeptides activate muscles and glands. T or F?
9. Enkephalins are neuropeptides. T or F?
10. A neuropeptide can affect the neuron that released it. T or F?

Check Your Memory: Pages 57-59

11. The neurilemma helps damaged nerve cell fibers regenerate after an injury. T or F?
12. Damage to neurons in the brain and spinal cord is usually permanent. T or F?
13. To date, grafting brain tissue has only been done in lower animals. T or F?
14. Parkinson's disease is related to a loss of brain cells that produce dopamine. T or F?
15. The sympathetic system generally controls voluntary behavior. T or F?

16. Thirty-one cranial nerves leave the brain directly. T or F?
17. "Fight-or-flight" emergency reactions are produced by the autonomic nervous system. T or F?
18. Activity in the parasympathetic system increases heart rate and respiration. T or F?
19. In a reflex arc, motor neurons carry messages to effector cells. T or F?

Check Your Memory: Pages 60-65

20. Dolphins have brain-body ratios similar to those of humans. T or F?
21. The term neocortex means "new" cortex.
22. The cerebellum makes up a large part of the neocortex. T or F?
23. Much of the cerebral cortex is made up of gray matter. T or F?
24. In general, smart brains tend to be the hardest working brains. T or F?
25. The right half of the brain mainly controls left body areas. T or F?
26. Roger Sperry won a Nobel prize for his work on corticalization. T or F?
27. Cutting the reticular formation produces a "split brain." T or F?
28. Information from the right side of vision is sent directly to the right cerebral hemisphere. T or F?
29. The right hemisphere tends to be good at manipulo-spatial skills. T or F?
30. The left hemisphere is mainly involved with analysis. T or F?
31. People making decisions are more likely to take a risk when their left hemisphere is more active than the right. T or F?
32. The motor cortex is found on the occipital lobes. T or F?
33. The somatosensory area is located on the parietal lobes. T or F?
34. Electrically stimulating the motor cortex causes movement in various parts of the body. T or F?

Check Your Memory: Pages 65-67

35. Large parts of the frontal lobes are made up of association cortex. T or F?
36. Damage to the left cerebral hemisphere usually causes spatial neglect. T or F?
37. Persons with right hemisphere damage tend to miss the emotional tone in what others say. T or F?
38. A person with Broca's aphasia might say "pear" when shown an apple. T or F?
39. Damage to Wernicke's area causes the condition known as mindblindness. T or F?
40. Women are much more likely than men to use both cerebral hemispheres for language processing. T or F?

Check Your Memory: Pages 68-70

41. The cerebrum makes up much of the hindbrain. T or F?
42. Injury to the medulla may affect breathing. T or F?
43. Injury to the cerebellum affects attention and wakefulness. T or F?
44. Smell is the only major sense that does not pass through the thalamus. T or F?
45. Stimulating various parts of the limbic system can produce rage, fear, pleasure, or aversion. T or F?
46. The hippocampus is associated with hunger and eating. T or F?

Check Your Memory: Pages 71-74

47. Androgens ("male" hormones) are related to the sex drive in both men and women. T or F?
48. "Normal short" children grow faster when given synthetic growth hormone, but their final height is not taller. T or F?
49. Activity of the pituitary is influenced by the hypothalamus. T or F?
50. A person who is slow, sleepy, and overweight could be suffering from hypothyroidism. T or F?

51. Virilism and premature puberty may be caused by problems with the adrenal glands. T or F?
52. Steroid drugs may cause sexual impotence and breast enlargement in males. T or F?

Check Your Memory: APPLICATIONS

53. Left-handers have an advantage in fencing, boxing, and baseball. T or F?
54. Most left-handed persons produce speech from their right hemispheres. T or F?
55. Left or right handedness is inherited from one's parents. T or F?
56. On average, left-handed persons die at younger ages than right-handed persons do. T or F?

Check Your Memory: EXPLORATION

57. Deep lesioning in the brain is usually done surgically. T or F?
58. Micro-electrodes are needed in order to record from single neurons. T or F?
59. CT scans form "maps" of brain activity. T or F?
60. The MANSCAN technique is based, in part, on information from the EEG. T or F?
61. Radioactive oxygen is used to make MEG scans. T or F?

FINAL SURVEY AND REVIEW

● *How do nerve cells operate and communicate?*

1. _____ is the study of how biological processes relate to behavior.
2. The brain and nervous system are made up of linked nerve cells called _____, which pass information from one to another through _____.
3. The basic conducting fibers of neurons are axons, but _____ (a receiving area), the _____ (the cell body and also a receiving area), and axon terminals (the branching ends of an axon) are also involved in communication.
4. The firing of an _____ _____ (nerve impulse) is basically electrical, whereas communication between neurons is generally chemical.
5. An action potential occurs when the resting potential is altered enough to reach the _____ for firing. At that point, _____ ions flow into the axon, through ion channels.
6. After each action potential, the neuron has a brief negative _____. Next, _____ ions flow out of the axon, restoring the resting potential.
7. In chemical synapses, neurons release _____. These cross to receptor sites on the receiving cell. For example, the transmitter chemical _____ activates muscles.
8. Transmitters called _____ appear to regulate activity in other neurons, thereby affecting activity in the brain. Through _____ _____, the effects of neural regulators can be widespread.
9. _____ are made of axons and associated tissues. Neurons and nerves in the _____ nervous system can often regenerate; damage in the _____ nervous system is permanent, unless a repair is attempted by grafting or implanting healthy tissue.

● *What are the functions of major parts of the nervous system?*

10. The nervous system can be divided into the _____ nervous system (the brain and _____ _____) and the peripheral nervous system.

11. The CNS includes the _____ (bodily) and _____ (involuntary) nervous systems.

12. The autonomic system has two divisions: the _____ (emergency, activating) branch and the _____ (sustaining, conserving) branch.

13. Thirty one pairs of _____ nerves leave the spinal cord. Twelve pairs of _____ nerves leave the brain directly. Together, these nerves carry sensory and _____ messages between the brain and the body.

14. The simplest behavior is a _____ _____, which involves a sensory neuron, an _____, and a _____ neuron.

● *How is the brain organized and what do its higher structures do?*

15. The human brain is marked by advanced _____, or enlargement of the cerebral cortex, which covers the outside surface of the _____.

16. The right cerebral _____ contains speech or language "centers" in most people. It also specializes in writing, calculating, judging time and rhythm, and ordering complex _____.

17. The left hemisphere is largely non-verbal. It excels at _____ and perceptual skills, visualization, and recognition of patterns, _____, and melodies.

18. "Split brains" have been created by cutting the _____ _____. The split-brain individual shows a remarkable degree of independence between the right and left _____.

19. The most basic functions of the lobes of the cerebral _____ are as follows: occipital lobes-- vision; parietal lobes--bodily _____; temporal lobes--hearing and language; frontal lobes--motor control, _____, and abstract thought.

● *Why are the brain's association areas important? What happens when they are injured?*

20. Association areas on the cortex are neither _____ nor _____ in function. They are related to more complex skills such as _____, memory, recognition, and problem solving.

21. Damage to either Broca's area or Wernicke's area causes speech and language problems known as

_____.

22. Damage to _____ area causes problems with speech and pronunciation. Damage to _____ area causes problems with the meaning of words.

23. Damage in other association areas may cause _____, the inability to identify objects by sight. A special form of such "mindblindness" is _____ _____, an inability to recognize familiar persons.

● *What kinds of behaviors are controlled by the subcortex?*

24. The brain as a whole can be subdivided into the _____, midbrain, and hindbrain. The _____ includes several crucial brain structures found at all three levels, below the cortex.

25. The _____ contains centers essential for reflex control of heart rate, breathing, and other "vegetative" functions.

26. The _____ maintains coordination, posture, and muscle tone.

27. The _____ formation directs sensory and motor messages, and part of it, known as the RAS, acts as an activating system for the _____ _____.

28. The _____ carries sensory information to the cortex. The _____ exerts powerful control over eating, drinking, sleep cycles, body temperature, and other basic motives and behaviors.

29. The _____ system is strongly related to emotion. It also contains distinct reward and punishment areas and an area known as the _____ that is important for forming memories.

30. _____ _____ of the brain (ESB) has been used to study the functions of various areas. ESB holds promise as a medical treatment.

31. There is tremendous _____, or duplication of function, in many brain structures, so there are few brain "_____" for various functions.

32. The brains of young children show greater _____ of organization, allowing better recovery from brain injuries.

● *Does the glandular system affect behavior?*

33. The _____ system provides chemical communication in the body through the release of hormones into the _____.

34. Many of the endocrine glands are influenced by the _____ (the "master gland"), which is in turn influenced by the _____.

35. The _____ supplies growth hormone. Too little GH causes dwarfism; too much causes giantism or _____.

36. Body rhythms and sleep cycles are influenced by _____, secreted by the _____ gland.

37. The thyroid gland regulates metabolism. Hyperthyroidism refers to an _____ thyroid gland; hypothyroidism to an _____ thyroid.

38. The _____ glands supply adrenaline and noradrenaline to activate the body. They also regulate salt balance, responses to _____, and they are a secondary source of sex hormones.

● *In what ways do right- and left-handed individuals differ?*

39. _____ _____ ranges from strongly left- to strongly right-handed, with mixed handedness and _____ in between.

40. _____ percent of the population is basically right-handed, _____ percent left-handed.

41. The vast majority of people are _____ and therefore _____ brain dominant for motor skills. Ninety-seven percent of right-handed persons and 68 percent of the left-handed produce speech from the _____ hemisphere.

42. In general, the left-handed are less strongly _____ in brain function than are right-handed persons.

● *How do biopsychologists study the brain?*

43. Conventional brain research relies on _____ (separation into parts), staining, ablation, deep lesioning, electrical recording, electrical _____, micro-electrode recording, EEG recording, and clinical studies.

44. Computer-enhanced techniques are providing three-dimensional images of the living human brain and its activities. Examples of such techniques are CT and _____ scans, the MANSCAN technique, _____ scans and MEG.

MASTERY TEST

1. At times of emergency, anger, or fear, what part of the nervous system becomes more active?
   a. corpus callosum of the forebrain   b. sympathetic branch of the ANS
   c. parasympathetic branch of the PNS   d. Broca's area

2. The highest and largest brain area in humans is the
   a. cerebrum   b. cerebellum   c. frontal lobes   d. gray matter of the callosum

3. A tumor in which brain area would most likely cause blind spots in vision?
   a. occipital lobe   b. temporal lobe   c. somatosensory area   d. association cortex

4. Neurotransmitters are found primarily in
   a. the spinal cord   b. neurilemmas   c. synapses   d. motor neurons

5. Enkephalins are an example of
   a. acetylcholine blockers   b. neuropeptides   c. receptor sites   d. adrenal hormones

6. Electrically stimulating a portion of which brain area would produce movements in the body?
   a. occipital lobe   b. frontal lobe   c. parietal lobe   d. temporal lobe

7. When a neuron reaches its threshold, a/an _____ occurs.
   a. volume potential   b. ion potential   c. action potential   d. dendrite potential

8. A person's ability to work as a commercial artist would be most impaired by damage to the
   a. left temporal lobe   b. right cerebral hemisphere   c. left cerebral hemisphere
   d. frontal association cortex

9. ESB will most likely produce anger if it is applied somewhere in the
   a. association cortex   b. limbic system   c. parasympathetic branch   d. reticular activating system

10. Information in neurons usually flows in what order?
    a. soma, dendrites, axon   b. dendrites, soma, axon   c. dendrites, myelin, axon terminals
    d. axon, soma, axon terminals

11. Volume transmission affecting large groups of neurons is most characteristic of
    a. neuropeptides   b. acetylcholine   c. reflex arcs   d. resting potentials

12. Nerve impulses occur when _____ rush into the axon.
    a. sodium ions   b. potassium ions   c. negative charges   d. neurotransmitters

13. Grafting brain cells has been used most successfully in humans to treat
    a. Alzheimer's disease   b. Parkinson's disease   c. Addison's disease   d. the after-effects of strokes

14. Negative after-potentials are caused by the outward flow of _____ from the axon.
    a. negative charges   b. potassium ions   c. neurotransmitters   d. sodium ions

15. A person who says "bife" for bike and "seep" for sleep probably suffers from
    a. Broca's aphasia   b. Wernicke's aphasia   c. functional agnosia
    d. the condition known as "mindblindness"

16. Damage to which part of the limbic system would most likely impair memory?
    a. thalamus   b. hypothalamus   c. amygdala   d. hippocampus

17. Changes in heart rate, blood pressure, digestion, and sweating are controlled by the
    a. thoracic nerves   b. parietal lobes   c. somatic system   d. autonomic system

18. In which of the following pairs are both structures part of the forebrain?
    a. medulla, hypothalamus   b. cerebrum, cerebellum   c. medulla, thalamus   d. cerebrum, thalamus

19. A 3-year-old child and her mother both receive head injuries in an automobile accident. The child recovers
    more completely than her mother does, showing that the child has greater brain
    a. laterality   b. redundancy   c. plasticity   d. dominance

20. Which two problems are associated with the pituitary gland?
    a. dwarfism, acromegaly   b. virilism, acromegaly   c. mental retardation, dwarfism
    d. giantism, premature puberty

21. The cerebral hemispheres are interconnected by the
    a. reticular system   b. cerebellum   c. cerebrum   d. corpus callosum

22. Damage to which of the following would most likely make it difficult for a person to play catch with a
    ball?
    a. reticular formation   b. limbic system   c. cerebellum   d. association cortex

23. Speech, language, calculation, and analysis are special skills of the
    a. right cerebral hemisphere   b. limbic system   c. left cerebral hemisphere   d. right somatosensory area

24. The usual flow of information in a reflex arc is
    a. cranial nerve, connector neuron, spinal nerve   b. sensory neuron, interneuron, motor neuron
    c. effector cell, interneuron, connector neuron   d. sensory neuron, connector neuron, reflex neuron

25. A person will "hear" a series of sounds when which area of the cortex is electrically stimulated?
    a. frontal lobe b. parietal lobe c. occipital lobe d. temporal lobe

26. Which of the following pairs contains the "master gland" and its master?
    a. pineal--thalamus b. thyroid--RAS c. pituitary--hypothalamus d. adrenal--cortex

27. Many basic motives and emotions are influenced by the
    a. thalamus b. hypothalamus c. corpus callosum d. cerebellum

28. Both surgical ablation and _____ remove brain tissue.
    a. the MEG technique b. tomography c. micro-electrode sampling d. deep lesioning

29. Which of the following techniques requires access to the interior of the brain?
    a. micro-electrode recording b. EEG recordings c. PET scanning d. functional MRI

30. Which of the following statements about handedness is false?
    a. Handedness is inherited from one's parents. b. A majority of left-handers produce speech from the left hemisphere. c. The left-handed are less lateralized than the right-handed. d. Left-handedness is an advantage in boxing and fencing.

ANSWERS

Recite and Review

1. biological, behavior
2. brain, neurons
3. axons, axon
4. nerve impulse
5. resting, ions, ion
6. negative, axon
7. electrical
8. receptor, muscles
9. regulate, neuropeptides
10. axons, permanent
11. central, brain
12. bodily, involuntary
13. branch, branch
14. nerves, nerves
15. behavior, motor
16. brain, cortex
17. left, writing
18. right, patterns
19. cutting, hemispheres
20. vision, hearing
21. sensory, motor

22. speech
23. grammar, meaning
24. identify, familiar
25. midbrain, cortex
26. heart rate
27. coordination
28. activating
29. sensory, motives
30. emotion, memories
31. control
32. duplication
33. brain injuries
34. chemical, hormones
35. master
36. growth, dwarfism
37. sleep
38. metabolism
39. adrenaline, sex
40. mixed
41. right-handed, left-handed
42. left, speech
43. left-handed, right-handed
44. electrical, clinical

45. images, activity

Relate

1. g
2. d
3. e
4. c
5. a
6. f
7. b
8. c or b
9. e
10. f or g
11. a
12. f or g
13. c or b
14. d
15. d
16. g
17. f
18. b

19. c
20. a
21. e
22. d
23. e
24. a
25. g
26. i
27. b
28. h
29. f
30. c
31. g
32. j
33. e
34. h
35. c
36. i
37. a
38. d
39. f
40. b

Check Your Memory

1. F
2. T
3. F
4. T
5. T
6. F
7. T
8. F
9. T
10. T
11. T
12. T
13. F
14. T
15. F
16. F
17. T
18. F
19. T
20. T
21. T
22. F
23. T
24. F
25. T
26. F

27. F
28. F
29. F
30. T
31. T
32. F
33. T
34. T
35. T
36. F
37. T
38. F
39. F
40. T
41. F
42. T
43. F
44. T
45. T
46. F
47. T
48. T
49. T
50. T
51. T
52. T
53. F
54. F
55. F
56. F
57. F
58. T
59. F
60. T
61. F

Final Survey and Review

1. Biopsychology
2. neurons, synapses
3. dendrites, soma
4. action potential
5. threshold, sodium
6. after-potential, potassium
7. neurotransmitters, acetylcholine
8. neuropeptides, volume conduction
9. Nerves, peripheral, central
10. central, spinal cord
11. somatic, autonomic

12. sympathetic, parasympathetic
13. spinal, cranial, motor
14. reflex arc, interneuron, motor
15. corticalization, cerebrum
16. hemisphere, movements
17. spatial, faces
18. corpus callosum, hemispheres
19. cortex, sensation, speech
20. sensory, motor, language
21. aphasias
22. Broca's, Wernicke's
23. agnosia, facial agnosia
24. forebrain, subcortex
25. medulla
26. cerebellum
27. reticular, cerebral cortex
28. thalamus, hypothalamus
29. limbic, hippocampus
30. Electrical stimulation
31. redundancy, centers
32. plasticity
33. endocrine, bloodstream
34. pituitary, hypothalamus
35. pituitary, acromegaly
36. melatonin, pineal
37. overactive, underactive
38. adrenal, stress
39. Hand dominance, ambidexterity
40. Ninety, 10
41. right-handed, left, left
42. lateralized
43. dissection, stimulation
44. MRI, PET

Mastery Test

1. b (p. 59)
2. a (p. 60-61)
3. a (p. 64)
4. c (p. 54)
5. b (p. 55)
6. b (p. 64-65)
7. c (p. 52-53)
8. b (p. 63)
9. b (p. 69)
10. b (p. 52-54)
11. a (p. 55-56)

12. a (p. 54)
13. b (p. 57)
14. b (p. 54)
15. a (p. 66)
16. d (p. 70)
17. d (p. 57-58)
18. d (p. 68)
19. c (p. 71)
20. a (p. 71-73)
21. d (p. 61)
22. c (p. 68)
23. c (p. 63)
24. b (p. 59)
25. d (p. 64)
26. c (p. 73)
27. b (p. 69)
28. d (p. 79)
29. a (p. 79)
30. a (p. 76)

Chapter 4

Child Development

CHAPTER OVERVIEW

Human newborns have adaptive reflexes, are capable of learning, and have visual preferences, especially for familiar faces. Maturation underlies the orderly sequence of motor, cognitive, language, and emotional development. Heredity affects personal characteristics, including temperament, and it organizes the human growth sequence. Most psychologists accept that heredity and environment are inseparable and interacting forces. A child's developmental level reflects heredity, environment, and the effects of the child's own behavior.

Prenatal development is affected by diseases, drugs, radiation, and the mother's diet, health, and emotions. Both conventional birth and natural (prepared) childbirth produce healthy babies.

Caregiving styles affect emotional and intellectual development. Optimal caregiving includes proactive involvement, a good fit between the temperaments of parent and child, and responsiveness to a child's needs and signals. Emotional attachment of infants to their caregivers is a critical event in social development.

Language development is based on a biological predisposition, which is augmented by learning. Language acquisition begins with prelanguage communication between parent and child.

Jean Piaget theorized that children go through a series of cognitive stages as they develop intellectually. Learning principles provide an alternate explanation which does not assume that cognitive development occurs in stages.

Lawrence Kohlberg theorized that moral development also occurs in stages. Some psychologists question whether moral development is based only on a sense of justice.

Early perceptual, intellectual, and emotional deprivation seriously retards development. Deliberate enrichment of the environment has a beneficial effect on early development.

Recent advances in genetics and reproduction raise ethical and social questions.

RECITE AND REVIEW

● *What can newborn babies do?*

Recite and Review: Pages 85-88

1. The human _____ (newborn) has a number of _____ reflexes, including the grasping, rooting, sucking, and Moro reflexes.

43

2. Newborns begin to _____ immediately, they appreciate the consequences of their actions, they remember events, and they _____ (mimic) adults.
3. Tests in a looking chamber reveal a number of _____ preferences in the newborn. The neonate is drawn to complex, _____, curved, and brightly-lighted designs.
4. Infants prefer human face patterns, especially _____ _____. In later infancy, interest in the unfamiliar emerges.

● *What influence does maturation have on early development?*

Recite and Review: Pages 88-91

5. Maturation of the body and nervous system underlies the orderly _____ of motor, cognitive, language, and emotional development.
6. While the rate of maturation varies from child to child, the _____ is nearly universal.
7. The development of _____ control (motor development) is cephalocaudal (from head to toe) and proximodistal (from the _____ of the body to the extremities).
8. Emotional development begins with a capacity for _____ excitement. After that the first pleasant and unpleasant emotions develop.
9. Some psychologists believe that basic emotional expressions are _____ and that some appear as early as 2.5 months of age.
10. By age 10 months, babies display a social smile when other _____ are nearby.
11. Many early _____ are subject to the principle of readiness (or motor primacy).

● *How do heredity and environment affect development?*

Recite and Review: Pages 91-98

12. The nature-nurture controversy concerns the relative contributions to development of heredity (_____) and environment (_____).
13. Hereditary instructions are carried by _____ (deoxyribonucleic acid) in the form of chromosomes and _____ in each cell of the body.
14. Most characteristics are polygenic (influenced by a combination of _____) and reflect the combined effects of dominant and recessive _____.
15. Two *X* chromosomes produce a _____; an *X* plus a *Y* chromosome produces a
_____.
16. Heredity organizes the general human growth sequence—the general pattern of _____ _____ from birth to death.
17. Heredity also influences differences in temperament (the physical core of _____). Most infants fall into one of three temperament categories: easy children, _____ children, and slow-to-warm-up children.
18. Most psychologists accept that _____ and environment are inseparable and interacting forces.
19. A child's developmental level (current state of development) reflects heredity, environment, and the effects of the child's _____ _____.
20. Prenatal development is subject to _____ influences in the form of diseases, drugs, radiation, and the mother's diet, health, and emotions.
21. Prenatal damage to the fetus may cause congenital problems, or _____ _____. In contrast, genetic problems are inherited from one's parents.

22. Healthy children are produced by both conventional birth and by natural (prepared) childbirth. However, _____ births do have the advantage of _____ the use of anesthetics.
23. Postpartum depression is a mild to moderate depressive disorder that affects many women after they give birth. Postpartum depression is more serious than the more common _____
_____.
24. The father's presence at birth appears to be desirable, although his attitude toward _____ may be of more basic importance.

● *How important are parenting styles?*

Recite and Review: Pages 98-100

25. Caregiving styles (patterns of parental care) have a substantial impact on emotional and intellectual _____.
26. Maternal influences (the effects _____ have on their children) tend to center on caregiving.
27. Paternal influences differ in their impact because _____ tend to function as a playmate for the infant.
28. Optimal caregiving includes proactive maternal _____, a good fit between the temperaments of parent and child, and responsiveness to a child's needs and _____.

● *Of what significance is a child's emotional attachment to parents?*

Recite and Review: Pages 100-103

29. _____ development refers to the emergence of self-awareness and forming relationships with parents and others.
30. Self-awareness (consciousness of oneself as a person) and _____ referencing (obtaining guidance from others) are elements of early _____ development.
31. A variety of critical periods (times of increased _____ to environmental influences) exist in development, as illustrated by imprinting in birds and other animals.
32. Emotional attachment of human infants to their _____ is a critical early event.
33. Infant attachment is reflected by _____ anxiety (distress when infants are away from parents).
34. The quality of attachment can be classified as _____, insecure-avoidant, or insecure-ambivalent.
35. High-quality day care does not _____ children; high-quality care can, in fact, accelerate some areas of development.
36. Although the issue is debated, it is doubtful that immediate mother-infant _____ is crucial for forming lasting emotional bonds.

● *How do children acquire language and thinking abilities?*

Recite and Review: Pages 104-111

37. Language development proceeds from control of _____, to cooing, then babbling, the use of single words, and then to telegraphic _____.
38. The patterns of early speech suggest a _____ predisposition to acquire language.

39. Psycholinguists (psychologists who study _____) believe that innate language predispositions are augmented by _____.

40. Prelanguage communication between parent and child involves shared rhythms, non-verbal _____, and turn-taking.

41. Parents help children learn language by using distinctive caretaker _____ or parentese.

42. The intellects of children are _____ abstract than those of adults. Jean Piaget theorized that _____ growth occurs through a combination of assimilation and accommodation.

43. Piaget also held that children go through a fixed series of cognitive _____.

44. These are: sensorimotor (0-2), preoperational (2-7), _____ operational (7-11), and formal _____ (11-adult).

45. Learning theorists dispute the idea that cognitive development occurs in _____. Recent studies suggest infants are capable of levels of thinking beyond that observed by _____.

● *How do children develop morals and values?*

Recite and Review: Pages 112-114

46. Lawrence Kohlberg theorized that _____ development passes through a series of stages revealed by _____ reasoning about _____ dilemmas.

47. Kohlberg identified preconventional, conventional, and postconventional levels of moral _____.

48. Some psychologists have questioned whether measures of moral development should be based only on a morality of _____. Adults appear to base moral choices on either _____ or caring, depending on the situation.

● *What are the effects of a poor early environment?*

Recite and Review: Pages 114-118

49. Early perceptual, intellectual, and emotional deprivation seriously retards development. Even physical _____ may be affected, as is the case in deprivation dwarfism.

50. Poverty greatly increases the likelihood that children will experience various forms of _____.

51. Research on deprivation suggests that attachment and perceptual stimulation are essential for _____ development.

52. Harry Harlow's work with rhesus _____ and surrogate (_____) mothers identified contact comfort as an important source of infant stimulation and attachment.

53. Deliberate enrichment of the _____ in infancy and early childhood has a beneficial effect on development.

54. Early childhood education programs, such as Program Head Start, are designed to _____ the environments of disadvantaged children.

● *What can be done to enhance early development?*

Recite and Review: APPLICATIONS

55. Parents should take steps to encourage _____ infant attachment.

56. Effective parents avoid overindulgence while encouraging _____ of surroundings.

57. Parents must respect individual differences and be aware of the distinction between the statistical child and a _____ child.
58. It is desirable to provide enrichment that is responsive to a child's _____ and _____.
59. Parents should _____ forced teaching (artificially paced learning).
60. A one-step-ahead strategy that takes into account the child's level of _____ development helps adapt instruction to a child's needs.

● *How has new genetic knowledge affected parenthood?*

Recite and Review: EXPLORATION

61. Many recent developments in _____ and reproduction raise ethical and social questions.
62. Examples of such developments are _____ insemination (medically engineered pregnancy) and in vitro fertilization (test-tube _____).
63. _____ selection techniques, amniocentesis (testing of the _____ fluid) and chorionic _____ testing also create ethical dilemmas.
64. Mapping of the human genome (entire set of human _____), eugenics (breeding for _____ characteristics), and genetic counseling pose particularly difficult questions for scientists and the general public.

RELATE

1. _____ grasping reflex   a. motor primacy
2. _____ rooting reflex   b. DNA area
3. _____ Moro reflex   c. old age
4. _____ readiness   d. nature
5. _____ gene   e. palm grip
6. _____ chromosome   f. nurture
7. _____ senescence   g. startled embrace
8. _____ heredity   h. conception to birth
9. _____ environment   i. colored body
10. _____ prenatal period   j. food search

11. _____ FAS   a. control of muscles and movement
12. _____ Lamaze   b. caregiving style
13. _____ motor development   c. love and attention
14. _____ super mother   d. vowel sounds
15. _____ critical period   e. prenatal alcohol
16. _____ attachment   f. natural birth
17. _____ affectional needs   g. vowels and consonants
18. _____ cooing   h. emotional bond
19. _____ babbling   i. caretaker speech
20. _____ parentese   j. imprinting

21. _____	assimilation	a. changing mental patterns
22. _____	accommodation	b. egocentricism
23. _____	sensorimotor stage	c. applying mental patterns
24. _____	preoperational stage	d. abstract principles
25. _____	concrete operations	e. being good/authority
26. _____	formal operations	f. social contract/individual principles
27. _____	preconventional	g. hospitalism
28. _____	conventional	h. conservation
29. _____	postconventional	i. punishment or pleasure
30. _____	infant deprivation	j. object permanence

CHECK YOUR MEMORY

Check Your Memory: Pages 85-88

1. Developmental psychology is the study of progressive changes in behavior and abilities during childhood. T or F?

2. Newborn babies rapidly learn to prefer seeing their mother's face, rather than a stranger's. T or F?

3. As early as 9 weeks of age, infants can imitate actions a full day after seeing them. T or F?

4. After age 2, familiar faces begin to hold great interest for infants. T or F?

Check Your Memory: Pages 88-91

5. Most infants learn to stand alone before they begin crawling. T or F?

6. Motor development follows a top-down, center-outward pattern. T or F?

7. Anger and fear are the first two emotions to emerge in infancy. T or F?

8. Toilet training should begin soon after a child is 1 year old. T or F?

Check Your Memory: Pages 91-98

9. Each cell in the human body (except sperm cells and ova) contains 23 chromosomes. T or F?

10. The order of organic bases in DNA acts as a genetic code. T or F?

11. Two brown-eyed parents cannot have a blue-eyed child. T or F?

12. Most sex-linked traits are carried by recessive genes on the Y chromosome. T or F?

13. Identical twins have identical genes. T or F?

14. Embryonic development occurs during the neonatal period. T or F?

15. Teratogens are substances capable of causing birth defects. T or F?

16. An infant damaged by exposure to German measles or X-rays during the prenatal period suffers from a genetic problem. T or F?

17. Many drugs can reach the fetus within the intrauterine environment. T or F?

18. To prevent FAS, the best advice to pregnant women is to get plenty of rest, vitamins, and good nutrition. T or F?

19. One hit of cocaine taken by a pregnant women can injure the fetus. T or F?

20. Postpartum depression lasts from 24 to 48 hours after childbirth. T or F?

Check Your Memory: Pages 98-100

21. Early patterns of competence are well established by the time a child reaches age 3. T or F?

22. The "zoo-keeper" mother provides poor physical, emotional, and intellectual care for her child. T or F?
23. The goodness of fit between parents and children refers mainly to how compatible their temperaments are. T or F?
24. Responsive parents are sensitive to a child's feelings, need, rhythms, and signals. T or F?
25. Fathers typically spend about half their time in caregiving and half playing with the baby. T or F?
26. Paternal play tends to be more physically arousing for infants than maternal play is. T or F?

Check Your Memory: Pages 100-103

27. Most infants have to be 15 weeks old before they can recognize themselves in a mirror or on videotape. T or F?
28. Infants seek guidance from their mothers when they engage in social referencing. T or F?
29. The critical period for mastering a second language appears to be before adolescence. T or F?
30. Ducklings can be imprinted on inanimate objects, instead of their mothers. T or F?
31. Securely attached infants turn away from their mother when she returns after a period of separation. T or F?
32. A small number of children per caregiver is desirable in day care settings. T or F?
33. Children who spend too much time in poor quality day care tend to be insecure and aggressive. T or F?
34. The question of when secure attachment occurs is less important than the question of whether it occurs at all. T or F?

Check Your Memory: Pages 104-111

35. By about 8 weeks of age, babies begin cooing. T or F?
36. The single-word stage begins at about 6 months of age. T or F?
37. "That red ball mine," is an example of telegraphic speech. T or F?
38. Noam Chomsky believes that basic language patterns are innate. T or F?
39. The "I'm going to get you" game is an example of prelanguage communication. T or F?
40. Parentese is spoken in higher pitched tones with a musical inflection. T or F?
41. According to Piaget, children first learn to make transformations at about age 3. T or F?
42. Assimilation refers to modifying existing ideas to fit new situations or demands. T or F?
43. Cognitive development during the sensorimotor stage is mostly non-verbal. T or F?
44. Reversibility of thoughts and the concept of conservation both appear during the concrete operational stage. T or F?
45. An understanding of hypothetical possibilities develops during the preoperational stage. T or F?
46. Contrary to what Piaget observed, infants as young as 3 months of age show signs of object permanence. T or F?

Check Your Memory: Pages 112-114

47. Lawrence Kohlberg used moral dilemmas to assess children's levels of moral development. T or F?
48. At the preconventional level, moral decisions are guided by the consequences of actions, such as punishment or pleasure. T or F?
49. The traditional morality of authority defines moral behavior in the preconventional stage. T or F?
50. Most adults function at the conventional level of moral reasoning. T or F?
51. Both men and women may use justice or caring as a basis for making moral judgments. T or F?

Check Your Memory: Pages 114-118

52. Deprivation dwarfism is typically caused by hospitalism. T or F?

53. René Spitz attributed hospitalism to a lack of dependable mother figures. T or F?
54. Harry Harlow found that infant monkeys chose to spend most of their time with the surrogate mother that fed them. T or F?
55. Poverty is associated with retarded emotional and intellectual development. T or F?
56. Colostrum, supplied by breast-feeding, helps protect infants from infections. T or F?
57. In animals, enriched environments can actually increase brain size and weight. T or F?
58. One of the main goals of Program Head Start is to prevent hospitalism. T or F?

Check Your Memory: APPLICATIONS

59. Always giving in to a child's demands is a sign of overindulgence. T or F?
60. There is a wide range of normal variations around averages or typical standards for child development. T or F?
61. "Hothousing" is a good example of enrichment in early childhood. T or F?
62. Playing peekaboo is a good way to establish the permanence of objects for children in the sensorimotor stage. T or F?

Check Your Memory: EXPLORATION

63. Artificial insemination is formally known as in vitro fertilization. T or F?
64. Currently, sex selection techniques are not 100 percent successful in producing children of the desired sex. T or F?
65. A majority of people who would use sex-selection methods say they would choose to have a boy. T or F?
66. Amniocentesis can be done earlier in pregnancy than chorionic villus sampling can. T or F?
67. Eugenics cannot be done until cloning has been applied to humans. T or F?

FINAL SURVEY AND REVIEW

● *What can newborn babies do?*

1. The human neonate (newborn) has a number of adaptive reflexes, including the _____, rooting, _____, and _____ reflexes.
2. Newborns begin to learn immediately, they appreciate the _____ of their actions, they _____ events, and they imitate (mimic) adults.
3. Tests in a _____ _____ reveal a number of visual preferences in the newborn. The neonate is drawn to _____, circular, curved, and brightly-lighted designs.
4. Infants prefer _____ _____ patterns, especially familiar faces. In later infancy, interest in the _____ emerges.

● *What influence does maturation have on early development?*

5. _____ of the body and _____ _____ underlies the orderly sequence of motor, cognitive, language, and emotional development.
6. While the _____ of maturation varies from child to child, the order is nearly _____.

7. The development of muscular control (_____ development) is _____ (from head to toe) and _____ and from the center of the body to the extremities.

8. Emotional development begins with a capacity for general _____. After that the first _____ and _____ emotions develop.

9. Some psychologists believe that basic _____ expressions are innate and that some appear as early as 2.5 _____ of age.

10. By age 10 months, babies display a _____ smile when other people are nearby.

11. Many early skills are subject to the principle of _____ (or motor _____).

● *How do heredity and environment affect development?*

12. The nature-nurture controversy concerns the relative contributions to development of _____ (nature) and _____ (nurture).

13. Hereditary instructions are carried by DNA (_____ acid) in the form of _____ ("colored bodies") and genes in every cell.

14. Most characteristics are _____ (influenced by a combination of genes) and reflect the combined effects of dominant and _____ genes.

15. Two ___ chromosomes produce a female; an ___ plus a ___ chromosome produces a male.

16. Heredity organizes the general human _____ _____—the general pattern of physical development from birth to death.

17. Heredity also influences differences in _____ (the physical foundations of personality). Most infants fall into one of three categories: _____ children, difficult children, and _____ children.

18. Most psychologists accept that heredity and environment are inseparable and _____ forces.

19. A child's _____ _____ (current state of development) reflects heredity, environment, and the effects of the child's own behavior.

20. During pregnancy, _____ development is subject to environmental influences in the form of diseases, _____, _____, and the mother's diet, health, and emotions.

21. Prenatal damage to the fetus may cause _____ problems, or birth defects. In contrast, _____ problems are inherited from one's parents.

22. Healthy children are produced by both _____ birth and by natural (prepared) childbirth. However, prepared births do have the advantage of minimizing the use of _____.

23. _____ depression is a mild to moderate depressive disorder that affects many women after they give birth. It is more serious than the more common maternity blues.

24. The father's presence at birth appears to be desirable, although his _____ toward birth may be of more basic importance.

● *How important are parenting styles?*

25. _____ _____ (patterns of parental care) have a substantial impact on emotional and intellectual development.

26. _____ influences (the effects mothers have on their children) tend to center on _____.

27. _____ influences differ in their impact because fathers tend to function as a
_____ for the infant.
28. Optimal caregiving includes _____ maternal involvement, a good fit between the
_____ of parent and child, and responsiveness to a child's needs and signals.

● *Of what significance is a child's emotional attachment to parents?*

29. Social development refers to the emergence of self-_____ and forming
_____ with parents and others.
30. _____ (consciousness of oneself as a person) and social
_____ (obtaining guidance from others) are elements of early social development.
31. A variety of _____ periods (times of increased sensitivity to environmental influences)
exist in development, as illustrated by _____ in birds and other animals.
32. Emotional _____ of human infants to their caregivers is a critical early event.
33. Infant attachment is reflected by separation _____ (distress when infants are away from
parents).
34. The quality of attachment can be classified as secure, insecure-_____, or insecure-
_____.
35. _____ day care does not harm children; excellent care can, in fact,
_____ some areas of development.
36. Although the issue is debated, it is doubtful that immediate mother-infant contact is crucial for forming
lasting emotional _____.

● *How do children acquire language and thinking abilities?*

37. Language development proceeds from control of crying, to _____, then
_____, the use of single words, and then to _____ speech (two-word
sentences).
38. The patterns of early speech suggest a biological _____ to acquire language.
39. _____ (psychologists who study language) believe that innate language
predispositions are augmented by learning.
40. _____ communication between parent and child involves shared rhythms,
non-verbal signals, and _____-taking.
41. Parents help children learn language by using distinctive caretaker speech or _____.
42. The intellects of children are less _____ than those of adults. Jean Piaget theorized that
cognitive growth occurs through a combination of _____ and accommodation.
43. Piaget also held that children go through a fixed series of _____ stages.
44. The stages are: _____ (0-2), _____ (2-7), concrete
operational (7-11), and formal operations (11-adult).
45. _____ theorists dispute the idea that cognitive development occurs in stages. Recent
studies suggest infants are capable of levels of _____ beyond that observed by Piaget.

● *How do children develop morals and values?*

46. Lawrence Kohlberg theorized that moral development passes through a series of stages revealed by moral _____ about moral _____.

47. Kohlberg identified _____, conventional, and postconventional levels of moral reasoning.

48. Some psychologists have questioned whether measures of moral development should be based only on a morality of justice. Adults appear to base moral choices on either justice or _____, depending on the _____.

● *What are the effects of a poor early environment?*

49. Early perceptual, intellectual, and emotional _____ seriously retards development. Even physical growth may be affected, as is the case in _____ _____.

50. _____ greatly increases the likelihood that children will experience various forms of deprivation.

51. Research on deprivation suggests that secure _____ and perceptual _____ are essential for normal development.

52. Harry Harlow's work with rhesus monkeys and _____ (artificial) mothers identified _____ comfort as an important source of infant stimulation and attachment.

53. Deliberate _____ of the environment in infancy and early childhood has a beneficial effect on development.

54. _____ _____ _____ programs, such as Program Head Start, are designed to enrich the environments of disadvantaged children.

● *What can be done to enhance early development?*

55. Parents should take steps to encourage secure infant _____.

56. Effective parents avoid _____ while encouraging exploration of surroundings.

57. Parents must respect individual differences and be aware of the distinction between the _____ child and a particular child.

58. It is desirable to provide enrichment that is _____ to a child's interests and needs.

59. Parents should avoid _____ _____ (artificially paced learning).

60. A _____ strategy that takes into account the child's level of cognitive development helps adapt instruction to a child's needs.

● *How has new genetic knowledge affected parenthood?*

61. Many recent developments in genetics and reproduction raise _____ and social questions.

62. Examples of such developments are artificial _____ (medically engineered pregnancy) and _____ _____ fertilization (test-tube fertilization).

63. Sex selection techniques, _____ (testing of the amniotic fluid) and _____ villus testing also create ethical dilemmas.

64. Mapping of the human _____ (entire set of human genes), _____ (breeding for desirable characteristics), and genetic counseling pose particularly difficult questions for scientists and the general public.

MASTERY TEST

1. The universal patterns of the human growth sequence can be attributed to
    a. recessive genes b. environment c. polygenic imprinting d. heredity

2. Exaggerated or musical voice inflections are characteristic of
    a. prelanguage turn-taking b. parentese c. telegraphic speech d. prompting and expansion

3. The choice of whether to use justice or caring to make moral decisions depends on the
    _____ a person faces.
    a. situation b. punishment c. level of authority d. exchange

4. Explaining things abstractly or symbolically to a child becomes most effective during which stage of cognitive development?
    a. postconventional b. formal operations c. preoperational d. post-intuitive

5. An infant startled by a loud noise will typically display
    a. a Moro reflex b. a rooting reflex c. a Meltzoff reflex d. an imprinting reflex

6. If one identical twin has a *Y* chromosome, the other must have a
    a. recessive chromosome b. sex-linked trait c. dominant chromosome d. *Y* chromosome

7. Ideas about Piaget's stages and the cognitive abilities of infants are challenged by infants' reactions to
    a. hypothetical possibilities b. impossible events c. turn-taking d. separation anxiety

8. Aware parents recognize the difference between their particular child and the
    a. statistical child b. indulged child c. "hothouse" child d. formal child

9. The majority of children display what type of temperament?
    a. easy b. difficult c. slow-to-warm-up d. generic

10. Which of the following is a congenital problem?
    a. FAS b. sickle-cell anemia c. hemophilia d. muscular dystrophy

11. A child may begin to question the idea that Santa Claus' sack could carry millions of toys when the child has grasped the concept of
    a. assimilation b. egocentricism c. conservation d. reversibility of permanence

12. In most areas of development, heredity and environment are
    a. independent b. interacting c. conflicting d. responsible for temperament

13. The concept of imprinting in animals is most closely related to
    a. cognitive accommodation b. prelanguage communication c. attachment in humans
    d. motor primacy

14. Children who grow up in poverty run a high risk of
    a. dwarfism b. hospitalism c. deprivation d. colostrum

15. Which of the following techniques has not yet been done with humans?
    a. cloning b. amniocentesis c. in vitro fertilization d. artificial insemination

16. By definition, a trait that is controlled by a dominant gene cannot be
    a. eugenic b. hereditary c. carried by DNA d. polygenic

17. _____ development proceeds head-down and center-outward.
    a. Cognitive b. Motor c. Prelanguage d. Preoperational

18. You could test for _____ by rubbing a spot of rouge on a child's nose and placing the child in front of a mirror.
    a. social referencing b. self-awareness c. the quality of attachment d. the degree of imprinting

19. After age 2, infants become much more interested in
    a. bonding b. non-verbal communication c. familiar voices d. unfamiliar faces

20. According to Piaget, one of the major developments during the sensorimotor stage is emergence of the concept of
    a. assimilation b. accommodation c. object permanence d. transformation

21. Hospitalism is to deprivation as early childhood education is to
    a. imprinting b. enrichment c. responsiveness d. assimilation

22. Sex selection involves
    a. in vitro fertilization b. genetic engineering c. separating *X*- and *Y*-bearing sperm
    d. all of the preceding

23. Which principle is most relevant to the timing of toilet training?
    a. motor primacy b. critical periods c. non-verbal signals d. assimilation

24. The most widely used form of prepared childbirth is the _____ method.
    a. Leboyer b. Lamaze c. Moro d. Lorenz

25. Consonants first enter a child's language when the child begins
    a. babbling b. cooing c. the single word stage d. turn-taking

26. Harlow's studies with surrogate mothers demonstrated the importance of _____ for infant attachment and development.
    a. contact comfort b. colostrum c. perceptual stimulation d. enriched environments

27. Physically arousing play is typically an element of
    a. the zoo-keeper mother's caregiving style b. paternal influences c. proactive maternal involvement
    d. secure attachment

28. Insecure attachment is revealed by
a. separation anxiety   b. seeking to be near the mother after separation   c. turning away from the mother after separation   d. social referencing

29. Seeking approval and upholding law, order, and authority are characteristics of what stage of moral development?
a. preconventional   b. conventional   c. postconventional   d. postformal

30. Studies of infant imitation
a. are conducted in a looking chamber   b. confirm that infants mimic adult facial gestures   c. show that self-awareness precedes imitation   d. are used to assess the quality of infant attachment

ANSWERS

Recite and Review

1. neonate, adaptive
2. learn, imitate
3. visual, circular
4. familiar faces
5. sequence
6. order
7. muscular, center
8. general
9. innate
10. people
11. skills
12. nature, nurture
13. DNA, genes
14. genes, genes
15. female, male
16. physical development
17. personality, difficult
18. heredity
19. own behavior
20. environmental
21. birth defects
22. prepared (or natural), minimizing
23. maternity blues
24. birth
25. development
26. mothers
27. fathers
28. involvement, signals
29. Social
30. social, social
31. sensitivity
32. caregivers
33. separation
34. secure
35. harm
36. contact
37. crying, speech
38. biological
39. language, learning
40. signals
41. speech
42. less, intellectual
43. stages
44. concrete, operations
45. stages, Piaget
46. moral, moral, moral
47. reasoning
48. justice, justice
49. growth
50. deprivation
51. normal
52. monkeys, artificial
53. environment
54. enrich
55. secure
56. exploration
57. particular
58. interests, needs
59. avoid
60. cognitive
61. genetics
62. artificial, fertilization
63. Sex, amniotic, villus
64. genes, desirable

Relate

1. e
2. j
3. g
4. a
5. b
6. i
7. c
8. d
9. f
10. h
11. e
12. f
13. a

14. b
15. j
16. h
17. c
18. d
19. g
20. i
21. c
22. a
23. j
24. b
25. h
26. d
27. i
28. e
29. f
30. g

Check Your Memory

1. F
2. T
3. F
4. F
5. F
6. T
7. F
8. F
9. F
10. T
11. F
12. F
13. T
14. F
15. T
16. F
17. T
18. F
19. T
20. F
21. T
22. F
23. T
24. T
25. F
26. T
27. F
28. T
29. T
30. T
31. F
32. T
33. T
34. T
35. T
36. F
37. F
38. T
39. T
40. T
41. F
42. F
43. T
44. T
45. F
46. T
47. T
48. T
49. F
50. T
51. T
52. F
53. T
54. F
55. T
56. T
57. T
58. F
59. T
60. T
61. F
62. T
63. F
64. T
65. T
66. F
67. F

Final Survey and Review

1. grasping, sucking, Moro
2. consequences, remember
3. looking chamber, complex
4. human face, unfamiliar
5. Maturation, nervous system
6. rate, universal
7. motor, cephalocaudal, proximodistal
8. excitement, pleasant, unpleasant
9. emotional, months
10. social
11. readiness, primacy
12. heredity, environment
13. deoxyribonucleic, chromosomes
14. polygenic, recessive
15. *X, X, Y*
16. growth sequence
17. temperament, easy, slow-to-warm-up
18. interacting
19. developmental level
20. prenatal, drugs, radiation
21. congenital, genetic
22. conventional, anesthetics
23. postpartum
24. attitude
25. Caregiving styles
26. Maternal, caregiving
27. Paternal, playmate
28. proactive, temperaments
29. awareness, relationships
30. Self-awareness, referencing
31. critical, imprinting
32. attachment
33. anxiety
34. avoidant, ambivalent
35. High-quality, accelerate
36. bonds
37. cooing, babbling, telegraphic
38. predisposition
39. Psycholinguists
40. Prelanguage, turn
41. parentese
42. abstract, assimilation

43. cognitive
44. sensorimotor, preoperational
45. Learning, thinking
46. reasoning, dilemmas
47. preconventional
48. caring, situation
49. deprivation, deprivation dwarfism
50. Poverty
51. attachment, stimulation
52. surrogate, contact
53. enrichment
54. Early childhood education
55. attachment
56. overindulgence
57. statistical
58. responsive
59. forced teaching
60. one-step-ahead
61. ethical
62. insemination, in vitro
63. amniocentesis, chorionic
64. genome, eugenics

20. c (p. 108)
21. b (p. 115, 118)
22. c (p. 123)
23. a (p. 90)
24. b (p. 96)
25. a (p. 104)
26. a (p. 116)
27. b (p. 99)
28. c (p. 102)
29. b (p. 113)
30. b (p. 86)

Mastery Test

1. d (p. 88)
2. b (p. 10)
3. a (p. 114)
4. b (p. 121)
5. a (p. 86)
6. d (p. 94)
7. b (p. 111)
8. a (p. 120)
9. a (p. 94)
10. a (p. 95)
11. c (p. 109)
12. b (p. 93-94)
13. c (p. 101)
14. c (p. 116)
15. a (p. 125)
16. d (p. 91)
17. b (p. 88)
18. b (p. 100)
19. d (p. 88)

Chapter 5

From Birth to Death: Life-Span Development

CHAPTER OVERVIEW

Life-span psychologists study continuity and change in behavior, as well as tasks, challenges, milestones, and problems throughout life. According to Erikson, each life stage provokes a different psychosocial dilemma.

Three major parenting styles are authoritarian, permissive, and authoritative (effective). Some major problems in childhood are toilet training, feeding disturbances, speech disturbances, learning disorders, and attention-deficit hyperactivity disorder. Childhood autism and child abuse are examples of the more severe problems that can occur.

Adolescence is culturally defined; puberty is a biological event. Early maturation is beneficial mostly for boys; its effects are mixed for girls. Adolescent identity formation is accelerated by cognitive development and influenced by parents and peer groups. Career development typically proceeds through several broad phases. Vocational counseling can greatly aid career decision making.

Adult development is marked by events that range from escaping parental dominance in the late teens to a noticeable acceptance of one's lot in life during the 50s. Some people experience a mid-life crisis, but this is not universal. Adjustment to later middle age is sometimes complicated by menopause and the climacteric. Biological aging begins between 25 and 30, but peak performance in specific pursuits may come at any point in life. Intellectual declines due to aging are limited. Two major theories of successful aging are disengagement and activity. Activity theory appears to apply to more people. Ageism is especially damaging to older people. Impending death and bereavement both produce a series of typical emotional reactions.

Effective parental discipline tends to emphasize child management techniques, rather than power assertion or withdrawal of love. Responsibility, mutual respect, consistency, love, encouragement, and clear communication are features of effective parenting.

New approaches to death include the hospice movement, living wills, and cryonic suspension. A continuing controversy concerns the ethics of passive euthanasia and active euthanasia.

RECITE AND REVIEW

● *What are the typical tasks and dilemmas through the life span?*

Recite and Review: Pages 128-132

1. Life-span psychologists study continuity and _____ over the life span.
2. They are also interested in _____ milestones, or prominent landmarks in personal development.
3. According to Erik Erikson, each life stage provokes a specific psychosocial _____.
4. During childhood these are: trust versus mistrust, autonomy versus _____ and doubt, initiative versus _____, and industry versus _____.
5. In _____, identity versus role confusion is the principal dilemma.
6. In young adulthood we face the dilemma of intimacy versus _____. Later, generativity versus _____ becomes prominent.
7. Old age is a time when the dilemma of integrity versus _____ must be faced.
8. In addition, each life stage requires successful mastery of certain _____ tasks (personal changes required for optimal development).

● *What is the nature of effective parenting?*

Recite and Review: Pages 133-135

9. Authoritarian parents enforce rigid _____ and demand strict obedience to _____.
10. Overly permissive parents give little _____ and don't hold children accountable for their actions.
11. Authoritative (_____) parents supply firm and consistent guidance, combined with love and affection.

● *What are some of the more serious childhood problems?*

Recite and Review: Pages 135-139

12. Few children grow up without experiencing some of the normal problems of childhood, including negativism, clinging, specific fears, sleep _____, general dissatisfaction, regression, sibling _____, and rebellion.
13. Major areas of difficulty in childhood are _____ _____ (including enuresis and encopresis) and _____ disturbances, such as overeating, anorexia nervosa (self-starvation), and pica (eating non-food substances).
14. Other problems include _____ disturbances (delayed speech, stuttering); _____ disorders, including dyslexia (an inability to read with understanding); and attention-deficit hyperactivity _____ (ADHD).
15. Childhood _____ is a severe problem involving mutism, sensory disturbances, tantrums, and a lack of responsiveness to other people.
16. Some cases of autism are being treated successfully with _____ modification.

17. Child abuse (physically or emotionally _____ a child) is a major problem. Roughly _____ percent of all abused children become abusive adults. Emotional support and therapy can help break the cycle of abuse.

● *Why is adolescent development especially challenging?*

Recite and Review: Pages 140-143

18. Adolescence is a culturally defined _____ status. Puberty is a _____ event.
19. On average, the peak growth spurt during puberty occurs earlier for _____ than for _____.
20. Early maturation is beneficial mostly for _____; its effects are mixed for _____.
21. Establishing a clear sense of personal identity is a major task of _____. One danger of _____ maturation is premature identity formation.
22. Many adolescents become self-conscious and preoccupied with imaginary _____ (imagined viewers).
23. Adolescent identity formation is accelerated by cognitive development and influenced by _____ and peer groups (age mates).

● *How do people select careers for themselves?*

Recite and Review: Pages 143-144

24. The first period in _____ development is the exploration phase, during which career possibilities are examined.
25. The exploration phase can be further divided into a fantasy stage, a tentative stage, and a _____ stage.
26. During the establishment phase the person enters a career and builds _____.
27. The midcareer phase is marked by high _____ and full status within the person's chosen career.
28. In the later career phase, preceding retirement, the person serves as a respected expert and mentor for _____ _____.
29. Vocational counseling can greatly aid career _____ making.

● *What happens psychologically during adulthood?*

Recite and Review: Pages 145-148

30. Certain relatively consistent events mark _____ _____ in our society.
31. In order these are: _____ from parental dominance, leaving the _____, building a workable life, a crisis of questions, a crisis of urgency, attaining stability, and mellowing.
32. A midlife crisis affects many people in the 37-41 age range, but this is by no means _____.
33. Some approaches to making career decisions are: the vigilant style, the complacent style, the defensive-avoidant style, and the hypervigilant style. The _____ style is most effective.
34. Adjustment to later middle age is sometimes complicated for _____ by menopause and for _____ by a climacteric.

● *What are some of the psychological challenges of aging?*

Recite and Review: Pages 148-153

35. The elderly are the _____ growing segment of society in North America..
36. Biological _____ begins between 25 and 30, but peak performance in specific pursuits may come at various points throughout life.
37. The length of human lives is limited by the _____ life span. _____ expectancy (the average number of years people live) is much shorter.
38. Intellectual declines associated with aging are limited, at least through one's _____. This is especially true of individuals who remain mentally _____.
39. The greatest losses occur for fluid abilities (which require _____ or rapid learning); crystallized abilities (stored up _____ and skills) show much less decline and may actually improve.
40. Gerontologists (those who study _____) have proposed the disengagement theory of successful _____. It holds that withdrawal from society is necessary and desirable in old age.
41. The activity theory states that optimal adjustment to aging is tied to continuing _____ and involvement. The activity theory applies to more people than disengagement does.
42. Ageism refers to prejudice, discrimination, and stereotyping on the basis of _____. It affects people of all ages, but is especially damaging to _____ people.

● *How do people typically react to death and bereavement?*

Recite and Review: Pages 153-156

43. Older people fear the circumstances of _____ more than the fact that it will occur.
44. Typical emotional reactions to impending death are denial, _____, bargaining, _____, and acceptance.
45. Near-death _____ (NDEs) frequently result in significant changes in personality, _____, and life goals.
46. Bereavement also brings forth a typical series of _____ reactions.
47. Initial shock is followed by pangs of _____. Later, apathy, dejection, and depression may occur. Eventually, grief moves toward _____, an acceptance of the loss.
48. Grief _____ helps people adapt to their loss and integrate changes into their lives.

● *How do effective parents discipline their children?*

Recite and Review: APPLICATIONS

49. Effective child _____ is based on a consistent framework of guidelines for acceptable behavior.
50. Good discipline tends to emphasize child management techniques (especially communication), rather than _____ assertion or withdrawal of _____.
51. _____ techniques tend to produce the highest levels of self-esteem in children.
52. Responsibility, mutual _____, consistency, love, encouragement, and clear _____ are features of effective parenting.

53. Much misbehavior can be managed by use of I-_____ and by applying _____ and logical consequences to children's behavior.

● *In what ways are attitudes toward death changing?*

Recite and Review: EXPLORATION

54. One approach to death is the hospice movement, which is devoted to providing humane care to persons who are _____.

55. A living will may help a person ensure that his or her life will not be artificially prolonged during a _____ illness.

56. Cryonic suspension has been attempted as a way of preserving people after death for possible future _____.

57. A continuing controversy concerns the ethics of passive euthanasia (allowing _____ to occur) and active euthanasia (inducing _____).

RELATE

1. _____	Erik Erikson	a.	"smother love"
2. _____	overprotection	b.	"soiling"
3. _____	regression	c.	reading disorder
4. _____	enuresis	d.	autism symptom
5. _____	encopresis	e.	psychosocial dilemmas
6. _____	pica	f.	hyperactive
7. _____	dyslexia	g.	bed wetting
8. _____	echolalia	h.	clinical death
9. _____	NDE	i.	eating disorder
10. _____	ADHD	j.	infantile behavior

11. _____	child abuse	a.	sexual maturation
12. _____	adolescence	b.	career dreams
13. _____	puberty	c.	narrowed career plans
14. _____	social marker	d.	broad career plans
15. _____	fantasy stage	e.	desired career
16. _____	tentative stage	f.	career guidance
17. _____	realistic stage	g.	life change
18. _____	vocational aspiration	h.	cultural status
19. _____	career center	i.	status or role clue
20. _____	transition period	j.	shaken baby

21.	_____	menopause	a. self-esteem studies
22.	_____	climacteric	b. expert on death
23.	_____	Roger Gould	c. parent-child communication
24.	_____	Elizabeth Kübler-Ross	d. care for dying
25.	_____	ageism	e. expert on aging
26.	_____	gerontologist	f. common prejudice
27.	_____	thanatologist	g. end of menstruation
28.	_____	Stanley Coopersmith	h. reactions to dying
29.	_____	Haim Ginott	i. significant physical change
30.	_____	hospice	j. adult development

CHECK YOUR MEMORY

Check Your Memory: Pages 128-132

1. Learning to read in childhood and establishing a vocation as an adult are typical life stages. T or F?
2. Psychosocial dilemmas occur when a person is in conflict with his or her social world. T or F?
3. Initiative versus guilt is the first psychosocial dilemma a child faces. T or F?
4. Answering the question "Who am I?" is a primary task during adolescence. T or F?
5. Generativity is expressed through taking an interest in the next generation. T or F?

Check Your Memory: Pages 133-135

6. Authoritarian parents view children as having adult-like responsibilities. T or F?
7. Permissive parents basically give their children the message "Do it because I say so." T or F?
8. The children of authoritarian parents tend to be independent, assertive, and inquiring. T or F?
9. It is best for parents to protect children from all stressful stimulation, as much as possible. T or F?

Check Your Memory: Pages 135-139

10. Clinging is one of the more serious problems of childhood. T or F?
11. Supportive and affectionate fathers tend to minimize sibling rivalry. T or F?
12. Toilet training is typically completed by age 3 or earlier. T or F?
13. A child who eats mud, buttons, or rubber bands suffers from enuresis nervosa. T or F?
14. Stuttering is more common among girls than boys. T or F?
15. Autism can be described as "word blindness." T or F?
16. ADHD affects 5 times as many boys as girls and may be partly hereditary. T or F?
17. Eating too much sugar is one of the main causes of hyperactivity in children. T or F?
18. The first signs of autism often appear in infancy, when autistic children may be extremely aloof and withdrawn. T or F?
19. Ritalin is used primarily to treat delayed speech. T or F?
20. The risk of committing child abuse is highest for young parents. T or F?
21. Abusive mothers tend to believe that their children are intentionally annoying them. T or F?

22. One third of abused children become abusive adults. T or F?
23. Parents Anonymous is an organization for parents who have autistic children. T or F?

Check Your Memory: Pages 140-143

24. The length of adolescence varies in different cultures. T or F?
25. The average onset of puberty is age 12 for boys and age 14 for girls. T or F?
26. Early maturation tends to enhance self-image for boys. T or F?
27. Early-maturing girls tend to date sooner and are more likely to get into trouble. T or F?
28. David Elkind believes that today's adolescents should be "hurried into adulthood" to maximize their potentials. T or F?
29. The term *imaginary audience* refers to adolescent peer groups and the influence they have on personal identity. T or F?
30. Being able to think about hypothetical possibilities helps adolescents in their search for identity. T or F?
31. Increased conflict with parents tends to occur early in adolescence. T or F?
32. Minority adolescents run an elevated risk of adopting a foreclosed identity. T or F?

Check Your Memory: Pages 143-144

33. During the establishment phase of career development, an initial search for career possibilities is made. T or F?
34. A person is most likely to serve as a mentor for other workers during the realistic stage of career development. T or F?
35. The fantasy stage of career development occurs early in the exploration phase. T or F?
36. The best predictor of what job category a person will enter is that person's vocational aspiration. T or F?
37. Vocational counselors give vocational interest and aptitude tests. T or F?

Check Your Memory: Pages 145-148

38. According to Gould, building a workable life is the predominant activity between ages 16 to 18. T or F?
39. A crisis of urgency tends to hit people around the age of 30. T or F?
40. Maintaining good health is a prominent goal among the elderly. T or F?
41. Levinson places the midlife transition in the 40-55 age range. T or F?
42. Only a small minority of the men studied by Levinson experienced any instability or urgency at midlife. T or F?
43. During the mid-life transition, women are less likely than men to define success in terms of a key event. T or F?
44. People who are uncomfortable making decisions tend to have a defensive-avoidant style of making career choices. T or F?
45. Over half of all women have serious emotional problems during menopause. T or F?
46. After the climacteric has occurred, men become infertile. T or F?
47. Having a sense of purpose in life is one element of well-being during adulthood. T or F

Check Your Memory: Pages 148-153

48. By the year 2020, 1 out of every 5 North Americans will be over age 65. T or F?
49. Peak functioning in most physical capacities occurs between ages 25 and 30. T or F?

50. The maximum human life span is around 120 years. T or F?
51. Life expectancy has increased dramatically in the last 200 years. T or F?
52. Crystallized abilities are the first to decline as a person ages. T or F?
53. Perceptual speed declines steadily after age 25. T or F?
54. For many people, successful aging requires a combination of activity and disengagement. T or F?
55. Ageism refers to prejudice and discrimination toward the elderly. T or F?
56. Few elderly persons become senile or suffer from mental decay. T or F?

Check Your Memory: Pages 153-156

57. Most of the deaths portrayed on television are homicides. T or F?
58. The "Why me" reaction to impending death is an expression of anger. T or F?
59. Trying to be "good" in order to live longer is characteristic of the denial reaction to impending death. T or F?
60. It is best to go through all the stages of dying described by Kübler-Ross in the correct order. T or F?
61. Medical explanations of NDEs attribute them to brain activities caused by oxygen starvation. T or F?
62. Bereaved persons should work through their grief as quickly as possible. T or F?

Check Your Memory: APPLICATIONS

63. Consistency of child discipline is more important than whether limits on children's behavior are strict or lenient. T or F?
64. As a means of child discipline, power assertion refers to rejecting a child. T or F?
65. Severely punished children tend to be defiant and aggressive. T or F?
66. Punishment is most effective when it is given immediately after a disapproved act. T or F?
67. Encouragement means giving recognition for effort and improvement. T or F?
68. Logical consequences should be stated as you-messages. T or F?

Check Your Memory: EXPLORATION

69. Hospice care can be provided at home, as well as in medical centers. T or F?
70. Hospice programs are designed to avoid the use of painkilling drugs. T or F?
71. A living will is not legally binding in most states in the U.S. T or F?
72. There is currently no way to freeze human bodies so their organs will resume functioning when thawed. T or F?

FINAL SURVEY AND REVIEW

● *What are the typical tasks and dilemmas through the life span?*

1. _____ psychologists study _____ and change from birth to death.
2. They are also interested in developmental _____, or prominent landmarks in personal development.

3. According to Erik _____, each life stage provokes a specific _____ dilemma.

4. During childhood these are: _____ versus mistrust, _____ versus shame and doubt, initiative versus guilt, and _____ versus inferiority.

5. In adolescence, _____ versus _____ confusion is the principal dilemma.

6. In young adulthood we face the dilemma of _____ versus isolation. Later, _____ versus stagnation becomes prominent.

7. Old age is a time when the dilemma of _____ versus despair must be faced.

8. In addition, each life stage requires successful mastery of certain developmental _____ (personal changes required for optimal development).

● *What is the nature of effective parenting?*

9. _____ parents enforce rigid rules and demand strict obedience to authority.

10. Overly _____ parents give little guidance and don't hold children accountable for their actions.

11. _____ (effective) parents supply firm and consistent guidance, combined with love and affection.

● *What are some of the more serious childhood problems?*

12. Few children grow up without experiencing some of the normal problems of childhood, including _____, _____, specific _____, sleep disturbances, general dissatisfaction, regression, sibling rivalry, and rebellion.

13. Major areas of difficulty in childhood are toilet training (including _____ and _____) and feeding disturbances, such as overeating, anorexia nervosa (self-starvation), and _____ (eating non-food substances).

14. Other problems include speech disturbances (delayed speech, _____); learning disorders, including _____ (an inability to read with understanding); and attention-deficit _____ disorder (ADHD).

15. Childhood autism is a severe problem involving _____ (failure to speak), sensory disturbances, tantrums, and a lack of responsiveness to _____ _____.

16. Some cases of autism are being treated successfully with behavior _____.

17. _____ _____ (physically or emotionally harming a child) is a major problem. Roughly 30 percent of all abused children become abusive _____. Emotional support and therapy can help break the cycle of abuse.

● *Why is adolescent development especially challenging?*

18. _____ is a culturally defined social status. _____ is a biological event.

19. On average, the peak _____ spurt during _____ occurs earlier for girls than for boys.

20. Early _____ is beneficial mostly for boys; its effects are mixed for girls.

21. Establishing a clear sense of personal _____ is a major task of adolescence. One danger of early maturation is premature _____ formation.

22. Many adolescents become self-conscious and preoccupied with _____ audiences.

23. Adolescent identity formation is accelerated by _____ development and influenced by parents and _____ groups (age mates).

● *How do people select careers for themselves?*

24. The first period in career development is the _____ phase, during which career possibilities are examined.

25. This phase can be further divided into a _____ stage, a _____ stage, and a realistic stage.

26. During the _____ phase the person enters a career and builds competence.

27. The _____ phase is marked by high competence and full status within the person's chosen career.

28. In the _____ _____ phase, preceding retirement, the person serves as a respected expert and _____ (role model and guide) for younger workers.

29. _____ counseling can greatly aid career decision making.

● *What happens psychologically during adulthood?*

30. Certain relatively _____ events mark adult development in our society.

31. In order these are: escape from parental _____, leaving the family, building a workable life, a crisis of _____, a crisis of _____, attaining stability, and mellowing.

32. A _____ _____ affects many people in the 37-41 age range, but this is by no means universal.

33. Some approaches to making career decisions are: the vigilant style, the _____ style, the _____-avoidant style, and the hypervigilant style. The vigilant style is most effective.

34. Adjustment to later middle age is sometimes complicated for women by menopause and for men by a _____.

● *What are some of the psychological challenges of aging?*

35. The _____ are the fastest growing segment of society in North America.

36. Biological aging begins between 25 and 30, but _____ _____ in specific pursuits may come at various points throughout life.

37. The length of human lives is limited by the maximum _____ _____. Life _____ (the average number of years people live) is much shorter.

38. _____ declines associated with aging are limited, at least through one's 70s. This is especially true of individuals who remain mentally active.

39. The greatest losses occur for _____ abilities (which require speed or rapid learning); _____ abilities (stored up knowledge and skills) show much less decline and may actually improve.

40. _____ (those who study aging) have proposed the _____ theory of successful aging. It holds that withdrawal from society is necessary and desirable in old age.

41. The _____ theory states that optimal adjustment to aging is tied to continuing action and involvement. This theory applies to more people than withdrawal from society does.

42. _____ refers to prejudice, discrimination, and stereotyping on the basis of age. It affects people of all ages, but is especially damaging to older people.

● *How do people typically react to death and bereavement?*

43. Older people fear the _____ of death more than the fact that it will occur.

44. Typical emotional reactions to impending death are _____, anger, _____, depression, and acceptance.

45. _____ experiences (NDEs) frequently result in significant changes in personality, values, and life goals.

46. _____ also brings forth a typical series of grief reactions.

47. Initial _____ is followed by _____ of grief. Later, apathy, dejection, and _____ may occur. Eventually, grief moves toward resolution, an acceptance of the loss.

48. _____ work helps people adapt to their loss and _____ changes into their lives.

● *How do effective parents discipline their children?*

49. Effective child discipline is based on a _____ framework of _____ for acceptable behavior.

50. Good discipline tends to emphasize child _____ techniques (especially communication), rather than power _____ or withdrawal of love.

51. Management techniques tend to produce the highest levels of _____ in children.

52. Responsibility, mutual respect, _____, love, _____, and clear communication are features of effective parenting.

53. Much misbehavior can be managed by use of I-messages and by applying natural and _____ _____ to children's behavior.

● *In what ways are attitudes toward death changing?*

54. One approach to death is the _____ movement, which is devoted to providing humane care to persons who are dying.

55. A _____ _____ may help a person ensure that his or her life will not be artificially prolonged during a terminal illness.

56. _____ suspension has been attempted as a way of preserving people after death for possible future revival; however, both suspension and revival are presently impossible.

57. A continuing controversy concerns the ethics of passive _____ (allowing death to occur) and active _____ (inducing death).

MASTERY TEST

1. Procrastination, inaction, and indecision are most characteristic of the _____ style of career
    decision making.
    a. vigilant   b. complacent   c. defensive-avoidant   d. hypervigilant

2. Identity formation during adolescence is aided by
    a. cognitive development   b. attaining the preoperational stage   c. emotional bargaining
    d. you-messages from parents

3. Which of the following is not a normal, relatively mild childhood problem?
    a. negativism   b. clinging   c. sibling rivalry   d. delayed speech

4. Infancy, childhood, adolescence, and young adulthood are
    a. developmental tasks   b. life stages   c. psychosocial dilemmas   d. biologically defined social statuses

5. Premature identity formation is one of the risks of early
    a. generativity   b. preoccupation with imaginary audiences   c. trust-mistrust resolution   d. puberty

6. The thought, "It's all a mistake" would most likely occur as part of which reaction to impending death?
    a. anger   b. freezing up   c. denial   d. bargaining

7. High self-esteem is most often a product of what style of child discipline?
    a. power assertion   b. child management   c. withdrawal of love   d. the natural consequences method

8. Which of the following is a correct match?
    a. enuresis--eating disorder   b. anorexia--speech disturbance   c. dyslexia--learning disorder
    d. pica--autism

9. According to Erikson, the first dilemma a newborn infant must resolve is
    a. independence versus dependence   b. initiative versus guilt   c. trust versus mistrust
    d. attachment versus confusion

10. People are most likely to imagine themselves in unrealistic vocations during the _____ stage
    of career development.
    a. preliminary   b. tentative   c. fantasy   d. mentoring

11. A living will that calls for the removal of life-support equipment is basically a request for
    a. cryonic suspension   b. passive euthanasia   c. active euthanasia   d. hospice care

12. For both boys and girls, a growth spurt corresponds with _____.
    a. adolescence   b. puberty   c. cognitive maturation   d. less prestige with peers

13. Autonomy, environmental mastery, a purpose in life, and continued personal growth help maintain
    well-being in old age. This observation supports the _____ theory of successful aging.
    a. disengagement   b. re-engagement   c. activity   d. re-activity

14. A healthy balance between the rights of parents and their children is characteristic of
    a. authoritarian parenting   b. permissive parenting   c. authoritative parenting   d. consistent parenting

15. According to Erikson, developing a sense of integrity is a special challenge in
    a. adolescence   b. young adulthood   c. middle adulthood   d. late adulthood

16. The event for males that is most comparable to menopause in women is the
    a. climacteric   b. midlife crisis   c. generativity transition   d. genophase

17. Grief following bereavement typically begins with _____ and ends with _____.
    a. anger, disengagement   b. dejection, disengagement   c. isolation, depression   d. shock, resolution

18. Physicians typically use the stimulant drug Ritalin to control
    a. encopresis   b. ADHD   c. echolalia   d. anorexia nervosa

19. The smallest number of Levinson's subjects experienced midlife as a(an)
    a. last chance   b. period of serious decline   c. time to start over   d. escape from dominance

20. One thing that all forms of effective child discipline have in common is that they
    a. are consistent   b. make use of punishment   c. involve temporary withdrawal of love
    d. emphasize you-messages

21. Which combination would lead to the highest risk of child abuse?
    a. young parent, high income, child over 3 years   b. young parent, low income, abused as a child
    c. older parent, low income, child over 3 years   d. older parent, high income, abused as a child

22. Foreclosed identity formation is a special risk for
    a. late maturing boys   b. minority adolescents   c. late maturing girls   d. adolescents in the
    preoperational stage

23. Oxygen deprivation in the brain best accounts for which element of a NDE?
    a. the tunnel of light   b. the pangs of grief   c. the period of depression   d. the life review and
    personality changes

24. The realistic stage of choosing a career usually comes immediately before the _____ phase.
    a. establishment   b. exploration   c. midcareer   d. preliminary

25. Overprotective parenting ignores the fact that _____ is a normal part of life.
    a. rebellion   b. punishment   c. rejection   d. stress

26. Ivar Lovaas has successfully used _____ to treat _____.
    a. Ritalin, echolalia   b. operant shaping, dyslexia   c. restricted sugar diets, ADHD
    d. behavior modification, autism

27. Skills that rely on fluid abilities could be expected to show declines beginning in
    a. adolescence   b. young adulthood   c. middle adulthood   d. late adulthood

28. Threatening, accusing, bossing, and lecturing children is most characteristic of
   a. PET   b. you-messages   c. applying natural consequences   d. management techniques

29. Gould's study of adult development found that a crisis of _____ is common between the ages of 35 and 43.
   a. urgency   b. questions   c. dominance   d. stability

30. With respect to aging, it is least possible to modify which of the following?
   a. life expectancy   b. crystallized abilities   c. mental abilities   d. maximum life span

ANSWERS

Recite and Review

1. change
2. developmental
3. dilemma
4. shame, guilt, inferiority
5. adolescence
6. isolation, stagnation
7. despair
8. developmental
9. rules, authority
10. guidance
11. effective
12. disturbances, rivalry
13. toilet training, feeding
14. speech, learning, disorder
15. autism
16. behavior
17. harming, 30
18. social, biological
19. girls, boys
20. boys, girls
21. adolescence, early
22. audiences
23. parents
24. career
25. realistic
26. competence
27. competence

28. younger workers
29. decision
30. adult development
31. escape, family
32. universal
33. vigilant
34. women, men
35. fastest
36. aging
37. maximum, Life
38. 70s, active
39. speed, knowledge
40. aging, aging
41. activity
42. age, older
43. death
44. anger, depression
45. experiences, values
46. grief
47. grief, resolution
48. work
49. discipline
50. power, love
51. Management
52. respect, communication
53. messages, natural
54. dying
55. terminal
56. revival
57. death, death

Relate

1. e
2. a
3. j
4. g
5. b
6. i
7. c
8. d
9. h
10. f
11. j
12. h
13. a
14. i
15. b
16. d
17. c
18. e
19. f
20. g
21. g
22. i
23. j
24. h
25. f
26. e
27. b
28. a
29. c
30. d

Check Your Memory

1. F
2. T
3. F
4. T
5. T
6. T
7. F
8. F
9. F
10. F
11. T
12. T
13. F
14. F
15. F
16. T
17. F
18. T
19. F
20. T
21. T
22. T
23. F
24. T
25. F
26. T
27. T
28. F
29. F
30. T
31. T
32. T
33. F
34. F
35. T
36. T
37. T
38. F
39. F
40. T
41. F
42. F
43. T
44. T
45. F
46. F
47. T
48. T
49. T
50. T
51. T
52. F
53. T
54. T
55. F
56. T
57. T
58. T
59. F
60. F
61. T
62. F
63. T
64. F
65. T
66. T
67. T
68. F
69. T
70. F
71. T
72. T

Final Survey and Review

1. Life-span, continuity
2. milestones
3. Erikson, psychosocial
4. trust, autonomy, industry
5. identity, role
6. intimacy, generativity
7. integrity
8. tasks
9. Authoritarian
10. permissive
11. Authoritative
12. negativism, clinging, fears
13. enuresis, encopresis, pica
14. stuttering, dyslexia, hyperactivity
15. mutism, other people
16. modification
17. Child abuse, adults
18. Adolescence, Puberty
19. growth, puberty
20. maturation
21. identity, identity
22. imaginary
23. cognitive, peer
24. exploration
25. fantasy, tentative
26. establishment
27. midcareer
28. later career, mentor
29. Vocational
30. consistent
31. dominance, questions, urgency
32. midlife crisis
33. complacent, defensive
34. climacteric
35. elderly
36. peak performance
37. life span, expectancy
38. Intellectual
39. fluid, crystallized
40. Gerontologists, disengagement
41. activity
42. Ageism
43. circumstances
44. denial, bargaining
45. Near-death
46. Bereavement
47. shock, pangs, depression
48. Grief, integrate
49. consistent, guidelines
50. management, assertion
51. self-esteem
52. consistency, encouragement
53. logical consequences
54. hospice
55. living will
56. Cryonic
57. euthanasia, euthanasia

Mastery Test

1. c (p. 147)
2. a (p. 142)
3. d (p. 134-136)
4. b (p. 129)
5. d (p. 141)
6. c (p. 153)
7. b (p. 159)
8. c (p. 136)
9. c (p. 129)
10. c (p. 144)
11. b (p. 163-164)
12. b (p. 140)
13. c (p. 151)

14. c (p. 133)
15. d (p. 131)
16. a (p. 148)
17. d (p. 155-156)
18. b (p. 136)
19. c (p. 146)
20. a (p. 158)
21. b (p. 138)
22. b (p. 143)
23. a (p. 154)
24. a (p. 144)
25. d (p. 134)
26. d (p. 137)
27. b (p. 150)
28. b (p. 161)
29. a (p. 145)
30. d (p. 149-150)

Chapter 6

Sensation and Reality

CHAPTER OVERVIEW

Sensory systems collect, select, transduce, analyze, and code information from the environment and send it to the brain. Psychophysics is the study of the relationship between physical stimuli and psychological sensations. Both absolute and difference thresholds have been identified for various senses. Subliminal perception occurs, but its impact tends to be weak.

Vision and visual problems can be partly understood by viewing the eyes as optical systems. However, the visual system also analyzes light stimuli to identify patterns and basic visual features. Color sensations are explained by the trichromatic theory (in the retina) and the opponent-process theory (for the rest of the visual system).

The inner ear is a sensory mechanism for transducing sound waves in the air into nerve impulses. The frequency and place theories of hearing explain how sound information is coded.

Olfaction is based on receptors that respond to gaseous molecules in the air. The lock-and-key theory and the locations of olfactory receptors activated by different scents explain how various odors are coded. Taste is another chemical sense. A lock-and-key match between dissolved molecules and taste receptors also explains many taste sensations.

The somesthetic, or bodily, senses include the skin senses, the kinesthetic senses, and the vestibular senses.

Our awareness of sensory information is altered by sensory adaptation, selective attention, and sensory gating. Pain sensations in particular are affected by anxiety, feelings of control, attention, and the interpretation given to aversive stimuli.

Various forms of motion sickness are related to mismatches between sensory information from the vestibular system, kinesthesis, and vision.

RECITE AND REVIEW

● *In general, how do sensory systems function?*

Recite and Review: Pages 168-170

~~chemical~~

1. Sensory organs transduce physical energies into _____nerve_____ impulses.

2. The senses act as _____ reduction systems that select, _____, and code sensory information.

3. A good example of sensory analysis is the identification of basic _____ features in a stimulus pattern.

4. In fact, many sensory systems act as feature _____.

5. Phosphenes and visual pop-out are examples of feature detection and _____ coding in action.

6. Sensory response can be partially understood in terms of localization of _____ in the brain. That is, the area of the brain _____ ultimately determines which type of sensory experience we have.

● *What are the limits of our sensory sensitivity?*

Recite and Review: Pages 170-173

7. Psychophysics is the study of _____ stimuli and the _____ they evoke.

8. The _____ amount of physical energy necessary to produce a _____ defines the absolute threshold.

9. The amount of _____ necessary to produce a just noticeable difference (or JND) in a stimulus defines a _____ threshold.

10. In general, the amount of change needed to produce a JND is a constant proportion of the original stimulus _____. This relationship is known as Weber's _____.

11. Threatening or anxiety-provoking stimuli may _____ the threshold for recognition, an effect called perceptual _____.

12. Any stimulus _____ the level of conscious awareness is said to be subliminal.

13. There is evidence that subliminal perception occurs, but subliminal advertising is largely

_____.

● *How is vision accomplished?*

Recite and Review: Pages 173-178

14. The _____ spectrum consists of electromagnetic radiation in a narrow range.

15. The electromagnetic spectrum ranges from violet, with a _____ of 400 nanometers, to red with a _____ of 700 nanometers.

16. Hue refers to a color's name, which corresponds to its _____. Saturated or "pure" colors come from a _____ band of wavelengths. Brightness corresponds to the amplitude of light waves.

17. The eye is in some ways like a camera. At its back lies an array of photoreceptors, called _____ and _____, that make up a light-sensitive layer called the retina.

18. Vision is focused by the _____ of the cornea and lens and by changes in the _____ of the lens, called accommodation.

19. Four common visual defects, correctable with glasses, are myopia (_____), hyperopia (farsightedness), presbyopia (loss of _____), and astigmatism (in which portions of vision are out of focus).

20. The amount of light entering the eye is controlled by movements of the iris, which dilates (_____) and constricts (_____) the pupil.

21. In the retina, the _____ specialize in night vision, black and white reception, and motion detection.

22. The _____, found exclusively in the fovea and otherwise toward the middle of the eye, specialize in _____ vision, acuity (perception of fine detail), and daylight vision.

23. Individual cells in the visual cortex of the brain act as feature _____ to analyze visual information.

24. The _____ supply much of our peripheral vision. Loss of peripheral vision is called tunnel vision.

● *How do we perceive colors?*

Recite and Review: Pages 178-182

25. The rods and cones differ in color _____. Yellow-green is brightest for cones; blue-green for the rods (although they will see it as colorless).

26. In the _____, color vision is explained by the trichromatic theory. The theory says that three types of _____ exist, each most sensitive to either red, green, or blue.

27. Three types of light-sensitive visual pigments are found in the _____, each pigment is most sensitive to either red, green, or blue light.

28. Beyond the retina, the visual system analyzes colors into _____ messages. According to the opponent-process theory, color information can be coded as either red or green, yellow or blue, and _____ _____ _____ messages.

29. _____ color blindness is rare, but 8 percent of males and 1 percent of females are red-green color blind or color weak.

30. Color blindness is a sex-linked trait carried on the *X* (_____) chromosome and passed from mother to son.

31. The Ishihara test is used to detect _____ _____.

32. Dark adaptation, an _____ in sensitivity to light, is caused by increased concentrations of visual pigments in the _____ and the _____.

33. Most dark adaptation is the result of increased rhodopsin concentrations in the _____. Vitamin A deficiencies may cause _____ blindness by impairing the production of rhodopsin.

● *What makes hearing possible?*

Recite and Review: Pages 183-187

34. Sound waves are the stimulus for hearing. Sound travels as waves of compression (_____) and rarefaction (_____) in the air.

35. The _____ of a sound corresponds to the frequency of sound waves. Loudness corresponds to the amplitude (_____) of sound waves.

36. Sound waves are transduced by the _____, auditory ossicles, oval window, cochlea, and ultimately, the _____ cells in the organ of Corti.

37. The frequency theory says that the _____ of nerve impulses in the auditory nerves matches the _____ of incoming sounds (up to 4000 hertz).

38. Place theory says that _____ tones register near the base of the cochlea and _____ tones near its tip.

39. Three basic types of deafness are _____ deafness, conduction deafness, and stimulation deafness.

40. Conduction deafness can often be overcome with a hearing aid. _____ deafness can sometimes be alleviated by cochlear implants.

41. Stimulation deafness can be prevented by avoiding excessive exposure to _____ sounds. Sounds above 120 decibels pose an immediate danger to hearing. Two warning signs of stimulation deafness are temporary threshold _____ and tinnitus.

● *How do the chemical senses operate?*

Recite and Review: Pages 187-190

42. Olfaction (_____) and gustation (_____) are chemical senses responsive to airborne or liquefied molecules.

43. It is suspected that humans are also sensitive to _____ signals called pheromones, although the evidence remains preliminary. Pheromones may be sensed by the vomeronasal

_____.

44. The lock and key theory partially explains smell. In addition, the _____ of the olfactory receptors in the nose helps identify various scents.

45. Specific areas on the tongue are more responsive to sweet, salty, sour, and _____ tastes. Taste also appears to be based in part on lock-and-key _____ of molecule shapes.

● *What are the somesthetic senses and why are they important?*

Recite and Review: Pages 190-192

46. The somesthetic senses include the _____ senses, vestibular senses, and kinesthetic senses (receptors that detect muscle and joint positioning).

47. The skin senses include touch, _____, pain, cold, and warmth. Sensitivity to each is related to the _____ of receptors found in an area of skin.

48. Distinctions can be made among various types of pain, including visceral pain, somatic pain, referred pain, warning system pain, and _____ system pain.

● *Why are we more aware of some sensations than others?*

Recite and Review: Pages 192-195

49. Incoming sensations are affected by sensory adaptation (a _____ in the number of nerve impulses sent).

50. Selective attention (selection and diversion of messages in the brain) and sensory _____ (blocking or alteration of messages flowing toward the brain) also alter sensations.

51. Selective gating of pain messages apparently takes place in the _____ _____. Gate control theory proposes an explanation for many pain phenomena.

52. "Runner's high," the painkilling effects of the Chinese medical art of acupuncture, and other pain phenomena appear to be explained by the release of a _____-like chemical in the brain, called beta-endorphin.

● *How can pain be reduced in everyday situations?*

Recite and Review: APPLICATIONS

53. Pain can be reduced by _____ anxiety and redirecting attention to stimuli other than the pain stimulus.

54. Feeling that you have control over a stimulus tends to _____ the amount of pain you experience.

55. The interpretation placed on a _____ affects how painful it is perceived to be.

56. Sending _____ pain messages to the spinal cord can close the gates to more severe pain. This effect is called counterirritation.

● *How is balance related to motion sickness?*

Recite and Review: EXPLORATION

57. Various forms of motion sickness are related to messages received from the vestibular system, which senses gravity and _____ movement.

58. The otolith organs detect the pull of _____ and rapid head movements.

59. The movement of _____ within the semicircular canals, and the movement of the _____ within each ampulla, detects head movement and positioning.

60. According to sensory conflict theory, motion sickness is caused by a _____ of visual, kinesthetic, and vestibular sensations. Motion sickness can be avoided by minimizing sensory conflict.

RELATE

1. _____ ciliary muscle

2. _____ iris

3. _____ cornea

4. _____ blind spot

5. _____ lens

6. _____ fovea

7. _____ retinal veins

8. _____ optic nerve

9. _____ aqueous humor

10. _____ pupil

11. _____ retina

12. _____   vestibular system

13. _____   cochlea

14. _____   round window

15. _____   auditory canal

16. _____   stapes

17. _____   auditory nerve

18. _____   incus

19. _____   oval window

20. _____   tympanic membrane

21. _____   malleus

22. _____   limen

23. _____   Landolt rings

24. _____   anosmia

25. _____   pressure

26. _____   eye tremors

27. _____   "bug detector"

28. _____   artificial vision

29. _____   hertz

30. _____   afterimages

31. _____   retinal

a. physiological nystagmus

b. visual acuity

c. perceptual features

d. localization of function

e. vibrations per second

f. vitamin A

g. opponent process theory

h. Pacinian corpuscle

i. threshold

j. "smell blindness"

CHECK YOUR MEMORY

Check Your Memory: Pages 168-170

1. The electromagnetic spectrum includes ultraviolet light and radio waves. T or F?
2. Each sensory organ is sensitive to a select range of physical energies. T or F?
3. The artificial vision system described in the text is based on electrodes implanted in the retina. T or F?
4. The retina responds to pressure, as well as light. T or F?

Check Your Memory: Pages 170-173

5. It takes only one photon striking the retina to produce a sensation of light. T or F?
6. Humans can hear sounds from 2 to 2,000 hertz. T or F?
7. It is possible to taste 1 teaspoon of sugar dissolved in 2 gallons of water. T or F?
8. Some music fans have been harmed by subliminal backmasking. T or F?

9. The JND for loudness is 1/10. T or F?
10. Weber's law applies mainly to stimuli in the mid-range. T or F?

Check Your Memory: Pages 173-178

11. A nanometer is one-millionth of a meter. T or F?
12. The lens of the eye is about the size and thickness of a postage stamp. T or F?
13. Farsightedness is corrected with a convex lens. T or F?
14. The myopic eye is longer than normal. T or F?
15. There are more rods than cones in the eyes. T or F?
16. Hubel and Wiesel directly recorded activity in single cells in the visual cortex. T or F?
17. The blind spot is the point where the optic nerve leaves the eye. T or F?
18. The fovea contains only retinal arteries and veins. T or F?
19. Vision rated at 20/200 is better than average. T or F?
20. Visual acuity decreases near the edges of the retina. T or F?

Check Your Memory: Pages 178-182

21. Blue emergency lights and taxiway lights are used because at night they are more visible to the cones. T or F?
22. The trichromatic theory of color vision assumes that black and white sensations are produced by the rods. T or F?
23. According to the opponent-process theory it is impossible to have a reddish green or yellowish blue. T or F?
24. The afterimage produced by staring at a red object is green. T or F?
25. Visual pigments bleach, or breakdown chemically, when struck by light. T or F?
26. Yellow-blue color weakness is very rare. T or F?
27. In the U.S. and Canada, stoplights are always on the bottom of traffic signals. T or F?
28. Compete dark adaptation takes about 12 minutes. T or F?
29. Dark adaptation can be preserved by working in an area lit with red light. T or F?

Check Your Memory: Pages 183-187

30. Sound cannot travel in a vacuum. T or F?
31. The visible, external portion of the ear is the malleus. T or F?
32. The hair cells are part of the organ of Corti. T or F?
33. Hunter's notch occurs when the auditory ossicles are damaged by the sound of gunfire. T or F?
34. Cochlear implants stimulate the auditory nerve directly. T or F?
35. A 40 decibel sound could be described as quiet. T or F?
36. A 100 decibel sound can damage hearing in less than 8 hours. T or F?
37. Every 20 decibels increases sound energy by a factor of 10. T or F?

Check Your Memory: Pages 187-190

38. At least 1000 different types of olfactory receptors exist. T or F?
39. Etherish odors smell like garlic. T or F?
40. Ansomia can be caused by exposure to chemical odors. T or F?
41. Human pheromones (if they exist) are sensed as a subtle, perfume-like odor. T or F?
42. Flavors are greatly influenced by odor, as well as taste. T or F?

43. Taste buds are found throughout the mouth, not just on the tongue. T or F?
44. Aspartame and saccharin are only half as sweet as common sugar. T or F?
45. Women are more likely to be supertasters. T or F?
46. PTC tastes bitter to about 70 percent of those tested. T or F?
47. The sense of taste tends to be weaker in early childhood than it is later as the body matures. T or F?

Check Your Memory: Pages 190-192

48. Free nerve endings can produce any of the basic skin sensations. T or F?
49. Vibration is one of the five basic skin sensations. T or F?
50. Areas of the skin that have high concentrations of pain receptors are no more sensitive to pain than other areas of the body. T or F?
51. Visceral pain is often felt at a location on the surface of the body. T or F?
52. Small nerve fibers generally carry warning-system pain messages. T or F?
53. Pain originating in the heart may be felt all the way down the left arm. T or F?
54. Most physical skills rely on dynamic touch, which combines touch sensations with kinesthetic information. T or F?

Check Your Memory: Pages 192-195

55. Unlike other receptor cells, the rods and cones do not undergo sensory adaptation. T or F?
56. If you wear a ring, you are rarely aware of it because of sensory gating. T or F?
57. The "seat-of-your pants" phenomenon is related to selective attention. T or F?
58. Stabilized visual images appear brighter and more intense than normal. T or F?
59. Mild electrical stimulation of the skin can block reminding system pain. T or F?
60. Mild electrical stimulation of the skin causes a release of endorphins in free nerve endings. T or F?

Check Your Memory: APPLICATIONS

61. High levels of anxiety tend to amplify the amount of pain a person experiences. T or F?
62. Prepared childbirth training helps women feel in control of the birth process. T or F?
63. Physical relaxation exercises can be used to lower anxiety in situations involving pain. T or F?
64. As a means of reducing pain, hot-water bottles are an example of counterirritation. T or F?

Check Your Memory: EXPLORATION

65. Space sickness tends to occur more suddenly than other types of motion sickness. T or F?
66. The semicircular canals are especially sensitive to the pull of gravity. T or F?
67. Motion sickness is believed to be related to the body's reactions to being poisoned. T or F?
68. A horizontal body position tends to intensify motion sickness. T or F?

FINAL SURVEY AND REVIEW

● *In general, how do sensory systems function?*

1. Sensory organs _____ physical energies into nerve impulses.

2. The senses act as data _____ systems that select, analyze, and _____ sensory information.

3. A good example of _____ _____ is the identification of basic perceptual features in a stimulus pattern.

4. In fact, many sensory systems act as _____ detectors.

5. _____ and visual pop-out are examples of feature detection and sensory _____ in action.

6. Sensory response can be partially understood in terms of _____ of function in the brain. That is, the _____ of the brain activated ultimately determines which type of sensory experience we have.

● *What are the limits of our sensory sensitivity?*

7. _____ is the study of physical stimuli and the sensations they evoke.

8. The minimum amount of physical energy necessary to produce a sensation defines the _____ threshold.

9. The amount of change necessary to produce a _____ _____ difference (or JND) in a stimulus defines a _____ threshold.

10. In general, the amount of change needed to produce a JND is a _____ _____ of the original stimulus intensity. This relationship is known as _____ law.

11. Threatening or anxiety-provoking stimuli may raise the _____ for recognition, an effect called _____ defense.

12. Any stimulus below the level of conscious awareness is said to be _____.

13. There is evidence that subliminal perception occurs, but subliminal _____ is largely ineffective.

● *How is vision accomplished?*

14. The visible spectrum consists of _____ radiation in a narrow range.

15. The visible spectrum ranges from violet, with a wavelength of _____ _____, to red with a wavelength of _____ _____.

16. _____ refers to a color's name, which corresponds to its wavelength. Saturated or "pure" colors come from a narrow band of wavelengths. Brightness corresponds to the _____ of light waves.

17. The eye is in some ways like a camera. At its back lies an array of _____, called rods and cones, that make up a light-sensitive layer called the _____.

18. Vision is focused by the shape of the _____ and lens and by changes in the shape of the lens, called _____.

19. Four common visual defects, correctable with glasses, are _____ (nearsightedness), hyperopia (farsightedness), presbyopia (loss of accommodation), and _____ (in which portions of vision are out of focus).

20. The amount of light entering the eye is controlled by movements of the _____, which _____ (enlarges) and _____ (narrows) the pupil.

21. In the retina, the rods specialize in night vision, black and white reception, and _____ detection.

22. The cones, found exclusively in the _____ and otherwise toward the middle of the eye, specialize in color vision, _____ (perception of fine detail), and daylight vision.

23. Individual cells in the visual _____ of the brain act as feature detectors to analyze visual information.

24. The rods supply much of our _____ vision. Loss of _____ vision is called tunnel vision.

● *How do we perceive colors?*

25. The rods and cones differ in color sensitivity. _____-green is brightest for cones; _____-green for the rods (although they will see it as colorless).

26. In the retina, color vision is explained by the _____ theory. The theory says that three types of cones exist, each most sensitive to either red, green, or blue.

27. Three types of light-sensitive visual _____ are found in the cones, each is most sensitive to either red, green, or blue light.

28. Beyond the retina, the visual system analyzes colors into either-or messages. According to the _____ theory, color information can be coded as either _____ _____ _____, yellow or blue, and black or white messages.

29. Total color blindness is rare, but 8 percent of males and 1 percent of females are _____ color blind or color weak.

30. Color blindness is a _____ trait carried on the *X* (female) chromosome and passed from _____ to son.

31. The _____ test is used to detect color blindness.

32. Dark adaptation, an increase in sensitivity to light, is caused by increased concentrations of _____ _____ in the rods and the cones.

33. Most dark adaptation is the result of increased _____ concentrations in the rods. Vitamin _____ deficiencies may cause night blindness.

● *What makes hearing possible?*

34. Sound waves are the stimulus for hearing. Sound travels as waves of _____ (peaks) and _____ (valleys) in the air.

35. The pitch of a sound corresponds to the _____ of sound waves. Loudness corresponds to the _____ (height) of sound waves.

36. Sound waves are transduced by the eardrum, auditory _____, oval window, cochlea, and ultimately, the hair cells in the organ of _____.

37. The frequency theory says that the frequency of nerve impulses in the _____ _____ matches the frequency of incoming sounds (up to 4000 hertz).

38. Place theory says that high tones register near the _____ of the cochlea and low tones near its _____.

39. Three basic types of deafness are nerve deafness, conduction deafness, and _____ deafness.

40. Conduction deafness can often be overcome with a hearing aid. Nerve deafness can sometimes be alleviated by _____ implants.

41. Stimulation deafness can be prevented by avoiding excessive exposure to loud sounds. Sounds above _____ _____ pose an immediate danger to hearing. Two warning signs of stimulation deafness are temporary threshold shift and a ringing in the ears, called _____.

● *How do the chemical senses operate?*

42. _____ (smell) and _____ (taste) are chemical senses responsive to airborne or liquefied molecules.

43. It is suspected that humans are also sensitive to chemical signals called _____, which may be sensed by the _____ organ.

44. The _____ _____ _____ theory partially explains smell. In addition, the location of the olfactory receptors in the nose helps identify various scents.

45. Specific areas on the tongue are more responsive to _____, _____, _____, and bitter tastes. Taste also appears to be based in part on lock-and-key coding of _____ shapes.

● *What are the somesthetic senses and why are they important?*

46. The somesthetic senses include the skin senses, vestibular senses, and _____ senses (receptors that detect muscle and joint positioning).

47. The skin senses include touch, pressure, _____, cold, and warmth. Sensitivity to each is related to the number of _____ found in an area of skin.

48. Distinctions can be made among various types of pain, including visceral pain, somatic pain, _____ pain, _____ system pain, and reminding system pain.

● *Why are we more aware of some sensations than others?*

49. Incoming sensations are affected by sensory _____ (a decrease in the number of nerve impulses sent).

50. Selective _____ (selection and diversion of messages in the brain) and sensory gating (blocking or alteration of messages flowing toward the brain) also alter sensations.

51. Selective gating of pain messages apparently takes place in the spinal cord. _____ _____ theory proposes an explanation for many pain phenomena.

52. "Runner's high," the painkilling effects of the Chinese medical art of _____, and other pain phenomena appear to be explained by the release of a morphine-like chemical in the brain, called beta-_____.

● *How can pain be reduced in everyday situations?*

53. Pain can be reduced by lowering anxiety and redirecting _____ to stimuli other than the pain stimulus.

54. Feeling that you have _____ over a stimulus tends to reduce the amount of pain you experience.

55. The _____ or meaning placed on a stimulus affects how painful it is perceived to be.

56. Sending mild pain messages to the spinal cord can close the gates to more severe pain. This effect is called _____.

● *How is balance related to motion sickness?*

57. Various forms of motion sickness are related to messages received from the _____ system, which senses gravity and head movement.

58. The _____ organs detect the pull of gravity and rapid head movements.

59. The movement of fluid within the _____ canals, and the movement of the crista within each _____, detects head movement and positioning.

60. According to _____ _____ theory, motion sickness is caused by a mismatch of visual, kinesthetic, and vestibular sensations. Motion sickness can be avoided by minimizing sensory conflict.

MASTERY TEST

1. A person with tunnel vision has mainly lost the ability to use the
   a. cones   b. photoreceptors   c. iris   d. rods

2. Sensory conflict theory attributes motion sickness to mismatches between what three systems?
   a. olfaction, kinesthesis, and audition   b. vision, kinesthesis, and the vestibular system
   c. kinesthesis, audition, and the somesthetic system   d. vision, gustation, and the skin senses

3. Which of the following types of color blindness is most common?
   a. yellow-blue, male   b. yellow-blue, female   c. red-green, female   d. red-green, male

4. A reasonable conclusion about subliminal perception is that
   a. subliminal stimuli have weak effects
   b. backmasking poses a serious threat to listeners
   c. subliminal tapes are more effective than subliminal advertising
   d. subliminal perception applies to hearing, but not to vision

5. Which of the following does not belong with the others?
   a. Pacinian corpuscle   b. Merkle's disk   c. vomeronasal organ   d. free nerve endings

6. The fact that the eyes are only sensitive to a narrow band of electromagnetic energies shows that vision acts as a (an) _____ system.
   a. opponent-process   b. gate-control   c. central biasing   d. data reduction

7. Which theory of color vision best explains the fact that we do not see yellowish blue?
   a. trichromatic   b. chromatic gating   c. Ishihara hypothesis   d. opponent process

8. A person with inflamed kidneys feels pain in her hips. This is an example of
   a. warning system pain   b. referred pain   c. somatic pain   d. vestibular pain

9. Hubel and Wiesel found that nerve cells in the visual cortex of the brain respond most to specific
   a. phosphenes   b. perceptual features   c. areas of the visible spectrum   d. numbers of photons

10. Which of the following pain control strategies makes use of gate control theory?
    a. counterirritation   b. distraction and reinterpretation   c. anxiety reduction
    d. gaining control over pain stimuli

11. New mothers who are depressed take longer than usual to recognize pictures of babies. This is an example of
    a. backmasking   b. visual accommodation   c. difference thresholds   d. perceptual defense

12. Forty ceiling lights are on in a large room. Four lights must be turned off before the room becomes noticeably darker. According to Weber's law, if you start with 10 lights on, how many must you turn off to make the room just noticeably darker?
    a. 1/4   b. 1   c. 2   d. 4

13. Dark adaptation is closely related to concentrations of _____ in the _____.
    a. retinal, aqueous humor   b. photopsin, cones   c. rhodopsin, rods   d. photons, optic nerve

14. Sensory analysis tends to extract perceptual _____ from stimulus patterns.
    a. thresholds   b. features   c. transducers   d. amplitudes

15. Which pair of terms is most closely related?
    a. hyperopia--color blindness   b. astigmatism--presbyopia   c. myopia--astigmatism
    d. hyperopia--presbyopia

16. The painkilling effects of acupuncture are partly explained by _____ theory and the release of
    _____.
    a. lock-and-key, pheromones   b. gate control, pheromones   c. gate control, endorphins
    d. lock-and-key, endorphins

17. Three photons of light striking the _____ defines the _____ for vision.
    a. retina, absolute threshold   b. cornea, difference threshold   c. iris, upper limen   d. cornea, JND

18. According to the _____ theory of hearing, low tones cause the greatest movement near the _____ of the cochlea.
    a. place, outer tip   b. frequency, outer tip   c. place, base   d. frequency, base

19. Where vision is concerned, physiological nystagmus helps prevent
    a. sensory gating   b. tunnel vision   c. sensory adaptation   d. night blindness

20. Which of the following best represents the concept of a transducer?
    a. Translating English into Spanish.   b. Copying a computer file from one floppy disk to another.
    c. Speaking into a telephone receiver.   d. Turning water into ice.

21. Visual pop-out is closely related to which sensory process?
    a. transduction   b. feature detection   c. difference thresholds   d. perception below the limen

22. Rods and cones are to vision as _____ are to hearing.
    a. auditory ossicles b. vibrations c. pinnas d. hair cells

23. You lose the ability to smell floral odors. This is called _____ and it is compatible with the _____ theory of olfaction.
    a. anosmia, lock-and-key b. anhedonia, place c. tinnitus, gate-control
    d. sensory adaptation, molecular

24. The main problem with current artificial vision systems is
    a. the retina's lack of an absolute threshold b. the danger of damaging the eyes while producing phosphenes c. their inability to transduce letters d. the rejection of implanted electrodes

25. Which two dimensions of color are related to the wavelength of electromagnetic energy?
    a. hue and saturation b. saturation and brightness c. brightness and hue d. brightness and amplitude

26. Temporary threshold shifts are related to
    a. conduction deafness b. nerve deafness c. stimulation deafness d. damage to the ossicles

27. The existence of the blind spot is explained by a lack of
    a. rhodopsin b. peripheral vision c. photoreceptors d. activity in the fovea

28. Which of the following normally has the most effect on the amount of light entering the eye?
    a. fovea b. iris c. aqueous humor d. cornea

29. In vision, a loss of accommodation is most associated with aging of the
    a. iris b. fovea c. lens d. cornea

30. Visual acuity and color vision are provided by the _____ found in large numbers in the _____ of the eye.
    a. cones, fovea b. cones, periphery c. rods, fovea d. rods, periphery

ANSWERS

Recite and Review

1. nerve
2. data, analyze
3. perceptual
4. detectors
5. sensory
6. function, activated
7. physical, sensations
8. minimum, sensation
9. change, difference
10. intensity, law
11. raise, defense
12. below
13. ineffective
14. visible
15. wavelength, wavelength
16. wavelength, narrow
17. rods, cones
18. shape, shape
19. nearsightedness, accommodation
20. enlarges, narrows
21. rods
22. cones, color
23. detectors
24. rods
25. sensitivity
26. retina, cones
27. cones
28. either-or, black or white
29. Total
30. female

31. color blindness
32. increase, rods, cones
33. rods, night
34. peaks, valleys
35. pitch, height
36. eardrum, hair
37. frequency, frequency
38. high, low
39. nerve
40. Nerve
41. loud, shifts
42. smell, taste
43. chemical, organ
44. location
45. bitter, coding
46. skin
47. pressure, number
48. reminding
49. reduction (or decrease)
50. gating
51. spinal cord
52. morphine (or opiate)
53. lowering
54. reduce
55. stimulus
56. mild
57. head
58. gravity
59. fluid, crista
60. mismatch

Relate

1. d
2. f
3. h
4. b
5. i
6. c
7. k
8. a
9. e
10. g
11. j
12. e
13. g
14. h
15. a
16. d
17. f
18. c
19. i
20. j
21. b
22. i
23. b
24. j
25. h
26. a
27. c
28. d
29. e
30. g
31. f

Check Your Memory

1. T
2. T
3. F
4. T
5. F
6. F
7. T
8. F
9. T
10. T
11. F
12. F
13. T
14. T
15. T
16. T
17. T
18. F
19. F
20. T
21. F
22. T
23. T
24. T
25. T
26. T
27. F
28. F
29. T
30. T
31. F
32. T
33. F
34. T
35. T
36. T
37. T
38. T
39. F
40. T
41. F
42. T
43. T
44. F
45. T
46. T
47. F
48. T
49. F
50. F
51. T
52. F
53. T
54. T
55. F
56. F
57. T
58. F
59. T
60. F
61. T
62. T
63. T
64. T
65. T
66. F
67. T
68. F

Final Survey and Review

1. transduce
2. reduction, code
3. sensory analysis
4. feature
5. Phosphenes, coding
6. localization, area
7. Psychophysics
8. absolute
9. just noticeable, difference
10. constant proportion, Weber's
11. threshold, perceptual
12. subliminal
13. advertising
14. electromagnetic

15. 400 nanometers, 700 nanometers
16. Hue, amplitude
17. photoreceptors, retina
18. cornea, accommodation
19. myopia, astigmatism
20. iris, dilates, constricts
21. motion
22. fovea, acuity
23. cortex
24. peripheral, peripheral
25. Yellow, blue
26. trichromatic
27. pigments
28. opponent-process, red or green
29. red-green
30. sex-linked, mother
31. Ishihara
32. visual pigments
33. rhodopsin, A
34. compression, rarefaction
35. frequency, amplitude
36. ossicles, Corti
37. auditory nerves
38. base, tip
39. stimulation
40. cochlear
41. 120 decibels, tinnitus
42. Olfaction, gustation
43. pheromones, vomeronasal
44. lock and key
45. sweet, salty, sour, molecule
46. kinesthetic
47. pain, receptors
48. referred, warning
49. adaptation
50. attention
51. Gate control
52. acupuncture, endorphin
53. attention
54. control
55. interpretation
56. counterirritation
57. vestibular
58. otolith
59. semicircular, ampulla
60. sensory conflict

Mastery Test

1. d (p. 178)
2. b (p. 198)
3. d (p. 179)
4. a (p. 172)
5. c (p. 188, 191)
6. d (p. 169)
7. d (p. 179)
8. b (p. 191)
9. b (p. 177)
10. a (p. 197)
11. d (p. 171)
12. b (p. 172)
13. c (p. 180)
14. b (p. 169)
15. d (p. 174-175)
16. c (p. 193-194)
17. a (p. 171)
18. a (p. 184)
19. c (p. 192)
20. c (p. 169)
21. b (p. 170)
22. d (p. 175, 183)
23. a (p. 187)
24. d (p. 170)
25. a (p. 173)
26. c (p. 185)
27. c (p. 175)
28. b (p. 175)
29. c (p. 175)
30. a (p. 175)

Chapter 7

Perceiving the World

CHAPTER OVERVIEW

Perception involves organizing sensations into meaningful patterns. Perceptions are hypotheses about sensory events or models of the world. Visual perceptions are stabilized by size, shape, and brightness constancies. The most basic perceptual pattern (in vision) is figure-ground organization. Sensations tend to be organized on the basis of nearness, similarity, continuity, closure, contiguity, and common region.

Depth perception depends on accommodation, convergence, retinal disparity, and various pictorial cues. The pictorial cues include linear perspective, relative size, light and shadow, overlap, texture gradients, aerial haze, and relative motion.

Learning, in the form of perceptual habits, influences perceptions. Perceptual judgments are related to stimulus context and to internal frames of reference, such as one's adaptation level. Perceptions are also greatly affected by attention, motives, values, and expectations. Selective attention and divided attention influence what information we are aware of at any moment. So do habituation, motives and values, and perceptual sets.

Because perceptions are reconstructions of events, eyewitness testimony can be unreliable. Perceptual accuracy can be improved by reality testing, dishabituation, actively paying attention, breaking perceptual habits, using broad frames of reference, and being aware of perceptual sets.

Parapsychology is the study of purported psi phenomena, including clairvoyance, telepathy, precognition, and psychokinesis. The bulk of the evidence to date is against the existence of extrasensory perception. Stage ESP is based on deception and tricks.

RECITE AND REVIEW

● *What are perceptual constancies, and what is their role in perception?*

Recite and Review: Pages 202-205

1. Perception is the process of assembling sensations into _____ that provide a usable mental _____ of the world.

2. In vision, the retinal _____ changes from moment to moment, but the external world appears stable and undistorted because of _____ constancies.

3. In size and shape _____, the perceived sizes and shapes of objects remain the same even though their retinal images change size and shape. The apparent brightness of objects remains stable (a property called brightness constancy) because each reflects a _____ proportion of light.

4. Perceptual constancies are partly native (_____) and partly empirical (_____).

● *What basic principles do we use to group sensations into meaningful patterns?*

Recite and Review: Pages 205-208

5. The most basic organization of sensations is a division into figure and ground (_____ and _____). Reversible figures, however, allow figure-ground organization to be reversed.

6. A number of factors, identified by the Gestalt psychologists, contribute to the _____ of sensations. These are nearness, _____, continuity, closure, contiguity, _____ region, and combinations of the preceding.

7. Stimuli near one another tend to be perceptually _____ together. So, too, do stimuli that are similar in _____. Continuity refers to the fact that perceptions tend to be organized as simple, uninterrupted patterns.

8. Closure is the tendency to _____ a broken or incomplete pattern. Contiguity refers to nearness in _____ and space. Stimuli that fall in a defined area, or common region, also tend to be grouped together.

9. _____ psychologists are also known as human factors _____.

10. These specialists make machine _____ and controls compatible with human _____ and motor capacities.

11. The most effective _____ _____ engineering follows the principles of natural design.

12. Basic elements of line drawings, especially the edges of _____ and parallel edges, appear to be universally recognized.

13. A perceptual organization may be thought of as an _____ held until evidence contradicts it. Camouflage patterns disrupt perceptual _____, especially figure-ground perceptions.

14. Perceptual organization shifts for ambiguous _____, which may have more than one interpretation. An example is Necker's _____. Impossible figures resist stable organization altogether.

● *How is it possible to see depth and judge distance?*

Recite and Review: Pages 209-216

15. _____ perception is the ability to perceive three-dimensional space and judge distances.

16. Depth perception is present in basic form soon after _____ as shown by testing with the visual cliff and other methods. As soon as infants become active _____ they refuse to cross the visual cliff.

17. Depth perception depends on the muscular cues of accommodation (bending of the _____) and convergence (inward movement of the _____).

18. The area of binocular vision is _____ in some birds than in humans. However, birds and other animals may have extremely _____ field of view.

19. A number of pictorial _____, which will work in _____ paintings, drawings, and photographs, also underlie normal depth perception.

20. Some pictorial cues are: linear perspective (the apparent convergence of _____ _____), relative size (more distant objects appear _____), height in the _____ plane, light and shadow (shadings of light), and overlap or interposition (one object overlaps another).

21. Additional pictorial cues include: texture gradients (textures become _____ in the distance), aerial haze (loss of color and detail at large distances), and relative _____ or _____ parallax (differences in the apparent movement of objects when a viewer is moving).

22. All the pictorial cues are monocular depth cues (only _____ _____ is needed to make use of them).

23. The moon illusion refers to the fact that the moon appears _____ near the horizon than it does when overhead.

24. The moon illusion is at least partially explained by the apparent _____ hypothesis, which emphasizes the greater number of depth cues present when the moon is on the _____. Changes in accommodation within the eyes also contribute to the moon illusion.

● *What effect does learning have on perception?*

Recite and Review: Pages 217-222

25. Organizing and interpreting sensations is greatly influenced by learned perceptual _____. An example is the Ames room, which looks rectangular but is actually distorted so that objects in the room appear to change _____.

26. Sensitivity to perceptual _____ is also partly learned. Studies of inverted vision show that even the most basic organization is subject to a degree of change. Active _____ speeds adaptation to new perceptual environments.

27. Perceptual judgments are almost always related to the _____ surrounding a stimulus, or to an internal frame of reference called the adaptation _____, which is a personal _____ point for making judgments.

28. Perceptual _____ (misleading perceptions) differ from hallucinations (perceptions of non-existent stimuli).

29. Illusions are often related to perceptual _____. One of the most familiar of all illusions, the Müller-Lyer illusion, seems to be related to perceptual learning based on experience with box-shaped _____ and rooms.

30. Linear perspective, _____ invariance relationships, and mislocating the end-points of the _____ also contribute to the Müller-Lyer illusion.

● *How is perception altered by attention, motives, values, and expectations?*

Recite and Review: Pages 222-226

31. _____ attention refers to giving priority to some sensory messages while excluding others.

32. Attention acts like a _____ or narrowing of the information channel linking the senses to perception.

33. Attention may also be divided among various activities. Divided attention suggests that our
_____ for storing and thinking about information is limited.

34. Attention is aroused by _____ stimuli, by repetition (with variation), by stimulus contrast,
_____, or incongruity.

35. Attention is accompanied by an orientation response (OR). When a stimulus is repeated without
_____, the orientation response _____, an effect known as habituation.

36. Personal motives and _____ often alter perceptions by changing the evaluation of what is
seen or by altering attention to specific details.

37. Perceptions may be based on _____ or bottom-up processing of information.

38. Bottom-up processing, perceptions begin with the organization of low-level _____. In
top-down processing, previous knowledge is used to rapidly _____ sensory information.

39. Attention, prior experience, suggestion, and motives combine in various ways to create perceptual sets, or
_____. A perceptual set is a readiness to perceive in a particular way, induced by strong
expectations.

● *How reliable are eyewitness reports?*

Recite and Review: APPLICATIONS

40. Perception is an _____ reconstruction of events. This is one reason why eyewitness
testimony is surprisingly _____.

41. In many crimes, eyewitness accuracy is further damaged by weapon _____. Similar factors,
such as observer stress, brief exposure times, cross-racial inaccuracies, and the wording of questions can
_____ eyewitness accuracy.

42. Perceptual accuracy is enhanced by reality _____, dishabituation, and conscious efforts to
pay _____.

43. It is also valuable to break perceptual habits, to _____ frames of reference, to beware of
perceptual sets, and to be aware of the ways in which motives and emotions influence perceptions.

● *Is extrasensory perception possible?*

Recite and Review: EXPLORATION

44. Parapsychology is the study of purported _____ phenomena, including clairvoyance (perceiving
events at a distance), _____ ("mind reading"), precognition (perceiving future events),
and psychokinesis (mentally influencing inanimate objects).

45. Clairvoyance, telepathy, and precognition are purported types of extrasensory _____.

46. Research in parapsychology remains controversial owing to a variety of problems.
_____ and after-the-fact reinterpretation are problems with "natural" ESP episodes.

47. Many studies of ESP overlook the impact of statistically unusual outcomes that are no more than runs of
_____.

48. The bulk of the evidence to date is _____ the existence of ESP. Very few positive results in
ESP research have been replicated (_____) by independent scientists.

49. Stage ESP is based on _____ and tricks.

RELATE

1. _____ texture gradients
2. _____ stereoscopic vision
3. _____ convergence
4. _____ continuity
5. _____ light and shadow
6. _____ common region
7. _____ relative size
8. _____ closure
9. _____ overlap
10. _____ retinal disparity
11. _____ linear perspective
12. _____ nearness
13. _____ similarity

14. _____ reversible figure
15. _____ visual cliff
16. _____ binocular cue
17. _____ mismatch
18. _____ woodcock
19. _____ Ponzo illusion
20. _____ motion pictures
21. _____ OR
22. _____ Zulus

a. convergence
b. stereogram
c. 360 degree view
d. moon illusion
e. Müller-Lyer illusion
f. infant depth perception
g. figure-ground
h. stroboscopic movement
i. double take

23. _____ advertising
24. _____ top-down
25. _____ perceptual awareness
26. _____ dishabituation
27. _____ psi events
28. _____ decline effect
29. _____ stage ESP
30. _____ Zener cards

a. perceptual expectancy
b. Zen and attention
c. run of luck
d. sex and anxiety
f. J. B. Rhine
g. Uri Geller
h. clairvoyance test
i. surrender to experience

CHECK YOUR MEMORY

Check Your Memory: Pages 202-205

1. Perception involves selecting, organizing, and integrating sensory information. T or F?
2. Some perceptual abilities must be learned after sight is restored to the previously blind. T or F?
3. Newborn babies show some evidence of size constancy. T or F?
4. Houses and cars look like toys from a low-flying airplane because of shape constancy. T or F?
5. Drunkenness impairs brightness constancy, but size and shape constancy are not usually affected. T or F?
6. Brightness constancy does not apply to objects illuminated by different amounts of light. T or F?

Check Your Memory: Pages 205-208

7. Basic figure-ground organization is learned at about age 2. T or F?
8. Illusory figures are related to the principle of closure. T or F?
9. Contiguity refers to our tendency to see lines as continuous. T or F?
10. A user-friendly camera must have displays and controls that are compatible with human sensory and motor capacities. T or F?
11. Natural design minimizes feedback so that people are not distracted by unnecessary information. T or F?
12. Pre-existing ideas actively guide our interpretation of sensations in many cases. T or F?
13. Necker's cube and the "three-pronged widget" are impossible figures. T or F?
14. Color boundaries on objects in drawings are intuitively understood by just about everyone. T or F?

Check Your Memory: Pages 209-216

15. Depth perception is partly learned and partly innate. T or F?
16. Human depth perception typically emerges at about 4 months of age. T or F?
17. All depth cues are basically binocular. T or F?
18. Accommodation and convergence are muscular depth cues. T or F?
19. Accommodation acts as a depth cue primarily for distances greater than 4 feet from the eyes. T or F?
20. Convergence acts as a depth cue primarily for distances less than 4 feet from the eyes. T or F?
21. The brain is sensitive to mismatches in information received from the right and left eyes. T or F?
22. Depth perception is actually as good when using just one eye as it is when both eyes are open. T or F?
23. Pigeons, ducks, and hummingbirds can see ultraviolet light. T or F?
24. With one eye closed, the pictorial depth cues no longer provide information about depth and distance. T or F?
25. Changing the image size of an object implies that its distance from the viewer has changed, too. T or F?
26. In a drawing, the closer an object is to the horizon line, the nearer it appears to be to the viewer. T or F?
27. Aerial perspective is most powerful when the air is exceptionally clear. T or F?
28. When an observer is moving forward, objects beyond the observer's point of fixation appear to move forward too. T or F?
29. Accommodation is a binocular depth cue. T or F?
30. Some familiarity with drawings is required to use overlap as a depth cue. T or F?
31. The moon's image is magnified by the dense atmosphere near the horizon. T or F?
32. More depth cues are present when the moon is viewed near the horizon. T or F?

Check Your Memory: Pages 217-222

33. A lack of relevant perceptual experience makes it difficult to judge upside-down faces. T or F?

34. The Ames room is primarily used to test the effects of inverted vision. T or F?

35. Cats who grow up surrounded by horizontal stripes are unusually sensitive to vertical stripes when they reach maturity. T or F?

36. People who wear inverting goggles say that eventually the visual world turns right side up again. T or F?

37. Divers must learn to compensate for visual distortions while underwater. T or F?

38. Perception is most accurate during active interactions with one's surroundings. T or F?

39. If your adaptation level for judging weight is 30 pounds, you would judge a 30-pound object as "heavy." T or F?

40. Hearing voices when no one is speaking is an example of a perceptual illusion. T or F?

41. Perceptual illusions are usually not noticeable until measurements reveal that our perceptions are inaccurate or distorted. T or F?

42. According to Richard Gregory, the arrowhead-tipped line in the Müller-Lyer illusion looks like the outside corner of a building. T or F?

43. Zulus rarely see round shapes and therefore fail to experience the Müller-Lyer illusion. T or F?

Check Your Memory: Pages 222-226

44. Messages passing through the "bottleneck" of selective attention appear to prevent other messages from passing through. T or F?

45. As skills become automated, they free mental capacity for other activities. T or F?

46. Repetitious stimuli must vary a little to gain attention, otherwise repetition leads to habituation. T or F?

47. Enlarged pupils and brain-wave changes typically accompany the OR. T or F?

48. Humans are especially sensitive to slow, gradual changes that occur over very long time periods. T or F?

49. Emotional stimuli can shift attention away from other information. T or F?

50. Analyzing information into small features and then building a recognizable pattern is called top-up processing. T or F?

51. Perceptual sets are frequently created by suggestion. T or F?

52. You could use a tachistoscope to flash stimuli on a screen for very brief periods. T or F?

53. Labels and categories have been shown to have little real effect on perceptions. T or F?

Check Your Memory: APPLICATIONS

54. In many ways we see what we believe, as well as believe what we see. T or F?

55. The more confident an eyewitness is about the accuracy of his or her testimony, the more likely it is to be accurate. T or F?

56. The testimony of crime victims is generally more accurate than the testimony of bystanders. T or F?

57. Police officers and other trained observers are more accurate eyewitnesses than the average person. T or F?

58. Reality testing is the process Abraham Maslow described as a "surrender" to experience. T or F?

59. Perceptually, Zen masters have been shown to habituate more rapidly than the average person. T or F?

Check Your Memory: EXPLORATION

60. Uri Geller was one of the first researchers in parapsychology to use the Zener cards. T or F?

61. Psychokinesis is classified as a psi event, but not a form of ESP. T or F?
62. Prophetic dreams are regarded as a form of precognition. T or F?
63. Strange coincidences are strong evidence for the existence of ESP. T or F?
64. The Zener cards eliminated the possibility of fraud and "leakage" of information in ESP experiments. T or F?
65. "Psi missing" is perhaps the best current evidence for ESP. T or F?
66. Belief in psi events has declined among parapsychologists in recent years. T or F?

FINAL SURVEY AND REVIEW

● *What are perceptual constancies, and what is their role in perception?*

1. Perception is the process of assembling _____ into patterns that provide a usable _____ _____ of the world.
2. In vision, the _____ image changes from moment to moment, but the external world appears stable and undistorted because of perceptual _____.
3. In size and shape constancy, the perceived sizes and shapes of objects remain the same even though their retinal images change size and shape. The apparent _____ of objects remains stable (a property called brightness constancy) because each reflects a constant _____ of _____.
4. Perceptual constancies are partly _____ (inborn) and partly _____ (learned).

● *What basic principles do we use to group sensations into meaningful patterns?*

5. The most basic organization of sensations is a division into _____ and _____ (object and background).
6. A number of factors, identified by the _____ psychologists, contribute to the organization of sensations. These are _____, similarity, continuity, _____, contiguity, common region, and combinations of the preceding.
7. Stimuli near one another tend to be perceptually grouped together. So, too, do stimuli that are similar in appearance. _____ refers to the fact that perceptions tend to be organized as simple, uninterrupted patterns.
8. _____ refers to nearness in time and space. Stimuli that fall in a defined area, or common region, also tend to be grouped together.
9. Engineering psychologists are also known as _____ _____ engineers.
10. These specialists make machine displays and _____ compatible with human sensory and _____ capacities.
11. The most effective human factors engineering follows the principles of _____ _____.
12. Basic elements of line drawings, especially the edges of surfaces and _____ _____, appear to be universally recognized.
13. A perceptual organization may be thought of as an hypothesis held until evidence contradicts it. _____ patterns disrupt perceptual organization, especially figure-ground perceptions.

14. Perceptual organization shifts for _____ stimuli, which may have more than one interpretation. An example is _____ cube. Impossible _____ resist stable organization altogether.

● *How is it possible to see depth and judge distance?*

15. Depth perception is the ability to perceive _____ space and judge distances.
16. Depth perception is present in basic form soon after birth as shown by testing with the _____ _____ and other methods. As soon as infants become active crawlers they refuse to cross the deep side of the _____ _____.
17. Depth perception depends on the muscular cues of _____ (bending of the lens) and _____ (inward movement of the eyes).
18. The area of _____ vision is smaller in some birds than in humans. However, birds and other animals may have extremely wide _____ _____ _____.
19. A number of _____ cues, which will work in flat paintings, drawings, and photographs, also underlie normal depth perception.
20. Some of these cues are: _____ _____ (the apparent convergence of parallel lines), relative size (more distant objects appear smaller), height in the picture plane, light and shadow (shadings of light), and overlap or _____ (one object overlaps another).
21. Additional pictorial cues include: texture _____ (textures become finer in the distance), aerial haze (loss of color and detail at large distances), and relative motion or motion _____ (differences in the apparent movement of objects when a viewer is moving).
22. All the pictorial cues are _____ depth cues (only one eye is needed to make use of them).
23. The moon illusion refers to the fact that the moon appears larger near the _____.
24. The moon illusion is at least partially explained by the _____ distance hypothesis, which emphasizes the greater number of depth cues present when the moon is on the horizon. Changes in _____ within the eyes also contribute to the moon illusion.

● *What effect does learning have on perception?*

25. Organizing and interpreting sensations is greatly influenced by learned _____ _____. An example is the _____ room, which looks rectangular but is actually distorted so that objects in the room appear to change size.
26. Sensitivity to perceptual features is also partly learned. Studies of _____ vision show that even the most basic organization is subject to a degree of change. Active movement speeds _____ to new perceptual environments.
27. Perceptual judgments are almost always related to the context surrounding a stimulus, or to an internal _____ _____ _____ called the _____ level, which is a personal medium point for making judgments.
28. Perceptual _____ (misleading perceptions) differ from _____ (perceptions of non-existent stimuli).
29. Illusions are often related to perceptual habits. One of the most familiar of all illusions, the _____ illusion, involves two equal-length lines tipped with arrowheads and V's. This illusion seems to be related to perceptual learning based on experience with box-shaped buildings and rooms.

30. Linear perspective, size-distance _____ relationships, and mislocating the _____ of the lines also contribute to the Müller-Lyer illusion.

● *How is perception altered by attention, motives, values, and expectations?*

31. _____ _____ refers to giving priority to some sensory messages while excluding others.

32. Attention acts like a bottleneck or narrowing of the information _____ linking the senses to perception.

33. Attention may also be split among various activities. _____ attention suggests that our capacity for storing and thinking about information is limited.

34. Attention is aroused by intense stimuli, by repetition (with variation), by stimulus _____, change, or _____.

35. Attention is accompanied by an _____ _____ (OR). When a stimulus is repeated without change, the OR decreases, an effect known as _____.

36. Personal _____ and values often alter perceptions by changing the evaluation of what is seen or by altering attention to specific details.

37. Perceptions may be based on top-down or bottom-up _____ of information.

38. _____ perceptions begin with the organization of low-level features. In _____ processing, previous knowledge is used to rapidly organize sensory information.

39. Attention, prior experience, suggestion, and motives combine in various ways to create _____ _____, or expectancies. A _____ _____ is a readiness to perceive in a particular way, induced by strong expectations.

● *How reliable are eyewitness reports?*

40. Perception is an active _____ of events. This is one reason why eyewitness testimony is surprisingly inaccurate.

41. In many crimes, eyewitness accuracy is further damaged by _____ focus. Similar factors, such as observer _____, brief exposure times, cross-racial inaccuracies, and the wording of questions can lower eyewitness accuracy.

42. Perceptual accuracy is enhanced by reality testing, _____, and conscious efforts to pay attention.

43. It is also valuable to break _____ _____, to broaden frames of reference, to beware of perceptual sets, and to be aware of the ways in which motives and emotions influence perceptions.

● *Is extrasensory perception possible?*

44. _____ is the study of purported psi phenomena, including clairvoyance (perceiving events at a distance), telepathy ("mind reading"), _____ (perceiving future events), and psychokinesis (mentally influencing inanimate objects).

45. Clairvoyance, telepathy, and precognition are purported types of _____ perception.

46. Research in parapsychology remains controversial owing to a variety of problems. Coincidence and after-the-fact _____ are problems with "natural" ESP episodes.

47. Many studies of ESP overlook the impact of _____ unusual outcomes that are no more than runs of luck.

48. The bulk of the evidence to date is against the existence of ESP. Very few positive results in ESP research have been _____ (repeated) by independent scientists.

49. _____ ESP is based on deception and tricks.

Mastery Test

1. The Ames room creates a conflict between
   a. horizontal features and vertical features   b. attention and habituation   c. top-down and bottom-up processing   d. shape constancy and size constancy

2. Weapon focus tends to lower eyewitness accuracy because it affects
   a. selective attention   b. the adaptation level   c. perceptions of contiguity   d. dishabituation

3. Stereograms create an illusion of depth by mimicking the effects of
   a. accommodation   b. convergence   c. retinal disparity   d. stroboscopic motion

4. Which perceptual constancy is most affected by sitting in the front row at a movie theater?
   a. size constancy   b. shape constancy   c. brightness constancy   d. depth constancy

5. The warning "Look right" at crosswalks in London is designed to counteract the _____ of tourists.
   a. habituation   b. perceptual habits   c. adaptation levels   d. unconscious transference

6. Fans of opposing sports teams often act as if they had seen two entirely different games. This is explained by the effects of _____ on perception.
   a. pictorial cues   b. motives   c. habituation   d. figure-ground organization

7. Size constancy
   a. emerges at about 4 months of age   b. is affected by experience with the sizes of objects
   c. requires that objects be illuminated by light of the same intensity   d. all of the preceding

8. Adaptation to visual distortions is most rapid if people are allowed to
   a. remain immobile   b. move actively   c. move their eye muscles   d. habituate their adaptation levels

9. Perceptual categories and perceptual expectancies tend to promote
   a. top-down processing   b. bottom-up processing   c. divided attention   d. reality testing

10. Both internal frames of reference and external _____ alter the interpretation given to a stimulus.
    a. reconstructions   b. bottlenecks   c. accommodations   d. contexts

11. Which of the following cues would be of greatest help to a person trying to thread a needle?
   a. light and shadow   b. texture gradients   c. linear perspective   d. overlap

12. The American woodcock has a narrow band of _____ but an unusually wide

   _____.
   a. monocular vision, spectral sensitivity   b. accommodation, field of view   c. binocular vision, field of view   d. spectral sensitivity, binocular range

13. Which of the following purported paranormal phenomena is not a form of ESP?
   a. clairvoyance   b. telepathy   c. precognition   d. psychokinesis

14. Size-distance invariances contribute to which of the following?
   a. Müller-Lyer illusion   b. the stroboscopic illusion   c. perceptual hallucinations
   d. changes in a person's adaptation level

15. The visual cliff is used primarily to test infant
   a. size constancy   b. figure-ground perception   c. depth perception   d. adaptation to spatial distortions

16. Which of the following organizational principles is based on nearness in time and space?
   a. continuity   b. closure   c. contiguity   d. size constancy

17. Which of the following is both a muscular and a monocular depth cue?
   a. convergence   b. relative motion   c. aerial perspective   d. accommodation

18. "Natural" ESP occurrences cannot usually be
   a. replicated   b. evaluated   c. reinterpreted   d. explained as coincidences

19. Which of the following is not part of the explanation of the Müller-Lyer illusion?
   a. aerial perspective   b. accommodation   c. living in a "square" culture   d. mislocating the
   ends of the lines

20. The term _____ refers to our limited capacity for storing and thinking about information.
   a. selective attention   b. habituated attention   c. divided attention   d. selective expectancy

21. A previously blind person has just had her sight restored. Which of the following perceptual experiences is
   she most likely to have?
   a. perceptual set   b. size constancy   c. linear perspective   d. figure-ground

22. An artist manages to portray a face with just a few unconnected lines. Apparently the artist has capitalized
   on
   a. closure   b. contiguity   c. the reversible figure effect   d. the principle of camouflage

23. The "boiled frog syndrome" is related to the idea that _____ elicit attention.
   a. repetition, habituation, and categories   b. expectancies, constancies, and ambiguities
   c. change, contrast, and incongruity   d. continuity, camouflage, and similarity

24. The most basic source of stereoscopic vision is
    a. accommodation b. retinal disparity c. convergence d. stroboscopic motion

25. Necker's cube is a good example of
    a. an ambiguous stimulus b. an impossible figure c. camouflage d. a binocular depth cue

26. Enlarged pupils, a pause in breathing, and increased blood flow to the head are associated with
    a. brightness constancy b. the onset of habituation c. reality testing d. an orientation response

27. Skeptics regard the decline effect as evidence that _____ occurred in an ESP test?
    a. replication b. cheating c. a run of luck d. leakage

28. Which of the following is a binocular depth cue?
    a. accommodation b. convergence c. linear perspective d. motion parallax

29. Ambiguous stimuli allow us to hold more than one perceptual
    a. gradient b. parallax c. constancy d. hypothesis

30. Increased perceptual awareness is especially associated with
    a. dishabituation b. unconscious transference c. high levels of stress d. stimulus repetition without variation

31. Effective, natural design provides
    a. clear feedback b. behavioral settings c. participative displays d. lifelike models

ANSWERS

Recite and Review

1. patterns, model
2. image, perceptual
3. constancy, constant
4. inborn, learned
5. object, background
6. organization, similarity, common
7. grouped, appearance
8. complete, time
9. Engineering, engineers
10. displays, sensory
11. human factors
12. surfaces
13. hypothesis, organization
14. stimuli, cube
15. Depth
16. birth, crawlers
17. lens, eyes
18. smaller, wide
19. cues, flat
20. parallel lines, smaller, picture
21. finer, motion, motion
22. one eye
23. larger
24. distance, horizon
25. habits, size
26. features, movement
27. context, level, medium
28. illusions
29. habits, buildings
30. size-distance, lines
31. Selective
32. bottleneck
33. capacity
34. intense, change
35. change, decreases
36. values
37. top-down
38. features, organize
39. expectancies
40. active, inaccurate
41. focus, lower
42. testing, attention
43. broaden
44. psi, telepathy
45. perception
46. Coincidence
47. luck

48. against, repeated
49. deception

Relate

1. m
2. g
3. f
4. c
5. l
6. e
7. j
8. d
9. k
10. h
11. i
12. a
13. b
14. g
15. f
16. a
17. b
18. c
19. d
20. h
21. i
22. e
23. d
24. a
25. i
26. b
27. f
28. c
29. g
30. h

Check Your Memory

1. T
2. T
3. T
4. F
5. F
6. T
7. F
8. T
9. F
10. T
11. F
12. T

13. T
14. F
15. T
16. T
17. F
18. T
19. F
20. F
21. T
22. F
23. T
24. F
25. T
26. F
27. F
28. T
29. F
30. F
31. F
32. T
33. T
34. F
35. F
36. F
37. T
38. T
39. F
40. F
41. T
42. T
43. F
44. T
45. T
46. T
47. T
48. F
49. T
50. F
51. T
52. T
53. F
54. T
55. F
56. F
57. F
58. F
59. F
60. F
61. T
62. T
63. F
64. F

65. F
66. T

Final Survey and Review

1. sensations, mental model
2. retinal, constancies
3. brightness, proportion, light
4. native, empirical
5. figure, ground
6. Gestalt, nearness, closure
7. Closure
8. Contiguity,
9. human factors
10. controls, motor
11. natural design
12. parallel edges
13. Camouflage
14. ambiguous, Necker's, figures
15. three-dimensional
16. visual cliff, visual cliff
17. accommodation, convergence
18. binocular, field of view
19. pictorial
20. linear perspective, interposition
21. gradients, parallax
22. monocular
23. horizon
24. apparent, accommodation
25. perceptual habits, Ames
26. inverted, adaptation
27. frame of reference, adaptation
28. illusions, hallucinations
29. Müller-Lyer
30. invariance, end-points
31. Selective attention
32. channel
33. Divided
34. contrast, incongruity
35. orientation response, habituation
36. motives
37. processing
38. Bottom-up, top-down
39. perceptual sets, perceptual set

40. reconstruction
41. weapon, stress
42. dishabituation
43. perceptual habits
44. Parapsychology, precognition
45. extrasensory
46. reinterpretation
47. statistically
48. replicated
49. Stage

Mastery Test

1. d (218)
2. a (227)
3. c (210-211)
4. b (204)
5. b (217)
6. b (224)
7. b (204)
8. b (219)
9. a (225)
10. d (219)
11. d (214)
12. c (213)
13. d (230)
14. a (221)
15. c (209)
16. c (206)
17. d (210)
18. a (231-232)
19. a (221)
20. c (223)
21. d (205)
22. a (205)
23. c (224)
24. b (210)
25. a (208)
26. d (223)
27. c (232)
28. b (210)
29. d (208)
30. a (229)
31. a (206-207)

Chapter 8

States of Consciousness

CHAPTER OVERVIEW

Consciousness consists of everything you are aware of at a given instant. Altered states of consciousness (ASCs) differ significantly from normal waking consciousness. Many conditions produce ASCs, which frequently have culturally defined meanings.

Sleep is an innate biological rhythm characterized by changes in consciousness and brain activity. Brain-wave patterns and sleep behaviors define four stages of sleep. The two most basic forms of sleep are rapid eye movement (REM) sleep and non-rapid eye movement (NREM) sleep. Dreams and nightmares occur primarily in REM sleep. Sleepwalking, sleeptalking, and night terrors are NREM events. Insomnia and other sleep disturbances are common, but generally treatable. Dreaming is emotionally restorative and it may help form adaptive memories. The psychodynamic view portrays dreams as a form of wish fulfillment; the activation-synthesis hypothesis says that dreaming is a physiological process with little meaning.

Hypnosis is characterized by narrowed attention and increased openness to suggestion. People vary in hypnotic susceptibility. Most hypnotic phenomena are related to the basic suggestion effect. Hypnosis can relieve pain and it has other useful effects, but it is not magic. Stage hypnotists simulate hypnosis in order to entertain.

Sensory deprivation refers to any major reduction in external stimulation. Sensory deprivation produces deep relaxation and a variety of perceptual effects. It can be used to help people enhance creative thinking and to change bad habits.

Psychoactive drugs are substances that alter consciousness. Most can be placed on a scale ranging from stimulation to depression, although some drugs are better classified as hallucinogens. The potential for abuse is high for drugs that lead to physical dependence, but psychological dependence can also be a serious problem.

Various strategies, ranging from literal to highly symbolic, can be used to reveal the meanings of dreams. Dreaming--especially lucid dreaming--can be a source of creativity and it may be used for problem solving and personal growth.

Drug abuse is supported by immediate pleasure (but delayed consequences), by false expectancies about the benefits of drug taking, and by cultural values that encourage drug abuse.

RECITE AND REVIEW

● *What is an altered state of consciousness?*

Recite and Review: Pages 236-238

1. States of _____ that differ from normal, alert, _____ consciousness are called altered states of consciousness (ASCs).

2. ASCs involve distinct shifts in the quality and _____ of mental activity.
3. Altered states are especially associated with _____ and _____, hypnosis, _____ deprivation, and psychoactive drugs.
4. Cultural conditioning greatly affects what altered states a person recognizes, seeks, considers _____, and attains.

● *What are the effects of sleep loss and changes in sleep patterns?*

Recite and Review: Pages 238-240

5. Sleep is an innate biological _____ essential for _____.
6. Higher animals and people deprived of sleep experience _____ microsleeps.
7. Moderate sleep loss mainly affects vigilance and self-motivated performance on _____ or boring tasks.
8. Extended sleep _____ can (somewhat rarely) produce a _____ sleep-deprivation psychosis, marked by confusion, delusions, and possibly hallucinations.
9. Sleep patterns show some flexibility, but 7 to 8 hours remains average. The unscheduled human sleep-waking cycle averages _____ hours, but cycles of _____ and _____ tailor it to 24-hour days.
10. The amount of daily sleep _____ steadily from birth to old age and switches from multiple sleep-wake cycles to once-a-day sleep periods.
11. Once-a-day sleep patterns, with a 2-to-1 ratio of _____ and _____, are most efficient for most people.

● *Are there different stages of sleep?*

Recite and Review: Pages 240-241

12. Sleepiness is associated with the accumulation of a sleep hormone in the _____ and spinal cord.
13. Sleep depends on which of _____ opposed sleep and waking systems in the _____ is dominant at any given moment.
14. Sleep occurs in _____ stages defined by changes in behavior and brain _____ recorded with an electroencephalograph (EEG).
15. Stage 1, _____ sleep, has small irregular brain waves. In stage 2, _____ spindles appear. _____ waves appear in stage 3. Stage 4, or deep sleep, is marked by almost pure delta waves.
16. Sleepers _____ between stages 1 and 4 (passing through stages 2 and 3) several times each night.

● *How does dream sleep differ from dreamless sleep?*

Recite and Review: Pages 241-242

17. There are two basic sleep states, rapid eye _____ (REM) sleep and non-REM (NREM) sleep.
18. REM sleep is much more strongly associated with _____ than non-REM sleep is.
19. _____ and REMs occur mainly during stage 1 sleep, but usually not during the first stage 1 period.

20. Dreaming is accompanied by sexual and _____ arousal but relaxation of the skeletal _____. People who move about violently while asleep may suffer from _____ behavior disorder.

● *What are the causes of sleep disorders and unusual sleep events?*

Recite and Review: Pages 243-244

21. _____ (somnambulism) and sleeptalking occur during NREM sleep in stages 3 and 4.
22. Night terrors occur in _____ sleep, whereas nightmares occur in _____ sleep.
23. Nightmares can be eliminated by the method called imagery _____.
24. Narcolepsy (_____ _____) and cataplexy (sudden muscle paralysis) are caused by a shift to stage-1 REM patterns of brain activity during normal waking hours.

● *Can insomnia be prevented?*

Recite and Review: Pages 244-246

25. Insomnia, which is difficulty in getting to sleep or staying asleep, may be _____ or chronic.
26. When insomnia is treated with drugs, sleep quality is often _____ and drug-dependency _____ may develop.
27. The amino acid tryptophan, found in milk and other foods, helps promote _____.
28. Behavioral approaches to managing insomnia, such as relaxation, sleep restriction, _____ control, and paradoxical _____ are quite effective.
29. Sleep apnea (interrupted _____) is one source of insomnia and daytime hypersomnia (_____).
30. Apnea is suspected as one cause of sudden _____ _____ syndrome (SIDS). With only a few exceptions, healthy infants should sleep face-up or on their _____.

● *Do dreams have meaning?*

Recite and Review: Pages 247-249

31. People deprived of dream sleep show a _____ rebound when allowed to sleep without interruption. However, total sleep loss seems to be more important than loss of a single sleep _____.
32. One of the more important functions of REM sleep appears to be the processing of adaptive _____.
33. Calvin Hall found that most dream content is about _____ settings, people, and actions. Dreams more often involve negative _____ than positive _____.
34. The Freudian, or psychodynamic, view is that dreams express unconscious _____, frequently hidden by dream symbols.
35. Allan Hobson and Robert McCarley's _____-synthesis model portrays dreaming as a physiological process. The brain, they say, creates dreams to explain _____ and motor messages that occur during REM sleep.

● *How is hypnosis done, and what are its limitations?*

Recite and Review: Pages 249-252

36. Hypnosis is an altered state characterized by narrowed attention and _____ suggestibility.
37. In the 1700s, Franz Mesmer (whose name is the basis for the term mesmerize) practiced "_____ magnetism," which was actually a demonstration of the power of _____.
38. The term _____ was first used by James Braid, an English doctor.
39. People vary in hypnotic susceptibility; _____ out of 10 can be hypnotized, as revealed by scores on the Stanford Hypnotic Susceptibility _____.
40. The core of hypnosis is the _____ suggestion effect—a tendency to carry out suggested actions as if they were involuntary.
41. Hypnosis appears capable of producing relaxation, controlling _____, and altering perceptions.
42. Stage hypnotism takes advantage of typical stage behavior, _____ suggestibility, responsive subjects, disinhibition, and _____ to simulate hypnosis.

● *How does sensory deprivation affect consciousness?*

Recite and Review: Pages 252-253

43. Sensory deprivation takes place when there is a major reduction in the amount or variety of sensory _____ available to a person.
44. Prolonged sensory deprivation is stressful and disruptive, leading to _____ distortions and vivid hypnogogic _____.
45. Brief or mild sensory deprivation can enhance sensory sensitivity and induce deep _____.
46. Sensory deprivation also appears to aid the breaking of long-standing _____ and promotes creative thinking. This effect is the basis for Restricted Environmental Stimulation Therapy (REST).

● *What are the effects of the more commonly used psychoactive drugs?*

Recite and Review: Pages 254-268

47. A psychoactive drug is a substance that affects the _____ in ways that alter consciousness.
48. Most psychoactive drugs can be placed on a scale ranging from stimulation to _____. Some, however, are best described as hallucinogens (drugs that alter _____ impressions).
49. Drugs may cause a physical dependence (_____) or a psychological dependence, or both.
50. The physically addicting drugs are heroin, morphine, codeine, methadone, barbiturates, alcohol, amphetamines, tobacco, and cocaine. All psychoactive drugs can lead to _____ dependence.
51. Drug use can be classified as experimental, recreational, situational, intensive, and _____. Drug abuse is most often associated with the last three.
52. Stimulant drugs are readily abused because of the period of _____ that often follows stimulation. The greatest risks are associated with amphetamines, cocaine, and nicotine, but even _____ can be a problem.
53. "Designer drugs," such as MDMA, are chemical _____ of other drugs. Their long-term _____ effects are not known.
54. _____ includes the added risk of lung cancer, heart disease, and other health problems.
55. Barbiturates are _____ drugs whose overdose level is close to the intoxication dosage, making them dangerous drugs. Mixing barbiturates and alcohol may result in a fatal _____ interaction (in which the joint effect of two drugs exceeds the effects of adding one drug's effects to the other's).

56. Benzodiazepine tranquilizers, such as _____, are used to lower anxiety. When abused, they have a strong _____ potential.

57. Alcohol is the most heavily abused drug in common use today. The development of a drinking problem is usually marked by an _____ phase of increasing consumption, a crucial phase, in which a _____ drink can set off a chain reaction, and a chronic phase, in which a person lives to drink and drinks to live.

58. Marijuana is a hallucinogen subject to an _____ pattern similar to alcohol. Studies have linked chronic marijuana use with memory impairment, lung cancer, reproductive problems, immune system disorders, and other health problems.

● *How are dreams used to promote personal understanding?*

Recite and Review: APPLICATIONS

59. Freud held that the meaning of dreams is _____ by four dream _____ he called condensation, displacement, symbolization, and secondary elaboration.

60. Calvin Hall emphasizes the setting, cast, _____, and emotions of a dream.

61. Rosalind Cartwright's view of dreams as feeling statements and Fritz Perls' technique of _____ for dream elements are also helpful.

62. Dreams may be used for _____ problem solving, especially when dream control is achieved through lucid dreaming (a dream in which the dreamer feels capable of normal thought and action).

● *Why is drug abuse so widespread?*

Recite and Review: EXPLORATION

63. Drug abuse is related to personal and social maladjustment, attempts to cope, and the _____ reinforcing qualities of psychoactive drugs.

64. Peer group influences, false expectations about the effects of drugs, and cultural _____ also encourage drug abuse.

65. Proposed remedies for drug abuse range from severe punishment to _____. The search for a solution continues.

RELATE

1. _____	John Lilly	a. daytime worries
2. _____	Randy Gardner	b. infancy
3. _____	long sleepers	c. reflex
4. _____	sleep patterns	d. awake, alert
5. _____	short sleep cycles	e. womb tank
6. _____	beta waves	f. restless legs
7. _____	alpha waves	g. relaxed
8. _____	hypnic jerk	h. sleep deprivation
9. _____	myoclonus	i. sexual arousal
10. _____	REM sleep	j. 2 to 1 ratio

11. _____	sleep drunkenness	a. violent actions
12. _____	hypersomnia	b. sleeping pill
13. _____	REM behavior disorder	c. unconscious meanings
14. _____	narcolepsy	d. slow awakening
15. _____	triazolam	e. hypnogogic images
16. _____	tryptophan	f. sudden daytime REM sleep
17. _____	dream symbols	g. sensory deprivation
18. _____	hidden observer	h. hypnosis
19. _____	theta waves	i. food supplement
20. _____	flotation tank	j. excessive sleepiness

21. _____	drug tolerance	a. cocaine rush
22. _____	amphetamine	b. cancer agent
23. _____	dopamine	c. addiction
24. _____	nicotine	d. sedative
25. _____	carcinogen	e. hallucinogen
26. _____	barbiturate	f. detoxification
27. _____	alcohol myopia	g. loss of pleasure
28. _____	alcohol treatment	h. stimulant
29. _____	THC	i. loss of restraint
30. _____	anhedonia	j. insecticide

CHECK YOUR MEMORY

Check Your Memory: Pages 236-238

1. William James characterized consciousness as an ever-changing stream of awareness. T or F?
2. All people experience at least some ASCs. T or F?
3. Both sensory overload and monotonous stimulation can produce ASCs. T or F?
4. Almost every known religion has accepted some ASCs as desirable. T or F?

Check Your Memory: Pages 238-240

5. Through sleep learning it is possible to master a foreign language. T or F?
6. A total inability to sleep results in death. T or F?
7. Even after extended sleep loss, most symptoms are removed by a single night's sleep. T or F?
8. Hallucinations and delusions are the most common reaction to extended sleep deprivation. T or F?
9. Without scheduled light and dark periods, the human free-running sleep rhythm will slowly advance around the clock. T or F?
10. Very short sleep-waking cycles are actually more efficient than the standard 24-hour day. T or F?

Check Your Memory: Pages 240-241

11. Sleep is promoted by a chemical that accumulates in the bloodstream.
12. Body temperature drops as a person falls asleep. T or F?
13. A hypnic jerk is a sign of serious problems. T or F?
14. Delta waves typically first appear in stage 2 sleep. T or F?

Check Your Memory: Pages 241-242

15. About 45 percent of awakenings during REM periods produce reports of dreams.
16. REM sleep occurs mainly in stages 3 and 4. T or F?
17. REM sleep increases when a person is subjected to daytime stress. T or F?
18. Most people change positions in bed during REM sleep. T or F?

Check Your Memory: Pages 243-244

19. It is dangerous to awaken a person who is sleepwalking. T or F?
20. Sleepwalking occurs during NREM periods, sleeptalking during REM periods. T or F?
21. People who have NREM night terrors usually have amnesia for the episode. T or F?
22. Susceptibility to narcolepsy appears to be hereditary. T or F?

Check Your Memory: Pages 244-246

23. Cashews, chicken, turkey, and milk all contain triazolam. T or F?
24. Caffeine, alcohol, and tobacco can all contribute to insomnia. T or F?
25. The two most effective behavioral treatments for insomnia are sleep restriction and stimulus control. T or F?
26. A CPAP mask is commonly used to treat sleep apnea. T or F?
27. Small, premature babies who breathe through the mouth and whose mothers are smokers are at greater risk for SIDS. T or F?

Check Your Memory: Pages 247-249

28. The average dream only lasts 3 to 4 minutes. T or F?
29. Alcoholics who quit drinking often experience a REM rebound. T or F?
30. Newborn babies spend 8 or 9 hours a day in REM sleep. T or F?
31. The favorite dream setting is outdoors. T or F?
32. According to Freud, dreams represent thoughts and wishes expressed as images. T or F?
33. The activation-synthesis hypothesis emphasizes the unconscious meanings of dream symbols. T or F?

Check Your Memory: Pages 249-252

34. The Greek word hypnos means "magnetism." T or F?
35. Only about 4 people out of 10 can be hypnotized. T or F?
36. The "finger-lock" is an example of the hidden observer effect. T or F?
37. Physical strength cannot be increased with hypnosis. T or F?
38. Hypnosis is better at changing subjective experiences than behaviors. T or F?
39. Stage hypnotists look for responsive volunteers who will cooperate and not spoil the show. T or F?

Check Your Memory: Pages 252-253

40. Hallucinations are rare during sensory deprivation. T or F?
41. Sensory sensitivity temporarily increases after a period of sensory deprivation. T or F?
42. Prolonged sensory deprivation produces deep relaxation. T or F?
43. REST is a form of brainwashing used during the Vietnam war. T or F?

Check Your Memory: Pages 254-268

44. Abuse of any psychoactive drug can produce physical dependence. T or F?

45. Amphetamines are used to treat narcolepsy and hyperactivity. T or F?
46. Amphetamine is more rapidly metabolized by the body than cocaine is. T or F?
47. Cocaine decreases the amount of noradrenaline in the brain. T or F?
48. Disregarding consequences is a sign of cocaine abuse. T or F?
49. Caffeine can increase the risk of miscarriage during pregnancy. T or F?
50. Twenty-five cigarettes could be fatal for a non-smoker. T or F?
51. Regular use of nicotine leads to drug tolerance, and often to physical addiction. T or F?
52. Every cigarette reduces a smoker's life expectancy by 7 minutes. T or F?
53. In order to stop smoking, tapering off is generally more successful than quitting abruptly. T or F?
54. One of the most effective ways to stop smoking is to schedule the number of cigarettes smoked each day. T or F?
55. There have been no known deaths caused by barbiturate overdoses. T or F?
56. It is legal and safe to drive as long as blood alcohol level does not exceed .8. T or F?
57. Children of alcoholics have a higher risk of becoming alcohol abusers. T or F?
58. At any weight, women tend to become more intoxicated than men do from a given amount of alcohol. T or F?
59. The goal of paced drinking is to maintain a blood alcohol level of .5 or less. T or F?
60. Hallucinogens generally affect brain transmitter systems. T or F?
61. THC receptors are found in large numbers in the cerebellum of the brain. T or F?

Check Your Memory: APPLICATIONS

62. Displacement refers to representing two or more people with a single dream image. T or F?
63. Secondary elaboration is the tendency to make a dream more logical when remembering it. T or F?
64. According to Calvin Hall, the overall emotional tone of a dream is the key to its meaning. T or F?
65. Alcohol decreases REM sleep. T or F?
66. It is basically impossible to solve daytime problems in dreams. T or F?
67. Lucid dreams either occur or they don't; there is no way to increase their frequency. T or F?

Check Your Memory: EXPLORATION

68. Drug abuse is frequently a symptom, rather than a cause, of personal maladjustment. T or F?
69. Heavy drinkers expect positive effects from drinking, but realize that severe negative consequences will follow. T or F?
70. Abuse of legally prescribed drugs is widespread. T or F?
71. Thomas Szasz believes that, where drug abuse is concerned, we should "legislate morality." T or F?

FINAL SURVEY AND REVIEW

● *What is an altered state of consciousness?*

1. States of awareness that differ from normal, alert, waking _____ are called altered states of _____ (ASCs).
2. ASCs involve distinct shifts in the quality and pattern of _____ _____.
3. Altered states are especially associated with sleep and dreaming, _____, sensory _____, and psychoactive drugs.

4. _____ conditioning greatly affects what altered states a person recognizes, seeks, considers normal, and attains.

● *What are the effects of sleep loss and changes in sleep patterns?*

5. Sleep is an _____ _____ rhythm essential for survival.
6. Higher animals and people deprived of sleep experience involuntary _____ (a brief shift to sleep patterns in the brain).
7. Moderate sleep loss mainly affects _____ and self-motivated performance on routine or boring tasks.
8. Extended sleep loss can (somewhat rarely) produce a temporary sleep-deprivation _____, marked by confusion, _____, and possibly hallucinations.
9. Sleep patterns show some flexibility, but 7 to 8 hours remains average. The unscheduled human _____ _____ averages 25 hours, but cycles of light and dark tailor it to 24-hour days.
10. The amount of daily sleep decreases steadily from birth to _____ _____ and switches from _____ sleep-wake cycles to once-a-day sleep periods.
11. Once-a-day sleep patterns, with a _____ ratio of sleep and waking, are most efficient for most people.

● *Are there different stages of sleep?*

12. Sleepiness is associated with the accumulation of a sleep _____ in the brain and _____ _____.
13. Sleep depends on which of two _____ sleep and waking _____ in the brain is dominant at any given moment.
14. Sleep occurs in 4 stages defined by changes in behavior and brain waves recorded with an _____ (EEG).
15. Stage 1, light sleep, has small irregular brain waves. In stage 2, sleep _____ appear. Delta waves appear in stage 3. Stage 4, or deep sleep, is marked by almost pure _____ _____.
16. Sleepers alternate between stages _____ and _____ (passing through stages _____ and _____) several times each night.

● *How does dream sleep differ from dreamless sleep?*

17. There are two basic sleep states, _____ _____ movement (REM) sleep and non-REM (NREM) sleep.
18. _____ sleep is much more strongly associated with dreaming than _____ sleep is.
19. Dreams and REMs occur mainly during _____ ____ sleep, but usually not during the first _____ ____ period.
20. Dreaming is accompanied by sexual and emotional _____ but _____ of the skeletal muscles. People who move about violently while asleep may suffer from REM behavior _____.

● *What are the causes of sleep disorders and unusual sleep events?*

21. Sleepwalking (_____) and sleeptalking occur during _____ sleep in stages 3 and 4.
22. Night terrors occur in _____ sleep, whereas nightmares occur in _____ sleep.
23. Nightmares can be eliminated by the method called _____ _____.
24. _____ (sleep attacks) and _____ (sudden muscle paralysis) are caused by a shift to stage-1 REM patterns of brain activity during normal waking hours.

● *Can insomnia be prevented?*

25. Insomnia, which is difficulty in getting to sleep or staying asleep, may be temporary or _____.
26. When insomnia is treated with drugs, sleep quality is often lowered and drug-_____ insomnia may develop.
27. The amino acid _____, found in milk and other foods, helps promote sleep.
28. Behavioral approaches to managing insomnia, such as relaxation, sleep _____, stimulus control, and _____ intention are quite effective.
29. Sleep _____ (interrupted breathing) is one source of insomnia and daytime _____ (sleepiness).
30. Apnea is suspected as one cause of _____ infant death _____ (SIDS). With only a few exceptions, healthy infants should sleep _____-up or on their sides.

● *Do dreams have meaning?*

31. People deprived of dream sleep show a REM _____ when allowed to sleep without interruption. However, _____ sleep loss seems to be more important than loss of a single sleep stage.
32. One of the more important functions of _____ _____ appears to be the processing of adaptive memories.
33. Calvin _____ found that most dream content is about familiar settings, people, and actions. Dreams more often involve _____ emotions than _____ emotions.
34. The Freudian, or _____, view is that dreams express unconscious wishes, frequently hidden by dream _____.
35. Allan Hobson and Robert McCarley's activation-_____ model portrays dreaming as a physiological process. The brain, they say, creates dreams to explain sensory and _____ messages that occur during REM sleep.

● *How is hypnosis done, and what are its limitations?*

36. Hypnosis is an altered state characterized by narrowed attention and increased
_____.
37. In the 1700s, Franz _____ (whose name is the basis for the term _____) practiced "animal magnetism," which was actually a demonstration of the power of suggestion.
38. The term hypnosis was first used by James _____, an English doctor.
39. People vary in hypnotic susceptibility; 8 out of 10 can be hypnotized, as revealed by scores on the _____ Hypnotic Susceptibility Scale.

40. The core of hypnosis is the basic _____ effect—a tendency to carry out suggested actions as if they were _____.

41. Hypnosis appears capable of producing _____, controlling pain, and altering perceptions.

42. _____ _____ takes advantage of typical stage behavior, waking suggestibility, responsive subjects, disinhibition, and deception to _____ hypnosis.

● *How does sensory deprivation affect consciousness?*

43. Sensory deprivation takes place when there is a major reduction in the amount or variety of _____ _____ available to a person.

44. Prolonged sensory deprivation is stressful and disruptive, leading to perceptual distortions and vivid _____ images.

45. Brief or mild sensory deprivation can enhance _____ sensitivity and induce deep relaxation.

46. Sensory deprivation also appears to aid the breaking of long-standing habits and promotes creative thinking. This effect is the basis for _____ _____ Stimulation Therapy (REST).

● *What are the effects of the more commonly used psychoactive drugs?*

47. A psychoactive drug is a substance that affects the brain in ways that alter _____.

48. Most psychoactive drugs can be placed on a scale ranging from _____ to _____. Some, however, are best described as _____ (drugs that alter sensory impressions).

49. Drugs may cause a physical _____ (addiction) or a psychological _____, or both.

50. The _____ _____ drugs are heroin, morphine, codeine, methadone, barbiturates, alcohol, amphetamines, tobacco, and cocaine. All psychoactive drugs can lead to psychological dependence.

51. Drug use can be classified as experimental, _____, situational, intensive, and compulsive. Drug abuse is most often associated with the last three.

52. Stimulant drugs are readily abused because of the period of depression that often follows stimulation. The greatest risks are associated with amphetamines, _____, and nicotine, but even caffeine can be a problem.

53. "_____ drugs," such as MDMA, are chemical variations of other drugs. Their long-term health effects are not known.

54. _____ includes the added risk of lung cancer, heart disease, and other health problems.

55. Barbiturates are depressant drugs whose overdose level is close to the intoxication dosage, making them dangerous drugs. Mixing barbiturates and _____ may result in a fatal drug _____ (in which the joint effect of two drugs exceeds the effects of adding one drug's effects to the other's).

56. _____ tranquilizers, such as Valium, are used to lower anxiety. When abused, they have a strong addictive potential.

57. _____ is the most heavily abused drug in common use today. The development of a drinking problem is usually marked by an initial phase of increasing consumption, a _____ phase, in which a single drink can set off a chain reaction, and a chronic phase, in which a person lives to drink and drinks to live.

58. Marijuana is a _____ subject to an abuse pattern similar to alcohol. Studies have linked chronic marijuana use with memory impairment, _____ cancer, reproductive problems, immune system disorders, and other health problems.

● *How are dreams used to promote personal understanding?*

59. Freud held that the meaning of dreams is hidden by the dream processes he called _____, displacement, symbolization, and _____ elaboration.
60. Calvin Hall emphasizes the _____, _____, plot, and emotions of a dream.
61. Rosalind Cartwright's view of dreams as _____ statements and Fritz _____ technique of speaking for dream elements are also helpful.
62. Dreams may be used for creative problem solving, especially when dream control is achieved through _____ dreaming (a dream in which the dreamer feels capable of normal thought and action).

● *Why is drug abuse so widespread?*

63. Drug abuse is related to personal and social _____, attempts to cope, and the immediate reinforcing qualities of psychoactive drugs.
64. Peer group influences, false _____ about the effects of drugs, and cultural values also encourage drug abuse.
65. Proposed remedies for drug abuse range from severe _____ to legalization. The search for a solution continues.

MASTERY TEST

1. Delirium, ecstasy, and daydreaming all have in common the fact that they are
   a. forms of normal waking consciousness b. caused by sensory deprivation c. perceived as subjectively real d. ASCs

2. Alcoholics who quit drinking and people who have been prevented from dreaming typically experience
   a. sleep apnea b. REM rebound c. cataplexy d. sleep-deprivation psychosis

3. Which of the following does not belong with the others?
   a. nicotine b. caffeine c. cocaine d. codeine

4. Sleep spindles usually first appear in stage _____, whereas delta waves first appear in stage _____.
   a. 1, 2   b. 2, 3   c. 3, 4   d. 1, 4

5. Which of the following is NOT one of the dream processes described by Freud?
   a. condensation b. illumination c. displacement d. symbolization

6. Which of the following most clearly occurs under hypnosis?
   a. unusual strength b. memory enhancement c. pain relief d. age regression

7. Alcohol, amphetamines, cocaine, and marijuana have in common the fact that they are all
   a. physically addicting b. psychoactive c. stimulants d. hallucinogens

8. Emotional arousal, blood pressure changes, and sexual arousal all primarily occur during
   a. REM sleep b. NREM sleep c. Delta sleep d. stage 4 sleep

9. The REST technique makes use of
   a. sensory deprivation b. hypodynamic imagery c. hallucinogens d. a CPAP mask

10. Mesmerism, hypnosis, hypnotic susceptibility scales, and stage hypnotism all rely in part on
    a. disinhibition b. the hidden observer c. suggestibility d. imagery rehearsal

11. Shortened sleep-waking cycles overlook the fact that sleep
    a. must match a 3 to 1 ratio of time awake and time asleep b. is an innate biological rhythm c. is caused by a sleep-promoting substance in the blood d. cycles cannot be altered by external factors

12. Morning drinking appears during the _____ phase in the development of a drinking problem.
    a. initial b. crucial c. chronic d. rebound

13. Which of the following statements about sleep is true?
    a. Learning math or a foreign language can be accomplished during sleep. b. Some people can learn to do without sleep. c. John Lilly had hallucinations during a sleep deprivation experiment. d. Randy Gardner slept for 14 hours after ending his sleep deprivation.

14. Amphetamine is very similar in effects to
    a. narcotics and tranquilizers b. methaqualone c. codeine d. cocaine

15. Microsleeps would most likely occur
    a. in stage 4 sleep b. in a 3 to 1 ratio to microawakenings c. in conjunction with delusions and hallucinations d. during sleep deprivation

16. Adolescents who abuse drugs tend to be
    a. suffering from brain dysfunctions b. high in self-esteem but unrealistic about consequences
    c. maladjusted and impulsive d. similar in most respects to non-abusers

17. Sleepwalking, sleeptalking, and severe nightmares all have in common the fact that they
    a. are REM events b. are NREM events c. are sleep disorders d. can be controlled with imagery rehearsal

18. Sensory deprivation sometimes produces vivid, dream-like images called
    a. cataplectic images b. hypnogogic images c. tryptophanic images d. REM symbolizations

19. The basic suggestion effect is closely related to
    a. hypnosis b. sensory enhancement after sensory deprivation c. hypersomnia d. the frequency of dreaming during REM sleep

20. Apnea can be especially dangerous in
    a. infancy b. cataplexy c. rebound insomnia d. cases of sleep drunkenness

21. Which of the following is a hallucinogen?
    a. LSD b. THC c. hashish d. all of the preceding

22. The two most basic states of sleep are
    a. stage 1 sleep and stage 4 sleep   b. REM sleep and NREM sleep   c. Alpha sleep and Delta sleep
    d. Alpha sleep and hypnic sleep

23. Thinking and perception become dulled in the condition known as
    a. alcohol rebound   b. alcohol apnea   c. alcohol anhedonia   d. alcohol myopia

24. Learning to use a computer would most likely be slowed if you were _____ each night.
    a. deprived of a half hour of NREM sleep   b. allowed to engage in extra REM sleep   c. prevented from dreaming   d. awakened three times at random

25. By definition, compulsive drug use involves
    a. dependence   b. experimentation   c. withdrawal symptoms   d. anhedonia

26. A particularly dangerous drug interaction occurs when _____ and _____ are combined.
    a. alcohol, amphetamine   b. barbiturates, nicotine   c. alcohol, barbiturates   d. amphetamine, codeine

27. Narcolepsy is closely associated with which of the following?
    a. night terrors   b. cataplexy   c. apnea   d. somnambulism

28. Sleep restriction and stimulus control techniques would most likely be used to treat
    a. insomnia   b. narcolepsy   c. sleepwalking   d. REM behavior disorder

29. In addition to the nicotine they contain, cigarettes release
    a. dopamine   b. tryptophan   c. noradrenaline   d. carcinogens

30. Disguised dream symbols are to psychodynamic dream theory as sensory and motor messages are to
    a. the Freudian theory of dreams   b. the activation-synthesis hypothesis   c. Fritz Perls' methods of dream interpretation   d. paradoxical intention

ANSWERS

Recite and Review

1. awareness, waking
2. pattern
3. sleep, dreaming, sensory
4. normal
5. rhythm, survival
6. involuntary
7. routine
8. loss, temporary
9. 25, light, dark
10. decreases
11. waking, sleep
12. brain
13. two, brain
14. 4, waves
15. light, sleep, Delta
16. alternate
17. movement
18. dreaming
19. Dreaming
20. emotional, muscles, REM
21. Sleepwalking
22. NREM, REM
23. rehearsal
24. sleep attacks
25. temporary
26. lowered, insomnia
27. sleep
28. stimulus, intention
29. breathing, sleepiness
30. infant death, sides
31. REM, stage
32. memories
33. familiar, emotions, emotions
34. wishes
35. activation, sensory
36. increased
37. animal, suggestion
38. hypnosis
39. 8, Scale
40. basic
41. pain
42. waking, deception

43. stimulation
44. perceptual, images
45. relaxation
46. habits
47. brain
48. depression, sensory
49. addiction
50. psychological
51. compulsive
52. depression, caffeine
53. variations, health
54. Nicotine
55. depressant, drug
56. Valium, addictive
57. initial, single
58. abuse
59. hidden, processes
60. plot
61. speaking
62. creative
63. immediate
64. values
65. legalization

Relate

1. e
2. h
3. a
4. j
5. b
6. d
7. g
8. c
9. f
10. i
11. d
12. j
13. a
14. f
15. b
16. i
17. c
18. h
19. e
20. g
21. c
22. h
23. a
24. j
25. b

26. d
27. i
28. f
29. e
30. g

Check Your Memory

1. T
2. T
3. T
4. T
5. F
6. T
7. T
8. F
9. T
10. F
11. F
12. T
13. F
14. F
15. F
16. F
17. T
18. F
19. F
20. F
21. T
22. T
23. F
24. T
25. T
26. T
27. T
28. F
29. T
30. T
31. F
32. T
33. F
34. F
35. F
36. F
37. T
38. T
39. T
40. T
41. T
42. F
43. F

44. F
45. T
46. F
47. F
48. T
49. T
50. T
51. T
52. T
53. T
54. T
55. F
56. F
57. T
58. T
59. F
60. T
61. F
62. F
63. T
64. F
65. T
66. F
67. F
68. T
69. F
70. T
71. F

Final Survey and Review

1. consciousness, consciousness
2. mental activity
3. hypnosis, deprivation
4. Cultural
5. innate biological
6. microsleeps
7. vigilance
8. psychosis, delusions
9. sleep-waking cycle
10. old age, multiple
11. 2-to-1
12. hormone, spinal cord
13. opposed, systems
14. electroencephalograph
15. spindles, delta waves
16. 1, 4, 2, 3
17. rapid eye
18. REM, non-REM
19. stage 1, stage 1

20. arousal, relaxation, disorder
21. somnambulism, NREM
22. NREM, REM
23. imagery rehearsal
24. Narcolepsy, cataplexy
25. chronic
26. dependency
27. tryptophan
28. restriction, paradoxical
29. apnea, hypersomnia
30. sudden, syndrome, face
31. rebound, total
32. REM sleep
33. Hall, negative, positive
34. psychodynamic, symbols
35. synthesis, motor
36. suggestibility
37. Mesmer, mesmerize
38. Braid
39. Stanford
40. suggestion, involuntary
41. relaxation
42. Stage hypnotism, simulate
43. sensory stimulation
44. hypnogogic
45. sensory
46. Restricted Environmental
47. consciousness
48. stimulation, depression, hallucinogens
49. dependence, dependence
50. physically addicting
51. recreational
52. cocaine
53. Designer
54. Nicotine
55. alcohol, interaction
56. Benzodiazepine
57. Alcohol, crucial
58. hallucinogen, lung
59. condensation, secondary
60. setting, cast
61. feeling, Perls'
62. lucid
63. maladjustment
64. expectations
65. punishment

Mastery Test

1. d (p. 237)
2. b (p. 247)
3. d (p. 255)
4. b (p. 241)
5. b (p. 268)
6. c (p. 251)
7. b (p. 254)
8. a (p. 242)
9. a (p. 253)
10. c (p. 249-251)
11. b (p. 238)
12. a (p. 264)
13. d (p. 239)
14. d (p. 258)
15. d (p. 238)
16. c (p. 272)
17. c (p. 243)
18. b (p. 252)
19. a (p. 250)
20. a (p. 246)
21. d (p. 266)
22. b (p. 242)
23. d (p. 264)
24. c (p. 247-248)
25. a (p. 255)
26. c (p. 263)
27. b (p. 244)
28. a (p. 245)
29. d (p. 260)
30. b (p. 248-249)

Chapter 9

Conditioning and Learning

CHAPTER OVERVIEW

Learning is a relatively permanent change in behavior due to experience. Two basic forms of learning are classical conditioning and operant conditioning.

Classical conditioning is also called respondent or Pavlovian conditioning. Classical conditioning occurs when a neutral stimulus is associated with an unconditioned stimulus (which reliably elicits an unconditioned response). After many pairings of the NS and the US, the NS becomes a conditioned stimulus that elicits a conditioned response. Learning is reinforced during acquisition of a response. Withdrawing reinforcement leads to extinction (although some spontaneous recovery of conditioning may occur). Stimulus generalization has occurred when a stimulus similar to the CS also elicits a learned response. In stimulus discrimination, organisms learn to respond differently to two similar stimuli. Conditioning often involves simple reflex responses, but emotional conditioning is also possible.

In operant conditioning (or instrumental learning), the consequences that follow a response alter the probability that it will be made again. Positive and negative reinforcers increase responding; punishment suppresses responding; non-reinforcement leads to extinction. Various types of reinforcers and schedules of reinforcement greatly affect operant learning. Informational feedback (or knowledge of results) also facilitates learning and performance. Antecedent stimuli influence operant learning, through stimulus generalization and discrimination, and stimulus control.

Learning, even simple conditioning, is based on acquiring information. Higher level cognitive learning involves memory, thinking, problem solving, and language. At a simpler level, cognitive maps, latent learning, and discovery learning show that learning is based on acquiring information. Learning also occurs through observation and imitation of models. Observational learning imparts large amounts of information that would be hard to acquire in other ways.

Operant principles can be applied to manage one's own behavior and to break bad habits. A combination of operant principles and cognitive learning underlies self-regulated learning--a collection of techniques to improve learning in school.

Learning in animals is limited at times by various biological constraints and species-typical behaviors.

RECITE AND REVIEW

● *What is learning?*

Recite and Review: Pages 276-278

1. Learning is a relatively permanent change in _____ due to experience. To understand learning we must study antecedents (events that _____ responses) and consequences (events that _____ responses).

2. Classical, or respondent, _____ and instrumental, or operant, _____ are two basic types of learning.

3. In classical conditioning, a previously neutral _____ is associated with a stimulus that elicits a response. In operant conditioning, the pattern of voluntary _____ is altered by consequences.

4. Both types of conditioning depend on reinforcement. In classical conditioning, learning is _____ when a US follows the NS or CS. _____ reinforcement is based on the consequences that follow a response.

● *How does classical conditioning occur?*

Recite and Review: Pages 278-282

5. Classical conditioning, studied by Ivan Pavlov, occurs when a _____ stimulus (NS) is associated with an unconditioned stimulus (US). The US triggers a reflex called the unconditioned _____ (UR).

6. If the NS is consistently paired with the US, it becomes a conditioned _____ (CS) capable of producing a response by itself. This response is a conditioned (_____) response (CR).

7. During acquisition of classical conditioning, the conditioned stimulus must be consistently followed by the unconditioned _____ .

8. Higher-order conditioning occurs when a well-learned conditioned stimulus is used as if it were an unconditioned _____, bringing about further learning.

9. When the CS is repeatedly presented alone, extinction takes place. That is, _____ is weakened or inhibited.

10. After extinction seems to be complete, a rest period may lead to the temporary reappearance of a conditioned _____. This is called spontaneous recovery.

11. Through stimulus generalization, stimuli _____ to the conditioned stimulus will also produce a response.

12. Generalization gives way to _____ discrimination when an organism learns to respond to one stimulus, but not to similar stimuli.

13. From an informational view, conditioning creates expectancies (or expectations about events), which alter _____ patterns.

14. In classical conditioning, the CS creates an expectancy that the US will _____ it.

● *Does conditioning affect emotions?*

Recite and Review: Pages 282-283

15. Conditioning applies to visceral or emotional responses as well as simple _____. As a result, _____ emotional responses (CERs) also occur.

16. Irrational fears called phobias may be CERs that are extended to a variety of situations by _____ generalization.

17. The conditioning of emotional responses can occur vicariously (_____) as well as directly. Vicarious classical conditioning occurs when we _____ another person's emotional responses to a stimulus.

● *How does operant conditioning occur?*

Recite and Review: Pages 284-289

18. Operant conditioning (or instrumental _____) occurs when a voluntary action is followed by a reinforcer.

19. Reinforcement in operant conditioning _____ the frequency or probability of a response. This result is based on what Edward L. Thorndike called the law of _____.

20. An operant reinforcer is any event that follows a _____ and _____ its probability.

21. Learning in operant conditioning is based on the expectation that a response will have a specific _____.

22. To be effective, operant _____ must be _____ contingent.

23. Delay of reinforcement reduces its effectiveness, but long _____ of responses may be built up so that a _____ reinforcer maintains many responses.

24. Superstitious behaviors (unnecessary responses) often become part of _____ chains because they appear to be associated with reinforcement.

25. In a process called shaping, complex _____ responses can be taught by reinforcing successive approximations (ever closer matches) to a final desired response.

26. If an operant response is not reinforced, it may extinguish (disappear). But after extinction seems complete, it may temporarily reappear (spontaneous _____).

● *Are there different kinds of operant reinforcement?*

Recite and Review: Pages 289-293

27. In positive reinforcement, _____ or a pleasant event follows a response. In negative reinforcement, a response that _____ discomfort becomes more likely to occur again.

28. Punishment _____ responding. Punishment occurs when a response is followed by the onset of an aversive event or by the removal of a positive event (response _____).

29. Primary reinforcers are "natural," physiologically-based rewards. Intra-cranial stimulation of "_____ centers" in the _____ can also serve as a primary reinforcer.

30. Secondary reinforcers are _____. They typically gain their reinforcing value by association with primary reinforcers or because they can be _____ for primary reinforcers. Tokens and money gain their reinforcing value in this way.

31. Human behavior is often influenced by social reinforcers, which are based on learned desires for attention and _____ from others.

32. Feedback, or knowledge of _____, aids learning and improves performance.

33. Programmed instruction breaks learning into a series of small steps and provides immediate _____.

34. Computer-assisted _____ (CAI) does the same, but has the added advantage of providing alternate exercises and information when needed.
35. Four variations of CAI are drill and _____, instructional games, educational simulations, and interactive videodisc instruction.

● *How are we influenced by patterns of reward?*

Recite and Review: Pages 294-297

36. Reward or reinforcement may be given continuously (after every _____), or on a schedule of _____ reinforcement. The study of schedules of reinforcement was begun by B. F. Skinner.
37. Partial reinforcement produces greater resistance to extinction. This is the partial reinforcement _____.
38. The four most basic schedules of reinforcement are _____ ratio (FR), variable ratio (VR), _____ interval (FI), and variable interval (VI).
39. FR and VR schedules produce _____ rates of responding. An FI schedule produces moderate rates of responding with alternating periods of activity and inactivity. VI schedules produce _____, steady rates of responding and strong resistance to extinction.
40. Stimuli that _____ a reinforced response tend to control the response on future occasions (stimulus control).
41. Two aspects of stimulus control are generalization and _____.
42. In generalization, an operant response tends to occur when stimuli _____ to those preceding reinforcement are present.
43. In discrimination, responses are given in the presence of discriminative stimuli associated with reinforcement (_____) and withheld in the presence of stimuli associated with non-reinforcement (_____).

● *What does punishment do to behavior?*

Recite and Review: Pages 297-300

44. A punisher is any consequence that _____ the frequency of a target behavior.
45. Punishment is most effective when it is _____, consistent, and intense.
46. Mild punishment tends only to temporarily _____ responses that are also reinforced or were acquired by reinforcement.
47. The undesirable side effects of punishment include the conditioning of fear; the learning of _____ and avoidance responses; and the encouragement of aggression.
48. Reinforcement and non-reinforcement are a better way to change behavior than punishment. When punishment is used, it should be _____ and combined with reinforcement of alternate _____.

● *What is cognitive learning?*

Recite and Review: Pages 301-303

49. Cognitive learning involves higher mental processes, such as understanding, knowing, or anticipating. Evidence of cognitive learning is provided by cognitive _____ (internal representations of spatial relationships) and latent (hidden) _____.
50. Discovery learning emphasizes insight and _____, in contrast to rote learning.

● *Does learning occur by imitation?*

Recite and Review: Pages 303-305

51. Much human learning is achieved through _____, or modeling. Observational learning is influenced by the personal characteristics of the _____ and the success or failure of the _____ behavior.

52. Television characters can act as powerful _____ for observational learning. Televised violence increases the likelihood of aggression by viewers.

● *How does conditioning apply to practical problems?*

Recite and Review: APPLICATIONS

53. Operant principles can be readily applied to manage behavior in everyday settings. Self-management of behavior is based on self-reinforcement, self-recording, _____, and behavioral contracting.

54. Prepotent, or frequent, high-probability _____, can be used to reinforce low-frequency responses. This is known as the Premack _____.

55. Four strategies that can help change bad habits are: reinforcing alternate responses, promoting extinction, breaking response _____, and avoiding antecedent _____.

56. In school, self-regulated _____ typically involves all of the following: setting learning _____, planning learning strategies, using self-instruction, monitoring progress, evaluating yourself, reinforcing _____, and taking corrective action when required.

● *How does biology influence learning?*

Recite and Review: EXPLORATION

57. Many animals are born with _____ behavior patterns far more complex than reflexes. These are organized into fixed _____ patterns (FAPs), which are stereotyped, species-specific behaviors.

58. Learning in animals is limited at times by various _____ constraints and species-typical behaviors.

59. According to prepared _____ theory, some stimuli are especially effective conditioned stimuli.

60. Many operant responses are subject to instinctive drift--the tendency for learned responses to shift toward _____ response patterns.

RELATE

1. _____	respondent conditioning	a.	before responses
2. _____	instrumental learning	b.	Pavlov's CS
3. _____	antecedents	c.	after responses
4. _____	meat powder	d.	higher-order conditioning
5. _____	bell	e.	Pavlovian conditioning
6. _____	salivation	f.	US missing
7. _____	consequences	g.	reinforcement period
8. _____	CS used as US	h.	UR
9. _____	extinction	i.	Pavlov's US
10. _____	acquisition	j.	operant conditioning

11. _____	phobia	a. CER
12. _____	desensitization	b. conditioning chamber
13. _____	Skinner	c. increased responding
14. _____	shaping	d. decreased responding
15. _____	negative reinforcement	e. social reinforcer
16. _____	punishment	f. Chimp-O-Mat
17. _____	tokens	g. approximations
18. _____	approval	h. resistance to extinction
19. _____	partial reinforcement	i. antecedent stimuli
20. _____	stimulus control	j. extinction of fear

21. _____	punishment	a. species-specific
22. _____	expectancies	b. reinforcement schedule
23. _____	KR	c. miserly raccoons
24. _____	CAI	d. escape and avoidance
25. _____	discovery learning	e. informational view
26. _____	modeling	f. educational simulations
27. _____	self-instruction	g. feedback
28. _____	FAP	h. insight
29. _____	instinctive drift	i. self-regulated learning
30. _____	fixed interval	j. imitation

CHECK YOUR MEMORY

Check Your Memory: Pages 276-278

1. Learning to press the buttons on a vending machine is based on operant conditioning. T or F?
2. In classical conditioning, the consequences that follow responses become associated with one another. T or F?
3. Getting compliments from friends could serve as reinforcement for operant learning. T or F?

Check Your Memory: Pages 278-282

4. Ivan Pavlov studied digestion and operant conditioning in dogs. T or F?
5. Pavlov used meat powder to reinforce conditioned salivation to the sound of a bell. T or F?
6. During successful conditioning, the NS becomes a CS. T or F?
7. During acquisition, the CS is presented repeatedly without the US. T or F?
8. The optimal delay between the CS and the US is 5 to 15 seconds. T or F?
9. Spontaneous recovery occurs when a CS becomes strong enough to be used like a US. T or F?
10. Discriminations are learned when generalized responses to stimuli similar to the CS are extinguished. T or F?

Check Your Memory: Pages 282-283

11. Narrowing of the pupils in response to bright lights is learned in early infancy. T or F?

12. Emotional conditioning involves autonomic nervous system responses. T or F?

13. Stimulus generalization helps convert some CERs into phobias. T or F?

14. Pleasant music can be used as a UR to create a CER. T or F?

15. To learn a CER vicariously, you would observe the actions of another person and try to imitate them. T or F?

Check Your Memory: Pages 284-289

16. In operant conditioning, learners actively emit responses. T or F?

17. Rewards are the same as reinforcers. T or F?

18. The Skinner box is primarily used to study classical conditioning. T or F?

19. Reinforcement in operant conditioning alters how frequently involuntary responses are elicited. T or F?

20. Operant reinforcers are most effective when they are response-contingent. T or F?

21. Rent reductions were the final reinforcers in the Experimental Living Project. T or F?

22. Operant learning is most effective if you wait a minute or two after the response is over before reinforcing it. T or F?

23. Response chains allow delayed reinforcers to support learning. T or F?

24. Superstitious responses appear to be associated with reinforcement, but they are not. T or F?

25. Teaching a pigeon to play Ping-Pong would most likely make use of the principle of response cost. T or F?

26. Children who misbehave may be reinforced by attention from parents. T or F?

27. Negative reinforcement is a type of punishment that is used to strengthen learning. T or F?

28. Both response cost and negative reinforcement decrease responding. T or F?

Check Your Memory: Pages 289-293

29. Food, water, grades, and sex are primary reinforcers. T or F?

30. ICS is a good example of a secondary reinforcer. T or F?

31. Social reinforcers are secondary reinforcers. T or F?

32. Attention and approval can be used to shape another person's behavior. T or F?

33. The effects of primary reinforcers may quickly decline as the person becomes satiated. T or F?

34. The Chimp-O-Mat accepted primary reinforcers and dispensed secondary reinforcers. T or F?

35. CAI is another term for informational feedback. T or F?

36. In sports, feedback is most effective when a skilled coach directs attention to important details. T or F?

37. The final level of skill and knowledge is almost always higher following CAI than it is with conventional methods. T or F?

Check Your Memory: Pages 294-297

38. Continuous reinforcement means that reinforcers are given continuously, regardless of whether or not responses are made. T or F?

39. A FR-3 schedule means that each correct response produces 3 reinforcers. T or F?
40. The time interval in FI schedules is measured from the last reinforced response. T or F?
41. In business, commissions and profit sharing are examples of FI reinforcement. T or F?
42. Antecedent stimuli tend to control when and where previously rewarded responses will occur. T or F?
43. Stimulus generalization is the primary method used to train dogs to detect contraband. T or F?

Check Your Memory: Pages 297-300

44. Like reinforcement, punishment should be response-contingent. T or F?
45. Punishment is most effective if it is unpredictable. T or F?
46. Speeding tickets are an example of response cost. T or F?
47. Mild punishment causes reinforced responses to extinguish more rapidly. T or F?
48. Generally, punishment should be the last resort for altering behavior. T or F?
49. An apparatus known as a shuttle box is used to study escape and avoidance learning. T or F?
50. Avoidance learning involves both classical and operant conditioning. T or F?
51. Punishment frequently leads to increases in aggression by the person who is punished. T or F?
52. Punishing children can be habit forming because it is negatively reinforced by an end to the adult's feelings of irritation. T or F?

Check Your Memory: Pages 301-303

53. Cognitive learning involves thinking, memory, and problem solving. T or F?
54. Animals learning their way through a maze memorize the correct order of right and left turns to make. T or F?
55. Typically, reinforcement must be provided in order to make latent learning visible. T or F?
56. In many situations, discovery learning produces better understanding of problems. T or F?

Check Your Memory: Pages 303-305

57. Modeling is another term for discovery learning. T or F?
58. After a new response is acquired through modeling, normal reinforcement determines if it will be repeated. T or F?
59. Children imitate aggressive acts performed by other people, but they are not likely to imitate cartoon characters. T or F?
60. Violence on television causes children to be more violent. T or F?

Check Your Memory: APPLICATIONS

61. Choosing reinforcers is the first step in behavioral self-management. T or F?
62. Self-recording can be an effective way to change behavior, even without using specific reinforcers. T or F?
63. A prepotent response is one that occurs frequently. T or F?
64. In a behavioral contract, you spell out what response chains you are going to extinguish. T or F?
65. Self-regulated learners actively seek feedback in both formal and informal ways. T or F?

Check Your Memory: EXPLORATION

66. A cat's face-washing routine is an example of an FAP. T or F?

67. Other than reflexes, humans generally lack rigidly programmed species-specific behaviors. T or F?
68. Biological constraints influence human learning, but animals are rarely affected by them. T or F?
69. Biological constraints affect both classical and operant conditioning. T or F?

FINAL SURVEY AND REVIEW

● *What is learning?*

1. Learning is a relatively permanent change in behavior due to experience. To understand learning we must study _____ (events that precede responses) and _____ (events that follow responses).
2. Classical, or _____, conditioning and instrumental, or _____, conditioning are two basic types of learning.
3. In classical conditioning, a previously _____ stimulus is associated with another stimulus that elicits a response. In operant conditioning, the pattern of voluntary responses is altered by _____.
4. Both types of conditioning depend on _____. In classical conditioning, learning is reinforced when a _____ follows the NS or CS. Operant reinforcement is based on the consequences that follow a response.

● *How does classical conditioning occur?*

5. Classical conditioning, studied by _____ _____, occurs when a neutral stimulus (NS) is associated with an _____ stimulus (US). The US triggers a _____ called the unconditioned response (UR).
6. If the NS is consistently paired with the US, it becomes a _____ stimulus (CS) capable of producing a response by itself. This response is a _____ (learned) response (CR).
7. During acquisition of classical conditioning, the conditioned stimulus must be consistently followed by the _____ _____.
8. _____ conditioning occurs when a well-learned conditioned stimulus is used as if it were an unconditioned stimulus, bringing about further learning.
9. When the CS is repeatedly presented alone, _____ takes place (learning is weakened or inhibited).
10. After extinction seems to be complete, a rest period may lead to the temporary reappearance of a conditioned response. This is called _____ _____.
11. Through stimulus _____, stimuli similar to the conditioned stimulus will also produce a response.
12. Generalization gives way to stimulus _____ when an organism learns to respond to one stimulus, but not to similar stimuli.
13. From an _____ view, conditioning creates expectancies (or expectations about events), which alter response patterns.
14. In classical conditioning, the _____ creates an expectancy that the _____ will follow it.

● *Does conditioning affect emotions?*

15. Conditioning applies to visceral or emotional responses as well as simple reflexes. As a result, conditioned _____ _____ (CERs) also occur.
16. Irrational fears called _____ may be CERs that are extended to a variety of situations by stimulus _____.
17. The conditioning of emotional responses can occur secondhand as well as directly. _____ classical conditioning occurs when we observe another person's emotional responses to a stimulus.

● *How does operant conditioning occur?*

18. Operant conditioning (or _____ learning) occurs when a voluntary action is followed by a reinforcer.
19. Reinforcement in operant conditioning increases the frequency or _____ of a response. This result is based on what Edward L. _____ called the law of effect.
20. An operant reinforcer is any event that follows a _____ and _____ its probability.
21. Learning in operant conditioning is based on the _____ that a response will have a specific effect.
22. To be effective, operant reinforcers must be response _____.
23. Delay of reinforcement _____ its effectiveness, but long chains of responses may be built up so that a single _____ maintains many responses.
24. _____ behaviors (unnecessary responses) often become part of response chains because they appear to be associated with reinforcement.
25. In a process called _____, complex operant responses can be taught by reinforcing successive _____ (ever closer matches) to a final desired response.
26. If an operant response is not reinforced, it may _____ (disappear). But after extinction seems complete, it may temporarily reappear (_____ recovery).

● *Are there different kinds of operant reinforcement?*

27. In _____ reinforcement, reward or a pleasant event follows a response. In _____ reinforcement, a response that ends discomfort becomes more likely to occur again.
28. Punishment decreases responding. Punishment occurs when a response is followed by the onset of an _____ event or by the removal of a _____ event (response cost).
29. _____ reinforcers are "natural," physiologically-based rewards. Intra-cranial _____ of "pleasure centers" in the brain can also serve as a reinforcers of this type.
30. _____ reinforcers are learned. They typically gain their reinforcing value by association with _____ reinforcers or because they can be exchanged for _____ reinforcers. Tokens and money gain their reinforcing value in this way.
31. Human behavior is often influenced by _____ reinforcers, which are based on learned desires for attention and approval from others.
32. Feedback, or _____ of results, aids learning and improves performance.
33. Programmed _____ breaks learning into a series of small steps and provides immediate feedback.

34. _____ _____ (CAI) does the same, but has the added advantage of providing alternate exercises and information when needed.

35. Four variations of _____ are drill and practice, instructional games, educational simulations, and interactive videodisc instruction.

● *How are we influenced by patterns of reward?*

36. Reward or reinforcement may be given continuously (after every response), or on a _____ of partial reinforcement like those studied by B. F. _____.

37. Partial reinforcement produces greater resistance to _____. This is the _____ reinforcement effect.

38. The four most basic schedules of reinforcement are fixed and variable _____ (FR and VR) and fixed and variable _____ (FI and VI).

39. _____ and _____ schedules produce high rates of responding. An _____ schedule produces moderate rates of responding with alternating periods of activity and inactivity. VI schedules produce slow, steady rates of responding and strong resistance to _____.

40. Stimuli that precede a reinforced response tend to control the response on future occasions. This is called _____ _____.

41. Two aspects of stimulus control are _____ and discrimination.

42. In _____, an operant response tends to occur when stimuli similar to those preceding reinforcement are present.

43. In _____, responses are given in the presence of stimuli associated with reinforcement (S+) and withheld in the presence of stimuli associated with non-reinforcement (S−).

● *What does punishment do to behavior?*

44. A _____ is any consequence that lowers the frequency of a target behavior.

45. Punishment is most effective when it is immediate, _____, and intense.

46. Mild punishment tends only to temporarily suppress responses that are also _____ in some way.

47. The undesirable side effects of punishment include the conditioning of fear; the learning of escape and _____ responses; and the encouragement of _____ against others.

48. _____ and _____ are a better way to change behavior than punishment.

● *What is cognitive learning?*

49. Cognitive learning involves higher mental processes, such as understanding, knowing, or anticipating. Evidence of cognitive learning is provided by _____ _____ (internal representations of spatial relationships) and _____ (hidden) learning.

50. Discovery learning emphasizes insight and understanding, in contrast to _____ learning.

● *Does learning occur by imitation?*

51. Much human learning is achieved through observation, or _____.
_____ learning is influenced by the personal characteristics of the model and the success or failure of the model's behavior.
52. Television characters can act as powerful models for _____ learning. Televised violence increases the likelihood of aggression by viewers.

● *How does conditioning apply to practical problems?*

53. Operant principles can be readily applied to manage behavior in everyday settings. Self-management of behavior is based on self-reinforcement, self-recording, feedback, and behavioral _____.
54. Prepotent, or frequent, high-probability responses, can be used to _____ low-frequency responses. This is known as the _____ principle.
55. Four strategies that can help change bad habits are: reinforcing alternate _____, promoting extinction, breaking response chains, and avoiding _____ cues.
56. In school, self-regulated learning typically involves all of the following: setting learning goals, planning learning _____, using self-instruction, monitoring progress, evaluating yourself, _____ successes, and taking corrective action when required.

● *How does biology influence learning?*

57. Many animals are born with innate behavior patterns far more complex than _____. These are organized into fixed action patterns (FAPs), which are stereotyped, _____-specific behaviors.
58. Learning in animals is limited at times by various biological _____ and species-typical behaviors.
59. According to _____ fear theory, some stimuli are especially effective conditioned stimuli.
60. Many operant responses are subject to instinctive _____—the tendency for learned responses to shift toward innate response patterns.

MASTERY TEST

1. Tokens are a good example of
   a. secondary reinforcers b. the effects of ICS on behavior c. non-contingent reinforcers
   d. generalized reinforcers

2. The principle of feedback is of particular importance to
   a. CERs b. ICS c. CAI d. higher-order conditioning

3. Biological constraints to learning are exemplified by
   a. instinctive drift b. spontaneous recovery c. the law of effect d. vicarious conditioning

4. To teach a pet dog to use a new dog door, it would be helpful to use
   a. the Premack principle b. shaping c. respondent conditioning d. delayed reinforcement

5. To test for the presence of classical conditioning you would omit the
   a. CS   b. US   c. CR   d. S+

6. Which of the following does not belong with the others?
   a. Thorndike   b. Skinner   c. Pavlov   d. instrumental learning

7. To teach a child to say "Please" when she asks for things, you should make getting the requested item
   a. the CS   b. a token   c. a negative reinforcer   d. response-contingent

8. Money is to secondary reinforcer as food is to
   a. ICS   b. prepotent responses   c. primary reinforcer   d. negative reinforcer

9. Whether a model is reinforced has a great impact on
   a. discovery learning   b. latent learning   c. observational learning   d. self-regulated learning

10. One thing that classical and operant conditioning have in common is that both
    a. were discovered by Pavlov   b. depend on reinforcement   c. are affected by the consequences of making a response   d. permanently change behavior

11. To shape the behavior of a teacher in one of your classes you would probably have to rely on
    a. tokens   b. primary reinforcers   c. negative attention seeking   d. social reinforcers

12. The concept that best explains persistence at gambling is
    a. partial reinforcement   b. continuous reinforcement   c. fixed interval reinforcement
    d. fixed ratio reinforcement

13. Which of the following is NOT a common side effect of mild punishment?
    a. escape learning   b. avoidance learning   c. aggression   d. accelerated extinction

14. With respect to televised violence it can be said that TV violence
    a. causes viewers to be more aggressive   b. makes aggression more likely   c. has no effect on the majority of viewers   d. vicariously lowers aggressive urges

15. Which of the following types of learning is most related to the consequences of making a response?
    a. Pavlovian conditioning   b. classical conditioning   c. operant conditioning   d. respondent conditioning

16. Which combination would most likely make a CER into a phobia?
    a. CER-discrimination   b. CER-desensitization   c. CER-response cost   d. CER-generalization

17. Active, goal-oriented learning in school is called _____ learning.
    a. two-factor   b. respondent   c. vicarious   d. self-regulated

18. A loud, unexpected sound causes a startle reflex; thus, a loud sound could be used as a _____ in conditioning.
    a. NS   b. CR   c. UR   d. US

19. Antecedents are to _____ as consequences are to _____.
a. discriminative stimuli, reinforcers b. shaping, response chaining c. conditioned stimuli, cognitive maps d. punishment, negative reinforcement

20. The use of self-recording to change personal behavior is closely related to the principle of
a. response chaining b. feedback c. two-factor reinforcement d. stimulus control

21. _____ typically only temporarily suppresses reinforced responses.
a. negative reinforcement b. extinction c. mild punishment d. stimulus generalization

22. In general, the highest rates of responding are associated with
a. delayed reinforcement b. continuous reinforcement c. interval reinforcement
d. fixed ratio reinforcement

23. A child who has learned, through classical conditioning, to fear sitting in a dentist's chair becomes frightened when he is placed in a barber's chair. This illustrates the concept of
a. stimulus generalization b. spontaneous recovery c. higher-order discrimination
d. vicarious conditioning

24. The informational view of learning places emphasis on the creation of mental
a. expectancies b. reinforcement schedules c. contracts d. antecedents

25. For some adults, blushing when embarrassed or ashamed is probably a _____ first formed in childhood.
a. conditioned stimulus b. CAI c. discriminative stimulus d. CER

26. Learning to obey traffic signals is related to the phenomenon called
a. stimulus control b. spontaneous recovery c. avoidance learning d. modeling

27. To be most effective, punishment should be combined with
a. response costs b. aversive stimuli c. delayed feedback d. reinforcement

28. Involuntary responses are to _____ conditioning as voluntary responses are to _____ conditioning.
a. classical, respondent b. classical, operant c. operant, classical d. operant, instrumental

29. Negative attention seeking by children demonstrates the impact of _____ on behavior.
a. operant extinction b. social reinforcers c. response costs d. prepotent responses

30. Which consequence increases the probability that a response will be repeated?
a. punishment b. response cost c. non-reinforcement d. negative reinforcement

ANSWERS

Recite and Review

1. behavior, precede, follow
2. conditioning, conditioning
3. stimulus, responses
4. reinforced, Operant
5. neutral, response
6. stimulus, learned
7. stimulus
8. stimulus
9. conditioning
10. response
11. similar
12. stimulus
13. response
14. follow
15. reflexes, conditioned
16. stimulus
17. secondhand, observe
18. learning
19. increases, effect
20. response, increases
21. effect
22. reinforcement, response
23. chains, single
24. response
25. operant
26. recovery
27. reward, ends
28. decreases, cost
29. pleasure, brain
30. learned, exchanged
31. approval
32. results
33. feedback
34. instruction
35. practice
36. response, partial
37. effect
38. fixed, fixed
39. high, slow
40. precede
41. discrimination
42. similar
43. S+, S−
44. decreases
45. immediate

46. suppress
47. escape
48. mild, responses
49. maps, learning
50. understanding
51. imitation, model, model's
52. models
53. feedback
54. responses, principle
55. chains, cues
56. learning, goals, successes
57. innate, action
58. biological
59. fear
60. innate

Relate

1. e
2. j
3. a
4. i
5. b
6. h
7. c
8. d
9. f
10. g
11. a
12. j
13. b
14. g
15. c
16. d
17. f
18. e
19. h
20. i
21. d
22. e
23. g
24. f
25. h
26. j
27. i
28. a

29. c
30. b

Check Your Memory

1. T
2. F
3. T
4. F
5. T
6. T
7. F
8. F
9. F
10. T
11. F
12. T
13. T
14. F
15. F
16. T
17. F
18. F
19. F
20. T
21. T
22. F
23. T
24. T
25. F
26. T
27. F
28. F
29. F
30. F
31. T
32. T
33. T
34. F
35. F
36. T
37. F
38. F
39. F
40. T
41. F

42. T
43. F
44. T
45. F
46. T
47. F
48. T
49. T
50. T
51. T
52. T
53. T
54. F
55. T
56. T
57. F
58. T
59. F
60. F
61. F
62. T
63. T
64. F
65. T
66. T
67. T
68. F
69. T

Final Survey and Review

1. antecedents, consequences
2. respondent, operant
3. neutral, consequences
4. reinforcement, US
5. Ivan Pavlov, unconditioned, reflex
6. conditioned, conditioned
7. unconditioned stimulus
8. Higher-order
9. extinction
10. spontaneous recovery
11. generalization
12. discrimination
13. informational
14. CS, US
15. emotional responses
16. phobias, generalization
17. Vicarious
18. instrumental
19. probability, Thorndike

20. response, increases
21. expectation
22. contingent
23. decreases, reinforcer
24. Superstitious
25. shaping, approximations
26. extinguish, spontaneous
27. positive, negative
28. aversive, positive
29. Primary, stimulation
30. Secondary, primary, primary
31. social
32. knowledge
33. instruction
34. Computer-assisted
35. CAI
36. schedule, Skinner
37. extinction, partial
38. ratio, interval
39. FR, VR, FI, extinction
40. stimulus control
41. generalization
42. generalization
43. discrimination
44. punisher
45. consistent
46. reinforced
47. avoidance, aggression
48. Reinforcement, non-reinforcement
49. cognitive maps, latent
50. rote
51. modeling, Observational
52. observational
53. contracting
54. reinforce, Premack
55. responses, antecedent
56. strategies, reinforcing
57. reflexes, species
58. constraints
59. prepared
60. drift

Mastery Test

1. a (p. 290)
2. c (p. 292)
3. a (p. 310)
4. b (p. 287-288)
5. b (p. 279)
6. c (p. 284-285)
7. d (p. 286)
8. c (p. 289-290)
9. c (p. 303)
10. b (p. 277)
11. d (p. 291)
12. a (p. 294)
13. d (p. 298)
14. b (p. 304)
15. c (p. 278)
16. d (p. 283)
17. d (p. 308)
18. d (p. 282)
19. a (p. 284, 296)
20. b (p. 307)
21. c (p. 298)
22. d (p. 294)
23. a (p. 281)
24. a (p. 281)
25. d (p. 283)
26. a (p. 295)
27. d (p. 298)
28. b (p. 285)
29. b (p. 288, 291)
30. d (p. 288)

Chapter 10

Memory

CHAPTER OVERVIEW

Memory systems encode and store information for later retrieval. A popular model divides memory into 3 systems: sensory memory, short-term memory (STM), and long-term memory (LTM). Sensory memory stores exact copies of sensory information for very brief periods. STM is limited to about 7 bits of information, but chunking and recoding allow more information to be stored. LTM has nearly unlimited storage. Short-term memories last only a short time; long-term memories are relatively permanent. Long-term memories can be further divided into declarative memories (which may be semantic or episodic) and procedural memories.

Explicit memories are revealed by recall, recognition, and relearning tasks. Implicit memories are revealed by priming. Eidetic imagery (photographic memory) is fairly common in children, but rare among adults. Many people have internal memory images and some have exceptional memory based on internal imagery. Exceptional memory capacity is based on both learned strategies and natural abilities.

Forgetting is most rapid immediately after learning. Some "forgetting" is based on a failure to encode information. Short-term forgetting is partly explained by the decay (weakening) of memory traces. Some long-term forgetting may also occur this way. Some forgetting is related to a lack of memory cues. Much forgetting is related to interference among memories. Clinical psychologists believe that memories are sometimes repressed (unconsciously held out of awareness).

In the brain, memory traces (engrams) must be consolidated before they become relatively permanent. The hippocampus is a structure involved in memory consolidation. Information appears to be stored in the brain through changes in nerve cells.

Memory can be improved by the use of mnemonic systems and by attention to factors that affect memory, such as overlearning, serial position, organization, and the like.

The core of the recovered memory debate is the fact that there is usually no way to separate true memories from fantasies.

RECITE AND REVIEW

● *Is there more than one type of memory?*

Recite and Review: Pages 314-317

1. Memory is an active _____. _____ is first encoded (changed into the form in which it will be retained).

 2. Next it is _____ in memory. Later it must be retrieved to be put to use.

3. Humans appear to have _____ interrelated memory systems. These are sensory memory, _____ memory (STM), and _____ memory (LTM).

4. Sensory memory holds an _____ copy of what is seen or heard, in the form of an icon (_____) or echo (sound sensation).

5. Short-term memories tend to be stored as _____. Long-term memories are stored on the basis of _____, or importance.

6. STM acts as a _____ storehouse for small amounts of information. It provides a working memory where thinking, mental arithmetic, and the like take place. LTM acts as a _____ storehouse for meaningful information.

What are the features of each type of memory?

Recite and Review: Pages 317-321

7. Sensory memory is exact, but very brief, lasting only 2 _____ or less. Through selective attention, some information is transferred to _____.

8. The digit-span test reveals that STM has an average upper limit of about 7 _____ of information. However, this can be extended by chunking, or recoding information into _____ units or groups.

9. Short-term memories are brief and very sensitive to _____, or interference; however, they can be prolonged by maintenance rehearsal (silent _____).

10. Elaborative rehearsal, which emphasizes meaning, helps transfer information from _____ to LTM. Elaborative rehearsal links new information with existing _____.

11. LTM seems to have an almost unlimited storage capacity. However, LTM is subject to constructive processing, or ongoing revision and _____. As a result, people often have pseudo-memories (_____ memories) that they believe are true.

12. LTM is highly _____ to allow retrieval of needed information. The pattern, or structure, of memory networks is the subject of current memory research. Network _____ portray LTM as a system of linked ideas.

13. Redintegrative memories unfold as each added memory provides a cue for retrieving the next _____. Seemingly forgotten memories may be reconstructed in this way.

Is there more than one type of long-term memory?

Recite and Review: Pages 322-323

14. Within long-term memory, declarative memories for _____ seem to differ from procedural memories for _____.

15. _____ memories may be further categorized as semantic memories or episodic memories.

16. Semantic memories consist of basic factual knowledge that is almost immune to _____.

17. Episodic memories record _____ experiences that are associated with specific times and places.

How is memory measured?

Recite and Review: Pages 323-325

18. The tip-of-the-tongue _____ shows that memory is not an all-or-nothing event. Memories may be revealed by _____, recognition, or relearning.

19. In recall, memory proceeds without specific cues, as in an _____ exam. Recall of listed information often reveals a serial position effect (_____ items on the list are most subject to errors).

20. A common test of _____ is the multiple-choice question. _____ is very sensitive to the kinds of distractors (wrong choices) used.

21. In relearning, "forgotten" material is learned again, and memory is indicated by a _____ score.

22. Recall, recognition, and relearning mainly measure explicit _____ that we are aware of having. Other techniques, such as priming, are necessary to reveal implicit _____, which are unconscious.

● *What are "photographic" memories?*

Recite and Review: Pages 325-328

23. Eidetic imagery (photographic memory) occurs when a person is able to project an _____ onto an external surface. Such images allow brief, nearly complete recall by some children.

24. Eidetic imagery is rarely found in _____. However, many adults have internal images, which can be very vivid and a basis for remembering.

25. Exceptional memory can be learned by finding ways to directly store information in _____. Learning has no effect on the limits of _____. Some people may have naturally superior memory abilities that that exceed what can be achieved through learning.

● *What causes forgetting?*

Recite and Review: Pages 328-332

26. Forgetting and memory were extensively studied by Herman Ebbinghaus, whose _____ of forgetting shows that forgetting is typically most rapid immediately _____ learning.

27. Ebbinghaus used nonsense syllables to study memory. The forgetting of _____ material is much _____ than shown by his curve of forgetting.

28. Failure to encode _____ is a common cause of "forgetting."

29. Forgetting in sensory memory and STM probably reflects decay of memory _____ in the nervous system. Decay or _____ of memories may also account for some LTM loss, but most forgetting cannot be explained this way.

30. Often, forgetting is cue dependent. The power of cues to trigger memories is revealed by state-dependent _____, in which bodily _____ at the time of learning and of retrieval affect memory.

31. Much _____ in both STM and LTM can be attributed to interference of memories with one another.

32. When recent learning _____ with retrieval of prior learning, retroactive interference has occurred. If old memories _____ with new memories, proactive interference has occurred.

33. Depending on the relationship between prior learning and a new task, skills may show _____ transfer or _____ transfer (carryover to a new situation).

● *How accurate are everyday memories?*

Recite and Review: Pages 332-333

34. Repression is the _____ of painful, embarrassing, or traumatic memories.
35. Repression is thought to be unconscious, in contrast to suppression, which is a _____ attempt to avoid thinking about something.
36. Flashbulb memories, which seem especially vivid, are created at emotionally significant times. While such memories may not be accurate, we tend to place great _____ in them.

● *What happens in the brain when memories are formed?*

Recite and Review: Pages 334-336

37. Retrograde _____ and the effects of electroconvulsive _____ (ECS) may be explained by the concept of consolidation.
38. Consolidation theory holds that engrams (permanent _____ _____) are formed during a critical period after learning. Until they are consolidated, long-term memories are easily destroyed.
39. The hippocampus is a _____ structure associated with the consolidation of memories.
40. The search within the brain for engrams has now settled on changes in individual _____ cells.
41. The best-documented changes are alterations in the amounts of transmitter _____ released by nerve cells and the number of receptor sites on each cell.

● *How can memory be improved?*

Recite and Review: Pages 336-339 & APPLICATIONS

42. Memory can be improved by using feedback, recitation, and rehearsal, by selecting and _____ information, and by using the progressive _____ method, spaced practice, overlearning, and active search strategies.
43. The effects of serial _____, sleep, review, cues, and elaboration should also be kept in mind when studying or memorizing.
44. Mnemonic systems, such as the _____ method, use mental images and unusual associations to link new information with familiar memories already stored in _____. Such strategies give information personal meaning and make it easier to recall.

● *What is the "recovered-memory" debate?*

Recite and Review: EXPLORATION

45. Experts are currently debating the validity of childhood memories of _____ that reappear after apparently being repressed for decades.
46. Independent evidence has verified that some recovered memories are _____. However, others have been shown to be _____.
47. In the absence of confirming or disconfirming _____, there is currently no way to separate true memories from fantasies. Caution is advised for all concerned with attempts to retrieve supposedly hidden memories.

RELATE

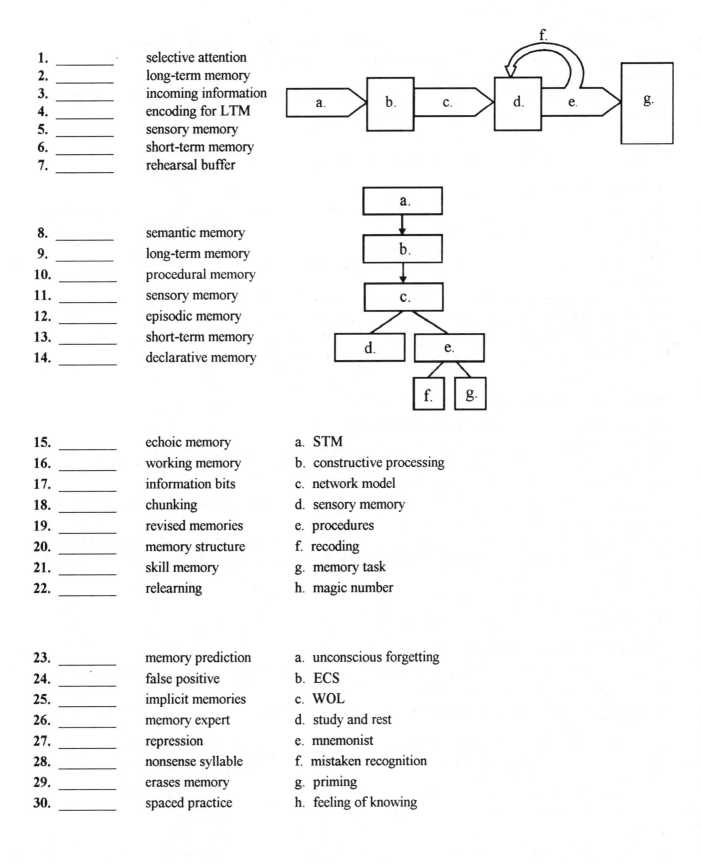

1. _____ selective attention
2. _____ long-term memory
3. _____ incoming information
4. _____ encoding for LTM
5. _____ sensory memory
6. _____ short-term memory
7. _____ rehearsal buffer

8. _____ semantic memory
9. _____ long-term memory
10. _____ procedural memory
11. _____ sensory memory
12. _____ episodic memory
13. _____ short-term memory
14. _____ declarative memory

15. _____ echoic memory   a. STM
16. _____ working memory   b. constructive processing
17. _____ information bits   c. network model
18. _____ chunking   d. sensory memory
19. _____ revised memories   e. procedures
20. _____ memory structure   f. recoding
21. _____ skill memory   g. memory task
22. _____ relearning   h. magic number

23. _____ memory prediction   a. unconscious forgetting
24. _____ false positive   b. ECS
25. _____ implicit memories   c. WOL
26. _____ memory expert   d. study and rest
27. _____ repression   e. mnemonist
28. _____ nonsense syllable   f. mistaken recognition
29. _____ erases memory   g. priming
30. _____ spaced practice   h. feeling of knowing

CHECK YOUR MEMORY

Check Your Memory: Pages 314-317

1. Incoming information must be encoded before it is stored in memory. T or F?
2. Sensory memories last for a few minutes or less. T or F?
3. A memory that cannot be retrieved has little value. T or F?
4. Selective attention influences what information enters STM. T or F?
5. Working memory is another name for sensory memory. T or F?
6. Errors in long-term memory tend to focus on the sounds of words. T or F?
7. Generally, the more you know, the more new information you can store in long-term memory. T or F?

Check Your Memory: Pages 317-321

8. For many kinds of information, STM can store an average of 5 bits of information. T or F?
9. Chunking recodes information into smaller units that are easier to fit into STM. T or F?
10. The more times a short-term memory is rehearsed, the better its chance of being stored in LTM. T or F?
11. On average, short-term memories last only about 18 minutes, unless they are rehearsed. T or F?
12. Maintenance rehearsal keeps memories active in sensory memory. T or F?
13. The surface of the brain records the past like a movie, complete with sound track. T or F?
14. Being confident about a memory tells little about the true accuracy of the memory. T or F?
15. Hypnosis increases false memories more than it does true ones. T or F?
16. Long-term memories appear to be organized alphabetically for speedy access. T or F?

Check Your Memory: Pages 322-323

17. Knowing how to swing a golf club is a type of declarative memory. T or F?
18. A person lacking declarative memory might still remember how to solve a mechanical puzzle. T or F?
19. Semantic memories are almost immune to forgetting. T or F?
20. Semantic memories are a type of declarative memory. T or F?
21. Episodic memories have no connection to particular times and places. T or F?

Check Your Memory: Pages 323-325

22. Remembering the first sound of a name you are trying to recall is an example of the tip-of-the-tongue state. T or F?
23. Tests of recognition require verbatim memory. T or F?
24. The serial position effect measures the strength of the feeling of knowing. T or F?
25. Recognition tends to be a more sensitive test of memory than recall. T or F?
26. False positives and distractors greatly affect the accuracy of relearning tests. T or F?
27. Recall, recognition, and relearning are used to measure explicit memories. T or F?
28. Priming is used to activate explicit (hidden) memories. T or F?

Check Your Memory: Pages 325-328

29. Eidetic images last for 30 seconds or more. T or F?
30. About 8 percent of all children have eidetic images. T or F?
31. Eidetic imagery becomes rare by adulthood. T or F?
32. Word memories can sometimes actually impair memories based on images. T or F?

33. Mr. S (the mnemonist) had virtually unlimited eidetic imagery. T or F?
34. Practice in remembering one type of information increases the capacity of STM to store other types of information, too. T or F?
35. All contestants in the World Memory Championship performed poorly on tasks that prevented the use of learned strategies. T or F?

Check Your Memory: Pages 328-332

36. Ebbinghaus chose to learn nonsense syllables so that they would all be the same length. T or F?
37. Ebbinghaus' curve of forgetting levels off after 2 days, showing little further memory loss after that. T or F?
38. Decay of memory traces clearly applies to information in STM. T or F?
39. Disuse theories of forgetting address the question: Have I been storing the information in the first place? T or F?
40. The presence of memory cues almost always improves memory. T or F?
41. Information learned under the influence of a drug may be best remembered when the drugged state occurs again. T or F?
42. If you are in a bad mood, you are more likely to remember unpleasant events. T or F?
43. Sleeping tends to interfere with the retention of new memories. T or F?
44. You learn information A and then information B. If your memory of B is lowered by having first learned A, you have experienced retroactive interference. T or F?
45. If knowing how to skateboard helps you rapidly learn to snowboard, then positive transfer occurred. T or F?

Check Your Memory: Pages 332-333

46. Unconsciously forgetting painful memories is called negative transfer. T or F?
47. A conscious attempt to put a memory out of mind is called repression. T or F?
48. Flashbulb memories tend to be formed when an event is surprising or emotional. T or F?
49. The confidence we have in flashbulb memories is well placed—they are much more accurate than most other memories. T or F?

Check Your Memory: Pages 334-336

50. Retrograde amnesia is a gap in memories of events preceding a head injury. T or F?
51. Stimulant drugs may speed up consolidation, but at high doses they disrupt memory. T or F?
52. People with damage to the hippocampus typically cannot remember events that occurred before the damage. T or F?
53. In the early 1920s, Karl Lashley found the location of engrams in the brain. T or F?
54. Storing memories alters the activity, structure, and chemistry of the brain. T or F?

Check Your Memory: Pages 336-339 & APPLICATIONS

55. Recitation is a good way to generate feedback while studying. T or F?
56. Elaborative rehearsal involving "why" questions improves memory. T or F?
57. Overlearning is inefficient; you should stop studying at the point of initial mastery of new information. T or F?
58. Massed practice is almost always superior to spaced practice. T or F?
59. Recalling events from different viewpoints is part of doing a cognitive interview. T or F?
60. *Roy G. Biv* is a mnemonic for the notes on a musical staff. T or F?

61. Many mnemonics make use of mental images or pictures. T or F?
62. Mnemonics often link new information to familiar memories. T or F?
63. The keyword method is superior to rote learning for memorizing vocabulary words in another language. T or F?

Check Your Memory: Exploration

64. Childhood memories of most atrocities are carried for life. T or F?
65. Everyday memories are unreliable and easily altered. T or F?
66. Suggestion and fantasy are elements of many techniques used in attempts to recover repressed memories. T or F?
67. Unless a memory can be independently confirmed, there is no way to tell if it is real or not. T or F?

FINAL SURVEY AND REVIEW

● *Is there more than one type of memory?*

1. Memory is an active system. Information is first _____ (changed into the form in which it will be retained).
2. Next it is stored in memory. Later it must be _____ to be put to use.
3. Humans appear to have 3 interrelated memory systems. These are _____ memory, _____ memory (STM), and long-term memory (LTM).
4. Sensory memory holds an exact copy of what is seen or heard, in the form of an _____ (image) or _____ (sound sensation).
5. _____ memories tend to be stored as sounds. _____ memories are stored on the basis of meaning, or importance.
6. _____ acts as a temporary storehouse for small amounts of information. It provides a _____ memory where thinking, mental arithmetic, and the like take place. LTM acts as a permanent storehouse for _____ information.

● *What are the features of each type of memory?*

7. _____ memory is exact, but very brief, lasting only 2 seconds or less. Through _____ _____, some information is transferred to STM.
8. The _____ test reveals that STM has an average upper limit of about 7 bits of information. However, this can be extended by chunking, or _____ information into larger units or groups.
9. Short-term memories are brief and very sensitive to interruption , or _____; however, they can be prolonged by _____ rehearsal (silent repetition).
10. _____ rehearsal, which emphasizes meaning, helps transfer information from STM to LTM.
11. LTM seems to have an almost unlimited storage capacity. However, LTM is subject to _____ processing, or ongoing revision and updating. As a result, people often have _____ (false memories) that they believe are true.

12. LTM is highly organized to allow retrieval of needed information. The pattern, or structure, of memory _____ is the subject of current memory research. _____ models portray LTM as a system of linked ideas.

13. _____ memories unfold as each added memory provides a cue for retrieving the next memory. Seemingly forgotten memories may be reconstructed in this way.

● *Is there more than one type of long-term memory?*

14. Within long-term memory, _____ memories for facts seem to differ from _____ memories for skills.

15. Declarative memories may be further categorized as _____ memories or _____ memories.

16. _____ memories consist of basic factual knowledge that is almost immune to forgetting.

17. _____ memories record personal experiences that are associated with specific times and places.

● *How is memory measured?*

18. The _____-of-the-_____ state shows that memory is not an all-or-nothing event. Memories may be revealed by recall, _____, or relearning.

19. In _____, memory proceeds without specific cues, as in an essay exam. Remembering a list of information often reveals a _____ _____ effect (middle items on the list are most subject to errors).

20. A common test of recognition is the _____-choice question. Recognition is very sensitive to the kinds of _____ (wrong choices) used.

21. In _____, "forgotten" material is learned again, and memory is indicated by a savings score.

22. Recall, recognition, and relearning mainly measure _____ memories that we are aware of having. Other techniques, such as priming, are necessary to reveal _____ memories, which are unconscious.

● *What are "photographic" memories?*

23. _____ _____ (photographic memory) occurs when a person is able to project an image onto an external surface. Such images allow brief, nearly complete recall by some children.

24. _____ _____ is rarely found in adults. However, many adults have internal images, which can be very vivid and a basis for remembering.

25. _____ memory can be learned by finding ways to directly store information in LTM. Learning has no effect on the _____ of STM. Some people may have naturally superior memory abilities that that exceed what can be achieved through learning.

● *What causes forgetting?*

26. Forgetting and memory were extensively studied by Herman _____, whose curve of forgetting shows that forgetting is typically most rapid immediately after learning.

27. He used _____ syllables to study memory. The forgetting of meaningful material is much slower than shown by his curve of forgetting.

28. Failure to _____ information is a common cause of "forgetting."

29. Forgetting in _____ memory and _____ probably reflects decay of memory traces in the nervous system. Decay or disuse of memories may also account for some _____ loss, but most forgetting cannot be explained this way.

30. Often, forgetting is _____ dependent. The power of _____ to trigger memories is revealed by _____ learning, in which bodily states at the time of learning and of retrieval affect memory.

31. Much forgetting in both STM and LTM can be attributed to _____ of memories with one another.

32. When recent learning interferes with retrieval of prior learning, _____ interference has occurred. If old memories interfere with new memories, _____ interference has occurred.

33. Depending on the relationship between prior learning and a new task, skills may show _____ transfer or _____ transfer (carryover to a new situation).

• *How accurate are everyday memories?*

34. _____ is the motivated forgetting of painful, embarrassing, or traumatic memories.

35. _____ is thought to be unconscious, in contrast to _____, which is a conscious attempt to avoid thinking about something.

36. _____ memories, which seem especially vivid, are created at emotionally significant times. While such memories may not be _____, we tend to place great confidence in them.

• *What happens in the brain when memories are formed?*

37. _____ amnesia and the effects of _____ shock (ECS) may be explained by the concept of consolidation.

38. Consolidation theory holds that _____ (permanent memory traces) are formed during a critical period after learning. Until they are _____, long-term memories are easily destroyed.

39. The _____ is a brain structure associated with the consolidation of memories.

40. The search within the brain for engrams has now settled on changes in individual _____ _____.

41. The best-documented changes are alterations in the amounts of _____ chemicals released by nerve cells and the number of _____ sites on each cell.

• *How can memory be improved?*

42. Memory can be improved by using _____ (knowledge of results), recitation, and rehearsal, by _____ and organizing information, and by using the progressive part method, spaced practice, overlearning, and active _____ strategies.

43. The effects of _____ position, sleep, review, cues, and _____ (connecting new information to existing knowledge) should also be kept in mind when studying or memorizing.

44. _____ systems, such as the keyword method, use mental images and unusual associations to link new information with familiar memories already stored in LTM. Such strategies give information personal meaning and make it easier to recall.

● *What is the "recovered-memory" debate?*

45. Experts are currently debating the validity of childhood memories of abuse that reappear after apparently being _____ for decades.

46. Independent evidence has verified that some _____ memories are true. However, others have been shown to be false.

47. In the absence of confirming or disconfirming evidence, there is currently no way to separate true memories from _____. Caution is advised for all concerned with attempts to retrieve supposedly hidden memories.

MASTERY TEST

1. The meaning and importance of information has a strong impact on
   a. sensory memory   b. eidetic memory   c. long-term memory   d. procedural memory

2. Pseudo-memories are closely related to the effects of
   a. repression   b. suppression   c. semantic forgetting   d. constructive processing

3. The occurrence of _____ implies that consolidation has been prevented.
   a. retrograde amnesia   b. hippocampal transfer   c. suppression   d. changes in the activities of individual nerve cells

4. Most of the techniques used to recover supposedly repressed memories involve
   a. redintegration and hypnosis   b. suggestion and fantasy   c. reconstruction and priming
   d. coercion and fabrication

5. Most daily memory chores are handled by
   a. sensory memory and LTM   b. STM and working memory   c. STM and LTM
   d. STM and declarative memory

6. Three key processes in memory systems are
   a. storage, organization, recovery   b. encoding, attention, reprocessing   c. storage, retrieval, encoding
   d. retrieval, reprocessing, reorganization

7. Procedural memories are to skills as _____ memories are to facts.
   a. declarative   b. short-term   c. redintegrative   d. eidetic

8. An ability to answer questions about distances on a map you have seen only once implies that some memories are based on
   a. constructive processing b. redintegration c. internal images d. episodic processing

9. The first potential cause of forgetting that may occur is
   a. engram decay b. disuse c. cue-dependent forgetting d. encoding failure

10. The persistence of icons and echoes is the basis for
    a. sensory memory b. short-term memory c. long-term memory d. working memory

11. Priming is most often used to reveal
    a. semantic memories b. episodic memories c. implicit memories d. eidetic memories

12. "Projection" onto an external surface is most characteristic of
    a. sensory memories b. eidetic images c. flashbulb memories d. mnemonic images

13. Chunking helps especially to extend the capacity of
    a. sensory memory b. STM c. LTM d. declarative memory

14. There is presently no way to tell if a "recovered" memory is true or false unless independent _____ exists.
    a. evidence b. amnesia c. elaboration d. consolidation

15. Taking an essay test inevitably requires a person to use
    a. recall b. recognition c. relearning d. priming

16. A savings score is used in what memory task?
    a. recall b. recognition c. relearning d. priming

17. _____ rehearsal helps link new information to existing memories by concentrating on meaning.
    a. Redintegrative b. Constructive c. Maintenance d. Elaborative

18. Middle items are neither held in STM nor moved to LTM. This statement explains the
    a. feeling of knowing b. serial position effect c. tip-of-the-tongue state d. semantic forgetting curve

19. According to the curve of forgetting, the greatest decline in the amount recalled occurs during the _____ after learning.
    a. first hour b. second day c. third to sixth days d. retroactive period

20. Work with brain stimulation, truth serums, and hypnosis suggests that long-term memories are
    a. stored in the hippocampus b. relatively permanent c. unaffected by later input
    d. always redintegrative

21. Which of the following is most likely to improve the accuracy of memory?
    a. hypnosis b. constructive processing c. the serial position effect d. memory cues

22. To qualify as repression, forgetting must be
  a. retroactive b. proactive c. unconscious d. explicit

23. Which of the following typically is NOT a good way to improve memory?
  a. massed practice b. overlearning c. rehearsal d. recall strategies

24. The first time they try, many people have trouble backing a car with a trailer attached to it. This occurs because of
  a. retroactive interference b. procedural repression c. negative redintegration d. negative transfer

25. One thing that is clearly true about flashbulb memories is that
  a. they are unusually accurate b. we place great confidence in them c. they apply primarily to public tragedies d. they are recovered by using visualization and hypnosis

26. One common mnemonic strategy is the
  a. serial position technique b. feeling of knowing tactic c. network procedure d. keyword method

27. A perspective that helps explain redintegrative memories is
  a. the feeling of knowing model b. recoding and chunking c. the network model d. mnemonic models

28. Which of the following is NOT considered a part of long-term memory?
  a. echoic memory b. semantic memory c. episodic memory d. declarative memory

29. You are very thirsty. Suddenly you remember a time years ago when you became very thirsty while hiking. This suggests that your memory is
  a. proactive b. state dependent c. still not consolidated d. eidetic

30. After memorizing 5 lists of words you recall less of the last list than a person who only memorized list number five. This observation is explained by
  a. reactive processing b. reconstructive processing c. proactive interference d. retroactive interference

ANSWERS

Recite and Review

1. system, Information
2. stored
3. 3, short-term, long-term
4. exact, image
5. sounds, meaning
6. temporary, permanent
7. seconds, STM
8. bits, larger
9. interruption, repetition
10. STM, memories
11. updating, false
12. organized, models
13. memory
14. facts, skills
15. Declarative
16. forgetting
17. personal
18. state, recall
19. essay, middle
20. recognition, Recognition
21. savings
22. memories, memories
23. image
24. adults
25. LTM, STM
26. curve, after
27. meaningful, slower
28. information
29. traces, disuse
30. learning, states
31. forgetting

32. interferes, interfere
33. positive, negative
34. forgetting
35. conscious
36. confidence
37. amnesia, shock
38. memory traces
39. brain
40. nerve
41. chemicals
42. organizing, part
43. position
44. keyword, LTM
45. abuse
46. true, false
47. evidence

Relate

1. c
2. g
3. a
4. e
5. b
6. d
7. f
8. f or g
9. c
10. d
11. a
12. f or g
13. b
14. e
15. d
16. a
17. h
18. f
19. b
20. c
21. e
22. g
23. h
24. f
25. g
26. e
27. a
28. c
29. b
30. d

Check Your Memory

1. T
2. F
3. T
4. T
5. F
6. F
7. T
8. T
9. F
10. T
11. F
12. F
13. F
14. T
15. T
16. F
17. F
18. T
19. T
20. T
21. F
22. T
23. F
24. F
25. T
26. F
27. T
28. F
29. T
30. T
31. T
32. T
33. F
34. F
35. F
36. F
37. T
38. T
39. F
40. T
41. T
42. T
43. F
44. F
45. T
46. F
47. F
48. T
49. F
50. T
51. T
52. F
53. F
54. T
55. T
56. T
57. F
58. F
59. T
60. F
61. T
62. T
63. T
64. T
65. T
66. T
67. T

Final Survey and Review

1. encoded
2. retrieved
3. sensory, short-term
4. icon, echo
5. Short-term, Long-term
6. STM, working, meaningful
7. Sensory, selective attention
8. digit-span, recoding
9. interference, maintenance
10. Elaborative
11. constructive, pseudo-memories
12. networks, Network
13. Redintegrative
14. declarative, procedural
15. semantic, episodic
16. Semantic
17. Episodic
18. tip, tongue, recognition
19. recall, serial position
20. multiple, distractors
21. relearning
22. explicit, implicit
23. Eidetic imagery
24. Eidetic imagery
25. Exceptional, limits
26. Ebbinghaus
27. nonsense
28. encode
29. sensory, STM, LTM
30. cue, cues, state-dependent

31. interference
32. retroactive, proactive
33. positive, negative
34. Repression
35. Repression, suppression
36. Flashbulb, accurate
37. Retrograde, electroconvulsive
38. engrams, consolidated
39. hippocampus
40. nerve cells
41. transmitter, receptor
42. feedback, selecting, search
43. serial, elaboration
44. Mnemonic
45. repressed
46. recovered
47. fantasies

Mastery Test

1. c (p. 316)
2. d (p. 320)
3. a (p. 334-335)
4. b (p. 343)
5. c (p. 317)
6. c (p. 315)
7. a (p. 322)
8. c (p. 326)
9. d (p. 329)
10. a (p. 315-316)
11. c (p. 325)
12. b (p. 326)
13. b (p. 318)
14. a (p. 344)
15. a (p. 324)
16. c (p. 329)
17. d (p. 318)
18. b (p. 324)
19. a (p. 329)
20. b (p. 319)
21. d (p. 337)
22. c (p. 333)
23. a (p. 338)
24. d (p. 332)
25. b (p. 334)
26. d (p. 340)
27. c (p. 321)
28. a (p. 322)
29. b (p. 330)
30. c (p. 331)

Chapter 11

Cognition and Creativity

CHAPTER OVERVIEW

Thinking is the mental manipulation of images, concepts, and language (or symbols). Most people use internal images for thinking. Kinesthetic images come from remembered actions and implicit actions. A concept is a generalized idea of a class of objects or events. We learn concepts from positive and negative instances and from rules. Prototypes are often used to identify concepts. Language translates events into symbols, which are combined using the rules of grammar and syntax. True languages are productive. Studies suggest that primates are capable of some language use.

The solution to a problem may be arrived at mechanically (by trial and error or by rote). Solutions by understanding usually begin with discovering the general properties of an answer. Next, functional solutions are proposed. Problem solving is frequently aided by heuristics, which narrow the search for solutions. When understanding leads to a rapid solution, it is said that insight has occurred. Insight can be blocked by fixations. Work on artificial intelligence has focused on computer simulations and expert systems. Computer simulations of human problem solving are usually based on a means-ends analysis. Human expertise is based on organized knowledge and acquired strategies.

Creative solutions are practical, sensible, and original. Creative thinking requires divergent thought, characterized by fluency, flexibility, and originality. Tests of creativity measure these qualities. Five stages often seen in creative problem solving are orientation, preparation, incubation, illumination, and verification. However, much creative work is simply based on incremental problem solving. Studies suggest that there is little correlation between IQ and creativity.

Intuitive thinking often leads to errors. Wrong conclusions may be drawn when an answer seems highly representative of what we already believe is true. A second problem is ignoring the base rate of an event. Clear thinking is usually aided by stating or framing a problem in broad terms. Major sources of thinking errors include rigid mental sets, faulty logic, and over-simplifications. Various strategies, including brainstorming, tend to enhance creative problem solving.

Animals reveal a rudimentary capacity for thought when they solve delayed response problems and, in some cases, problems that appear to require understanding or insight. There is also evidence that higher animals, such as chimpanzees, can learn to use basic symbolic thought.

RECITE AND REVIEW

● *What is the nature of thought?*

Recite and Review: Pages 347-349

1. Cognitive psychology is the study of _____, language, problem solving, and _____ processing.
2. Thinking is the manipulation of _____ representations of external problems or situations.
3. Three basic units of thought are images, concepts, and _____ or symbols.

● *In what ways are images related to thinking?*

Recite and Review: Pages 349-352

4. Most people have internal images of one kind or another. Images may be based on information stored in memory or they may be _____.
5. Sometimes images cross normal _____ boundaries in a type of imagery called synesthesia.
6. The size of images used in problem solving may _____. Images may be three-dimensional and they may be rotated in _____ to answer questions.
7. Many of the systems in the brain that are involved in processing _____ images work in reverse to create mental images.
8. Kinesthetic images are created by memories of _____ or by implicit (unexpressed) _____. Kinesthetic sensations and micromovements seem to help structure thinking for many people.

● *How are concepts learned? Are there different kinds of concepts?*

Recite and Review: Pages 352-353

9. A concept is a generalized idea of a _____ of objects or events.
10. Forming concepts may be based on experiences with _____ and negative instances.
11. Concepts may also be acquired by learning rules that define the _____.
12. In practice, we frequently use prototypes (general _____ of the concept class) to identify concepts.
13. Concepts may be classified as conjunctive ("_____" concepts), disjunctive ("_____" concepts), or relational concepts.
14. The denotative meaning of a word or concept is its dictionary _____. Connotative meaning is _____ or emotional.
15. Connotative meaning can be measured with the semantic differential. Most connotative meaning involves the dimensions _____, strong-weak, and active-passive.

● *What is the role of language in thinking?*

Recite and Review: Pages 354-356

16. Language allows events to be encoded into _____ for easy mental manipulation.
17. Language is built out of phonemes (basic speech _____) and morphemes (speech sounds collected into _____ units).

18. Thinking in language is influenced by meaning. The study of _____ is called semantics.

19. Language carries meaning by combining a set of symbols or signs according to a set of _____ (grammar), which includes rules about word _____ (syntax).

20. Various sentences are created by applying transformation _____ to simple statements.

21. A true language is productive, and can be used to generate new ideas or possibilities. American Sign Language (ASL) and other _____ languages used by the deaf are true languages.

● *Can animals be taught to use language?*

Recite and Review: Pages 356-357

22. Animal communication is relatively limited because it lacks symbols that can be _____ easily.

23. Attempts to teach chimpanzees ASL and other non-verbal systems suggest to some that primates are capable of language use. However, others believe that the chimps are merely using _____ responses to get food and other reinforcers.

24. Studies that make use of lexigrams (_____ word-symbols) provide the best evidence yet of animal language use.

● *What do we know about problem solving?*

Recite and Review: Pages 358-361

25. The solution to a problem may be found mechanically (by trial and error or by _____ application of rules). However, mechanical solutions are frequently inefficient or ineffective, except where aided by _____.

26. Solutions by understanding usually begin with discovery of the _____ properties of an answer. Next comes proposal of a number of functional _____.

27. Problem solving is frequently aided by heuristics. These are strategies that typically _____ the search for solutions. The _____ strategy (identify, define, explore, act, look and learn) is a general heuristic.

28. When understanding leads to a rapid _____, insight has occurred. Three elements of insight are _____ encoding, selective combination, and selective comparison.

29. Insights and other problem solving attempts can be blocked by fixation (a tendency to repeat _____ solutions).

30. Functional fixedness is a common _____, but emotional blocks, cultural values, learned conventions, and perceptual _____ are also problems.

● *What is artificial intelligence?*

Recite and Review: Pages 362-364

31. Artificial intelligence refers to any artificial _____ that can perform tasks that require _____ when done by people.

32. Two principal areas of artificial intelligence research are _____ simulations and expert systems.

33. Computer simulations of human problem solving are usually based on a means-ends _____ (finding ways to reduce the difference between the present state and the desired goal).

34. Expert human problem solving is based on organized _____ and acquired strategies, rather than some general improvement in thinking ability. Expertise also allows more automatic _____ of problems.

● *What is the nature of creative thinking?*

Recite and Review: Pages 364-369

35. To be creative, a solution must be _____ and sensible as well as original.

36. _____ may be deductive or inductive, logical or illogical.

37. Creative thinking requires divergent thought, characterized by fluency, flexibility, and _____. Creativity is also marked by problem _____, the active discovery of problems to be solved.

38. Daydreaming and _____ are a source of much divergent thinking. Two very common daydream plots are the conquering _____ and the suffering martyr.

39. Tests of _____, such as the *Unusual Uses Test*, the *Consequences Test*, and the *Anagrams Test*, measure the capacity for divergent thinking.

40. Five stages often seen in creative problem solving are orientation, _____, incubation, illumination, and verification.

41. Not all creative thinking fits this pattern. Much creative activity is based on incremental problem solving (many small _____).

42. Studies suggest that creative persons share a number of identifiable general traits, _____ abilities, thinking _____, and personality characteristics. There is little or no correlation between IQ and creativity.

● *How accurate is intuition?*

Recite and Review: Pages 369-370

43. Intuitive thinking often leads to _____. Wrong conclusions may be drawn when an answer seems highly representative of what we already believe is _____. (That is, when people apply the representativeness heuristic.)

44. A second problem is ignoring the base rate (or underlying _____) of an event.

45. Clear thinking is usually aided by stating or framing a problem in _____ terms.

● *What can be done to improve thinking and to promote creativity?*

Recite and Review: APPLICATIONS

46. Major sources of thinking _____ include rigid mental set, faulty logic, and over-simplification.

47. Syllogisms can be evaluated for the _____ of their premises, the validity of the reasoning, and the truth of the _____.

48. Two common examples of over-simplification are _____ thinking (thinking in black and white terms) and stereotyped thinking (relying on inaccurate and oversimplified images of social groups).

49. Creativity can be enhanced by defining problems _____, by establishing a creative atmosphere, by allowing _____ for incubation, by seeking _____ input, and by looking for analogies.

50. Brainstorming, in which the production and criticism of ideas is kept _____, also tends to enhance creative problem solving.

● *Do animals think?*

Recite and Review: EXPLORATION

51. Animals reveal a rudimentary capacity for thought when they solve _____ response problems.

52. Köhler's chimp solved multiple-stick problems that appeared to require understanding or _____. Some natural "problem solving" by animals appears to be versatile and appropriate enough to qualify as _____.

53. In a recent study, three kinds of apes showed evidence of understanding in a problem that involved using _____ to obtain food hidden in a transparent plastic tube.

54. There is also evidence that higher animals, such as chimpanzees, can learn to use rudimentary symbolic _____. For the moment, however, some psychologists remain unconvinced about such abilities.

RELATE

1. _____	cognition	a. 3-D images
2. _____	language	b. remembered perceptions
3. _____	synesthesia	c. brain imaging
4. _____	mental rotation	d. mental class
5. _____	reverse vision	e. implicit actions
6. _____	stored images	f. thinking
7. _____	kinesthetic imagery	g. ideal or model
8. _____	concept	h. semantic differential
9. _____	prototype	i. crossed senses
10. _____	connotative meaning	j. symbols and rules

11. _____	word meanings	a. meaningful unit
12. _____	morpheme	b. ASL
13. _____	phoneme	c. semantics
14. _____	"hidden" grammar	d. lexigrams
15. _____	Washoe	e. language sound
16. _____	if-then statement	f. mechanical solution
17. _____	Kanzi	g. thinking strategy
18. _____	trial-and-error	h. element of insight
19. _____	heuristic	i. conditional relationship
20. _____	selective comparison	j. transformation rules

21. _____	fixation	a. knowledge plus rules
22. _____	expert system	b. many types of solutions
23. _____	fluency	c. one correct answer
24. _____	flexibility	d. moment of insight
25. _____	originality	e. underlying odds
26. _____	convergent thinking	f. analysis of logic
27. _____	Anagrams Test	g. many solutions
28. _____	illumination	h. blind to alternatives
29. _____	base rate	i. measures divergent thinking
30. _____	syllogism	j. novelty of solutions

CHECK YOUR MEMORY

Check Your Memory: Pages 347-349

1. Cognitive psychology is the study of sensation, memory, and learning. T or F?
2. Images, concepts, and language may be used to mentally represent problems. T or F?
3. Images are generalized ideas of a class of related objects or events. T or F?
4. Blindfolded chess players mainly use concepts to represent chess problems and solutions. T or F?

Check Your Memory: Pages 349-352

5. Experiencing color sensations while listening to music is an example of mental rotation. T or F?
6. Mental images may be used to improve memory and skilled actions. T or F?
7. In an imagined space, it is easiest to locate objects placed above and below yourself. T or F?
8. The visual cortex is activated when a person has a mental image. T or F?
9. The more the image of a shape as to be rotated in space, the longer it takes to tell if it matches another view of the same shape. T or F?
10. People who have good imaging abilities tend to score high on tests of creativity. T or F?
11. The smaller a mental image is, the harder it is to identify its details. T or F?
12. People with good synesthetic imagery tend to learn sports skills faster than average. T or F?

Check Your Memory: Pages 352-353

13. Concept formation is typically based on examples and rules. T or F?
14. Prototypes are very strong negative instances of a concept. T or F?
15. "Greater than" and "lopsided" are relational concepts. T or F?
16. The semantic differential is used to rate the objective meanings of words and concepts. T or F?

Check Your Memory: Pages 354-356

17. Encoding is the study of the meanings of language. T or F?
18. The Stroop interference test shows that thought is greatly influenced by language. T or F?
19. Morphemes are the basic speech sounds of a language. T or F?
20. Syntax is a part of grammar. T or F?
21. Noam Chomsky believes that a child who says, "I drinked my juice," has applied the semantic differential to a simple, core sentence. T or F?

22. Similar universal language patterns are found in both speech and gestural languages, such as ASL. T or F?

23. ASL has 600,000 root signs. T or F?

24. True languages are productive, thus ASL is not a true language. T or F?

Check Your Memory: Pages 356-357

25. Animal communication can be described as productive. T or F?

26. Chimpanzees have never learned to speak even a single word. T or F?

27. One of Sarah chimpanzee's outstanding achievements was mastery of sentences involving transformational rules. T or F?

28. Some "language" use by chimpanzees appears to be no more than simple operant responses. T or F?

29. Only a minority of the things that language-trained chimps "say" have anything to do with food. T or F?

30. Language-trained chimps have been known to hold conversations when no humans were present. T or F?

31. Kanzi's use of grammar is on a par with that of a 2-year-old child. T or F?

Check Your Memory: Pages 358-361

32. Except for the simplest problems, mechanical solutions are typically best left to computers. T or F?

33. Karl Dunker's famous tumor problem could only be solved by trial-and-error. T or F?

34. In solutions by understanding, functional solutions are usually discovered by use of a random search strategy. T or F?

35. Working backward from the desired goal to the starting point can be a useful heuristic. T or F?

36. In problem solving, rapid insights are more likely to be correct than those that develop slowly. T or F?

37. Selective encoding refers to bringing together seemingly unrelated bits of useful information. T or F?

38. Functional fixedness is an inability to see new uses for familiar objects. T or F?

Check Your Memory: Pages 362-364

39. In general, artificial intelligence lacks the creativity and common sense of human intelligence. T or F?

40. AI is frequently based on a set of rules applied to a body of information. T or F?

41. Computer simulations are used to test models of human cognition. T or F?

42. Most computer-based models of human problem solving rely on the principle of automatic processing. T or F?

43. Much human expertise is based on acquired strategies for solving problems. T or F?

44. Chess experts have an exceptional ability to remember the positions of chess pieces placed at random on a chessboard. T or F?

Check Your Memory: Pages 364-369

45. In inductive thinking, a general rule is inferred from specific examples. T or F?

46. Fluency and flexibility are measures of convergent thinking. T or F?

47. About half of our waking thoughts are occupied by daydreams. T or F?

48. Fantasy contributes to divergent thinking and creativity. T or F?

49. Creative thinkers typically apply reasoning and critical thinking to novel ideas after they produce them. T or F?

50. Creative ideas combine originality with feasibility. T or F?

51. Creative problem solving temporarily stops during the incubation period. T or F?

52. Much creative problem solving is incremental, rather than being based on sudden insights or breakthroughs. T or F?

53. Creative people have an openness to experience and they have a wide range of knowledge and interests. T or F?

Check Your Memory: Pages 369-370

54. Intuition is a quick, impulsive insight into the true nature of a problem and its solution. T or F?

55. The probability of two events occurring together is lower than the probability of either one occurring alone. T or F?

56. The representativeness heuristic is the strategy of stating problems in broad terms. T or F?

57. Framing refers to the way in which a problem is stated or structured. T or F?

Check Your Memory: APPLICATIONS

58. It is possible to draw true conclusions using faulty logic. T or F?

59. It is possible to draw false conclusions using valid logic. T or F?

60. Classifying things as absolutely right or wrong may lead to all-or-nothing thinking. T or F?

61. Exposure to creative models tends to increase creativity among observers. T or F?

62. Delaying evaluation during the early stages of creative problem solving tends to lead to poor thinking. T or F?

63. The cross-stimulation effect is a important part of brainstorming in groups. T or F?

Check Your Memory: EXPLORATION

64. Wolfgang Köhler believed that solving multiple-stick problems revealed insight in chimpanzees. T or F?

65. Animal thinking is implied by actions that appear to be planned with an awareness of likely results. T or F?

66. Apes attempting to use tools to obtain food from a plastic tube made more errors with "practice," suggesting that their successes reflect random trial and error. T or F?

67. Learning to use symbols appeared to free Sheba chimpanzee to ignore the powerful allure of visible food. T or F?

FINAL SURVEY AND REVIEW

● *What is the nature of thought?*

1. _____ psychology is the study of thinking, language, _____
_____, and information processing.

2. Thinking is the manipulation of internal _____ of external problems or situations.

3. Three basic units of thought are _____, _____, and language or
_____.

● *In what ways are images related to thinking?*

4. Most people have internal images of one kind or another. Images may be based on
_____ _____ in memory or they may be created.

5. Sometimes images cross normal sense boundaries in a type of imagery called

_____.

6. The _____ of images used in problem solving may change. Images may be three-dimensional and they may be _____ in space to answer questions.

7. Many of the systems in the _____ that are involved in processing _____ images work in reverse to create _____ images.

8. Kinesthetic images are created by memories of actions or by _____ (unexpressed) actions. Kinesthetic sensations and _____ seem to help structure thinking for many people.

● *How are concepts learned? Are there different kinds of concepts?*

9. A concept is a _____ idea of a class of objects or events.

10. Forming concepts may be based on experiences with positive and _____

_____.

11. Concepts may also be acquired by learning _____ that define the concept.

12. In practice, we frequently use _____ (general models of the concept class) to identify concepts.

13. Concepts may be classified as _____ ("and" concepts), _____ ("either-or" concepts), or relational concepts.

14. The _____ meaning of a word or concept is its dictionary definition. _____ meaning is personal or emotional.

15. Connotative meaning can be measured with the _____ differential. Most connotative meaning involves the dimensions good-bad, _____, and

_____.

● *What is the role of language in thinking?*

16. Language allows events to be _____ into symbols for easy mental manipulation.

17. Language is built out of _____ (basic speech sounds) and _____ (speech sounds collected into meaningful units).

18. Thinking in language is influenced by meaning. The study of meaning is called

_____.

19. Language carries meaning by combining a set of symbols or signs according to a set of rules (_____), which includes rules about word order (_____).

20. Various sentences are created by applying _____ rules to simple statements.

21. A true language is _____, and can be used to generate new ideas or possibilities. _____ _____ Language (ASL) and other gestural languages used by the deaf are true languages.

● *Can animals be taught to use language?*

22. Animal communication is relatively limited because it lacks _____ that can be rearranged easily.

23. Attempts to teach chimpanzees ASL and other non-verbal systems suggest to some that _____ are capable of language use. However, others believe that the chimps are merely using operant responses to get food and other _____.
24. Studies that make use of _____ (geometric word-symbols) provide the best evidence yet of animal language use.

● *What do we know about problem solving?*

25. The solution to a problem may be found _____ (by trial and error or by rote application of rules). However, _____ solutions are frequently inefficient or ineffective, except where aided by computer.
26. Solutions by _____ usually begin with discovery of the general properties of an answer. Next comes proposal of a number of _____ (workable) solutions.
27. Problem solving is frequently aided by _____. These are strategies that typically narrow the search for solutions. An example is the ideal strategy (_____, define, _____, act, look and learn).
28. When understanding leads to a rapid solution, _____ has occurred. Three elements of _____ are selective _____, selective combination and selective comparison.
29. Insights and other problem solving attempts can be blocked by _____ (a tendency to repeat wrong solutions).
30. _____ fixedness is a common fixation, but emotional _____, cultural _____, learned conventions, and perceptual habits are also problems.

● *What is artificial intelligence?*

31. Artificial intelligence refers to any _____ _____ that can perform tasks that require intelligence when done by _____.
32. Two principal areas of artificial intelligence research are computer simulations and _____.
33. Computer simulations of human problem solving are usually based on a _____ analysis (finding ways to reduce the difference between the present state and the desired goal).
34. Expert human problem solving is based on _____ knowledge and acquired _____, rather than some general improvement in thinking ability. Expertise also allows more _____ processing of problems.

● *What is the nature of creative thinking?*

35. To be creative, a solution must be practical and sensible as well as _____.
36. Thinking may be deductive or _____, _____ or illogical.
37. Creative thinking requires _____ thought, characterized by _____, flexibility, and originality. Creativity is also marked by _____ _____, the active discovery of problems to be solved.
38. Daydreaming and fantasy are a source of much divergent thinking. Two very common daydream plots are the _____ hero and the suffering _____.

39. Tests of creativity, such as the *Unusual _____ Test,* the *Consequences Test,* and the *Anagrams Test,* measure the capacity for _____ thinking.

40. Five stages often seen in creative problem solving are orientation, preparation, _____, _____, and verification.

41. Not all creative thinking fits this pattern. Much creative activity is based on _____ problem solving (many small steps).

42. Studies suggest that creative persons share a number of identifiable general traits, thinking abilities, thinking styles, and _____ characteristics. There is little or no _____ between IQ and creativity.

● *How accurate is intuition?*

43. Intuitive thinking often leads to errors. Wrong conclusions may be drawn when an answer seems highly _____ of what we already believe is true. (That is, when people apply the representativeness _____.)

44. A second problem is ignoring the _____ _____ (or underlying probability) of an event.

45. Clear thinking is usually aided by stating or _____ a problem in broad terms.

● *What can be done to improve thinking and to promote creativity?*

46. Major sources of thinking errors include rigid mental _____, faulty _____, and over-simplification.

47. Syllogisms can be evaluated for the truth of their _____, the validity of the _____, and the truth of the conclusions.

48. Two common examples of _____ are all-or-nothing thinking (thinking in black and white terms) and _____ thinking (relying on inaccurate and oversimplified images of social groups).

49. Creativity can be enhanced by defining problems broadly, by establishing a creative atmosphere, by allowing time for _____, by seeking varied _____, and by looking for analogies.

50. _____, in which the production and criticism of ideas is kept separate, also tends to enhance creative problem solving.

● *Do animals think?*

51. Animals reveal a rudimentary capacity for thought when they solve delayed _____ problems.

52. Köhler's chimp solved _____ problems that appeared to require understanding or insight. Some natural "problem solving" by animals appears to be _____ and appropriate enough to qualify as thinking.

53. In a recent study, three kinds of apes showed evidence of _____ in a problem that involved using tools to obtain food hidden in a transparent plastic tube.

54. There is also evidence that higher animals, such as chimpanzees, can learn to use rudimentary _____ thought. For the moment, however, some psychologists remain unconvinced about such abilities.

MASTERY TEST

1. The mark of a true language is that it must be
   a. spoken b. productive c. based on spatial grammar and syntax d. capable of encoding conditional relationships

2. Computer simulations and expert systems are two major applications of
   a. AI b. ASL c. brainstorming d. problem framing

3. Failure to wear automobile seat belts is an example of which intuitive thinking error?
   a. allowing too much time for incubation b. framing a problem broadly c. ignoring base rates
   d. recognition that two events occurring together are more likely than either one alone

4. One thing that images, concepts, and symbols all have in common is that they are
   a. morphemes b. internal representations c. based on reverse vision d. translated into micromovements

5. To decide if a container is a cup, bowl, or vase, most people compare it to
   a. a prototype b. its connotative meaning c. a series of negative instances d. a series of relevant phonemes

6. During problem solving, being "cold," "warm," or "very warm" is closely associated with
   a. insight b. fixation c. automatic processing d. rote problem solving

7. The *Anagrams Test* measures
   a. mental sets b. inductive thinking c. logical reasoning d. divergent thinking

8. "Either-or" concepts are
   a. conjunctive b. disjunctive c. relational d. prototypical

9. Which term does not belong with the others?
   a. selective comparison b. functional fixedness c. learned conventions d. emotional blocks

10. The IDEAL thinking strategy is basically a
    a. prototype b. heuristic c. functional solution d. form of intuitive thought

11. An incremental view of creative problem solving CONTRASTS most directly with which stage of creative thought?
    a. orientation b. preparation c. illumination d. verification

12. Daydreaming and fantasy are two principal sources of
    a. intuition b. divergent thinking c. feasible solutions d. selective comparison

13. The difference between prime beef and dead cow is primarily a matter of
    a. syntax b. conjunctive meaning c. semantics d. the productive nature of language

14. Synesthesia is an unusual form of
    a. imagery   b. heuristic   c. insight   d. daydreaming

15. Which of the listed terms does NOT correctly complete this sentence: Insight involves selective

    _____.
    a. encoding   b. combination   c. comparison   d. fixation

16. Which of the following is LEAST likely to predict that a person is creative?
    a. high IQ   b. a preference for complexity   c. fluency in combining ideas   d. use of mental images

17. A major premise, minor premise, and conclusion are elements of
    a. brainstorming   b. a syllogism   c. selective comparison   d. the representativeness heuristic

18. Language allows events to be _____ into _____.
    a. translated, concepts   b. fixated, codes   c. rearranged, lexigrams   d. encoded, symbols

19. "A triangle must be a closed shape with three sides made of straight lines." This statement is an example of a
    a. prototype   b. positive instance   c. concept rule   d. disjunctive concept

20. Fluency, flexibility, and originality are all measures of
    a. inductive thinking   b. selective comparison   c. intuitive framing   d. divergent thinking

21. The form of imagery that is especially important in music, sports, dance, and martial arts is
    a. kinesthetic imagery   b. synesthetic imagery   c. prototypical imagery   d. conjunctive imagery

22. Among animals trained to use language, Kanzi has been unusually accurate at
    a. using proper syntax   b. substituting gestures for lexigrams   c. expressing conditional relationships
    d. forming chains of operant responses

23. Random search strategies are most similar to
    a. selective encoding   b. automatic processing   c. trial-and-error problem solving   d. the orientation phase of problem solving

24. Looking for analogies and delaying evaluation are helpful strategies for increasing
    a. divergent thinking   b. convergent thinking   c. functional fixedness   d. concept formation

25. Comparing 2 three-dimensional shapes to see if they match is easiest if only a small amount of
    _____ is required.
    a. conceptual recoding   b. mental rotation   c. concept formation   d. kinesthetic transformation

26. The good-bad dimension on the semantic differential is closely related to a concept's
    a. disjunctive meaning   b. conjunctive meaning   c. connotative meaning   d. denotative meaning

27. Most computer-based models of human problem solving are based on some form of
    a. base rate framing   b. means-ends analysis   c. divergent search strategy
    d. representativeness heuristic

28. The directions "modify, magnify, rearrange, and suspend judgment" could be expected to aid a group engaged in
a. a means-ends analysis   b. base rate framing   c. brainstorming   d. solving delayed response problems

29. According to Noam Chomsky, surface sentences are created by applying _____ to simple sentences.
a. encoding grammars   b. transformation rules   c. conditional prototypes   d. selective conjunctions

30. The occurrence of an insight corresponds to which stage of creative thinking?
a. verification   b. incubation   c. illumination   d. fixation

ANSWERS

Recite and Review

1. thinking, information
2. internal
3. language
4. created
5. sense
6. change, space
7. visual
8. actions, actions
9. class
10. positive
11. concept
12. models
13. and, either-or
14. definition, personal
15. good-bad
16. symbols
17. sounds, meaningful
18. meaning
19. rules, order
20. rules
21. gestural
22. rearranged
23. operant
24. geometric
25. rote, computer
26. general, solutions
27. narrow, ideal
28. solution, selective
29. wrong
30. fixation, habits
31. system, intelligence
32. computer
33. analysis
34. knowledge, processing
35. practical
36. Thinking
37. originality, finding
38. fantasy, hero
39. creativity
40. preparation
41. steps
42. thinking, styles
43. errors, true
44. probability
45. broad
46. errors
47. truth, conclusion
48. all-or-nothing
49. broadly, time, varied
50. separate
51. delayed
52. insight, thinking
53. tools
54. thought

Relate

1. f
2. j
3. i
4. a
5. c
6. b
7. e

8. d
9. g
10. h
11. c
12. a
13. e
14. j
15. b
16. i
17. d
18. f
19. g
20. h
21. h
22. a
23. g
24. b
25. j
26. c
27. i
28. d
29. e
30. f

Check Your Memory

1. F
2. T
3. F
4. F
5. F
6. T
7. T

8. T
9. T
10. T
11. T
12. F
13. T
14. F
15. T
16. F
17. F
18. T
19. F
20. T
21. F
22. T
23. F
24. F
25. F
26. F
27. F
28. T
29. T
30. T
31. T
32. T
33. F
34. F
35. T
36. T
37. F
38. T
39. T
40. T
41. T
42. F
43. T
44. F
45. T
46. F
47. T
48. T
49. T
50. T
51. F
52. T
53. T
54. F
55. T
56. F
57. T
58. T
59. T

60. T
61. T
62. F
63. T
64. T
65. T
66. F
67. T

Final Survey and Review

1. Cognitive, problem solving
2. representations
3. images, concepts, symbols
4. information stored
5. synesthesia
6. size, rotated
7. brain, visual, mental
8. implicit, micromovements
9. generalized
10. negative instances
11. rules
12. prototypes
13. conjunctive, disjunctive
14. denotative, Connotative
15. semantic, strong-weak, active-passive
16. encoded
17. phonemes, morphemes
18. semantics
19. grammar, syntax
20. transformation
21. productive, American Sign
22. symbols
23. primates, reinforcers
24. lexigrams
25. mechanically, mechanical
26. understanding, functional
27. heuristics, identify, explore
28. insight, insight, encoding
29. fixation
30. Functional, blocks, values
31. artificial system, people
32. expert systems
33. means-ends
34. organized, strategies, automatic
35. original
36. inductive, logical
37. divergent, fluency, problem finding
38. conquering, martyr

39. *Uses*, divergent
40. incubation, illumination
41. incremental
42. personality, correlation
43. representative, heuristic
44. base rate
45. framing
46. set, logic
47. premises, reasoning
48. over-simplification, stereotyped
49. incubation, input
50. Brainstorming
51. response
52. multiple-stick, versatile
53. understanding
54. symbolic

Mastery Test

1. b (p. 356)
2. a (p. 362)
3. c (p. 369)
4. b (p. 348)
5. a (p. 352)
6. a (p. 359)
7. d (p. 366)
8. b (p. 352)
9. a (p. 360-361)
10. b (p. 359)
11. c (p. 367)
12. b (p. 365)
13. c (p. 353, 354)
14. a (p. 349)
15. d (p. 360)
16. a (p. 368)
17. b (p. 372)
18. d (p. 348, 354)
19. c (p. 352)
20. d (p. 364)
21. a (p. 351)
22. a (p. 357)
23. c (p. 358)
24. a (p. 373)
25. b (p. 350)
26. c (p. 353)
27. b (p. 362)
28. c (p. 374)
29. b (p. 355)
30. c (p. 367)

Chapter 12

Intelligence

CHAPTER OVERVIEW

Intelligence refers to a general capacity to act purposefully, think rationally, and deal effectively with the environment. In practice, intelligence is operationally defined by creating tests. Aptitude tests measure a narrower range of abilities than general intelligence tests do. To be of value, an intelligence test must be reliable, valid, objective, and standardized.

The first practical individual intelligence test was assembled by Alfred Binet. A modern version is the Stanford-Binet Intelligence Scale. *A second major intelligence test is the* Wechsler Adult Intelligence Scale. *Group intelligence tests are also available. Intelligence is expressed as an intelligence quotient (IQ) or as a deviation IQ. The distribution of IQ scores approximates a normal curve. There are no overall differences between males and females in tested intelligence.*

People with IQs in the gifted or "genius" range tend to be superior in many respects. By criteria other than IQ, a large proportion of children might be considered gifted or talented in one way or another. The terms mentally retarded and developmentally disabled apply to persons with an IQ below 70 or who lack various adaptive behaviors. About 50 percent of the cases of mental retardation are organic; the remaining cases are of undetermined cause (many are thought to be familial).

Newer approaches relate intelligence to the speed with which information is processed in the nervous system. In addition, people who possess metacognitive skills tend to be superior at thinking and problem solving. As a result, they also tend to be more intelligent. Many psychologists now believe that several distinct types of intelligence exist.

Studies of animals and family relationships in humans demonstrate that intelligence reflects the combined effects of heredity and environment. Traditional IQ tests often suffer from a degree of cultural bias. For this and other reasons, it is wise to remember that IQ is merely an index of intelligence and that intelligence is narrowly defined by most tests.

RECITE AND REVIEW

● *How do psychologists define intelligence?*

Recite and Review: Pages 380-382

1. Intelligence refers to one's general capacity to act purposefully, think _____, and deal effectively with the _____.

2. In practice, writing an intelligence test provides an operational _____ of intelligence.

3. General _____ is distinguished from specific talents called aptitudes.

4. Special _____ tests and multiple _____ tests (such as the *Scholastic Assessment Test*) are used to assess a person's capacities for learning various abilities.

5. Aptitude tests measure a _____ range of abilities than general intelligence tests do.

● *What are the qualities of a good psychological test?*

Recite and Review: Page 382-383

6. To be of any value, a psychological test must be reliable (give _____ results).

7. Three types of reliability are test-retest, _____-half, and equivalent-_____.

8. A worthwhile test must also have validity, meaning that it _____ what it claims to _____. Validity is often measured by comparing test scores to actual performance at work or in school.

9. Widely used intelligence tests are objective (they give the same result when scored by _____ _____).

10. Intelligence tests are also standardized (the same procedures are always used in giving the test, and _____, or average scores, have been established so that scores can be interpreted).

● *What are typical IQ tests like?*

Recite and Review: Pages 383-387

11. The first practical _____ _____ was assembled in 1904, in Paris, by Alfred Binet.

12. A modern version of Binet's test is the *Stanford-Binet* _____ _____, Fourth Edition.

13. The Stanford-Binet measures _____ reasoning, quantitative reasoning, abstract/visual reasoning, and short-term _____.

14. A second major intelligence test is the *Wechsler* _____ *Intelligence Scale, Third Edition* (WAIS-III). The WAIS-III measures both verbal and performance (_____) intelligence.

15. Intelligence tests have also been produced for use with _____ of people. A _____ test of historical interest is the *Army Alpha*.

16. The *Scholastic Assessment Test* (SAT), the *American College Test* (ACT), and the *College Qualifications Test* (CQT) are _____ scholastic aptitude tests. Although narrower in scope than IQ tests, they bear some similarities to them.

● *How do IQ scores relate to gender, age, and occupation?*

Recite and Review: Pages 387-389

17. Intelligence is expressed in terms of an intelligence _____ (IQ). IQ is defined as mental age (MA) divided by chronological age (CA) and then multiplied by _____.

18. An "average" IQ of _____ occurs when mental age _____ chronological age.

19. Modern IQ tests no longer calculate _____ directly. Instead, the final score reported by the test is a deviation IQ, which gives a person's _____ intellectual standing in his or her age group.

20. IQ scores become fairly _____ at about age 6, and they become increasingly reliable thereafter.

21. On the average, IQ scores continue to gradually _____ until middle age. Later intellectual declines are moderate for most people until their _____.

22. Shortly before _____, a more significant terminal decline (sudden drop) in intelligence is often observed.

23. When graphed, the distribution (percentage of people receiving each score) of IQ scores approximates a normal (_____-shaped) _____.

24. There are no overall differences between males and females in tested _____.

25. However, very small _____ differences may result from the intellectual skills our culture encourages males and females to develop.

26. IQ is related to school _____ and job status. The second association may be somewhat artificial because educational credentials are required for entry into many _____.

● *What does IQ tell us about genius?*

Recite and Review: Pages 389-390

27. People with IQs above 140 are considered to be in the _____ or "genius" range.

28. Studies done by Lewis Terman showed that the gifted tend to be _____ in many respects, such as achievement, physical appearance, and mental health.

29. The most successful gifted persons tend to be those who are persistent and _____ to learn and succeed.

30. By criteria other than _____, a large proportion of children might be considered gifted or talented in one way or another.

31. Intellectually gifted children often have difficulties in average classrooms and benefit from special _____ and Talented Education (GATE) programs.

● *What causes mental retardation?*

Recite and Review: Pages 390-393

32. The terms mentally _____ and developmentally disabled are applied to those whose IQ falls below _____ or who lack various adaptive behaviors.

33. Further classifications of retardation are: _____ (50-55 to 70), moderate (35-40 to 50-55), _____ (20-25 to 35-40), and profound (below 20-25).

34. About _____ percent of the cases of mental retardation are organic, being caused by _____ injuries, fetal damage, metabolic disorders, or genetic abnormalities. The remaining cases are of undetermined cause.

35. Many cases of subnormal intelligence are thought to be the result of familial retardation (a low level of _____ stimulation in the home, poverty, and poor nutrition).

36. Three specialized forms of _____ retardation are phenylketonuria (PKU), microcephaly (small headedness), and hydrocephaly (excess cerebrospinal fluid).

37. Two additional sources of retardation are cretinism (insufficient thyroid _____), and Down syndrome (presence of an extra _____).

38. The second most common form of genetic mental retardation is fragile-*X* _____, a problem related to an abnormal area on the _____ chromosome.

● *How do heredity and environment affect intelligence?*

Recite and Review: Pages 393-395

39. Studies of eugenics (selective _____ for desirable characteristics) in animals suggest that intelligence is influenced by _____.

40. Studies of family relationships in humans, especially comparisons between fraternal twins and identical twins (who have identical _____), also suggest that intelligence is partly _____.

41. However, environment is also important, as revealed by changes in tested intelligence induced by _____ environments and improved education.

42. _____ therefore reflects the combined effects of heredity and environment.

● *How have views of intelligence changed in recent years?*

Recite and Review: Pages 395-397

43. To an extent, intelligence may represent the brain's _____ and efficiency, which is revealed by tasks that measure the _____ of processing.

44. How smart a person is probably depends on his or her neural intelligence, experiential intelligence (specialized _____ and skills), and reflective intelligence (the ability to become aware of one's own _____ patterns).

45. Metacognitive skills involve an ability to manage one's own _____ and problem solving efforts.

46. Howard Gardner believes that _____ IQ tests define intelligence too narrowly. According to Gardner, intelligence consists of abilities in language, logic and _____, _____ and spatial thinking, music, kinesthetic skills, intrapersonal skills, and interpersonal skills.

● *Are IQ tests fair to all racial and cultural groups?*

Recite and Review: APPLICATIONS and EXPLORATION

47. Traditional IQ tests often suffer from a degree of cultural _____ that makes them easier for some groups and harder for others.

48. Culture-fair tests try to measure intelligence in ways that are not strongly affected by _____ background, but no test is entirely _____-free.

49. Differences in the average IQ scores for various racial groups are based on environmental differences, not _____.

50. _____ is merely an index of intelligence based tests that offer a narrow definition of intelligence.

51. The Larry P. case raised questions about the use of IQ tests to place students into special education, or educable _____ _____ (EMR) classes.

52. Tests such as SOMPA (*System of Multicultural Pluralistic Assessment*) have been created to more accurately measure the intelligence of people from _____ cultural backgrounds.

53. However, the use of standard IQ tests, or even SOMPA, for educational placement of students has been prohibited by the _____ in some states.

RELATE

1. _____	savant syndrome	a. legitimate measure
2. _____	Binet	b. average score
3. _____	reliable	c. relative standing
4. _____	valid	d. calendar calculator
5. _____	norm	e. absurdities
6. _____	IQ	f. Wechsler test
7. _____	deviation IQ	g. first intelligence test
8. _____	verbal reasoning	h. block design
9. _____	memory test	i. *Army Alpha*
10. _____	WAIS	j. bell shape
11. _____	performance test	k. digit span
12. _____	group test	l. MA/CA * 100
13. _____	normal curve	m. consistent measure

14. _____	average IQ	a. phenylalanine
15. _____	mentally retarded	b. old parents
16. _____	Termites	c. small head
17. _____	general ability	d. smart rat
18. _____	PKU	e. 70
19. _____	hydrocephaly	f. deficient thyroid
20. _____	microcephaly	g. one egg
21. _____	cretinism	h. two eggs
22. _____	Down syndrome	i. gifted children
23. _____	maze-bright	j. 100
24. _____	fraternal twins	k. *g*-factor
25. _____	identical twins	l. education controversy
26. _____	Larry P.	m. fluid in brain

CHECK YOUR MEMORY

Check Your Memory: Pages 380-382

1. The savant syndrome refers to a person of normal intelligence who has a highly developed, but specific, mental ability. T or F?
2. Alfred Binet's first test was designed to measure mechanical aptitude. T or F?
3. Most psychologists list abstract reasoning ability as an important element of intelligence. T or F?
4. A test of clerical aptitude would measure your capacity for learning to do office work. T or F?
5. The SAT is a special aptitude test. T or F?

Check Your Memory: Page 382-383

6. A test is valid if it gives the same score, or close to the same score when given to the same person on two separate occasions. T or F?

7. To check for split-half reliability you would compare scores on two different versions of a test. T or F?
8. Criterion validity is shown by comparing scores on a test to actual performance in the "real world." T or F?
9. If a test is objective then by definition it is fair. T or F?
10. Standardizing a test helps ensure that it is the same for everyone who takes it. T or F?

Check Your Memory: Pages 383-387

11. Lewis Terman helped write the Stanford-Binet intelligence test. T or F?
12. Mental age refers to average mental ability for a person of a given age. T or F?
13. Mental age can't be higher than chronological age. T or F?
14. IQ is equal to MA times CA divided by 100. T or F?
15. An IQ will be greater than 100 when CA is larger than MA. T or F?
16. Average intelligence is defined as an IQ from 90 to 109. T or F?
17. Modern IQ tests give scores as deviation IQs. T or F?
18. The correlation between IQ scores obtained at ages 2 and 18 is 3.1. T or F?
19. On the average, changes in IQ are small after middle childhood. T or F?
20. The WISC is designed to test adult performance intelligence. T or F?
21. The digit symbol task is considered a performance subtest of the WAIS. T or F?
22. The Stanford-Binet, Wechsler's, and *Army Alpha* are all group intelligence tests. T or F?

Check Your Memory: Pages 387-389

23. In a normal curve, a majority of scores are found near the average. T or F?
24. An IQ above 130 is described as "bright normal." T or F?
25. The correlation between IQ scores and school grades is .5. T or F?
26. High IQ scores are strongly correlated with creativity. T or F?

Check Your Memory: Pages 389-390

27. Only 12 people out of 100 score above 130 on IQ tests. T or F?
28. Gifted children tend to get average IQ scores by the time they reach adulthood. T or F?
29. Gifted persons are more susceptible to mental illness. T or F?
30. Gifted persons are more likely to succeed in adulthood if they have a high degree of intellectual determination. T or F?
31. Talking in complete sentences at age 2 is regarded as a sign of giftedness. T or F?
32. Gifted children tend to become bored in classes designed for children of average abilities. T or F?

Check Your Memory: Pages 390-393

33. A person must have an IQ of 80 or below to be classified as mentally retarded. T or F?
34. The moderately retarded can usually learn routine self-help skills. T or F?
35. The borderline retarded are capable of living alone. T or F?
36. Familial retardation is a genetic condition that runs in families. T or F?
37. Mental retardation caused by birth injuries is categorized as an organic problem. T or F?
38. Phenylalanine is found in the artificial sweetener Aspartame. T or F?
39. Hydrocephaly cannot be treated. T or F?
40. Iodized salt has helped prevent cretinism. T or F?

41. The risk of having a Down syndrome child increases as the mother gets older, but is unaffected by the father's age. T or F?

42. Fragile-*X* males tend to be severely retarded as children but only mildly retarded during adulthood. T or F?

Check Your Memory: Pages 393-395

43. The correlation between the IQs of unrelated people reared apart is 0.0. T or F?

44. The IQs of fraternal twins reared together are more similar than those of other siblings. T or F?

45. The IQs of identical twins are more alike than those of fraternal twins. T or F?

46. Adult intelligence is approximately 50 percent hereditary. T or F?

47. Children adopted into higher status homes tend, on average, to have higher adult IQs. T or F?

48. IQ scores tend to rise the longer people stay in school. T or F?

Check Your Memory: Pages 393-395

49. The speed with which information is processed has been used as a measure of the speed and efficiency of the brain. T or F?

50. Longer inspection times have been shown to correspond with higher intelligence. T or F?

51. Experiential intelligence is a relatively fixed element of overall intelligence. T or F?

52. Metacognitive skills are a major part of what is meant by reflective intelligence. T or F?

53. Gardner's theory of multiple intelligences states that traditional measures of language, logic, and math skills have little to do with intelligence. T or F?

54. The g-factor is regarded by some psychologists as a sign that "general intelligence" underlies many different measures of intelligence. T or F?

Check Your Memory: APPLICATIONS

55. The Dove Test was designed to be culturally biased. T or F?

56. A book titled *The Bell Curve* states that as a group African Americans score below average on IQ tests because they are more likely to attend poor-quality schools. T or F?

57. The small difference in average IQ scores for African Americans and Anglo Americans is explained by cultural and environmental differences. T or F?

58. IQ scores predict later career success. T or F?

59. Standardized testing is used primarily to select people for school and employment. T or F?

60. Changing intelligence tests would result in a change in the IQ scores of people taking the tests. T or F?

Check Your Memory: EXPLORATION

61. Larry P. was a Latino child who was mistakenly placed in an EMR class on the basis of an IQ score. T or F?

62. SOMPA assumes that a child's true potential can be hidden by his or her cultural background. T or F?

63. IQ tests are legally banned from use in California for the purposes of screening children for placement in EMR classes. T or F?

64. IQ tests continue to predict school performance quite well. T or F?

FINAL SURVEY AND REVIEW

● *How do psychologists define intelligence?*

1. Intelligence refers to one's general capacity to act _____, _____ rationally, and deal effectively with the environment.
2. In practice, writing an intelligence test provides an _____ definition of intelligence.
3. General intelligence is distinguished from specific talents called _____.
4. _____ aptitude tests and _____ aptitude tests (such as the *Scholastic Assessment Test*) are used to assess a person's capacities for _____ various abilities.
5. _____ tests measure a narrower range of abilities than general _____ tests do.

● *What are the qualities of a good psychological test?*

6. To be of any value, a psychological test must be _____ (give consistent results).
7. Three types of reliability are _____, split-half, and _____- forms.
8. A worthwhile test must also have _____, meaning that it measures what it claims to measure. _____ is often measured by comparing test scores to actual _____ at work or in school.
9. Widely used intelligence tests are _____ (they give the same result when scored by different people).
10. Intelligence tests are also _____ (the same procedures are always used in giving the test, and norms have been established for _____).

● *What are typical IQ tests like?*

11. The first practical intelligence test was assembled in 1904, in Paris, by _____ _____.
12. A modern version of that test is the _____ *Intelligence Scale*, Fourth Edition.
13. The scale measures verbal reasoning, _____ reasoning, _____/visual reasoning, and short-term memory.
14. A second major intelligence test is the _____ *Adult Intelligence Scale-III* (WAIS-III). The WAIS-III measures both _____ and _____ (non-verbal) intelligence.
15. Intelligence tests have also been produced for use with groups of people. A group test of historical interest is the _____ _____.
16. The *Scholastic Assessment Test* (SAT), the *American College Test* (ACT), and the *College Qualifications Test* (CQT) are group _____ _____ tests. Although narrower in scope than IQ tests, they bear some similarities to them.

● *How do IQ scores relate to gender, age, and occupation?*

17. Intelligence is expressed in terms of an intelligence quotient (IQ). IQ is defined as _____ _____ (MA) divided by _____ _____ (CA) and then multiplied by 100.
18. An "average" IQ of 100 occurs when _____ age equals _____ age.

19. Modern IQ tests no longer calculate IQ directly. Instead, the final score reported by the test is a _____ _____, which gives a person's relative intellectual standing in his or her age group.

20. IQ scores become fairly stable at about age ___, and they become increasingly _____ thereafter.

21. On the average, IQ scores continue to gradually increase until middle age. Later intellectual _____ are moderate for most people until their 70s.

22. Shortly before death, a more significant _____ _____ (sudden drop) in intelligence is often observed.

23. When graphed, the _____ (percentage of people receiving each score) of IQ scores approximates a _____ (bell-shaped) curve.

24. There are no overall _____ between males and females in tested intelligence.

25. However, very small gender differences may result from the intellectual skills our _____ encourages males and females to develop.

26. IQ is related to school grades and _____ _____. The second association may be somewhat artificial because _____ credentials are required for entry into many vocations.

What does IQ tell us about genius?

27. People with IQs above _____ are considered to be in the gifted or "genius" range.

28. Studies done by Lewis _____ showed that the _____ tend to be superior in many respects, such as achievement, physical appearance, and mental health.

29. The most _____ gifted persons tend to be those who are _____ and motivated to learn and succeed.

30. By criteria other than IQ, a large proportion of children might be considered _____ or _____ in one way or another.

31. Intellectually gifted children often have difficulties in average classrooms and benefit from special Gifted and Talented _____ (GATE) programs.

What causes mental retardation?

32. The terms mentally retarded and _____ disabled are applied to those whose IQ falls below 70 or who lack various _____ behaviors.

33. Further classifications of retardation are: mild (50-55 to 70), _____ (35-40 to 50-55), severe (20-25 to 35-40), and _____ (below 20-25).

34. About 50 percent of the cases of mental retardation are _____, being caused by birth injuries, fetal damage, metabolic disorders, or _____ abnormalities. The remaining cases are of undetermined cause.

35. Many cases of subnormal intelligence are thought to be the result of _____ retardation (a low level of intellectual stimulation in the home, poverty, and poor nutrition).

36. Three specialized forms of organic retardation are _____ (PKU), _____ (small headedness), and hydrocephaly (excess cerebrospinal fluid).

37. Two additional sources of retardation are _____ (insufficient thyroid hormone), and _____ syndrome (presence of an extra chromosome).

38. The second most common form of genetic mental retardation is _____ syndrome, a problem related to an abnormal area on the male _____ .

● *How do heredity and environment affect intelligence?*

39. Studies of _____ (selective breeding for desirable characteristics) in animals suggest that intelligence is influenced by heredity.

40. Studies of family relationships in humans, especially comparisons between _____ twins and _____ twins, also suggest that intelligence is partly hereditary.

41. However, _____ is also important, as revealed by changes in tested intelligence induced by stimulating _____ and improved education.

42. Intelligence therefore reflects the combined effects of _____ and _____.

● *How have views of intelligence changed in recent years*

43. To an extent, intelligence may represent the _____ speed and efficiency, which is revealed by tasks that measure the speed of _____.

44. How smart a person is probably depends on his or her _____ intelligence, experiential intelligence (specialized knowledge and skills), and _____ intelligence (the ability to become aware of one's own thinking patterns).

45. _____ skills involve an ability to manage one's own thinking and problem solving efforts.

46. Howard _____ believes that traditional IQ tests define intelligence too narrowly. According to Gardner, intelligence consists of abilities in _____, logic and math, visual and spatial thinking, _____, kinesthetic skills, intrapersonal skills, and interpersonal skills.

● *Are IQ tests fair to all racial and cultural groups?*

47. Traditional IQ tests often suffer from a degree of _____ bias that makes them easier for some groups and harder for others.

48. _____ tests try to measure intelligence in ways that are not strongly affected by cultural background, but no test is entirely culture-free.

49. Differences in the average IQ scores for various racial groups are based on _____ differences, not heredity.

50. IQ is merely an _____ of intelligence based tests that offer a narrow definition of intelligence.

51. The _____ case raised questions about the use of IQ tests to place students into special education, or _____ mentally retarded (EMR) classes.

52. Tests such as SOMPA (System of _____ _____ *Assessment*) have been created to more accurately measure the intelligence of people from different cultural backgrounds.

53. However, the use of standard _____ _____, or even _____, for educational placement of students has been prohibited by the law in some states.

MASTERY TEST

1. The largest number of people are found in which IQ range?
   a. 80-89   b. 90-109   c. 110-119   d. below 70

2. Questions about vocabulary, comprehension, and absurdities would be found in which ability area of the Stanford-Binet?
a. verbal reasoning b. quantitative reasoning c. abstract/visual reasoning d. short-term memory

3. The *Scholastic Assessment Test* is really a
a. special aptitude test b. multiple aptitude test c. general intelligence test
d. test of performance intelligence

4. It is unlikely that a developmentally disabled person would benefit from
a. a sheltered workshop b. supervised education c. a GATE program d. learning self-help skills

5. The term "six-hour retardates" refers to children who appear to be intelligent
a. when given EMR training b. when they are not at home c. after Instrumental Enrichment
d. outside of school

6. Which of the following is NOT a group test?
a. SAT b. ACT c. WAIS d. *Army Alpha*

7. On the average, the smallest changes in IQ would be expected between the ages of
a. 2 and 10 b. 10 and 15 c. 2 and 18 d. 30 and 40

8. A combination of high ability and general retardation is found in
a. the savant syndrome b. Down syndrome c. the adapted developmentally disabled
d. maze-bright retardation

9. The distribution of IQ scores closely matches
a. an inverted U curve b. a normal curve c. a g-factor curve d. Bell's percentiles

10. Which of the following is fixed at birth?
a. IQ b. genes c. giftedness d. MA

11. Speed of neural processing has been measured by using an _____ task.
a. inspection time b. reflective c. metacognitive d. g-factor

12. Separate collections of verbal and performance subtests are a feature of the
a. WAIS b. *Dove Test* c. CQT d. Stanford-Binet

13. Fourteen nations have shown average IQ gains in a single generation. These findings support the idea that intelligence is influenced by
a. eugenics b. environment c. genetics d. the hereditary g-factor

14. Use of a test like _____ might have avoided the problem that led to the Larry P. case.
a. the WAIS-C b. SOMPA c. the WAIS-R d. the Binet-4

15. Mental retardation is formally defined by deficiencies in
a. aptitudes and self-help skills b. intelligence and scholastic aptitudes c. language and spatial thinking
d. IQ and adaptive behaviors

16. A 12-year-old child, with an IQ of 100, must have an MA of
a. 100   b. 12   c. 10   d. 15

17. The Stanford-Binet intelligence test was based on the work of Binet and
a. Terman   b. Wechsler   c. Gardner   d. Feuerstein

18. A test deliberately written to be culturally biased is the
a. WAIS   b. Binet-4   c. Dove Test   d. SOMPA test battery

19. A person's relative intellectual standing in his or her age group is revealed by
a. the age quotient   b. the digit symbol index   c. chronological age   d. deviation IQ

20. The age of parents may affect the risks of having a child suffering from
a. familial retardation   b. phenylketonuria   c. Down syndrome   d. the savant syndrome

21. Traditional intelligence tests are especially good at predicting
a. career success   b. performance in school   c. creative achievement   d. which children will benefit from eugenic programs

22. The validity of a test could be assessed by comparing
a. scores earned on one occasion to scores earned on another   b. scores based on the first half of the test to scores based on the second half   c. scores on two equivalent forms of the test   d. scores on the test to an external criterion of performance

23. Creating an intelligence test provides a/an _____ definition of intelligence.
a. valid   b. reliable   c. operational   d. chronological

24. For large groups, the greatest similarity in IQs would be expected between
a. identical twins   b. fraternal twins   c. siblings reared together   d. parents and their children

25. Both the *Scholastic Assessment Test* and the *Law School Admissions Test* are
a. tests of general intelligence   b. standardized aptitude tests   c. culture-fair tests of verbal comprehension   d. objective performance tests

26. An intelligence test specifically designed for use with children is the
a. WAIS-C   b. Dove Test   c. WISC   d. *Tester Developmental Scale*

27. Which statement about gifted persons is TRUE?
a. They tend to be shy and socially withdrawn.   b. They tend to be smaller and weaker than average.
c. They have above average mental health records.   d. They must score above 160 on IQ tests to be considered gifted.

28. Instrumental Enrichment is to _____ as eugenics is to _____.
a. environment, genetics   b. genetics, selective breeding   c. culture fairness, genetics   d. intelligence, culture

29. A type of retardation that appears to be based largely on the effects of poor environment is
    a. Down syndrome b. microcephaly c. PKU d. familial retardation

30. The idea that children can be gifted in ways other than having a high IQ is in agreement with
    a. Feuerstein's Instrumental Enrichment program b. Dove's Counterbalance model of intelligence
    c. Hernstein and Murray's bell curve model d. Gardner's seven intelligences

ANSWERS

Recite and Review

1. rationally, environment
2. definition
3. intelligence
4. aptitude, aptitude
5. narrower
6. consistent
7. split, forms
8. measures, measure
9. different people
10. norms
11. intelligence test
12. *Intelligence Scale*
13. verbal, memory
14. *Adult,* non-verbal
15. groups, group
16. group
17. quotient, 100
18. 100, equals
19. IQs, relative
20. stable
21. increase, 70s
22. death
23. bell, curve
24. intelligence
25. gender
26. grades, occupations
27. gifted
28. superior
29. motivated
30. IQ
31. Gifted

32. retarded, 70
33. mild, severe
34. 50, birth
35. intellectual
36. organic
37. hormone, chromosome
38. syndrome, *X* or male
39. breeding, heredity
40. genes, heredity
41. stimulating
42. Intelligence
43. speed, speed
44. knowledge, thinking
45. thinking
46. traditional, math, visual
47. bias
48. cultural, culture
49. genetics (or heredity)
50. IQ
51. mentally retarded
52. different
53. law

Relate

1. d
2. g
3. m
4. a
5. b
6. l
7. c

8. e
9. k
10. f
11. h
12. i
13. j
14. j
15. e
16. i
17. k
18. a
19. m
20. c
21. f
22. b
23. d
24. h
25. g
26. l

Check Your Memory

1. F
2. F
3. T
4. T
5. F
6. F
7. F
8. T
9. F
10. T

11. T
12. T
13. F
14. F
15. F
16. T
17. T
18. F
19. T
20. F
21. T
22. F
23. T
24. F
25. T
26. F
27. F
28. F
29. F
30. T
31. T
32. T
33. F
34. T
35. T
36. F
37. T
38. T
39. F
40. T
41. F
42. F
43. T
44. T
45. T
46. T
47. T
48. T
49. T
50. F
51. F
52. T
53. F
54. T
55. T
56. F

57. T
58. F
59. T
60. T
61. F
62. T
63. T
64. T

Final Survey and Review

1. purposefully, think
2. operational
3. aptitudes
4. Special, multiple, learning
5. Aptitude, intelligence
6. reliable
7. test-retest, equivalent
8. validity, Validity, performance
9. objective
10. standardized, scores
11. Alfred Binet
12. *Stanford-Binet*
13. quantitative, abstract
14. *Wechsler*, verbal, performance
15. *Army Alpha*
16. scholastic aptitude
17. mental age, chronological age
18. mental, chronological
19. deviation IQ
20. 6, reliable
21. declines
22. terminal decline
23. distribution, normal
24. differences
25. culture
26. job status, educational
27. 140
28. Terman, gifted
29. successful, persistent
30. gifted, talented
31. Education

32. developmentally, adaptive
33. moderate, profound
34. organic, genetic
35. familial
36. phenylketonuria, microcephaly
37. cretinism, Down
38. fragile-*X*, chromosome
39. eugenics
40. fraternal, identical
41. environment, environments
42. heredity, environment
43. brain's, processing
44. neural, reflective
45. Metacognitive
46. Gardner, language, music
47. cultural
48. Culture-fair
49. environmental
50. index
51. Larry P., educable
52. *Multicultural Pluralistic*
53. IQ tests, SOMPA

Mastery Test

1. b (p. 388)
2. a (p. 384)
3. b (p. 382)
4. c (p. 390)
5. d (p. 402)
6. c (p. 387)
7. d (p. 384-385)
8. a (p. 380)
9. b (p. 388)
10. b (p. 395)
11. a (p. 396)
12. a (p. 387)
13. b (p. 395)
14. b (p. 402)
15. d (p. 390)
16. b (p. 384)
17. a (p. 383)
18. c (p. 399)
19. d (p. 384)

20. c (p. 392)
21. b (p. 388, 400)
22. d (p. 383)
23. c (p. 382)
24. a (p. 394)
25. b (p. 400)
26. c (p. 386)
27. c (p. 389)
28. a (p. 393, 395)
29. d (p. 391)
30. d (p. 397)

Chapter 13

Motivation and Emotion

CHAPTER OVERVIEW

Motivation typically involves needs, drives, goals, and goal attainment. Three types of motives are primary, stimulus, and secondary motives. Most primary motives maintain homeostasis.

Hunger is influenced by the stomach, blood sugar levels, metabolism in the liver, fat stores in the body, activity in the hypothalamus, diet, and other factors. Eating disorders are serious and sometimes fatal problems.

Thirst and other basic motives are affected by many factors, but they are primarily controlled by the hypothalamus. Pain avoidance is episodic and partially learned. The sex drive is non-homeostatic.

The stimulus motives include drives for exploration, manipulation, change, and sensory stimulation. Drives for stimulation are partially explained by arousal theory. Optimal performance on a task usually occurs at moderate levels of arousal. Circadian rhythms are closely tied to sleep, activity, and energy cycles.

Social motives, which are learned, account for much of the diversity of human motivation. The need for achievement is a social motive correlated with success in many situations.

Maslow's hierarchy of motives categorizes needs as basic or growth oriented. Self-actualization, the highest and most fragile need, is reflected in meta-needs. In many situations, extrinsic motivation can lower intrinsic motivation, enjoyment, and creativity.

Emotions are linked to basic adaptive behaviors. Other major elements of emotion are bodily changes, emotional expressions, and emotional feelings. Physiological changes during emotion are caused by adrenaline and the autonomic nervous system (ANS). The sympathetic branch of the ANS arouses the body and the parasympathetic branch quiets it. Basic emotional expressions are unlearned. Facial expressions are central to emotion. Body gestures and movements (body language) also express feelings. A variety of theories have been proposed to explain emotion.

Behavioral dieting uses self-control techniques to change basic eating patterns and habits.

Sternberg's triangular theory describes love as a combination of passion, intimacy, and commitment.

RECITE AND REVIEW

● *What is motivation? Are there different types of motives?*

Recite and Review: Pages 406-409

  1. Motives _____ (begin), sustain (perpetuate), and direct _____ .

2. Motivation typically involves the sequence _____, drive, _____, and goal attainment (need reduction).

3. Behavior can be activated either by needs (_____) or by goals (_____).

4. The attractiveness of a _____ and its ability to initiate action are related to its incentive value (its value above and beyond its capacity to fill a _____).

5. Three principal types of motives are primary motives, stimulus motives, and _____ motives.

6. Most _____ motives operate to maintain a _____ state of bodily equilibrium called homeostasis.

● *What causes hunger? Overeating? Eating disorders?*

Recite and Review: Pages 409-416

7. Hunger is influenced by a complex interplay between distention (fullness) of the _____, hypoglycemia (low _____ sugar), metabolism in the _____, and fat stores in the body.

8. The most direct control of eating is exerted by the hypothalamus, which has areas that act like feeding (_____) and satiety (_____) systems for hunger and eating.

9. The lateral hypothalamus acts as a _____ system; the ventromedial hypothalamus is part of a _____ system; the paraventricular nucleus influences both hunger and satiety.

10. Other factors influencing hunger are the set point for the proportion of _____ in the body, external eating cues, the attractiveness and variety of _____.

11. Hunger is also influenced by emotions, learned _____ preferences and _____ aversions (such as bait shyness in animals), and cultural values.

12. Anorexia nervosa (self-inflicted _____) and bulimia nervosa (_____ and purging) are two prominent eating disorders.

13. Both eating disorders tend to involve conflicts about self-image, self-control, and _____.

● *Is there more than one type of thirst?*

Recite and Review: Pages 416-417

14. Like hunger, thirst and other basic motives are affected by a number of _____ factors, but are primarily under the central control of the hypothalamus in the _____.

15. Thirst may be either intracellular (when _____ is lost from inside _____) or extracellular (when _____ is lost from the spaces between _____).

● *In what ways are pain avoidance and the sex drive unusual?*

Recite and Review: Pages 417-418

16. Pain avoidance is unusual because it is episodic (associated with particular conditions) as opposed to cyclic (occurring in regular _____).

17. Pain avoidance and pain tolerance are partially _____ (influenced by training).

18. The sex drive in many lower animals is related to estrus (or "heat") in _____. The sex drive is unusual in that it is non-homeostatic (both its _____ and its reduction are sought).

● *How does arousal relate to motivation?*

Recite and Review: Pages 418-423

19. The stimulus motives include drives for exploration, manipulation, change, and _____ stimulation.
20. Drives for stimulation are partially explained by arousal theory, which states that an ideal level of _____ _____ will be maintained if possible.
21. The desired level of _____ or stimulation varies from person to person, as measured by the *Sensation-Seeking Scale*.
22. Optimal performance on a task usually occurs at _____ levels of arousal. This relationship is described by an inverted U function.
23. The Yerkes-Dodson law further states that for _____ tasks the ideal arousal level is higher, and for _____ tasks it is lower.
24. Circadian _____ within the body are closely tied to sleep, activity levels, and energy cycles. Time zone travel and shift work can seriously disrupt _____ and bodily rhythms.
25. Body rhythms and _____ cycles are strongly influenced by the release of melatonin, a _____ produced at night by the pineal gland.

● *What are social motives? Why are they important?*

Recite and Review: Pages 423-426

26. _____ motives are learned through socialization and cultural conditioning.
27. Opponent-process theory, which states that strong _____ tend to be followed by an opposite _____, explains some acquired motives.
28. One of the most prominent social motives is the _____ for achievement (nAch).
29. High nAch is correlated with _____ in many situations, with occupational choice, and with moderate _____ taking.
30. There is evidence that at times both men and women experience a _____ of success. This is especially true if achievement is seen as conflicting with social acceptance.

● *Are some motives more basic than others?*

Recite and Review: Pages 426-429

31. Maslow's hierarchy (rank ordering) of motives categorizes needs as _____ and growth oriented.
32. _____ needs in the hierarchy are assumed to be prepotent (dominant) over _____ needs.
33. _____-actualization, the highest and most fragile need, is reflected in meta-_____.
34. In many situations, extrinsic motivation (that which is induced by obvious _____ rewards) can reduce intrinsic motivation, enjoyment, and creativity.

● *What happens during emotion?*

Recite and Review: Pages 429-433

35. Emotions are linked to many basic adaptive _____, such a attacking, retreating, feeding, and reproducing.

36. Other major elements of emotion are physiological changes in the body, emotional expressions, and emotional _____.

37. The following are considered to be primary emotions: fear, surprise, _____, disgust, _____, anticipation, joy, and acceptance. Other emotions seem to represent mixtures of the primaries.

38. Physical changes associated with emotion are caused by the action of adrenaline, a _____ released into the bloodstream, and by activity in the autonomic _____ _____ (ANS).

39. The sympathetic _____ of the ANS is primarily responsible for arousing the body, the parasympathetic _____ for quieting it.

40. Sudden death due to prolonged and intense emotion is probably related to parasympathetic _____ (excess activity). Heart attacks caused by sudden intense emotion are more likely due to sympathetic _____.

● *Can "lie detectors" really detect lies?*

Recite and Review: Pages 433-434

41. The polygraph, or "lie detector," measures _____ _____ by monitoring heart rate, blood pressure, breathing rate, and the galvanic skin response (GSR).

42. Asking a series of _____ and irrelevant questions may allow the detection of _____, but overall, the accuracy of the lie detector has been challenged by many researchers.

● *How accurately are emotions expressed by "body language" and the face?*

Recite and Review: Pages 435-437

43. Basic emotional expressions, such as smiling or baring one's teeth when angry, appear to be _____.

44. Facial expressions of _____, anger, disgust, _____, and happiness are recognized by people of all cultures.

45. Body gestures and movements (body language) also express _____, mainly by communicating emotional _____.

46. Three dimensions of _____ expressions are pleasantness-unpleasantness, attention-rejection, and activation.

47. The study of _____ _____ is known as kinesics.

48. Lying can sometimes be detected from changes in illustrators (_____ used to express what a person is saying) or emblems (_____ that have clear cultural meanings) and from signs of general arousal.

● *How do psychologists explain emotions?*

Recite and Review: Pages 437-442

49. The James-Lange theory of emotion says that emotional experience _____ an awareness of the bodily reactions of emotion.

50. In contrast, the Cannon-Bard theory says that bodily reactions and emotional experience occur _____ _____ _____ _____ and that emotions are organized in the brain.

51. Schachter's cognitive theory of emotion emphasizes the importance of _____, or interpretations, applied to feelings of bodily arousal.

52. Also important is the process of attribution, in which bodily _____ is attributed to a particular person, object, or situation.

53. The facial feedback hypothesis holds that sensations and information from emotional _____ help define what emotion a person is feeling.

54. Contemporary views of emotion place greater emphasis on how _____ are appraised. Also, all of the elements of emotion are seen as interrelated and interacting.

● *Can psychology be applied to weight control?*

Recite and Review: APPLICATIONS

55. Because of the limitations of traditional dieting, changing basic eating patterns and _____ is usually more effective.

56. Behavioral _____ brings about such changes by use of self-control techniques.

● *What is the nature of love?*

Recite and Review: EXPLORATION

57. Sternberg's triangular theory describes love as a combination of _____, intimacy, and commitment.

58. Combinations of these three factors produce non-love, _____, infatuation, romantic love, fatuous love, companionate love, _____ love, and consummate love.

RELATE

1. _____   physiological needs
2. _____   safety and security
3. _____   self-actualization
4. _____   lateral hypothalamus
5. _____   basic needs
6. _____   esteem and self-esteem
7. _____   paraventricular nucleus
8. _____   growth needs
9. _____   love and belonging
10. _____   ventromedial hypothalamus

11. _____	need	a. steady state
12. _____	incentive value	b. lateral hypothalamus
13. _____	secondary motives	c. internal deficiency
14. _____	homeostasis	d. learned goals
15. _____	satiety system	e. estrogen levels
16. _____	feeding system	f. yo-yo dieting
17. _____	hunger and satiety	g. about a day
18. _____	weight cycling	h. paraventricular nucleus
19. _____	estrus	i. ventromedial hypothalamus
20. _____	circadian	j. goal desirability

21. _____	melatonin	a. standards of excellence
22. _____	nAch	b. prolonged mild emotion
23. _____	meta-needs	c. lie detection
24. _____	mood	d. pineal gland
25. _____	sympathetic branch	e. commitment and intimacy
26. _____	control questions	f. appraisal of loss
27. _____	body language	g. appraisal of threat
28. _____	sadness	h. self-actualization
29. _____	anxiety	i. kinesics
30. _____	companionate love	j. fight or flight

CHECK YOUR MEMORY

Check Your Memory: Pages 406-409

1. The terms need and drive are used interchangeably to describe motivation. T or F?
2. Incentive value refers to the "pull" of valued goals. T or F?
3. Primary motives are based on needs that must be met for survival. T or F?
4. Much of the time, homeostasis is maintained by automatic reactions within the body. T or F?

Check Your Memory: Pages 409-416

5. Cutting the sensory nerves from the stomach abolishes hunger. T or F?
6. Injecting a person with insulin can cause hunger and stomach contractions. T or F?
7. The body's hunger center is found in the thalamus. T or F?
8. The paraventricular nucleus is sensitive to neuropeptide Y. T or F?
9. Both glucagon-like peptide 1 (GLP-1) and leptin act as stop signals that inhibit eating. T or F?
10. People who become overweight in childhood have more fat cells than those who become overweight as adults. T or F?
11. Dieting speeds up the body's metabolic rate. T or F?
12. Taste aversions may be learned after longer time delays than in other forms of classical conditioning. T or F?
13. Many victims of anorexia nervosa overestimate their body size. T or F?

Check Your Memory: Pages 416-417

14. Bleeding, vomiting, or sweating can cause extracellular thirst. T or F?
15. Intracellular thirst is best satisfied by a slightly salty liquid. T or F?

Check Your Memory: Pages 417-418

16. Tolerance for pain is largely unaffected by learning. T or F?
17. Castration of a male animal typically abolishes the sex drive. T or F?
18. The Coolidge effect refers to a reappearance of the sex drive when an apparently satiated animal is provided with a new partner. T or F?

Check Your Memory: Pages 418-423

19. The effects of sensory deprivation suggest that drives for stimulation are learned.
20. It is uncomfortable to experience both very high and very low levels of arousal. T or F?
21. Disinhibition and boredom susceptibility are characteristics of sensation-seeking persons. T or F?
22. For nearly all activities, the best performance occurs at high levels of arousal. T or F?
23. Test anxiety is a combination of arousal and excessive worry. T or F?
24. Being overprepared is a common cause of test anxiety. T or F?
25. Changes in body temperature are closely related to circadian rhythms. T or F?
26. Adapting to rapid time zone changes is easiest when a person travels east, rather than west. T or F?
27. Studies show that biorhythms predict occupational accidents and sports performance. T or F?

Check Your Memory: Pages 423-426

28. Opponent-process theory assumes that emotional responses habituate when activities are repeated. T or F?
29. The need for achievement refers to a desire to have impact on other people. T or F?
30. People high in nAch generally prefer "long shots" or "sure things." T or F?
31. Subliminal motivational tapes are no more effective than placebo tapes that lack any "hidden messages." T or F?
32. Fears of success are often related to fears of rejection by others. T or F?
33. Benjamin Bloom found that high achievement is based as much on hard work as it is on talent. T or F?
34. For many activities, self-confidence is one of the most important sources of motivation. T or F?

Check Your Memory: Pages 426-429

35. Maslow's hierarchy of needs places self-esteem at the top of the pyramid. T or F?
36. Maslow believed that needs for safety and security are more potent than needs for love and belonging. T or F?
37. Meta-needs are the most basic needs in Maslow's hierarchy. T or F?
38. Intrinsic motivation occurs when obvious external rewards are provided for engaging in an activity. T or F?
39. People are more likely to be creative when they are intrinsically motivated. T or F?

Check Your Memory: Pages 429-433

40. Most physiological changes during emotion are related to the release of adrenaline into the brain. T or F?
41. Robert Plutchik's theory lists contempt as a primary emotion. T or F?
42. For most students, elevated moods tend to occur on Saturdays and Tuesdays. T or F?
43. Positive emotions are processed mainly in the left hemisphere of the brain. T or F?

44. A part of the brain called the amygdala specializes in producing fear. T or F?
45. The sympathetic branch of the ANS is under voluntary control and the parasympathetic branch is involuntary. T or F?
46. The parasympathetic branch of the ANS slows the heart and lowers blood pressure. T or F?
47. The pupils of the eyes dilate during both pleasant and unpleasant emotions. T or F?
48. Most sudden deaths due to strong emotion are associated with the traumatic disruption of a close relationship. T or F?

Check Your Memory: Pages 433-434

49. The polygraph measures the body's unique physical responses to lying. T or F?
50. Only a guilty person should react emotionally to irrelevant questions. T or F?
51. Control questions used in polygraph exams are designed to make almost everyone anxious. T or F?
52. The lie detector's most common error is to label innocent persons guilty. T or F?

Check Your Memory: Pages 435-437

53. Children born deaf and blind express emotions with their faces in about the same way as other people do. T or F?
54. The "A-okay" hand gesture means "everything is fine" around the world. T or F?
55. Facial blends mix two or more basic expressions. T or F?
56. Liking is expressed in body language by leaning back and relaxing the extremities. T or F?
57. When a person is successful, his or her posture is more erect. T or F?
58. Gestures such as rubbing hands, twisting hair, and biting lips are consistently related to lying. T or F?

Check Your Memory: Pages 437-442

59. The James-Lange theory of emotion says that we see a bear, feel fear, are aroused, and then run. T or F?
60. According to Schachter's cognitive theory, arousal must be labeled in order to become an emotion. T or F?
61. Making facial expressions can actually cause emotions to occur and alter physiological activities in the body. T or F?
62. Emotional appraisal refers to deciding if your own facial expressions are appropriate for the situation you are in. T or F?
63. Moving toward a desired goal is associated with the emotion of happiness. T or F?
64. Emotional intelligence refers to the ability to use primarily the right cerebral hemisphere to process emotional events. T of F?

Check Your Memory: APPLICATIONS

65. People who diet intensely every other day lose as much weight as those who diet moderately every day. T or F?
66. Exercise makes people hungry and tends to disrupt dieting and weight loss. T or F?
67. Behavioral dieting changes habits without reducing the number of calories consumed. T or F?
68. Charting daily progress is a basic behavioral dieting technique. T or F?

Check Your Memory: EXPLORATION

69. Robert Sternberg's triangular theory states that love consists of intimacy, passion, and contentment. T or F?
70. Passion refers mainly to physiological arousal. T or F?

71. Liking mainly emphasizes intimacy. T or F?
72. Romantic love combines intimacy and passion. T or F?
73. The passionate stage of love typically lasts about 6 to 30 months. T or F?

FINAL SURVEY AND REVIEW

● *What is motivation? Are there different types of motives?*

1. Motives initiate (begin), _____ (perpetuate), and _____ activities.
2. Motivation typically involves the sequence need, _____, goal, and goal _____ (need reduction).
3. Behavior can be activated either by _____ (push) or by _____ (pull).
4. The attractiveness of a goal and its ability to initiate action are related to its _____
_____.
5. Three principal types of motives are _____ motives, _____ motives, and _____ motives.
6. Most primary motives operate to maintain a steady state of bodily equilibrium called _____.

● *What causes hunger? Overeating? Eating disorders?*

7. Hunger is influenced by a complex interplay between _____ (fullness) of the stomach, _____ (low blood sugar), metabolism in the liver, and fat stores in the body.
8. The most direct control of eating is exerted by the _____, which has areas that act like feeding (start) and _____ (stop) systems for hunger and eating.
9. The _____ hypothalamus acts as a feeding system; the _____ hypothalamus is part of a satiety system; the paraventricular _____ influences both hunger and satiety.
10. Other factors influencing hunger are the _____ _____ for the proportion of fat in the body, external eating _____, the attractiveness and variety of diet.
11. Hunger is also influenced by emotions, learned taste preferences and taste _____ (such as _____ _____ in animals), and cultural values.
12. _____ nervosa (self-inflicted starvation) and _____ nervosa (gorging and purging) are two prominent eating disorders.
13. Both eating disorders tend to involve conflicts about _____, self-control, and anxiety.

● *Is there more than one type of thirst?*

14. Like hunger, thirst and other basic motives are affected by a number of bodily factors, but are primarily under the central control of the _____ in the brain.
15. Thirst may be either _____ (when fluid is lost from inside cells) or _____ (when fluid is lost from the spaces between cells).

● *In what ways are pain avoidance and the sex drive unusual?*

16. Pain avoidance is unusual because it is _____ (associated with particular conditions) as opposed to _____ (occurring in regular cycles).
17. Pain _____ and pain _____ are partially learned.
18. The sex drive in many lower animals is related to _____ (or "heat") in females. The sex drive is unusual in that it is non-_____ (both its arousal and its reduction are sought).

● *How does arousal relate to motivation?*

19. The _____ motives include drives for _____, manipulation, change, and sensory stimulation.
20. Drives for stimulation are partially explained by _____ _____, which states that an ideal level of bodily arousal will be maintained if possible.
21. The desired level of arousal or stimulation varies from person to person, as measured by the _____ *Scale.*
22. Optimal performance on a task usually occurs at moderate levels of arousal. This relationship is described by an _____ _____ function.
23. The _____ law further states that for simple tasks the ideal arousal level is higher, and for complex tasks it is lower.
24. _____ rhythms within the body are closely tied to sleep, activity levels, and energy cycles. Travel across _____ _____ and shift work can seriously disrupt sleep and bodily rhythms.
25. Body rhythms and sleep cycles are strongly influenced by the release of _____, a hormone produced at night by the _____ gland.

● *What are social motives? Why are they important?*

26. Social motives are learned through _____ and cultural conditioning.
27. _____ theory, which states that strong emotions tend to be followed by an opposite emotion, explains some acquired motives.
28. One of the most prominent social motives is the need for _____ (nAch).
29. _____ nAch is correlated with success in many situations, with occupational choice, and with _____ risk taking.
30. There is evidence that at times both men and women experience a fear of success. This is especially true if _____ is seen as conflicting with _____ acceptance.

● *Are some motives more basic than others?*

31. Maslow's _____ (rank ordering) of motives categorizes needs as basic and _____ oriented.
32. Lower needs in the hierarchy are assumed to be _____ (dominant) over higher needs.
33. Self-_____, the highest and most fragile need, is reflected in _____- needs.

34. In many situations, _____ motivation (that which is induced by obvious external rewards) can reduce _____ motivation, enjoyment, and creativity.

● *What happens during emotion?*

35. Emotions are linked to many basic _____ behaviors, such a attacking, retreating, feeding, and reproducing.

36. Other major elements of emotion are physiological changes in the body, emotional _____, and emotional feelings.

37. The following are considered to be _____ emotions: fear, surprise, sadness, disgust, anger, anticipation, joy, and acceptance.

38. Physical changes associated with emotion are caused by the action of _____, a hormone released into the bloodstream, and by activity in the _____ nervous system (ANS).

39. The _____ branch of the ANS is primarily responsible for arousing the body, the _____ branch for quieting it.

40. Sudden death due to prolonged and intense emotion is probably related to _____ rebound (excess activity). Heart attacks caused by sudden intense emotion are more likely due to _____ arousal.

● *Can "lie detectors" really detect lies?*

41. The _____, or "lie detector," measures emotional arousal by monitoring heart rate, blood pressure, breathing rate, and the _____ skin response (GSR).

42. Asking a series of _____ and _____ questions may allow the detection of lies, but overall, the accuracy of the lie detector has been challenged by many researchers.

● *How accurately are emotions expressed by "body language" and the face?*

43. Basic emotional _____, such as smiling or baring one's teeth when angry, appear to be unlearned.

44. _____ expressions of fear, anger, disgust, sadness, and happiness are recognized by people of all cultures.

45. Body _____ and movements (body language) also express feelings, mainly by communicating emotional tone.

46. Three dimensions of emotional expressions are pleasantness-unpleasantness, attention-rejection, and _____.

47. The study of body language is known as _____.

48. Lying can sometimes be detected from changes in _____ (gestures used to express what a person is saying) or _____ (gestures that have clear cultural meanings) and from signs of general arousal.

● *How do psychologists explain emotions?*

49. The _____-Lange theory of emotion says that emotional experience follows an awareness of the bodily reactions of emotion.
50. In contrast, the _____-Bard theory says that bodily reactions and emotional experience occur at the same time and that emotions are organized in the brain.
51. Schachter's _____ theory of emotion emphasizes the importance of labels, or interpretations, applied to feelings of bodily _____.
52. Also important is the process of _____, in which bodily arousal is attributed to a particular person, object, or situation.
53. The _____ _____ hypothesis holds that sensations and information from emotional expressions help define what emotion a person is feeling.
54. Contemporary views of emotion place greater emphasis on how situations are _____ (evaluated). Also, all of the elements of emotion are seen as interrelated and interacting.

● *Can psychology be applied to weight control?*

55. Because of the limitations of traditional dieting, changing basic _____ patterns and habits is usually more effective.
56. _____ dieting brings about such changes by use of _____-control techniques.

● *What is the nature of love?*

57. Sternberg's _____ theory describes love as a combination of passion, _____, and commitment.
58. Combinations of these three factors produce non-love, liking, infatuation, _____ love, fatuous love, _____ love, empty love, and consummate love.

MASTERY TEST

1. Which of the following is NOT one of the signs of emotional arousal recorded by a polygraph?
   a. heart rate b. blood pressure c. pupil dilation d. breathing rate

2. Plain water is most satisfying when a person has _____ thirst.
   a. intracellular b. hypothalamic c. extracellular d. homeostatic

3. Bait shyness is a type of
   a. taste aversion b. self-selection feeding pattern c. bulimia d. weight cycling

4. Strong external rewards tend to undermine
   a. extrinsic motivation b. intrinsic motivation c. prepotent motivation d. stimulus motivation

5. Activity in the ANS is directly responsible for which element of emotion?
   a. emotional feelings b. emotional expressions c. physiological changes d. misattributions

6. Sternberg's triangular theory classifies a combination of intimacy and commitment as _____ love.

a. romantic   b. consummate   c. companionate   d. fatuous

7. Motivation refers to the ways in which activities are initiated, sustained, and

a. acquired   b. valued   c. directed   d. aroused

8. The psychological state or feeling we call thirst corresponds to which element of motivation?

a. need   b. drive   c. deprivation   d. incentive value

9. People who score high on the SSS generally prefer

a. low levels of arousal   b. moderate levels of arousal   c. high levels of arousal   d. the middle of the V function

10. Which facial expression is NOT recognized by people of all cultures?

a. anger   b. disgust   c. optimism   d. fear

11. Learning to weaken eating cues is useful in

a. self-selection feeding   b. yo-yo dieting   c. rapid weight cycling   d. behavioral dieting

12. Jet lag occurs when a traveler's _____ are out of synchrony with local time.

a. biorhythms   b. circadian rhythms   c. sensation-seeking patterns   d. opponent processes

13. Which theory holds that emotional feelings, arousal, and behavior are generated simultaneously in the brain?

a. James-Lange   b. Cannon-Bard   c. cognitive   d. attribution

14. Fears of success directly undermine

a. needs for achievement   b. the need for affiliation   c. the curiosity drive   d. the need for homeostasis

15. Binge eating is most associated with

a. bulimia nervosa   b. bait shyness   c. low levels of NPY   d. anorexia nervosa

16. Goals that are desirable are high in

a. need reduction   b. incentive value   c. homeostatic valence   d. motivational "push"

17. _____ is to pain avoidance as _____ is to the sex drive.

a. Non-homeostatic, episodic   b. Episodic, non-homeostatic   c. Non-homeostatic, cyclic
d. Cyclic, non-homeostatic

18. A specialist in kinesics could be expected to be most interested in

a. facial blends   b. circadian rhythms   c. sensation seeking   d. primary motives

19. Coping statements are a way to directly correct which part of test anxiety?

a. overpreparation   b. under-arousal   c. excessive worry   d. compulsive rehearsal

20. Drives for exploration and activity are categorized as
    a. primary motives   b. secondary motives   c. stimulus motives   d. extrinsic motives

21. Sudden death following a period of intense fear may occur when _____ slows the heart to a stop.
    a. a sympathetic overload   b. adrenaline poisoning   c. opponent-process feedback
    d. a parasympathetic rebound

22. The reinforcing effects of skydiving and ski jumping are best explained by _____ theory.
    a. arousal   b. opponent-process   c. meta-needs   d. the Cannon-Bard

23. You could induce eating in a laboratory rat by activating the
    a. lateral hypothalamus   b. corpus callosum   c. rat's set point   d. ventromedial hypothalamus

24. People think cartoons are funnier if they see them while holding a pen crosswise in their teeth. This observation supports
    a. the James-Lange theory   b. the Cannon-Bard theory   c. Schachter's cognitive theory
    d. the facial feedback hypothesis

25. Basic biological motives are closely related to
    a. nAch   b. homeostasis   c. activity in the thalamus   d. levels of melatonin in the body

26. Self-actualization is to _____ needs as safety and security are to _____ needs.
    a. growth, basic   b. basic, meta-   c. prepotent, basic   d. meta-, extrinsic

27. Which of the following is NOT a core element of emotion?
    a. physiological changes   b. emotional expressions   c. emotional feelings   d. misattributions

28. The effects of a "supermarket diet" on eating are related to the effects of _____ on eating.
    a. anxiety and unhappiness   b. incentive value and eating cues   c. metabolic rates and external motives
    d. stomach distention

29. According to the Yerkes-Dodson law optimum performance occurs at _____ levels of arousal for simple tasks and _____ levels of arousal for complex tasks.
    a. higher, lower   b. lower, higher   c. minimum, high   d. average, high

30. Contemporary models of emotion place greater emphasis on _____, or the way situations are evaluated.
    a. appraisal   b. attribution   c. feedback   d. emotional tone

ANSWERS

Recite and Review

1. initiate, activities
2. need, goal
3. push, pull
4. goal, need
5. secondary
6. primary, steady
7. stomach, blood, liver
8. start, stop
9. feeding, satiety
10. fat, diet
11. taste, taste
12. starvation, gorging
13. anxiety
14. bodily, brain
15. fluid, cells, fluid, cells
16. cycles
17. learned
18. females, arousal
19. sensory
20. physical arousal
21. arousal
22. moderate
23. simple, complex
24. rhythms, sleep
25. sleep, hormone
26. Social
27. emotions, emotion
28. need
29. success, risk
30. fear
31. basic
32. Lower, higher
33. Self, needs
34. external
35. behaviors
36. feelings
37. sadness, anger
38. hormone, nervous system
39. branch, branch
40. rebound, arousal
41. emotional arousal
42. relevant, lying
43. unlearned
44. fear, sadness
45. feelings, tone

46. facial
47. body language
48. gestures, gestures
49. follows
50. at the same time
51. labels
52. arousal
53. expressions
54. situations
55. habits
56. dieting
57. passion
58. liking, empty

Relate

1. h
2. g
3. d
4. a
5. j
6. e
7. c
8. i
9. f
10. b
11. c
12. j
13. d
14. a
15. i
16. b
17. h
18. f
19. e
20. g
21. d
22. a
23. h
24. b
25. j
26. c
27. i
28. f
29. g
30. e

Check Your Memory

1. F
2. T
3. T
4. T
5. F
6. T
7. F
8. T
9. T
10. T
11. F
12. T
13. T
14. T
15. F
16. F
17. T
18. T
19. F
20. T
21. T
22. F
23. T
24. F
25. T
26. F
27. F
28. T
29. F
30. F
31. T
32. T
33. T
34. T
35. F
36. T
37. F
38. F
39. T
40. F
41. F
42. F
43. T
44. T
45. F

46. T
47. T
48. T
49. F
50. F
51. T
52. T
53. T
54. F
55. T
56. F
57. T
58. F
59. F
60. T
61. T
62. F
63. T
64. F
65. T
66. F
67. F
68. T
69. F
70. T
71. T
72. T
73. T

Final Survey and Review

1. sustain, direct
2. drive, attainment
3. needs, goals
4. incentive value
5. primary, stimulus, secondary
6. homeostasis
7. distention, hypoglycemia
8. hypothalamus, satiety
9. lateral, ventromedial, nucleus
10. set point, cues
11. aversions, bait shyness
12. Anorexia, bulimia
13. self-image
14. hypothalamus
15. intracellular, extracellular
16. episodic, cyclic
17. avoidance, tolerance
18. estrus, homeostatic

19. stimulus, exploration
20. arousal theory
21. *Sensation-Seeking*
22. inverted U
23. Yerkes-Dodson
24. Circadian, time zones
25. melatonin, pineal
26. socialization
27. Opponent-process
28. achievement
29. High, moderate
30. achievement, social
31. hierarchy, growth
32. prepotent
33. actualization, meta
34. extrinsic, intrinsic
35. adaptive
36. expressions
37. primary
38. adrenaline, autonomic
39. sympathetic, parasympathetic
40. parasympathetic, sympathetic
41. polygraph, galvanic
42. relevant, irrelevant
43. expressions
44. Facial
45. gestures
46. activation
47. kinesics
48. illustrators, emblems
49. James
50. Cannon
51. cognitive, arousal
52. attribution
53. facial feedback
54. appraised
55. eating
56. Behavioral, self
57. triangular, intimacy
58. romantic, companionate

Mastery Test

1. c (p. 433)
2. a (p. 416)
3. a (p. 414)
4. b (p. 428)
5. c (p. 431)
6. c (p. 445)
7. c (p. 407)
8. b (p. 407)
9. c (p. 419)
10. c (p. 435)
11. d (p. 443)
12. b (p. 421)
13. b (p. 438)
14. a (p. 425)
15. a (p. 414)
16. b (p. 408)
17. b (p. 417)
18. a (p. 436)
19. c (p. 421)
20. c (p. 408)
21. d (p. 433)
22. b (p. 423)
23. a (p. 410)
24. d (p. 439)
25. b (p. 409)
26. a (p. 427)
27. d (p. 429)
28. b (p. 408, 412)
29. a (p. 420)
30. a (p. 440)

Chapter 14

Health, Stress, and Coping

CHAPTER OVERVIEW

Health psychologists study behavioral risk factors and health-promoting behaviors. Stress is a major risk factor. At work, prolonged stress can lead to burnout. Emotional appraisals greatly affect our stress reactions and coping attempts.

Frustration and conflict are common sources of stress. Major behavioral reactions to frustration include persistence, more vigorous responding, circumvention, direct aggression, displaced aggression and escape or withdrawal. Five major types of conflict are approach-approach, avoidance-avoidance, approach-avoidance, double approach-avoidance, and multiple approach-avoidance.

Anxiety, threat, or feelings of inadequacy frequently lead to the use of defense mechanisms. Common defense mechanisms include compensation, denial, fantasy, intellectualization, isolation, projection, rationalization, reaction formation, regression, repression, and sublimation. Learned helplessness explains some depression and some failures to cope with threat. Mastery training acts as an antidote to helplessness.

A large number of life changes can increase susceptibility to illness. However, immediate health is more closely related to the severity of daily hassles or microstressors. Intense or prolonged stress may cause psychosomatic problems. Biofeedback may be used to combat stress and psychosomatic illnesses. People with Type A personalities run a heightened risk of suffering a heart attack. People with hardy personality traits are resistant to stress. The body reacts to stress in a pattern called the general adaptation syndrome (G.A.S.). In addition, stress may lower the body's immunity to disease.

A number of coping skills can be applied to manage stress. Most focus on bodily effects, ineffective behaviors, and upsetting thoughts. Meditation can also be used to reduce stress. Two benefits of meditation are its ability to interrupt anxious thoughts and its ability to elicit the relaxation response.

RECITE AND REVIEW

● *What is health psychology? How does behavior affect health?*

Recite and Review: Pages 449-453

1. Health psychologists are interested in _____ that helps maintain and promote health. The related field of behavioral medicine applies psychology to _____ treatment and problems.
2. Most people today die from lifestyle diseases caused by unhealthy personal _____.

3. Studies have identified a number of behavioral risk factors, which increase the chances of
_____ or injury.

4. A general disease-prone personality pattern also raises the risk of _____.

5. Health-promoting _____ tend to maintain good health.

6. Health psychologists attempt to promote wellness (a positive state of _____) through
community health _____ that educate people about risk factors and healthful behaviors.

● *What is stress? What factors determine its severity?*

Recite and Review: Pages 454-457

7. Stress occurs when we are forced to _____ or adapt to external demands.

8. Stress is more damaging in situations involving pressure (responding at full capacity for long periods), a
lack of _____, unpredictability of the stressor, and _____ or repeated emotional
shocks.

9. _____ is intensified when a situation is perceived as a threat and when a person does not feel
competent to cope with it.

10. In _____ settings, prolonged stress can lead to burnout, marked by emotional
_____, depersonalization (detachment from others), and reduced personal
accomplishment.

11. The _____ (initial) appraisal of a situation greatly affects our emotional response to it.
Stress reactions, in particular, are related to an appraisal of _____.

12. During a _____ appraisal some means of coping with a situation is selected.
Coping may be either problem-focused (managing the situation) or emotion-focused (managing one's emotional
reactions) or both.

● *What causes frustration and what are typical reactions to it?*

Recite and Review: Pages 457-459

13. Frustration is the negative emotional state that occurs when progress toward a _____ is
_____. Sources of frustration may be external or personal.

14. External frustrations are based on delay, failure, rejection, loss, and other direct blocking of motives.
Personal frustration is related to _____ characteristics over which one has little control.

15. Frustrations of all types become more _____ as the strength, urgency, or importance of
the blocked motive increases.

16. Major behavioral reactions to frustration include persistence, more _____ responding,
and circumvention of barriers.

17. Other reactions to frustration are _____ aggression, displaced aggression (including
scapegoating), and escape, or _____.

● *Are there different types of conflict? How do people react to conflict?*

Recite and Review: Pages 459-461

18. _____ occurs when we must choose between contradictory alternatives.

19. Three basic types of conflict are approach-approach (choice between two _____ alternatives), avoidance-avoidance (both alternatives are _____), and approach-avoidance (a goal or activity has both positive and negative aspects).

20. More complex conflicts are: double approach-avoidance (both alternatives have _____ and _____ qualities) and multiple approach-avoidance (several alternatives each have good and bad qualities).

21. Approach-approach conflicts are usually the _____ to resolve.

22. Avoidance conflicts are _____ to resolve and are characterized by inaction, indecision, freezing, and a desire to escape (called _____ the field).

23. People usually remain in approach-avoidance conflicts, but fail to fully resolve them. Approach-avoidance conflicts are associated with ambivalence (_____ feelings) and _____ approach.

24. Vacillation (wavering between choices) is the most common reaction to double _____ conflicts.

● *What are defense mechanisms?*

Recite and Review: Pages 461-463

25. Anxiety, threat, or feelings of _____ frequently lead to the use of psychological defense mechanisms. These are habitual strategies used to avoid or reduce anxiety.

26. A number of defense mechanisms have been identified, including denial, fantasy, intellectualization, isolation, projection, rationalization, _____ formation, regression, and _____ (motivated forgetting).

27. Two defense mechanisms that have some _____ qualities are compensation and sublimation.

● *What do we know about coping with feelings of helplessness and depression?*

Recite and Review: Pages 464-467

28. Learned helplessness is a learned inability to overcome obstacles or to _____ punishment.

29. Learned helplessness explains the failure to cope with some threatening situations. The symptoms of learned helplessness and depression are nearly _____.

30. Mastery _____ and hope act as antidotes to helplessness.

31. Depression (a state of deep sadness or despondency) is a serious emotional problem. Actions and thoughts that counter feelings of helplessness tend to _____ depression.

● *How is stress related to health and disease?*

Recite and Review: Pages 467-475

32. Work with the *Social Readjustment Rating Scale* (SRRS) indicates that a large number of life _____ units (LCUs) can increase susceptibility to _____ or illness.

33. Immediate health is more closely related to the intensity and severity of daily annoyances, known as _____ or microstressors.

34. People who move to a new culture frequently experience a period of acculturative stress (_____ shock).

35. Intense or prolonged stress may damage the body in the form of psychosomatic disorders (illnesses in which _____ factors play a part).

36. Psychosomatic (mind-body) disorders have no connection to hypochondria, the tendency to imagine that one has a _____.

37. During biofeedback training, bodily processes are _____ and converted to a signal that indicates what the body is doing.

38. Biofeedback allows alteration of many bodily activities. It shows promise for promoting _____, self-regulation, and for treating some psychosomatic illnesses.

39. People with Type A (_____ attack prone) personalities are competitive, striving, and frequently angry or hostile, and they have a chronic sense of _____ urgency.

40. _____ and hostility are especially likely to increase the chances of heart attack.

41. People who have traits of the hardy personality seem to be resistant to _____, even if they also have Type A traits.

42. The body reacts to stress in a series of stages called the _____ adaptation syndrome (G.A.S.).

43. The stages of the G.A.S. are alarm, resistance, and exhaustion. The G.A.S. contributes to the development of _____ disorders.

44. Stress weakens the immune system and lowers the body's resistance to _____.

● *What are the best strategies for managing stress?*

Recite and Review: APPLICATIONS

45. Most stress management skills focus on one of three areas: bodily effects, ineffective _____, and upsetting _____.

46. Bodily effects can be managed with exercise, meditation, progressive _____, and guided _____.

47. The impact of ineffective behavior can be remedied by slowing down, getting organized, striking a balance between "good stress" and _____, accepting your limits, and seeking social support.

48. A good way to control upsetting thoughts is to replace negative self-statements with _____ coping statements.

● *Is meditation useful for coping with stress?*

Recite and Review: EXPLORATION

49. Meditation is a self-control technique that can be used to reduce _____.

50. In receptive meditation, attention is _____ to include an awareness of one's entire moment-by-moment experience.

51. In concentrative meditation, attention is focused on a _____ object or thought.

52. Two major benefits of meditation are its ability to interrupt anxious thoughts and its ability to elicit the relaxation response (the pattern of changes that occur in the body at times of deep _____).

RELATE

1. _____	risk factors	a. leading cause of death
2. _____	tobacco	b. ANS arousal
3. _____	refusal skills	c. blocked motive
4. _____	stress reaction	d. lifestyle diseases
5. _____	burnout	e. psychological escape
6. _____	primary appraisal	f. scapegoat
7. _____	frustration	g. approach-avoidance
8. _____	displaced aggression	h. "Am I in trouble?"
9. _____	apathy	i. job stress
10. _____	ambivalence	j. smoking prevention

11. _____ compensation	a. Fulfilling unmet desires in imagined activities.
12. _____ denial	b. Separating contradictory thoughts into "logic-tight" mental compartments.
13. _____ fantasy	
14. _____ intellectualization	c. Preventing dangerous actions by exaggerating opposite behavior.
15. _____ isolation	d. Justifying your behavior by giving reasonable but false reasons for it.
16. _____ projection	
17. _____ rationalization	e. Unconsciously preventing painful thoughts from entering awareness.
18. _____ reaction formation	
19. _____ regression	f. Counteracting a real or imagined weakness by seeking to excel.
20. _____ repression	g. Retreating to an earlier level of development.
21. _____ sublimation .	h. Attributing one's own shortcomings or unacceptable impulses to others.
	i. Protecting oneself from an unpleasant reality by refusing to perceive it.
	j. Working off unacceptable impulses in constructive activities.
	k. Thinking about threatening situations in impersonal terms.

22. _____	learned helplessness	a. LCU
23. _____	mastery training	b. culture shock
24. _____	SRRS	c. mind-body
25. _____	hassle	d. self-regulation
26. _____	acculturative stress	e. cardiac personality
27. _____	psychosomatic	f. alarm reaction
28. _____	biofeedback	g. microstressor
29. _____	Type A	h. hope
30. _____	G.A.S.	i. shuttle box

CHECK YOUR MEMORY

Check Your Memory: Pages 449-453

1. Heart disease, lung cancer, and stroke are typical lifestyle diseases. T or F?
2. Illicit use of drugs is the second most common cause of death in the United States, after smoking. T or F?
3. People with disease-prone personalities are depressed, anxious, and hostile. T or F?
4. Unhealthy lifestyles typically involve multiple risks. T or F?
5. The Alameda County health study found that eating breakfast and not eating between meals are two of the most important health-promoting behaviors. T or F?
6. Community health campaigns provide refusal skills training to large numbers of people. T or F?
7. Wellness can be described as an absence of disease. T or F?

Check Your Memory: Pages 454-457

8. Unpleasant activities produce stress, whereas, pleasant activities do not. T or F?
9. Initial reactions to stressors are similar to those that occur during strong emotion. T or F?
10. Short-term stresses rarely do any damage to the body. T or F?
11. Unpredictable demands increase stress. T or F?
12. Pressure occurs when we are faced with a stressor we can control. T or F?
13. Burnout is especially a problem in helping professions. T or F?
14. Stress is often related to the meaning a person places on events. T or F?
15. The same situation can be a challenge or a threat, depending on how it is appraised. T or F?
16. In a secondary appraisal, we decide if a situation is relevant or irrelevant, positive or threatening. T or F?
17. When confronted by a stressor, it is best to choose one type of coping—problem focused or emotion focused. T or F?
18. Emotion-focused coping is best suited to managing stressors you cannot control. T or F?

Check Your Memory: Pages 457-459

19. Delays, rejections, and losses are good examples of personal frustrations. T or F?
20. Varied responses and circumvention attempt to directly destroy or remove barriers that cause frustration. T or F?
21. Scapegoating is a good example of escape or withdrawal. T or F?
22. Abuse of drugs can be a way of psychologically escaping frustration. T or F?

Check Your Memory: Pages 459-461

23. Approach-approach conflicts are fairly easy to resolve. T or F?
24. Indecision, inaction, and freezing are typical reactions to approach-approach conflicts. T or F?
25. People find it difficult to escape approach-avoidance conflicts. T or F?
26. Wanting to eat, but not wanting to be overweight, creates an approach-approach conflict. T or F?
27. People are very likely to vacillate when faced with a double approach-avoidance conflict. T or F?

Check Your Memory: Pages 461-463

28. Defense mechanisms are used to avoid or distort sources of threat or anxiety. T or F?
29. Denial is a common reaction to bad news, such as learning that a friend has died. T or F?
30. In reaction formation, a person fulfills unmet desires in imagined achievements. T or F?

31. A child who becomes homesick while visiting relatives may be experiencing a mild regression. T or F?
32. Denial and repression are the two most positive of the defense mechanisms. T or F?

Check Your Memory: Pages 464-467

33. The deep depression experienced by prisoners of war appears to be related to learned helplessness. T or F?
34. Learned helplessness occurs when events appear to be uncontrollable. T or F?
35. Attributing failure to specific factors in a specific situation tends to create the most damaging feelings of helplessness.
36. Mastery training restores feelings of control over the environment. T or F?
37. At any given time, 52 to 61 percent of all college students are experiencing the symptoms of depression. T or F?
38. Depression is more likely when students find it difficult to live up to idealized images of themselves. T or F?
39. Writing rational answers to self-critical thoughts can help counteract feelings of depression.

Check Your Memory: Pages 467-475

40. Scores on the SRRS are expressed as life control units. T or F?
41. A score of 300 LCUs on the SRRS is categorized as a major life crisis. T or F?
42. According to the SRRS, being fired at work involves more LCUs than divorce does. T or F?
43. Microstressors tend to predict changes in health 1 to 2 years after the stressful events took place. T or F?
44. Acculturative stress tends to be highest when a person is marginalized. T or F?
45. Functional dyspepsia is a type of hypochondria. T or F?
46. Psychosomatic disorders involve actual damage to the body or damaging changes in bodily functioning. T or F?
47. A person undergoing biofeedback can sleep if he or she desires—the machine does all the work. T or F?
48. Type B personalities are more than twice as likely to suffer heart attacks as Type A personalities. T or F?
49. People with the hardy personality type tend to see life as a series of challenges. T or F?
50. In the stage of resistance of the G.A.S., people have symptoms of headache, fever, fatigue, upset stomach, and the like. T or F?
51. Serious health problems tend to occur when a person reaches the stage of exhaustion in the G.A.S. T or F?
52. Stress management training can actually boost immune system functioning. T or F?

Check Your Memory: APPLICATIONS

53. The USQ was specifically written to assess the stress levels of older, more established adults. T or F?
54. Exercising for stress management is most effective when it is done daily. T or F?
55. Guided imagery is used to reduce anxiety and promote relaxation. T or F?
56. Merely writing down thoughts and feelings about daily events can provide some of the benefits of social support. T or F?
57. To get the maximum benefits, coping statements should be practiced in actual stressful situations. T or F?
58. Persistence must be flexible before it is likely to aid a person trying to cope with frustration. T or F?

Check Your Memory: EXPLORATION

59. Receptive meditation is typically harder to do than concentrative meditation. T or F?
60. A mantra is used as a focus for attention during receptive meditation. T or F?

61. Herbert Benson states that the physical benefits of meditation are based on evoking the body's relaxation response. T or F?
62. The harder you try to meditate the more likely you are to succeed. T or F?

FINAL SURVEY AND REVIEW

● *What is health psychology? How does behavior affect health?*

1. Health psychologists are interested in behavior that helps maintain and promote health. The related field of _____ _____ applies psychology to medical treatment and problems.
2. Most people today die from _____ diseases caused by unhealthy personal habits.
3. Studies have identified a number of behavioral _____ _____, which increase the chances of disease or injury.
4. A general _____ personality pattern also raises the risk of illness.
5. Health-_____ behaviors tend to maintain good health.
6. Health psychologists attempt to promote _____ (a positive state of health) through _____ _____ campaigns that educate people about risk factors and healthful behaviors.

● *What is stress? What factors determine its severity?*

7. Stress occurs when we are forced to adjust or _____ to external _____.
8. Stress is more damaging in situations involving _____ (responding at full capacity for long periods), a lack of control, unpredictability of the _____, and intense or repeated emotional shocks.
9. Stress is intensified when a situation is perceived as a _____ and when a person does not feel _____ to cope with it.
10. In work settings, prolonged stress can lead to _____, marked by emotional exhaustion, _____ (detachment from others), and reduced personal accomplishment.
11. The primary _____ of a situation greatly affects our emotional response to it. Stress reactions, in particular, are related to an _____ of threat.
12. During a secondary appraisal some means of coping with a situation is selected. Coping may be either _____-focused (managing the situation) or _____-focused (managing one's emotional reactions) or both.

● *What causes frustration and what are typical reactions to it?*

13. _____ is the negative emotional state that occurs when progress toward a goal is blocked. Sources of frustration may be external or _____.
14. _____ frustrations are based on delay, failure, rejection, loss, and other direct blocking of motives. _____ frustration is related to personal characteristics over which one has little control.

15. Frustrations of all types become more intense as the strength, urgency, or importance of the _____ _____ increases.

16. Major behavioral reactions to frustration include _____, more vigorous responding, and _____ of barriers.

17. Other reactions to frustration are direct aggression, _____ aggression (including _____), and escape, or withdrawal.

● *Are there different types of conflict? How do people react to conflict?*

18. Conflict occurs when we must choose between _____ alternatives.

19. Three basic types of conflict are _____ (choice between two positive alternatives), _____ (both alternatives are negative), and approach-avoidance (a goal or activity has both positive and negative aspects).

20. More complex conflicts are: _____ approach-avoidance (both alternatives have positive and negative qualities) and _____ approach-avoidance (several alternatives each have good and bad qualities).

21. _____ conflicts are usually the easiest to resolve.

22. _____ conflicts are difficult to resolve and are characterized by inaction, indecision, freezing, and a desire to escape (called leaving the field).

23. People usually remain in approach-avoidance conflicts, but fail to fully resolve them. Approach-avoidance conflicts are associated with _____ (mixed feelings) and partial approach.

24. _____ (wavering between choices) is the most common reaction to double approach-avoidance conflicts.

● *What are defense mechanisms?*

25. Anxiety, threat, or feelings of inadequacy frequently lead to the use of psychological _____ _____. These are habitual strategies used to avoid or reduce _____.

26. A number of defense mechanisms have been identified, including _____ (refusing to perceive an unpleasant reality), fantasy, intellectualization, isolation, projection, _____ (justifying one's behavior), reaction formation, regression, and repression.

27. Two defense mechanisms that have some positive qualities are _____ and _____.

● *What do we know about coping with feelings of helplessness and depression?*

28. Learned _____ is a learned inability to overcome obstacles or to avoid _____.

29. The symptoms of learned helplessness and _____ are nearly identical.

30. _____ training and hope act as antidotes to helplessness.

31. _____ (a state of deep sadness or despondency) is a serious emotional problem. Actions and thoughts that counter feelings of _____ tend to reduce depression.

● *How is stress related to health and disease?*

32. Work with the _____ _____ _____ *Scale* (SRRS) indicates that a large number of life change units (LCUs) can increase susceptibility to accident or illness.

33. Immediate health is more closely related to the intensity and severity of daily annoyances, known as hassles or _____.

34. People who move to a new culture frequently experience a period of _____ stress (culture shock).

35. Intense or prolonged stress may damage the body in the form of _____ disorders (illnesses in which psychological factors play a part).

36. _____ (mind-body) disorders have no connection to _____, the tendency to imagine that one has a disease.

37. During _____ training, bodily processes are monitored and converted to a _____ that indicates what the body is doing.

38. Biofeedback allows alteration of many bodily activities. It shows promise for promoting relaxation, self-_____, and for treating some psychosomatic illnesses.

39. People with _____ (heart attack prone) personalities are competitive, striving, and frequently _____ or hostile, and they have a chronic sense of time urgency.

40. Anger and hostility are especially likely to increase the chances of _____ _____.

41. People who have traits of the _____ personality seem to be resistant to stress, even if they also have Type A traits.

42. The body reacts to stress in a series of stages called the general _____ _____ (G.A.S.).

43. The stages of the G.A.S. are _____, resistance, and _____. The G.A.S. contributes to the development of psychosomatic disorders.

44. Stress weakens the _____ system and lowers the body's resistance to illness.

● *What are the best strategies for managing stress?*

45. Most stress management skills focus on one of three areas: bodily effects, _____ behavior, and _____ thoughts.

46. Bodily effects can be managed with exercise, meditation, _____ relaxation, and _____ imagery.

47. The impact of ineffective behavior can be remedied by slowing down, getting organized, striking a balance between "good stress" and relaxation, accepting your _____, and seeking _____ support.

48. A good way to control upsetting thoughts is to replace _____ self-statements with positive _____ statements.

● *Is meditation useful for coping with stress?*

49. _____ is a self-control technique that can be used to reduce stress.

50. In _____ meditation, attention is broadened to include an awareness of one's entire moment-by-moment experience.

51. In _____ meditation, attention is focused on a single object or thought.

52. Two major benefits of meditation are its ability to interrupt anxious thoughts and its ability to elicit the
_____ _____ (the pattern of changes that occur in the body at times of deep relaxation).

MASTERY TEST

1. When stressful events appear to be uncontrollable, two common reactions are
   a. apathy and acculturative stress   b. helplessness and depression   c. assimilation and marginalization
   d. psychosomatic disorders and hypochondria

2. The USQ is most closely related to the
   a. SRRS   b. G.A.S.   c. K.I.S.   d. disease-prone personality

3. We answer the question "Am I okay or in trouble" when making
   a. negative self-statements   b. coping statements   c. a primary appraisal   d. a secondary appraisal

4. Which of the following is NOT a major symptom of burnout?
   a. emotional exhaustion   b. depersonalization   c. reduced accomplishment
   d. dependence on co-workers

5. A child who displays childish speech and infantile play after his parents bring home a new baby shows signs of
   a. compensation   b. reaction formation   c. regression   d. sublimation

6. Persistent but inflexible responses to frustration can become
   a. stereotyped behaviors   b. imagined barriers   c. negative self-statements
   d. sublimated and depersonalized

7. The leading cause of death in the United States is
   a. tobacco   b. diet/inactivity   c. alcohol   d. infection

8. Both mountain climbing and marital strife
   a. are behavioral risk factors   b. are appraised as secondary threats   c. cause stress reactions
   d. produce the condition known as pressure

9. LCUs are used to assess
   a. burnout   b. social readjustments   c. microstressors   d. what stage of the G.A.S. a person is in

10. Use of a mantra is incompatible with
    a. receptive meditation   b. concentrative meditation   c. the relaxation response   d. Herbert Benson's approach to meditation

11. Lifestyle diseases are of special interest to _____ psychologists.
    a. health   b. community   c. wellness   d. psychosomatic

12. Which of the following is NOT characteristic of the hardy personality?
    a. commitment   b. a sense of control   c. accepting challenge   d. repression

13. Unhealthy lifestyles are marked by the presence of a number of
    a. health refusal factors   b. behavioral risk factors   c. acculturative stressors
    d. Type B personality traits

14. The most effective response to a controllable stressor is
    a. problem-focused coping   b. emotion-focused coping   c. leaving the field   d. depersonalization

15. Delay, rejection, failure, and loss are all major causes of
    a. pressure   b. frustration   c. conflict   d. helplessness

16. There is evidence that the core lethal factor of Type A behavior is
    a. time urgency   b. anger and hostility   c. competitiveness and ambition
    d. accepting too many responsibilities

17. According to Herbert Benson, the one thing that all types of meditation have in common is
    a. use of a mantra   b. the relaxation response   c. that meditation replaces sleep   d. that you should
    end meditation if distracting thoughts occur

18. A person is caught between "the frying pan and the fire" in an _____ conflict.
    a. approach-approach   b. avoidance-avoidance   c. approach-avoidance   d. double appraisal

19. Which of the following health-promoting behaviors has the LEAST impact on health?
    a. maintain ideal weight   b. get adequate sleep   c. get regular exercise   d. avoid eating between meals

20. Ambivalence and partial approach are very common reactions to what type of conflict?
    a. approach-approach   b. avoidance-avoidance   c. approach-avoidance   d. multiple avoidance

21. Which of the following terms does not belong with the others?
    a. Type A personality   b. stage of exhaustion   c. displaced aggression   d. psychosomatic disorder

22. Coping statements are a key element in
    a. stress inoculation   b. the K.I.S. technique   c. guided imagery   d. refusal skills training

23. Which of the following factors typically minimizes the amount of stress experienced?
    a. predictable stressors   b. repeated stressors   c. uncontrollable stressors   d. intense stressors

24. Scapegoating is closely related to which response to frustration?
    a. leaving the field   b. displaced aggression   c. circumvention   d. reaction formation

25. The study of the ways in which stress and the immune system affect susceptibility to disease is called
    a. neuropsychosymptomology   b. immunohypochondrology   c. psychosomatoneurology
    d. psychoneuroimmunology

26. Refusal skills training is typically used to teach young people how to
    a. avoid drug use   b. cope with burnout   c. resist stressors at home and at school   d. avoid forming habits that lead to heart disease

27. Which combination is most relevant to managing bodily reactions to stress?
    a. social support, self pacing   b. exercise, social support   c. exercise, negative self-statements
    d. progressive relaxation, guided imagery

28. Stress reactions are most likely to occur when a stressor is viewed as a _____ during the _____.
    a. pressure, primary appraisal   b. pressure, secondary appraisal   c. threat, primary appraisal
    d. threat, secondary appraisal

29. External symptoms of the body's adjustment to stress are least visible in which stage of the G.A.S?
    a. alarm   b. regulation   c. resistance   d. exhaustion

30. A perceived lack of control creates a stressful sense of threat when combined with a perceived
    a. sense of time urgency   b. state of sublimation   c. need to change secondary risk factors
    d. lack of competence

ANSWERS

Recite and Review

1. behavior, medical
2. habits
3. disease (or illness)
4. illness (or disease)
5. behaviors
6. health, campaigns
7. adjust
8. control, intense
9. Stress
10. work, exhaustion
11. primary, threat
12. secondary
13. goal, blocked
14. personal
15. intense
16. vigorous
17. direct, withdrawal
18. Conflict
19. positive, negative
20. positive, negative
21. easiest

22. difficult, leaving
23. mixed, partial
24. approach-avoidance
25. inadequacy
26. reaction, repression
27. positive
28. avoid
29. identical
30. training
31. reduce
32. change, accident
33. hassles
34. culture
35. psychological
36. disease
37. monitored
38. relaxation
39. heart, time
40. Anger
41. stress
42. general
43. psychosomatic
44. disease (or illness)

45. behavior, thoughts
46. relaxation, imagery
47. relaxation
48. positive
49. stress
50. widened
51. single
52. relaxation

Relate

1. d
2. a
3. j
4. b
5. i
6. h
7. c
8. f
9. e
10. g
11. f

12. i
13. a
14. k
15. b
16. h
17. d
18. c
19. g
20. e
21. j
22. i
23. h
24. a
25. g
26. b
27. c
28. d
29. e
30. f

Check Your Memory

1. T
2. F
3. T
4. T
5. F
6. F
7. F
8. F
9. T
10. T
11. T
12. F
13. T
14. T
15. T
16. F
17. F
18. T
19. F
20. F
21. F
22. T
23. T
24. F
25. T
26. F
27. T
28. T
29. T

30. F
31. T
32. F
33. T
34. T
35. F
36. T
37. F
38. T
39. T
40. F
41. T
42. F
43. F
44. T
45. F
46. T
47. F
48. F
49. T
50. F
51. T
52. T
53. F
54. T
55. T
56. T
57. T
58. T
59. T
60. F
61. T
62. F

Final Survey and Review

1. behavioral medicine
2. lifestyle
3. risk factors
4. disease-prone
5. promoting
6. wellness, community health
7. adapt, demands
8. pressure, stressor
9. threat, competent
10. burnout, depersonalization
11. appraisal, appraisal
12. problem, emotion
13. Frustration, personal
14. External, Personal

15. blocked motive
16. persistence, circumvention
17. displaced, scapegoating
18. contradictory
19. approach-approach, avoidance-avoidance
20. double, multiple
21. Approach-approach
22. Avoidance
23. ambivalence
24. Vacillation
25. defense mechanisms, anxiety
26. denial, rationalization
27. compensation, sublimation
28. helplessness, punishment
29. depression
30. Mastery
31. Depression, helplessness
32. *Social Readjustment Rating*
33. microstressors
34. acculturative
35. psychosomatic
36. Psychosomatic, hypochondria
37. biofeedback, signal
38. regulation
39. Type A, angry
40. heart attack
41. hardy
42. adaptation syndrome
43. alarm, exhaustion
44. immune
45. ineffective, upsetting
46. progressive, guided
47. limits, social
48. negative, coping
49. Meditation
50. receptive
51. concentrative
52. relaxation response

Mastery Test

1. b (p. 464-465)
2. a (p. 476)
3. c (p. 456)
4. d (p. 455)
5. c (p. 462)
6. a (p. 479)

7. a (p. 451)
8. c (p. 454)
9. b (p. 467)
10. a (p. 481)
11. a (p. 450)
12. d (p. 474)
13. b (p. 450)
14. a (p. 457)
15. b (p. 457)
16. b (p. 472)
17. b (p. 481)
18. b (p. 460)
19. d (p. 452)
20. c (p. 460)
21. c (p. 458)
22. a (p. 479)
23. a (p. 455)
24. b (p. 458)
25. d (p. 475)
26. a (p. 452)
27. d (p. 476)
28. c (p. 456)
29. c (p. 474)
30. d (p. 457)

Chapter 15

Gender and Sexuality

CHAPTER OVERVIEW

Gender consists of genetic sex, gonadal sex, hormonal sex, genital sex, and gender identity. The development of primary and secondary sexual characteristics is influenced by androgens and estrogens. Prenatal hormones may exert a biological biasing effect that combines with social factors to influence psychosexual development.

On most psychological dimensions, men and women are more alike than they are different. Social factors are especially apparent in learned gender identity and the effects of sex roles. Sex role socialization accounts for most observed male/female differences. Psychological androgyny is related to greater personal adaptability.

"Normal" sexual behavior is defined differently by various cultures. There is little difference in male and female sexual responsiveness. Sexual orientation refers to whether a person is heterosexual, homosexual, or bisexual. A combination of hereditary, biological, social, and psychological influences combine to produce one's sexual orientation.

Human sexual response can be divided into four phases: (1) excitement; (2) plateau; (3) orgasm; and (4) resolution, which apply to both males and females.

Attitudes toward sexual behavior have grown more liberal, but actual changes in behavior have been more gradual. During the last 20 years there has been a steady increase in the incidence of sexually transmitted diseases, which has altered patterns of sexual behavior.

The principal problems in sexual adjustment are desire disorders, arousal disorders, orgasm disorders, and sexual pain disorders. Behavioral methods and counseling techniques can alleviate each problem. However, communication skills that foster and maintain intimacy are the real key to successful relationships.

Patterns of touching vary from culture to culture, and they depend on the nature of the relationship between two people. Touch can therefore have a variety of meanings, most of which are non-sexual.

RECITE AND REVIEW

● *What are the basic dimensions of gender?*

Recite and Review: Pages 485-490

1. Physical differences between males and females can be divided into _____ and _____ sexual characteristics.

2. Primary sexual characteristics are the _____ and internal reproductive organs.

3. Secondary sexual characteristics are bodily features such as breast development, body _____, and facial hair.

4. Reproductive maturity in females is signaled by menarche (the onset of _____). Soon after, ovulation (the release of _____, or eggs) begins.

5. The development of sexual characteristics is influenced by androgens (_____ sex hormones) and estrogens (_____ sex hormones) secreted by the gonads (sex _____).

6. Gender can be broken down into genetic sex, gonadal sex, _____ sex, genital sex, and _____ identity.

7. Gender development begins with _____ sex (*XX* or *XY* chromosomes). Two *X* chromosomes normally produce a _____; an *X* plus a *Y* produces a _____.

8. During prenatal sexual development, the presence of testosterone produces _____ genitals; an absence of testosterone produces _____ genitals.

9. Androgen insensitivity, exposure to progestin, and the androgenital _____ result in _____ ambiguities called hermaphroditism.

10. Many researchers believe that prenatal _____ can exert a biological biasing _____ that combines with social factors present after birth to influence psychosexual development.

11. On most psychological dimensions, men and women are more _____ than they are _____.

● *How does one's sense of maleness or femaleness develop?*

Recite and Review: Pages 490-492

12. Social factors are especially apparent in learned gender identity (a private sense of _____ or _____) and the effect of sex roles (patterns of behavior defined as male or female within a particular culture).

13. Gender identity, which is based to a large extent on labeling, usually becomes stable by age ____ or ____ years.

14. Sex roles contribute to the development of _____ _____ stereotypes (oversimplified beliefs about the nature of men and women) that often distort perceptions about the kinds of occupations for which men and women are suited.

15. _____ _____ socialization (learning sex roles) seems to account for most observed male/female differences.

16. Parents tend to encourage _____ in instrumental behaviors and _____ in expressive behaviors.

● *What is psychological androgyny (and is it contagious)?*

Recite and Review: Pages 493-494

17. Research conducted by Sandra Bem indicates that roughly one third of all persons are androgynous (they possess both _____ and _____ traits).

18. Androgyny is measured with the *Bem* _____ _____ *Inventory* (BSRI).

19. Being _____ means that a person is independent and assertive.

20. Being _____ means that a person is nurturant and interpersonally oriented.

21. Psychological _____ appears related to greater adaptability or flexibility in behavior.

● *What are the most typical patterns of human sexual behavior?*

Recite and Review: Pages 495-500

22. Sexual behavior, including orgasm (sexual _____) is apparent soon after birth and expressed in various ways throughout life.

23. Sexual arousal is related to stimulation of the body's erogenous zones (areas that produce erotic _____), but cognitive elements such as _____ and images are equally important.

24. "Normal" sexual behavior is defined differently by various _____. Also, each person uses learned sexual scripts (plots or mental plans) to guide sexual behavior.

25. There is little difference in sexual _____ between males and females.

26. Evidence suggests that the sex drive peaks at a _____ age for females than it does for males, although this difference is diminishing.

27. Sex _____ in both males and females may be related to bodily levels of androgens.

28. Nocturnal _____ are a normal, but relatively minor, form of sexual release.

29. _____ (removal of the gonads) may or may not influence sex drive in humans, depending on how sexually experienced a person is. Sterilization (a vasectomy or tubal ligation) does not alter sex drive.

30. There is a gradual _____ in the frequency of sexual intercourse with increasing age.

31. Masturbation is a normal, harmless behavior practiced by a large percentage of the population. For many, masturbation is an important part of sexual self-_____.

32. Sexual orientation refers to one's degree of emotional and erotic attraction to members of the same _____, opposite _____, or both _____.

33. A person may be heterosexual, _____, or bisexual.

34. A combination of hereditary, biological, social, and psychological influences combine to produce one's _____ _____.

35. As a group, homosexual men and women do not differ psychologically from _____.

36. However, gay men and lesbians are frequently affected by homophobia (fear of _____) and heterosexism (the belief that heterosexuality is more natural than homosexuality).

● *To what extent do males and females differ in sexual response?*

Recite and Review: Pages 500-502

37. In a series of landmark studies, William _____ and Virginia Johnson directly observed sexual response in a large number of adults.

38. Human sexual response can be divided into four phases: (1) _____; (2) plateau; (3) _____; and (4) resolution.

39. Both males and females may go through all four stages in ____ or ____ minutes. But during lovemaking, most females typically take longer than this, averaging from 10 to 20 minutes.

40. Males experience a refractory period after _____ and ejaculation. Only 5 percent of men are _____-orgasmic.

41. Fifteen percent of women are consistently _____-orgasmic, and at least 48 percent are capable of _____ orgasm.

42. There do not appear to be any differences between "vaginal _____" and "clitoral _____" in the female.
43. Mutual _____ has been abandoned by most sex counselors as the ideal in lovemaking.

● *Have recent changes in attitudes affected sexual behavior?*

Recite and Review: Pages 503-505

44. Attitudes toward sexual behavior, especially the behavior of others, have become more liberal, but actual changes in sexual _____ have been more gradual.
45. Another change has been _____ and more frequent sexual activity among adolescents and young adults, including larger percentages of people who have premarital _____.
46. Also evident are a greater acceptance of _____ sexuality and a narrowing of differences in male and female patterns of sexual _____. In other words, the double standard is fading.
47. Acquaintance (_____) rape and _____-supportive myths and attitudes remain major problems.

● *What impacts have sexually transmitted diseases had on sexual behavior?*

Recite and Review: Pages 505-508

48. During the last 20 years there has been a steady increase in the incidence of sexually transmitted _____ (STDs).
49. Part of this increase is due to the emergence of _____ _____ deficiency syndrome (AIDS) caused by the human immunodeficiency _____ (HIV).
50. STDs have had a sizable impact on patterns of sexual behavior, including increased awareness of high-_____ behaviors and some curtailment of _____ taking.

● *What are the most common sexual adjustment problems? How are they treated?*

Recite and Review: APPLICATIONS

51. The principal problems in sexual adjustment are _____ disorders, arousal disorders, orgasm disorders, and sexual _____ disorders.
52. Desire disorders include hypoactive _____ _____ (a loss of sexual desire) and _____ aversion (fear or disgust about engaging in sex).
53. Arousal disorders include _____ erectile disorder and _____ sexual arousal disorder.
54. Orgasm disorders are male orgasmic disorder (retarded _____), premature _____, and female orgasm disorder (an inability to reach orgasm during lovemaking).
55. Sexual pain disorders are dyspareunia (_____ intercourse) and vaginismus (_____ _____ of the vagina).
56. Behavioral methods such as sensate _____ and the squeeze technique have been developed to alleviate each problem. In addition, counseling can be quite helpful.
57. However, most sexual adjustment problems are closely linked to the general health of a couple's _____.
58. For this reason, communication skills that foster and maintain _____ are the key to successful relationships.

● *What is the role of touching in personal relationships?*

Recite and Review: EXPLORATION

59. Patterns of touching vary from culture to culture, and they depend on the nature of the
_____ between two people.

60. During childhood, girls are touched more by _____ than boys are.

61. The vast majority of touching takes place between _____.

62. However, touch has a variety of meanings, most of which are non-sexual. A lack of human contact is one
of the consequences of equating touch with _____.

RELATE

1. _____	pelvic bone
2. _____	urethra
3. _____	labia minora
4. _____	ovary
5. _____	vagina
6. _____	uterus
7. _____	rectum
8. _____	fallopian tube
9. _____	clitoris
10. _____	labia majora
11. _____	urinary bladder
12. _____	cervix

13. _____	androgen	a.	ovaries or testes
14. _____	estrogen	b.	cultural pattern
15. _____	genetic sex	c.	self-perception
16. _____	gonadal sex	d.	AIDS
17. _____	hermaphroditism	e.	female hormone
18. _____	gender identity	f.	man-woman
19. _____	sex role	g.	pain disorder
20. _____	androgyny	h.	*XX* or *XY*
21. _____	STD	i.	androgenital syndrome
22. _____	dyspareunia	j.	testosterone

23. _____   Cowper's gland
24. _____   glans penis
25. _____   urethra
26. _____   seminal vesicle
27. _____   vas deferens
28. _____   pelvic bone
29. _____   urinary bladder
30. _____   testis
31. _____   rectum
32. _____   urethral orifice
33. _____   epididymis
34. _____   prostate

CHECK YOUR MEMORY

Check Your Memory: Pages 485-490

1. Primary sexual characteristics involve differences in the reproductive organs and the breasts. T or F?
2. The term menarche refers to the ending of regular monthly fertility cycles in females. T or F?
3. The female gonads are the ovaries. T or F?
4. Cowper's glands are female reproductive structures. T or F?
5. All individuals normally produce both androgens and testosterones. T or F?
6. Transsexuals are persons who have had their genetic sex altered medically. T or F?
7. Without testosterone, a human embryo will develop into a female. T or F?
8. Androgen insensitivity results in the development of female genitals. T or F?
9. Differences in male and female scores on the SAT have declined in recent years. T or F?
10. Observed differences in the abilities of males and females are based on averages, they tell nothing about a particular person. T or F?

Check Your Memory: Pages 490-492

11. Gender identity refers to all the behaviors that are defined as male or female by one's culture. T or F?
12. Babies are perceived differently and treated differently when they are labeled as males than when they are labeled as females. T or F?
13. Women continue to receive unequal pay for work comparable to that of men. T or F?
14. Even though their culture is quite different, the sex roles of Tchambuli men and women are almost identical to those in North America. T or F?
15. Boys are allowed to roam over wider areas than girls are. T or F?
16. Expressive behaviors are those that directly express a person's desire to attain a goal. T or F?

Check Your Memory: Pages 493-494

17. The BSRI consists of 20 masculine traits and 20 feminine traits. T or F?
18. About 50 percent of all people who take the BSRI are scored as androgynous. T or F?
19. Masculine men and feminine women consistently choose to engage in sex-appropriate activities. T or F?
20. Masculine men find it difficult to accept support from others. T or F?
21. Androgynous persons tend to be more satisfied with their lives than non-androgynous persons are. T or F?

Check Your Memory: Pages 495-500

22. Sexual scripts determine when, where, and with whom we are likely to express sexual feelings. T or F?
23. Women are less physically aroused by erotic stimuli than men are. T or F?
24. Women may engage in sexual activity at any time during their menstrual cycles. T or F?
25. More women than men have sexual dreams that result in orgasm. T or F?
26. Drunkenness lowers sexual arousal and performance. T or F?
27. Sterilization tends to abolish the sex drive in the sexually inexperienced. T or F?
28. Masturbation typically ends soon after people get married. T or F?
29. The average frequency of sexual intercourse declines dramatically between the ages of 30 and 39. T or F?
30. Your sexual orientation is revealed, in part, by who you have erotic fantasies about. T or F?
31. Gay males are converted to homosexuality during adolescence by other homosexuals. T or F?
32. Sexual orientation is a very stable personal characteristic. T or F?
33. Sexual orientation is influenced by heredity. T or F?
34. Hormone imbalances cause most instances of homosexuality and bisexuality. T or F?
35. Homosexual persons tend to discover their sexual orientation at a later age than heterosexual persons do. T or F?

Check Your Memory: Pages 500-502

36. Masters and Johnson's data on human sexuality was restricted to questionnaires and interviews. T or F?
37. During the excitement phase of sexual response, the nipples become erect in both males and females. T or F?
38. In males, orgasm is always accompanied by ejaculation. T or F?
39. Almost all women experience a short refractory period after ejaculation. T or F?
40. Both orgasm and resolution tend to last longer in females than they do in males. T or F?
41. Contemporary research has confirmed that clitoral orgasms are an inferior form of sexual response. T or F?
42. Women tend to go through the phases of sexual response more slowly than men do. T or F?
43. One woman in 3 does not experience orgasm during the first year of marriage. T or F?

Check Your Memory: Pages 503-505

44. In recent decades the gap between sexual values and actual behavior has narrowed. T or F?
45. A majority of young adults continue to believe that premarital sex is unacceptable. T or F?
46. The incidence of extramarital sex has not changed much in the last 40 years. T or F?
47. The majority of men and women have sexual experiences before marriage. T or F?
48. About 12 percent of all adult Americans are sexually abstinent. T or F?
49. Women who are raped usually asked for trouble by wearing sexy clothes. T or F?

Check Your Memory: Pages 505-508

50. The first symptoms of AIDS may not appear for up to 7 years. T or F?
51. HIV infections are spread by direct contact with body fluids. T or F?
52. The AIDS epidemic has dramatically altered the sexual behavior of college students. T or F?
53. Most women who contract the HIV virus today do so through intravenous drug use. T or F?
54. It is unwise to count on a partner for protection from HIV infection. T or F?
55. Gonorrhea can be prevented by vaccination. T or F?
56. Hepatitis B can be prevented by vaccination. T or F?
57. Chlamydia is now the most common STD among men. T or F?
58. Many people suffering from STDs are asymptomatic. T or F?

Check Your Memory: APPLICATIONS

59. In a desire disorder the person desires sex, but does not become sexually aroused. T or F?
60. A person who is repelled by sex and seeks to avoid it suffers from a sexual aversion. T or F?
61. Men suffering from primary erectile dysfunction have never had an erection. T or F?
62. The squeeze technique is the most commonly recommended treatment for erectile disorders. T or F?
63. The majority of erectile dysfunctions are psychogenic. T or F?
64. Treatment for female sexual arousal disorder usually involves sensate focus. T or F?
65. Female orgasmic disorder is the female equivalent of premature ejaculation in the male. T or F?
66. Both males and females can experience dyspareunia. T or F?
67. Masters and Johnson regard all sexual problems as mutual, or shared by both parties. T or F?
68. Gunnysacking is an important communication skill that all couples should master. T or F?
69. Rather than telling your partner what he or she thinks, you should ask her or him. T or F?

Check Your Memory: EXPLORATION

70. Very limited body contact is all that occurs outside of strictly sexual contexts. T or F?
71. College students are touched mainly on the head and arms by their parents. T or F?
72. Most regions of the body remain untouched unless one has a romantic partner. T or F?

FINAL SURVEY AND REVIEW

● *What are the basic dimensions of gender?*

1. Physical differences between males and females can be divided into primary and secondary

_____ _____ .

2. _____ refers to the genitals and internal _____ organs.

3. _____ refers to bodily features such as _____ development in females, body shape, and facial _____ .

4. Reproductive maturity in females is signaled by _____ (the onset of menstruation). Soon after, _____ (the release of eggs) begins.

5. The development of sexual characteristics is influenced by _____ (male sex hormones) and _____ (female sex hormones) secreted by the _____ (sex glands).

6. Gender can be broken down into _____ sex, _____ sex, hormonal sex, _____ sex, and gender identity.

7. Gender development begins with genetic sex (*XX* or *XY* _____). Two ___s normally produce a female ___ plus a ___ produces a male.

8. During prenatal sexual development, the presence of _____ produces male _____; its absence produces female _____.

9. _____ insensitivity, exposure to progestin, and the androgenital syndrome result in gender ambiguities called _____.

10. Many researchers believe that _____ hormones can exert a biological _____ effect that combines with social factors present after birth to influence psychosexual development.

11. On most _____ dimensions, men and women are more alike than they are different.

● *How does one's sense of maleness or femaleness develop?*

12. Social factors are especially apparent in learned _____ _____ (a private sense of maleness or femaleness) and the effect of _____ _____ (patterns of behavior defined as male or female within a particular culture).

13. Gender identity, which is based to a large extent on _____, usually becomes stable by age 3 or 4 years.

14. Sex roles contribute to the development of sex role _____ (oversimplified beliefs about the nature of men and women) that often distort perceptions about the kinds of occupations for which men and women are suited.

15. Sex role _____ (learning sex roles) seems to account for most observed male/female differences.

16. Parents tend to encourage boys in _____ behaviors (goal-directed actions) and girls in _____ (emotional) behaviors.

● *What is psychological androgyny (and is it contagious)?*

17. Research conducted by Sandra Bem indicates that roughly one _____ of all persons are _____ (they possess both masculine and feminine traits).

18. Androgyny is measured with the _____ *Sex Role* _____ (BSRI).

19. Being masculine means that a person is _____ and assertive.

20. Being feminine means that a person is _____ (helpful and comforting) and interpersonally oriented.

21. Psychological androgyny appears related to greater _____ or flexibility in behavior.

● *What are the most typical patterns of human sexual behavior?*

22. Sexual behavior, including _____ (sexual climax) is apparent soon after birth and expressed in various ways throughout life.

23. Sexual arousal is related to stimulation of the body's _____ zones (areas that produce erotic pleasure), but _____ elements such as thoughts and images are equally important.

24. "Normal" sexual behavior is defined differently by various cultures. Also, each person uses learned sexual _____ (plots or mental _____) to guide sexual behavior.

25. There is little _____ in sexual behavior between males and females.

26. Evidence suggests that the sex drive peaks at a later age for _____ than it does for _____, although this difference is diminishing.

27. Sex drive in both males and females may be related to bodily levels of _____.

28. _____ orgasms, which occur during sleep, are a normal form of sexual release.

29. Castration (removal of the gonads) may or may not influence sex drive in humans, depending on how sexually experienced a person is. _____ (a vasectomy or tubal ligation) does not alter sex drive.

30. There is a gradual decline in the _____ of sexual intercourse with increasing _____. However, many elderly persons remain sexually active and great variations exist at all ages.

31. _____ (sexual self-stimulation) is a normal, harmless behavior practiced by a large percentage of the population. For many, it is an important part of sexual self-discovery.

32. Sexual _____ refers to one's degree of emotional and erotic attraction to members of the same gender, opposite gender, or both genders.

33. A person may be _____, homosexual, or _____.

34. A combination of _____, biological, _____, and psychological influences combine to produce one's sexual orientation.

35. As a group, _____ men and women do not differ psychologically from _____.

36. However, gay men and lesbians are frequently affected by _____ (fear of homosexuality) and _____ (the belief that heterosexuality is better than homosexuality).

● *To what extent do males and females differ in sexual response?*

37. In a series of landmark studies, William Masters and Virginia _____ directly observed sexual response in a large number of adults.

38. Human sexual response can be divided into four phases: (1) excitement; (2) _____; (3) orgasm; and (4) _____.

39. Both males and females may go through all four stages in 4 or 5 minutes. But during lovemaking, most _____ typically take longer than this, averaging from 10 to 20 minutes.

40. Males experience a _____ period after orgasm and ejaculation. Only 5 percent of men are multi-_____.

41. _____ percent of women are consistently _____, and at least 48 percent are capable of multiple orgasm.

42. There do not appear to be any differences between "_____ orgasms" and "_____ orgasms" in the female.

43. _____ orgasm has been abandoned by most sex counselors as the ideal in lovemaking.

● *Have recent changes in attitudes affected sexual behavior?*

44. _____ toward sexual behavior, especially the behavior of others, have become more _____, but actual changes in sexual behavior have been more gradual.

45. Another change has been earlier and more frequent sexual activity among adolescents and young adults, including larger percentages of people who have _____ intercourse.

46. Also evident are a greater acceptance of female sexuality and a narrowing of differences in male and female patterns of sexual behavior. In other words, the _____ _____ is fading.

47. _____ (date) rape and rape-supportive _____ (false beliefs) and attitudes remain major problems.

● *What impacts have sexually transmitted diseases had on sexual behavior?*

48. During the last 20 years there has been a steady increase in the incidence of _____ _____ diseases (STDs).

49. Part of this increase is due to the emergence of acquired immune _____ syndrome (AIDS) caused by the human _____ virus (HIV).

50. _____ have had a sizable impact on patterns of sexual behavior, including increased awareness of high-risk behaviors and some curtailment of risk taking.

● *What are the most common sexual adjustment problems? How are they treated?*

51. The principal problems in sexual adjustment are desire disorders, _____ disorders, _____ disorders, and sexual pain disorders.

52. Desire disorders include _____ sexual desire (a loss of sexual desire) and sexual _____ (fear or disgust about engaging in sex).

53. Arousal disorders include male _____ disorder and female sexual _____ disorder.

54. Orgasm disorders are male orgasmic disorder (_____ ejaculation), _____ ejaculation, and female _____ disorder (an inability to reach orgasm during lovemaking).

55. Sexual pain disorders are _____ (painful intercourse) and _____ (muscle spasms of the vagina).

56. Behavioral methods such as _____ focus and the _____ technique for premature ejaculation have been developed to alleviate each problem. In addition, counseling can be quite helpful.

57. However, most sexual _____ problems are closely linked to the general health of a couple's relationship.

58. For this reason, _____ skills that foster and maintain intimacy are the key to successful relationships.

● *What is the role of touching in personal relationships?*

59. Patterns of touching vary in different _____, and they depend on the nature of the relationship between two people.

60. During childhood, _____ are touched more by parents than _____ are.

61. The _____ of touching takes place between lovers.

62. However, touch has a variety of meanings, most of which are non-_____. A lack of human contact is one of the consequences of equating touch with sexuality.

MASTERY TEST

1. The strength of the sex drive in both men and women is related to levels of
   a. androgens b. progestin c. estrogens d. androgenin

2. Worldwide, the main source of HIV infection is
   a. heterosexual sex b. homosexual sex c. intravenous drug use d. blood transfusions

3. Boys are encouraged to be strong, aggressive, dominant, and achieving through the process of
   a. biological biasing b. sexual orienting c. gender adaptation d. sex role socialization

4. Before birth, a genetic male will develop as a female if which condition exists?
   a. excessive progestin b. an androgen insensitivity c. the androgenital syndrome
   d. the testes produce testosterone

5. Concerning masturbation, it can be concluded that
   a. masturbation typically ceases after marriage b. after age 30, women masturbate more than men do
   c. those who are most sexually active masturbate the most d. masturbation slows psychosexual
   development

6. One of the greatest changes in attitudes toward sex is a tolerance for
   a. extramarital sex b. the sexual behavior of others c. the double standard d. STDs

7. The squeeze technique is typically used to treat
   a. dyspareunia b. vaginismus c. female sexual arousal disorder d. premature ejaculation

8. In a female, gonadal sex is determined by the presence of
   a. estrogens b. androgens c. ovaries d. a vagina and uterus

9. A man who accepts emotional support from others, especially from women, would most likely be scored
   as _____ on the BSRI.
   a. masculine b. feminine c. androgynous d. expressive-nurturant

10. Which of the following is POOR advice for couples who want to communicate effectively and maintain
    intimacy?
    a. Avoid gunnysacking. b. Avoid expressing anger. c. Don't try to win. d. Don't be a mind-reader.

11. The aspect of gender that is essentially formed by age 4 is
    a. gender identity b. sex roles c. sexual scripting d. psychological androgyny

12. In a female, broadening of the hips and breast development are
    a. primary sexual characteristics b. secondary sexual characteristics c. caused by the release of
    androgens d. associated with the presence of a *Y* chromosome

13. The first two phases of the sexual response cycle are
    a. excitement, arousal b. arousal, orgasm c. excitement, plateau d. stimulation, arousal

14. Patterns of touching by same-sex friends primarily avoid the
    a. head b. torso c. hands d. legs

15. The presence of a *Y* chromosome is associated with
    a. hermaphroditism b. prenatal testosterone c. menarche d. the presence of progestin

16. With respect to the behaviors parents encourage in their children, which is a correct match?
    a. controlling-female b. goal-oriented-female c. expressive-male d. instrumental-male

17. Which condition is LEAST likely to lower sexual performance?
    a. sterilization b. castration c. extreme alcohol intoxication d. sexual aversion

18. Prenatally masculinized females tend to be tomboys during childhood, and observation that supports the
    a. biological biasing effect b. estrogen paradox c. view that gender is genetically determined
    d. idea that sex role socialization is dominant

19. All but one of the following is a rape myth. Which is NOT a myth?
    a. Women who get raped ask for it in one way or another. b. A majority of rapes are committed by a
    friend or acquaintance of the victim. c. Rape is impossible unless a woman consents. d. Most women
    secretly want to be raped.

20. Sex role _____ treat learned sex role differences as if they were real gender
    differences.
    a. labels b. behavior patterns c. stereotypes d. templates

21. Regarding sexual response it can be said that
    a. orgasm and resolution tend to last longer in women b. a short refractory period occurs just before
    orgasm in males c. some women skip the arousal phase of the cycle d. men are incapable of having
    second orgasms

22. The decline of the double standard refers to abandoning different standards for
    a. risky sex and "safe" sex b. heterosexual relationships and homosexual relationships c. sexuality
    before and after marriage d. male and female sexual behavior

23. Declines in the differences in male and female scores on the SAT call into question which concept?
    a. the androgenital syndrome b. the biological biasing effect c. sex role socialization
    d. gender identity

24. When expectations of a friendly first date clash with an attempted seduction the problem can be attributed
    to differences in
    a. sex roles b. erogenous confrontation c. gender myths d. sexual scripts

25. Which statement concerning sexual orientation is TRUE?
    a. Sexual orientation is partly hereditary. b. Homosexuality is caused by a hormone imbalance.
    c. Sexual orientation can be changed fairly easily. d. Heterosexual persons tend to discover their sexual
    orientation at a later date than homosexual persons do.

ANSWERS

Recite and Review

1. primary, secondary
2. genitals
3. shape
4. menstruation, ova
5. male, female, glands
6. hormonal, gender
7. genetic, female, male
8. male, female
9. syndrome, gender
10. hormones, effect
11. alike, different
12. maleness, femaleness
13. 3, 4
14. sex role
15. Sex role
16. boys, girls
17. masculine, feminine
18. *Sex Role*
19. masculine
20. feminine
21. androgyny
22. climax
23. pleasure, thoughts
24. cultures
25. responsiveness
26. later
27. drive
28. orgasms
29. Castration
30. decline (or decrease)
31. discovery
32. gender, gender, genders
33. homosexual
34. sexual orientation
35. heterosexuals
36. homosexuality
37. Masters
38. excitement, orgasm
39. 4, 5
40. orgasm, multi
41. multi, multiple
42. orgasms, orgasms
43. orgasm
44. behavior
45. earlier, intercourse
46. female, behavior
47. date, rape
48. diseases
49. acquired immune, virus
50. risk, risk
51. desire, pain
52. sexual desire, sexual
53. male, female
54. ejaculation, ejaculation
55. painful, muscle spasms
56. focus
57. relationship
58. intimacy
59. relationship
60. parents
61. lovers
62. sexuality

Relate

1. d
2. h
3. f
4. b
5. j
6. l
7. i
8. a
9. e
10. g
11. c
12. k
13. j
14. e
15. h
16. a
17. i
18. c
19. b
20. f
21. d
22. g
23. d
24. g
25. i
26. a
27. j
28. k
29. l
30. e
31. c
32. f
33. h
34. b

Check Your Memory

1. F
2. F
3. T
4. F
5. F
6. F
7. T
8. T
9. T
10. T
11. F
12. T
13. T
14. F
15. T
16. F
17. F
18. F
19. T
20. T
21. T
22. T
23. F
24. T
25. F
26. T
27. F
28. F
29. F
30. T
31. F
32. T
33. T
34. F
35. T

36. F
37. T
38. F
39. F
40. T
41. F
42. T
43. T
44. T
45. F
46. T
47. T
48. T
49. F
50. T
51. T
52. F
53. F
54. T
55. F
56. T
57. F
58. T
59. F
60. T
61. T
62. F
63. T
64. T
65. F
66. T
67. T
68. F
69. T
70. T
71. T
72. T

Final Survey and Review

1. sexual characteristics
2. Primary, reproductive
3. Secondary, breast, hair
4. menarche, ovulation
5. androgens, estrogens, gonads
6. genetic, gonadal, genital
7. chromosomes, *X, X, Y*
8. testosterone, genitals, genitals
9. Androgen, hermaphroditism
10. prenatal, biasing
11. psychological
12. gender identity, sex roles
13. labeling
14. stereotypes
15. socialization
16. instrumental, expressive
17. third, androgynous
18. *Bem, Inventory*
19. independent
20. nurturant
21. adaptability
22. orgasm
23. erogenous, cognitive
24. scripts, plans
25. difference
26. females, males
27. androgens
28. Nocturnal
29. Sterilization
30. frequency, age
31. Masturbation
32. orientation
33. heterosexual, bisexual
34. hereditary, social
35. homosexual, heterosexuals
36. homophobia, heterosexism
37. Johnson
38. plateau, resolution
39. females
40. refractory, orgasmic
41. Fifteen, multi-orgasmic
42. vaginal, clitoral
43. Mutual
44. Attitudes, liberal
45. premarital
46. double standard
47. Acquaintance, myths
48. sexually transmitted
49. deficiency, immunodeficiency
50. STDs
51. arousal, orgasm
52. hypoactive, aversion
53. erectile, arousal
54. retarded, premature, orgasm
55. dyspareunia, vaginismus
56. sensate, squeeze
57. adjustment
58. communication
59. cultures
60. girls, boys
61. majority
62. sexual

Mastery Test

1. a (p. 496)
2. a (p. 505-508)
3. d (p. 491-492)
4. b (p. 488)
5. c (p. 497-498)
6. b (p. 503)
7. d (p. 512)
8. c (p. 487)
9. c (p. 494)
10. b (p. 513)
11. a (p. 490)
12. b (p. 486)
13. c (p. 500)
14. b (p. 515)
15. b (p. 488)
16. d (p. 492)
17. a (p. 497)
18. a (p. 489)
19. b (p. 505)
20. c (p. 491)
21. a (p. 502)
22. d (p. 504)
23. b (p. 489)
24. d (p. 495)
25. a (p. 499)

Chapter 16

Personality

CHAPTER OVERVIEW

Personality refers to unique and enduring behavior patterns. Character is personality evaluated. Temperament refers to the hereditary and physiological aspects of one's emotional nature. Personality traits are lasting personal qualities. Personality types are categories defined by groups of shared traits. Behavior is also influenced by self-concept. Personality theories combine various ideas and principles to explain personality.

Allport's trait theory classifies traits as common, individual, cardinal, central, or secondary. Cattell's trait theory attributes visible surface traits to the existence of 16 underlying source traits. The five-factor model reduces traits to 5 dimensions. Traits appear to interact with situations to determine behavior. Behavioral genetics suggests that heredity influences personality traits.

Like other psychodynamic approaches, Sigmund Freud's psychoanalytic theory emphasizes unconscious forces and conflicts within the personality. Behavioral theories of personality emphasize learning, conditioning, and the immediate effects of the environment. Social learning theory adds cognitive elements, such as perception, thinking, and understanding to the behavioral view. Humanistic theory emphasizes subjective experiences and needs for self-actualization.

Techniques typically used for personality assessment are interviews, direct observation, questionnaires, and projective tests.

Shyness is a mixture of social inhibition and social anxiety. It is marked by heightened public self-consciousness and a tendency to regard one's shyness as a lasting trait. Shyness can be lessened by changing self-defeating beliefs and by improving social skills.

People vary in their degree of self-monitoring. High self-monitoring persons try to fit their public image to various situations. Low self-monitors are interested in accurately expressing their feelings, beliefs, and values, regardless of the situation.

RECITE AND REVIEW

● *How do psychologists use the term personality?*

Recite and Review: Pages 518-519

1. Personality is made up of one's unique and relatively stable _____ patterns.

2. Character is personality that has been judged or _____. That is, it is the possession of desirable qualities.

3. Temperament refers to the _____ and physiological aspects of one's emotional nature.

● *What core concepts make up the psychology of personality?*

Recite and Review: Pages 519-522

4. Personality traits are lasting personal qualities that are inferred from _____.

5. A personality type is a style of personality defined by having a group of related _____ or similar characteristics.

6. Two widely recognized personality _____ are an introvert (shy, self-centered person) and an extrovert (bold, outgoing person).

7. Behavior is influenced by self-concept, which is a person's perception of his or her own _____ traits.

8. _____ theories combine interrelated assumptions, ideas, and principles to explain personality.

9. Four major types of personality theories are: _____, psychodynamic, behavioristic, and humanistic.

● *Are some personality traits more basic or important than others?*

Recite and Review: Pages 522-527

10. Trait _____ attempt to specify qualities of personality that are most lasting or characteristic of a person.

11. Gordon Allport made useful distinctions between common traits (which are shared by most members of a culture) and _____ traits (characteristics of a single person).

12. Allport also identified cardinal traits (a trait that influences nearly all of a person's activities), central traits (core traits of personality), and _____ traits (superficial traits).

13. The theory of Raymond Cattell attributes visible _____ traits to the existence of 16 underlying source traits (which he identified using factor _____).

14. Source traits are measured by the Sixteen _____ _____ Questionnaire (16 PF).

15. The outcome of the 16 PF and other personality tests may be graphically presented as a _____ profile.

16. The five-factor model of personality reduces traits to 5 _____ dimensions of personality.

17. The five factors are: extroversion, _____, conscientiousness, neuroticism, and openness to _____.

18. _____ interact with situations to determine behavior.

19. Behavioral genetics is the study of _____ behavioral traits.

20. Studies of separated _____ twins suggest that heredity contributes significantly to adult personality traits. Overall, however, personality is shaped as much, or more by differences in environment.

● *How do psychodynamic theories explain personality?*

Recite and Review: Pages 528-533

21. Psychodynamic theories focus on the inner workings of personality, especially hidden or _____ forces and internal conflicts.

22. According to Sigmund Freud's psychoanalytic theory, personality is made up of the id, _____, and superego.

23. The id operates on the pleasure _____. The ego is guided by the reality _____.

24. The _____ is made up of the conscience and the ego ideal.

25. Libido, derived from the _____ instincts, is the primary _____ running the personality.

26. Conflicts within the personality may cause neurotic _____ or moral _____ and motivate use of ego-defense mechanisms.

27. The personality operates on three levels, the _____, preconscious, and unconscious.

28. The id is completely _____; the ego and superego can operate at all three levels of awareness.

29. The Freudian view of personality development is based on a series of psychosexual _____: the _____, anal, phallic, and genital.

30. Fixations (unresolved emotional conflicts) at any stage can leave a lasting imprint on _____.

31. Personality theorists who altered or revised Freud's ideas are called neo-_____. Two prominent members of this group are Karen Horney and Carl Jung.

● *What do behaviorists emphasize in their approach to personality?*

Recite and Review: Pages 533-537

32. Behavioral theories of personality emphasize _____, conditioning, and immediate effects of the environment.

33. Learning theorists generally stress the effects of prior learning and _____ determinants of behavior.

34. Learning theorists John Dollard and Neal Miller consider _____ the basic core of personality. _____ express the combined effects of drive, cue, response, and _____.

35. _____ learning theory adds cognitive elements, such as perception, thinking, and understanding to the behavioral view of personality.

36. Examples of social learning concepts are the _____ situation (the situation as it is perceived), expectancies (expectations about what effects a response will have), and reinforcement _____ (the subjective value of a reinforcer or activity).

37. Some social learning theorists treat "conscience" as a case of _____-reinforcement.

38. The behavioristic view of personality development holds that social reinforcement in four situations is critical. The critical situations are _____, toilet or cleanliness training, sex training, and _____ or aggression training.

39. Identification (feeling emotionally connected to a person) and _____ (mimicking another person's behavior) are of particular importance in sex (or gender) training.

● *How do humanistic theories differ from other perspectives?*

Recite and Review: Pages 538-543

40. Humanistic theory views human nature as _____, and emphasizes subjective experience, _____ choice, and needs for self-actualization.

41. Abraham Maslow's study of self-actualizers identified characteristics they share, ranging from efficient perceptions of reality to frequent _____ _____ (temporary moments of self-actualization).

42. Carl Rogers' theory views the _____ as an entity that emerges when experiences that match the self-_____ are symbolized (admitted to consciousness), while those that are incongruent are excluded.

43. The incongruent person has a highly unrealistic _____ and/or a mismatch between the _____ and the ideal self.

44. The congruent or _____ functioning person is flexible and open to experiences and feelings.

45. In the development of personality, humanists are primarily interested in the emergence of a _____ and in self-evaluations.

46. As parents apply conditions of _____ (standards used to judge thoughts, feelings, and actions) to a child, the child begins to do the same.

47. Internalized conditions of worth contribute to incongruence, they damage _____ self-regard, and they disrupt the organismic _____ process.

● *How do psychologists measure personality?*

Recite and Review: Pages 543-550

48. Techniques typically used for personality assessment are _____, observation, questionnaires, and projective _____.

49. Structured and unstructured _____ provide much information, but they are subject to _____ bias and misperceptions. The halo effect may also _____ accuracy.

50. Direct observation, sometimes involving situational tests, behavioral assessment, or the use of _____ scales, allows evaluation of a person's actual _____.

51. Personality questionnaires, such as the _____ _____ *Personality Inventory-2* (MMPI-2), are objective and _____, but their validity is open to question.

52. Honesty tests, which are essentially personality _____, are widely used by businesses to make hiring decisions. Their validity is hotly debated.

53. Projective tests ask a subject to project thoughts or feelings to an ambiguous _____ or unstructured situation.

54. The *Rorschach*, or _____ test, is a well-known projective technique. A second is the _____ *Apperception Test* (TAT).

55. The validity and objectivity of projective tests are quite _____. Nevertheless, projective techniques are considered useful by many clinicians, particularly as part of a _____ battery.

● *What causes shyness? What can be done about it?*

Recite and Review: APPLICATIONS

56. Shyness is a mixture of _____ inhibition and _____ anxiety.
57. Shy persons tend to lack social skills and they feel social anxiety (because they believe they are being _____ by others).
58. Shy persons also have a self-defeating bias in their _____ (they tend to blame _____ for social failures).
59. Shyness is marked by heightened _____ self-consciousness (awareness of oneself as a _____ object) and a tendency to regard shyness as a lasting trait.
60. Shyness can be lessened by changing self-defeating _____ and by improving _____ skills.

● *How does self-monitoring affect behavior?*

Recite and Review: EXPLORATION

61. People vary in their degree of _____-monitoring or desire to control the impression they make on others.
62. _____ self-monitoring persons try to fit their public image to various situations.
63. _____ self-monitors are interested in accurately expressing their feelings, beliefs, and values, regardless of the situation.

RELATE

1. _____	character	a.	heart-attack risk
2. _____	trait	b.	hot-tempered
3. _____	Type A	c.	personality judged
4. _____	melancholic	d.	cheerful
5. _____	choleric	e.	source traits
6. _____	phlegmatic	f.	culturally typical
7. _____	sanguine	g.	sluggish
8. _____	16 PF	h.	universal dimensions
9. _____	common traits	i.	sad, gloomy
10. _____	Big Five	j.	lasting personal quality

11. _____	trait-situation	a. mouth
12. _____	Thanatos	b. pride
13. _____	Eros	c. genitals
14. _____	conscience	d. female conflict
15. _____	ego ideal	e. interaction
16. _____	oral stage	f. male conflict
17. _____	anal stage	g. death instinct
18. _____	phallic stage	h. elimination
19. _____	Oedipus	i. life instinct
20. _____	Electra	j. guilt

21. _____	Horney	a. interview problem
22. _____	Jung	b. evaluation fears
23. _____	Maslow	c. shoot-don't-shoot
24. _____	Rogers	d. personality questionnaire
25. _____	social learning	e. faking good
26. _____	halo effect	f. fully functioning person
27. _____	MMPI	g. self-actualization
28. _____	validity scale	h. archetypes
29. _____	social anxiety	i. cognitive behaviorism
30. _____	situational test	j. basic anxiety

CHECK YOUR MEMORY

Check Your Memory: Pages 518-519

1. The term personality refers to charisma or personal style. T or F?
2. Personality is a person's relatively stable pattern of attitudes. T or F?
3. Character refers to the inherited "raw material" from which personality is formed. T or F?

Check Your Memory: Pages 519-522

4. Traits are stable or lasting qualities of personality, displayed in most situations. T or F?
5. Personality traits typically become quite stable by age 30. T or F?
6. Paranoid, dependent, and antisocial personalities are regarded as personality types. T or F?
7. Two major dimensions of Eysenck's personality theory are stable-unstable and calm-moody. T or F?
8. Trait theories of personality stress subjective experience and personal growth. T or F?

Check Your Memory: Pages 522-527

9. Extroverted students tend to study in noisy areas of the library. T or F?
10. Nearly all of a person's activities can be traced to one or two common traits. T or F?
11. Roughly 7 central traits are needed, on the average, to describe an individual's personality. T or F?
12. Allport used factor analysis to identify central traits. T or F?
13. The 16 PF is designed to measure surface traits. T or F?

14. Judging from scores on the 16 PF, airline pilots have traits that are similar to creative artists. T or F?
15. As one of the Big Five factors, neuroticism refers to having negative, upsetting emotions. T or F?
16. The expression of personality traits tends to be influenced by external situations. T or F?
17. Intelligence, some mental disorders, temperament, and personality traits are all influenced by heredity. T or F?
18. Studies of identical twins show that personality traits are approximately 70 percent hereditary. T or F?
19. Some of the coincidences shared by identical twins appear to be based on the fallacy of positive instances. T or F?

Check Your Memory: Pages 528-533

20. The id is totally unconscious. T or F?
21. The ego is guided by the pleasure principle. T or F?
22. The superego is the source of feelings of guilt and pride. T or F?
23. Threats of punishment from the Thanatos cause moral anxiety. T or F?
24. Oral-dependent persons are gullible. T or F?
25. Vanity and narcissism are traits of the anal-retentive personality. T or F?
26. The genital stage occurs between the ages of 3 and 6, just before latency. T or F?
27. Boys are more likely to develop a strong conscience if their fathers are affectionate and accepting. T or F?
28. According to Jung, people control anxiety by moving toward, against, or away from others. T or F?
29. Jung called the male principle the animus. T or F?

Check Your Memory: Pages 533-537

30. Behaviorists view personality as a collection of learned behavior patterns. T or F?
31. Behaviorists attribute our actions to prior learning and specific situations. T or F?
32. According to Dollard and Miller, habits are acquired through observational learning. T or F?
33. Cues are signals from the environment that guide responses. T or F?
34. An expectancy refers to the anticipation that making a response will lead to reinforcement. T or F?
35. People who are depressed tend to engage in high rate of self-reinforcement to make themselves feel better. T or F?
36. Social reinforcement is based on attention and approval from others. T or F?
37. In elementary school, boys typically get more attention from teachers than girls do. T or F?

Check Your Memory: Pages 538-543

38. Humanists believe that humans are capable of free choice. T or F?
39. To investigate self-actualization, Maslow studied eminent men and women exclusively. T or F?
40. Self-actualizers usually try to avoid task centering. T or F?
41. Personal autonomy is a characteristic of the self-actualizing person. T or F?
42. Information inconsistent with one's self-image is described as incongruent. T or F?
43. Poor self-knowledge is associated with high self-esteem because people do not have to think about their own faults. T or F?
44. Congruence represents a close correspondence between self-image, the ideal self, and the true self. T or F?
45. Images of possible selves typically cause feelings of incongruence. T or F?
46. Rogers believed that organismic valuing is healthier than trying to meet someone else's conditions of worth. T or F?

Check Your Memory: Pages 543-550

47. Planned questions are used in a structured interview. T or F?
48. The halo effect may involve either a positive or a negative impression. T or F?
49. Personality questionnaires are used to do behavioral assessments. T or F?
50. Judgmental firearms training is a type of honesty test. T or F?
51. Items on the MMPI-2 were selected for their ability to identify persons with psychiatric problems. T or F?
52. The validity scale of the MMPI-2 is used to rate Type A behavior. T or F?
53. The psychasthenia scale of the MMPI-2 detects the presence of phobias and compulsive actions. T or F?
54. It is very easy to fake responses to a projective test. T or F?
55. The TAT is a situational test. T or F?
56. Habitually violent prison inmates are aggressive and overcontrolled. T or F?

Check Your Memory: APPLICATIONS

57. Shyness is closely related to private self-consciousness. T or F?
58. Non-shy persons believe that external situations cause their occasional feelings of shyness. T or F?
59. The odds of meeting someone interested in socializing are about the same wherever you are. T or F?
60. Flippant statements are consistently the best way to start conversations with strangers. T or F?
61. Open-ended questions help keep conversations going. T or F?

Check Your Memory: EXPLORATION

62. Self-monitoring refers to how much attention you pay to your ideal self. T or F?
63. High self-monitors would probably agree that they would make good actors. T or F?
64. High self-monitors vary their behavior, depending on who they are speaking to. T or F?
65. Low self-monitors tend to have friends who are all pretty much alike. T or F?

FINAL SURVEY AND REVIEW

● *How do psychologists use the term personality?*

1. _____ is made up of one's unique and relatively stable behavior

_____.

2. _____ is personality that has been judged or evaluated. That is, it is the possession of desirable qualities.

3. _____ refers to the hereditary and physiological aspects of one's emotional nature.

● *What core concepts make up the psychology of personality?*

4. Personality _____ are lasting personal qualities that are inferred from behavior.

5. A personality _____ is a style of personality defined by having a group of related traits or similar characteristics.

6. Two widely recognized personality types are an _____ (shy, self-centered person) and an _____ (bold, outgoing person).

7. Behavior is influenced by _____, which is a person's perception of his or her own personality traits.

8. Personality _____ combine interrelated assumptions, ideas, and principles to explain personality.

9. Four major types of personality theories are: trait, _____, behavioristic, and _____.

● *Are some personality traits more basic or important than others?*

10. _____ theories attempt to specify qualities of personality that are most lasting or characteristic of a person.

11. Gordon _____ made useful distinctions between _____ traits (which are shared by most members of a culture) and individual traits (characteristics of a single person).

12. He also identified _____ traits (a trait that influences nearly all of a person's activities), _____ traits (core traits of personality), and secondary traits (superficial traits).

13. The theory of Raymond _____ attributes visible surface traits to the existence of 16 underlying _____ traits (which he identified using _____ analysis).

14. _____ _____ are measured by the *Sixteen Personality Factor Questionnaire* (16 PF).

15. The outcome of the 16 PF and other personality tests may be graphically presented as a trait _____.

16. The _____ model of personality reduces traits to 5 universal dimensions of personality.

17. They are: _____, agreeableness, conscientiousness, _____, and openness to experience.

18. Traits _____ with _____ to determine behavior.

19. _____ _____ is the study of inherited behavioral traits.

20. Studies of separated identical twins suggest that _____ contributes significantly to adult personality traits. Overall, however, personality is shaped as much, or more by differences in _____.

● *How do psychodynamic theories explain personality?*

21. Psychodynamic theories focus on the inner workings of _____, especially hidden or unconscious forces and internal _____.

22. According to Sigmund Freud's _____ theory, personality is made up of the _____, ego, and _____.

23. The id operates on the _____ principle. The ego is guided by the _____ principle.

24. The superego is made up of the _____ and the _____ ideal.

25. _____, derived from the life _____, is the primary energy running the personality.

26. Conflicts within the personality may cause _____ anxiety or _____ anxiety and motivate use of ego-defense mechanisms.

27. The personality operates on three levels, the conscious, _____, and
_____.

28. The _____ is completely unconscious; the _____ and _____ can operate
at all three levels of awareness.

29. The Freudian view of personality development is based on a series of _____
stages: the oral, anal, _____, and genital.

30. _____ (unresolved emotional conflicts) at any stage can leave a lasting imprint on
personality.

31. Personality theorists who altered or revised Freud's ideas are called _____-Freudians. Two prominent
members of this group are Karen Horney and Carl _____.

● *What do behaviorists emphasize in their approach to personality?*

32. _____ theories of personality emphasize learning, conditioning, and immediate effects
of the environment.

33. Learning theorists generally stress the effects of prior learning and situational
_____ of behavior.

34. Learning theorists John Dollard and Neal Miller consider habits the basic core of personality. Habits
express the combined effects of _____, _____, response, and reward.

35. Social learning theory adds _____ elements, such as perception, thinking, and
understanding to the behavioral view of personality.

36. Examples of social learning concepts are the psychological situation (the situation as it is perceived),
_____ (expectations about what effects a response will have), and
_____ value (the subjective value of a reinforcer or activity).

37. Some social learning theorists treat "conscience" as a case of self-_____.

38. The behavioristic view of personality development holds that social reinforcement in four situations is
critical. The critical situations are feeding, _____ _____, sex training, and
anger or _____ training.

39. _____ (feeling emotionally connected to a person) and imitation (mimicking
another person's behavior) are of particular importance in sex (or gender) training.

● *How do humanistic theories differ from other perspectives?*

40. Humanistic theory views human nature as good, and emphasizes _____ experience,
free choice, and needs for self-_____.

41. Abraham _____ study of _____ identified
characteristics they share, ranging from efficient perceptions of reality to frequent peak experiences.

42. Carl Rogers' theory views the self as an entity that emerges when experiences that match the self-image are
_____ (admitted to consciousness), while those that are _____ are
excluded.

43. The _____ person has a highly unrealistic self-image and/or a mismatch
between the self-image and the _____ self.

44. The _____ or fully functioning person is flexible and open to experiences and
feelings.

45. In the development of personality, humanists are primarily interested in the emergence of a self-image and in _____.

46. As parents apply _____ of worth (standards used to judge thoughts, feelings, and actions) to a child, the child begins to do the same.

47. Internalized _____ ____ _____ contribute to incongruence, they damage positive self-regard, and they disrupt the _____ valuing process.

● *How do psychologists measure personality?*

48. Techniques typically used for personality assessment are interviews, direct _____, questionnaires, and _____ tests.

49. Structured and _____ interviews provide much information, but they are subject to interviewer _____ and misperceptions. The halo effect may also lower the accuracy of an interview.

50. Direct observation, sometimes involving _____ tests, _____ assessment, or the use of rating scales, allows evaluation of a person's actual behavior.

51. Personality questionnaires, such as the *Minnesota Multiphasic* _____ *-2* (MMPI-2), are objective and reliable, but their _____ is open to question.

52. _____ tests, which are essentially personality questionnaires, are widely used by businesses to measure integrity and make hiring decisions.

53. _____ tests ask subjects react to an ambiguous stimulus or unstructured situation.

54. The _____, or inkblot test, is a well-known projective technique. A second is the *Thematic* _____ *Test* (TAT).

55. The _____ and objectivity of projective tests are quite low. Nevertheless, projective techniques are considered useful by many clinicians, particularly as part of a test _____.

● *What causes shyness? What can be done about it?*

56. Shyness is a mixture of social _____ and social anxiety.

57. Shy persons tend to lack social _____ and they feel social anxiety (because they believe they are being evaluated by others).

58. Shy persons also have a _____ bias in their thinking (they tend to blame themselves for social failures).

59. Shyness is marked by heightened public self-_____ (awareness of oneself as a _____ object) and a tendency to regard shyness as a lasting _____.

60. Shyness can be lessened by changing _____ beliefs and by improving social _____.

● *How does self-monitoring affect behavior?*

61. People vary in their degree of self-monitoring or desire to control the _____ they make on _____.

62. High self-monitoring persons try to fit their _____ _____ to various situations.
63. Low self-monitors are interested in _____ expressing their feelings, beliefs, and values, regardless of the situation.

MASTERY TEST

1. The hereditary aspects of a person's emotional nature define his or her
  a. character b. personality c. cardinal traits d. temperament

2. Two parts of the psyche that operate on all three levels of awareness are the
  a. id and ego b. ego and superego c. id and superego d. id and ego ideal

3. The four critical situations Miller and Dollard consider important in the development of personality are feeding, toilet training,
  a. sex, and aggression b. cleanliness, and language c. attachment, and imitation d. social learning

4. Scales that rate a person's tendencies for depression, hysteria, paranoia, and mania are found on the
  a. MMPI-2 b. Rorschach c. TAT d. 16 PF

5. In the five-factor model, people who score high on openness to experience are
  a. intelligent b. extroverted c. choleric d. a personality type

6. Jung regarded mandalas as symbols of the
  a. animus b. anima c. self archetype d. persona

7. Maslow used the term _____ to describe the tendency to make full use of personal potentials.
  a. full functionality b. self-potentiation c. ego-idealization d. self-actualization

8. Studies of reunited identical twins support the idea that
  a. personality traits are 70 percent hereditary b. fixations influence the expression of personality traits
  c. personality traits are altered by selective mating d. personality is shaped more by environment than by heredity

9. A person's perception of his or her own personality is the core of
  a. temperament b. source traits c. self-concept d. trait-situation interactions

10. Which of the following concepts is NOT part of Dollard and Miller's behavioral model of personality?
  a. drive b. expectancy c. cue d. reward

11. The terms structured and unstructured apply most to
  a. the halo effect b. interviews c. questionnaires d. honesty tests

12. Persons low in self-monitoring usually
a. are concerned with outer appearances b. make a good actors c. prefer jobs where they can be themselves d. have different friends for various activities

13. Feelings of pride come from the _____, a part of the _____.
a. libido, conscience b. ego ideal, superego c. reality principle, superego d. superego, ego

14. Four types of temperament recognized by the early Greeks are: melancholic, choleric, phlegmatic and
a. sanguine b. sardonic c. sagittarian d. sagacious

15. Freud believed that boys identify with their fathers in order to resolve the _____ conflict.
a. Animus b. Electra c. Oedipus d. Persona

16. Maslow regarded peak experiences as temporary moments of
a. task-centering b. congruent selfhood c. self-actualization d. organismic valuing

17. Ambiguous stimuli are used primarily in the
a. MMPI-2 b. Shoot-Don't-Shoot Test c. Rorschach d. 16 PF

18. A person who is generally extroverted is more outgoing in some situations than in others. This observation supports the concept of
a. trait-situation interactions b. behavioral genetic determinants c. situational fixations
d. possible selves

19. Allport's concept of central traits is most closely related to Cattell's
a. surface traits b. source traits c. secondary traits d. cardinal traits

20. According to Freud, tendencies to be orderly, obstinate, and stingy are formed during the _____ stage.
a. genital b. anal c. oral d. phallic

21. Which of the following is NOT part of Carl Rogers' view of personality?
a. possible selves b. organismic valuing c. conditions of worth d. congruence

22. Rating scales are primarily used in which approach to personality assessment?
a. projective testing b. direct observation c. questionnaires d. the TAT technique

23. Which theory of personality places the greatest emphasis on the effects of the environment?
a. trait b. psychodynamic c. behavioristic d. humanistic

24. Freudian psychosexual stages occur in the order:
a. oral, anal, genital, phallic b. oral, phallic, anal, genital c. genital, oral, anal, phallic
d. oral, anal, phallic, genital

25. Rogers described mismatches between one's self-image and reality as a state of
a. moral anxiety b. incongruence c. basic anxiety d. negative symbolization

26. All but one of the following are major elements of shyness; which does not apply?
   a. private self-consciousness   b. social anxiety   c. self-defeating thoughts   d. belief that shyness is a lasting trait

27. People who all grew up in the same culture would be most likely to have the same _____ traits.
   a. cardinal   b. common   c. secondary   d. source

28. A trait profile is used to report the results of
   a. the 16 PF   b. situational tests   c. the TAT   d. the inkblot test

29. An emphasis on the situational determinants of actions is a key feature of _____ theories of personality.
   a. psychodynamic   b. projective   c. behaviorist   d. humanist

30. The behavioral concept most closely related to the superego is
   a. psychological situation   b. self-reinforcement   c. reinforcement value   d. self-concept

ANSWERS

Recite and Review

1. behavior
2. evaluated
3. hereditary
4. behavior
5. traits
6. types
7. personality
8. Personality
9. trait
10. theories
11. individual
12. secondary
13. surface, analysis
14. *Personality Factor*
15. trait
16. universal
17. agreeableness, experience
18. Traits
19. inherited
20. identical
21. unconscious
22. ego
23. principle, principle
24. superego

25. life, energy
26. anxiety, anxiety
27. conscious
28. unconscious
29. stages, oral
30. personality
31. Freudians
32. learning
33. situational
34. habits, Habits, reward
35. Social
36. psychological, value
37. self
38. feeding, anger
39. imitation
40. good, free
41. peak experiences
42. self, image
43. self-image, self-image
44. fully
45. self-image
46. worth
47. positive, valuing
48. interviews, tests
49. interviews, interviewer, lower

50. rating, behavior
51. *Minnesota, Multiphasic,* reliable
52. questionnaires
53. stimulus
54. inkblot, *Thematic*
55. low, test
56. social, social
57. evaluated
58. thinking, themselves
59. public, social
60. beliefs, social
61. self
62. High
63. Low

Relate

1. c
2. j
3. a
4. i
5. b
6. g
7. d

8. e
9. f
10. h
11. e
12. g
13. i
14. j
15. b
16. a
17. h
18. c
19. f
20. d
21. j
22. h
23. g
24. f
25. i
26. a
27. d
28. e
29. b
30. c

Check Your Memory

1. F
2. F
3. F
4. T
5. T
6. T
7. F
8. F
9. T
10. F
11. T
12. F
13. F
14. F
15. T
16. T
17. T
18. F
19. T
20. T
21. F
22. T
23. F
24. T
25. F

26. F
27. T
28. F
29. T
30. T
31. T
32. F
33. T
34. T
35. F
36. T
37. T
38. T
39. F
40. F
41. T
42. T
43. F
44. T
45. F
46. T
47. T
48. T
49. F
50. F
51. T
52. F
53. T
54. F
55. F
56. F
57. F
58. T
59. F
60. F
61. T
62. F
63. T
64. T
65. T

Final Survey and Review

1. Personality, patterns
2. Character
3. Temperament
4. traits
5. type
6. introvert, extrovert
7. self-concept
8. theories

9. psychodynamic, humanistic
10. Trait
11. Allport, common
12. cardinal, central
13. Cattell, source, factor
14. Source traits
15. profile
16. five-factor
17. extroversion, neuroticism
18. interact, situations
19. Behavioral genetics
20. heredity, environment
21. personality, conflicts
22. psychoanalytic, id, superego
23. pleasure, reality
24. conscience, ego
25. Libido, instincts
26. neurotic, moral
27. preconscious, unconscious
28. id, ego, superego
29. psychosexual, phallic
30. Fixations
31. neo, Jung
32. Behavioral
33. determinants
34. drive, cue
35. cognitive
36. expectancies, reinforcement
37. reinforcement
38. toilet training, aggression
39. Identification
40. subjective, actualization
41. Maslow's, self-actualizers
42. symbolized, incongruent
43. incongruent, ideal
44. congruent
45. self-evaluations
46. conditions
47. conditions of worth, organismic
48. observation, projective
49. unstructured, bias
50. situational, behavioral
51. *Personality Inventory*, validity
52. Honesty
53. Projective
54. *Rorschach, Apperception*
55. validity, battery

56. inhibition
57. skills
58. self-defeating
59. consciousness, social, trait
60. self-defeating, skills
61. impression, others
62. public image
63. accurately

Mastery Test

1. d (p. 519)
2. b (p. 530)
3. a (p. 536)
4. a (p. 547)
5. a (p. 524)
6. c (p. 533)
7. d (p. 538)
8. d (p. 526-527)
9. c (p. 521)
10. b (p. 535)
11. b (p. 543)
12. c (p. 553-554)
13. b (p. 529)
14. a (p. 522)
15. c (p. 531)
16. c (p. 539)
17. c (p. 548)
18. a (p. 525)
19. b (p. 523-524)
20. b (p. 531)
21. a (p. 540-541)
22. b (p. 545)
23. c (p. 543)
24. d (p. 530-531)
25. b (p. 540)
26. a (p. 551)
27. b (p. 523)
28. a (p. 524)
29. c (p. 534)
30. b (p. 535-536)

Chapter 17

Abnormal Behavior:
Deviance and Disorder

CHAPTER OVERVIEW

Abnormal behavior is defined by subjective discomfort, deviation from statistical norms, social non-conformity, and cultural or situational contexts. Disordered behavior is also maladaptive. Major categories of psychopathology described by DSM-IV include psychotic disorders, organic mental disorders, substance related disorders, mood disorders, anxiety disorders, somatoform disorders, dissociative disorders, personality disorders, and sexual or gender identity disorders. Insanity is a legal term, not a mental disorder.

Personality disorders are deeply ingrained maladaptive personality patterns, such as the antisocial personality. Troubling sexual disorders such as pedophilia and fetishism are called paraphilias. Rape is primarily a violent crime of aggression rather than a sex crime.

Anxiety disorders, dissociative disorders, and somatoform disorders are characterized by high levels of anxiety, rigid defense mechanisms, and self-defeating behavior patterns. Anxiety disorders include generalized anxiety disorder, panic disorder (with or without agoraphobia), agoraphobia, specific phobia, social phobia, obsessive-compulsive disorders, and post-traumatic or acute stress disorders.

Dissociative disorders may take the form of amnesia, fugue, or identity disorder (multiple personality). Somatoform disorders center on physical complaints that mimic disease or disability, such as hypochondriasis, somatization disorder, somatoform pain disorder, and conversion disorders.

The psychodynamic explanation of anxiety-based disorders emphasizes unconscious conflicts within the personality. The humanistic approach emphasizes the effects of a faulty self-image. The existential approach stresses a loss of meaning in one's life. The behavioral approach emphasizes the effects of previous learning, particularly avoidance learning.

David Rosenhan's use of pseudo-patients to study mental hospitals suggests that problems in diagnosis exist and that psychiatric labeling can affect our perceptions of others' behavior.

In Western law, the insanity defense evolved from the M'Naghten rule. Insanity is closely related to claims of diminished capacity or claims that a person had an irresistible impulse. Inconsistencies in the application of the insanity defense have fueled debate about its validity.

RECITE AND REVIEW

● *How is normality defined, and what are the major psychological disorders?*

Recite and Review: Pages 557-566

1. Psychopathology is defined as an inability to behave in ways that foster the _____ of the individual and ultimately of _____.

2. Formal definitions of abnormality usually take into account subjective _____ (private feelings of suffering or unhappiness).

3. Statistical definitions define abnormality as an extremely _____ or _____ score on some dimension or measure.

4. Social non-conformity is a failure to follow societal _____ or _____ standards for conduct.

5. Frequently, the _____ or situational context that a behavior takes place in affects judgments of normality and abnormality.

6. _____ of the preceding definitions are relative standards.

7. A key element in judgments of disorder is that a person's _____ must be maladaptive (it makes it difficult for the person to adapt to the _____).

8. A _____ disorder is a significant impairment in psychological functioning.

9. Major disorders and categories of psychopathology are described in the *Diagnostic and Statistical* _____ of _____ *Disorders* (DSM-IV).

10. Psychotic disorders are characterized by a retreat from _____, by hallucinations and delusions, and by _____ withdrawal.

11. Organic mental disorders are problems caused by _____ injuries and _____.

12. Substance related disorders are defined as abuse of or dependence on _____ - or behavior-altering _____.

13. Mood disorders involve disturbances in affect, or _____.

14. Anxiety disorders involve high levels of fear or _____ and distortions in behavior that are _____ related.

15. Somatoform disorders involve physical symptoms that mimic physical _____ or injury for which there is no identifiable _____.

16. Dissociative disorders include cases of sudden amnesia, multiple _____, or episodes of depersonalization.

17. Personality disorders are deeply ingrained, unhealthy _____ patterns.

18. Sexual and gender disorders include _____ identity disorders, paraphilias, and _____ dysfunctions.

19. In the past, the term neurosis was used to describe milder, _____ related disorders. However, the term is fading from use.

20. Insanity is a _____ term defining whether a person may be held responsible for his or her actions. Sanity is determined in _____ on the basis of testimony by expert witnesses.

● *What is a personality disorder?*

Recite and Review: Pages 566-568

21. Personality disorders are deeply ingrained _____ personality patterns.

22. The personality disorders are: antisocial, avoidant, _____, dependent, histrionic, narcissistic, obsessive-_____, paranoid, schizoid, and schizotypal.

23. Antisocial persons (sociopaths) seem to lack a _____. They are _____ "cold" or unresponsive, manipulative, and they have shallow interpersonal relationships.

● *What are the most common sexual disorders?*

Recite and Review: Pages 568-571

24. Definitions of sexual deviance are highly _____. Many "sexually deviant" behaviors are acceptable in private or in some _____.

25. Sexual _____ that often cause difficulty are called paraphilias.

26. Some paraphilias include: pedophilia (sex with children), _____ (sexual arousal associated with inanimate objects), voyeurism (viewing the genitals of others without their permission), and _____ (displaying the genitals to unwilling viewers).

27. Other paraphilias are: transvestic fetishism (achieving sexual arousal by wearing clothing of the opposite sex), sexual _____ (deriving sexual pleasure from inflicting pain), sexual _____ (desiring pain as part of the sex act), and frotteurism (sexually touching or rubbing against a non-consenting person).

28. Exhibitionists are rarely dangerous and can best be characterized as sexually _____ and immature.

29. The effects of child molestation vary greatly, depending on the _____ of the molestation and the child's relationship to the molester.

30. _____ is primarily a violent crime of aggression rather than a sex crime.

● *What problems result when a person suffers high levels of anxiety?*

Recite and Review: Pages 571-576

31. Anxiety disorders, dissociative disorders, and somatoform disorders are characterized by high levels of _____, rigid _____ mechanisms, and self-defeating behavior patterns.

32. The term nervous breakdown has no formal meaning. However, "emotional breakdowns" do correspond somewhat to adjustment disorders, in which the person is overwhelmed by ongoing _____ _____.

33. Anxiety disorders include generalized anxiety disorder (chronic _____ and worry) and panic disorder (anxiety attacks, panic, free-_____ anxiety).

34. Panic disorder may occur with or without agoraphobia (fear of _____ places, unfamiliar situations, or leaving the _____).

35. Other anxiety disorders are agoraphobia and _____ phobia (irrational fears of specific objects or situations).

36. In the anxiety disorder called social phobia, the person fears being _____, evaluated, embarrassed, or humiliated by others in _____ situations.

37. Obsessive-compulsive disorders (obsessions and compulsions), and post-traumatic stress disorder or acute stress disorder (emotional disturbances triggered by severe _____) are also classified as _____ disorders.

38. Dissociative disorders may take the form of dissociative amnesia (loss of _____ and personal identity) or _____ fugue (flight from familiar surroundings).

39. A more dramatic problem is dissociative identity disorder, in which a person develops _____ personalities.

40. Somatoform disorders center on physical complaints that mimic _____ or disability.

41. In hypochondriasis, persons think that they have specific diseases, when they are, in fact _____.

42. In a somatization disorder, the person has numerous _____ complaints. The person repeatedly seeks medical _____ for these complaints, but no organic problems can be found.

43. Somatoform pain refers to discomfort for which there is no identifiable _____ cause.

44. In conversion disorders, actual symptoms of disease or disability develop but their causes are actually _____.

● *How do psychologists explain anxiety-based disorders?*

Recite and Review: Pages 577-578

45. The psychodynamic approach emphasizes _____ conflicts within the personality as the cause of disabling anxiety.

46. The humanistic approach emphasizes the effects of a faulty _____.

47. The existential approach stresses a loss of _____ in one's life.

48. The behavioral approach emphasizes the effects of previous _____, particularly avoidance _____.

49. Some patterns in anxiety disorders can be explained by the _____ reduction hypothesis, which states that immediate _____ from anxiety rewards self-defeating behaviors.

50. The cognitive view of anxiety disorders states that distorted _____ causes people to _____ ordinary threats and failures, leading to distress.

● *Is psychiatric labeling damaging?*

Recite and Review: APPLICATIONS

51. David Rosenhan's use of pseudo-patients (_____ patients) to study _____ hospitals suggests that problems in diagnosis exist and that psychiatric labeling can affect perceptions of others' behavior.

● *What role does the concept of insanity play in criminal trials?*

Recite and Review: EXPLORATION

52. In Western law, the _____ defense evolved from the M'Naghten rule.

53. Insanity is closely related to claims of diminished _____ (impaired ability to control actions) or claims that a person had an irresistible _____ (uncontrollable urge to act).

54. Insanity is determined by courts of law, usually on the basis of _____ by expert witnesses (psychiatrists or psychologists).

55. Inconsistencies in applying the insanity defense have fueled debate about its _____.

RELATE

1. _____ DSM
2. _____ drapetomania
3. _____ psychosis
4. _____ mood disorder
5. _____ somatoform disorder
6. _____ insanity
7. _____ organic disorder
8. _____ neurosis
9. _____ paraphilia
10. _____ microphobia

a. phony disorder
b. physical symptoms
c. legal problem
d. outdated term
e. sexual deviation
f. diagnostic manual
g. retreat from reality
h. fear of germs
i. brain pathology
j. mania or depression

11. _____ dependent personality
12. _____ histrionic personality
13. _____ narcissistic personality
14. _____ antisocial personality
15. _____ obsessive-compulsive
16. _____ schizoid personality
17. _____ avoidant personality
18. _____ borderline personality
19. _____ paranoid personality
20. _____ schizotypal personality

a. self-importance
b. rigid routines
c. submissiveness
d. little emotion
e. attention seeking
f. unstable self-image
g. odd, disturbed thinking
h. suspiciousness
i. fear of social situations
j. no conscience

21. _____ adjustment disorder
22. _____ generalized anxiety
23. _____ panic disorder
24. _____ agoraphobia
25. _____ specific phobia
26. _____ social phobia
27. _____ PTSD
28. _____ acute stress disorder
29. _____ glove anesthesia
30. _____ fugue

a. afraid to leave the house
b. fears being observed
c. conversion disorder
d. one month after extreme stress
e. dissociation
f. within weeks after extreme stress
g. sudden attacks of fear
h. normal life stress
i. chronic worry
j. fears objects or activities

CHECK YOUR MEMORY

Check Your Memory: Pages 557-566

1. Psychopathology refers to the study of mental disorders and to disorders themselves. T or F?
2. One out of every 10 persons will require mental hospitalization during his or her lifetime. T or F?
3. Statistical definitions of abnormality attempt to measure a person's level of subjective discomfort. T or F?

4. Statistical definitions do not automatically tell us where to draw the line between normality and abnormality. T or F?

5. All cultures classify people as abnormal if they fail to communicate with others. T or F?

6. Gender is a common source of bias in judging normality. T or F?

7. All abnormal behavior is in some way maladaptive. T or F?

8. Being a persistent danger to oneself or others is regarded as a clear sign of disturbed psychological functioning. T or F?

9. DSM-IV lists the various types of insanity that can occur. T or F?

10. Depersonalization and mania are core features of psychotic disorders. T or F?

11. Poverty, abusive parents, low intelligence, and head injuries are risk factors for mental disorder. T or F?

12. "Organic mental disorders" is one of the major categories in DSM-IV. T or F?

13. Multiple personality is a dissociative disorder. T or F?

14. Neurosis is a legal term, not a type of mental disorder. T or F?

15. Only persons who are actively psychotic are more prone to violence than non-patients are. T or F?

Check Your Memory: Pages 566-568

16. Histrionic persons are preoccupied with their own self-importance. T or F?

17. Personality disorders usually appear suddenly in early adulthood. T or F?

18. The schizoid person shows little emotion and is uninterested in relationships with others. T or F?

19. The schizotypal person is socially isolated and displays extremely odd behavior and disturbed thinking. T or F?

20. "Psychopath" is another term for the borderline personality. T or F?

21. Sociopaths usually have a childhood history of emotional deprivation, neglect, and abuse. T or F?

22. Antisocial behavior typically declines somewhat after age 20. T or F?

Check Your Memory: Pages 568-571

23. Oral sex and masturbation are formally classified as paraphilias. T or F?

24. Frotteurism refers to sex with children. T or F?

25. Most exhibitionists are male and married. T or F?

26. An exhibitionist who approaches closer than arm's length may be dangerous. T or F?

27. In the majority of cases of child molesting, the offender is an acquaintance or relative of the child. T or F?

28. Child molesting is especially likely to be harmful if the molester is someone the child deeply trusts. T or F?

29. One woman in 70 will be raped in her lifetime. T or F?

30. The majority of rapists are friends or acquaintances of the victim. T or F?

31. Males high in sex role stereotyping are more aroused by stories about rape than males low in sex role stereotyping. T or F?

Check Your Memory: Pages 571-576

32. Anxiety is an emotional response to an ambiguous threat. T or F?

33. Seven percent of the adult population suffers from anxiety disorders. T or F?

34. Adjustment disorders occur when severe stresses outside the normal range of human experience push people to their breaking points. T or F?

35. Sudden, unexpected episodes of intense panic are a key feature of generalized anxiety disorder. T or F?
36. A person who fears he or she will have a panic attack in public places or unfamiliar situations suffers from acrophobia. T or F?
37. Arachnophobia, claustrophobia, and pathopobia are all specific phobias. T or F?
38. A person who fears eating, writing, or speaking in public suffers from an acute stress disorder. T or F?
39. Many people who have an obsessive-compulsive disorder are checkers or cleaners. T or F?
40. PTSD is a psychological disturbance lasting more than one month after exposure to severe stress. T or F?
41. Multiple personality is the most common form of schizophrenia. T or F?
42. Sybil suffered from dissociative identity disorder. T or F?
43. Depersonalization and fusion are the goals of therapy for dissociative identity disorders. T or F?
44. In a somatization disorder, people express their anxieties in the form of various bodily complaints. T or F?
45. The word somatoform means "body form." T or F?
46. An unusual lack of concern about the appearance of a sudden disability is a sign of a conversion reaction. T or F?

Check Your Memory: Pages 577-578

47. Anxiety disorders appear to be partly hereditary. T or F?
48. The psychodynamic approach characterizes anxiety disorders as a product of id impulses that threaten a loss of control. T or F?
49. Carl Rogers interpreted emotional disorders as the result of a loss of meaning in one's life. T or F?
50. According to the existential view, people with excessive anxiety are living in "bad faith." T or F?
51. Disordered behavior is paradoxical, because it makes the person more anxious and unhappy in the long run. T or F?
52. The cognitive view attributes anxiety disorders to distorted thinking that leads to avoidance learning. T or F?

Check Your Memory: APPLICATIONS

53. To gain admittance to mental hospitals, David Rosenhan complained of drug flashbacks and visual hallucinations. T or F?
54. Pseudo-patients were frequently detected by staff members who suspected they were journalists. T or F?
55. Daily contact of pseudo-patients with therapists averaged about 7 minutes. T or F?
56. The label "schizophrenic" was so powerful that pseudo-patients actually began to act "crazy." T or F?
57. It is usually more productive to label people, rather than their problems. T or F?

Check Your Memory: EXPLORATION

58. The insanity defense has been used in Western law for over 130 years. T or F?
59. The M'Naghten rule says that a person must intentionally harm others before he or she has committed a crime. T or F?
60. The "Twinkie defense" in the Dan White case was essentially a plea of diminished capacity. T or F?
61. Notorious serial killer Jeffrey Dahmer pleaded "guilty but insane." T or F?
62. In most cases, persons declared insane are hospitalized longer than they would have been imprisoned for the same crime. T or F?

FINAL SURVEY AND REVIEW

● *How is normality defined, and what are the major psychological disorders?*

1. _____ is defined as an inability to behave in ways that foster the well-being of the individual and ultimately of society.

2. Formal definitions of abnormality usually take into account _____ discomfort (private feelings of suffering or unhappiness).

3. _____ definitions define abnormality as an extremely high or low score on some dimension or measure.

4. _____ _____ is a failure to follow societal norms or minimum standards for conduct.

5. Frequently, the cultural or situational _____ that a behavior takes place in affects judgments of normality and abnormality.

6. All of the preceding definitions are _____ standards.

7. A key element in judgments of disorder is that a person's behavior must be _____ (it makes it difficult for the person to adapt to the environment).

8. A mental disorder is a significant impairment in _____ functioning.

9. Major disorders and categories of psychopathology are described in the _____ and _____ *Manual of Mental Disorders* (DSM-IV).

10. _____ disorders are characterized by a retreat from reality, by _____ and delusions, and by social withdrawal.

11. _____ mental disorders are problems caused by brain injuries and diseases.

12. _____ _____ disorders are defined as abuse of or dependence on mood- or behavior-altering drugs.

13. _____ disorders involve disturbances in _____, or emotion.

14. _____ disorders involve high levels of fear or anxiety and distortions in behavior that are anxiety related.

15. _____ disorders involve physical symptoms that mimic physical disease or injury for which there is no identifiable cause.

16. _____ disorders include cases of sudden _____, multiple personality, or episodes of depersonalization.

17. _____ disorders are deeply ingrained, unhealthy personality patterns.

18. Sexual and gender disorders include gender _____ disorders, paraphilias, and sexual - _____.

19. In the past, the term _____ was used to describe milder, anxiety related disorders. However, the term is fading from use.

20. _____ is a legal term defining whether a person may be held responsible for his or her actions. Sanity is determined in court on the basis of testimony by expert witnesses.

● *What is a personality disorder?*

21. Personality disorders are deeply _____ maladaptive personality patterns.

22. The personality disorders are: antisocial, avoidant, borderline, _____, histrionic, narcissistic, obsessive-compulsive, _____, schizoid, and _____.

23. Antisocial persons (_____) seem to lack a conscience. They are emotionally "cold" or unresponsive, manipulative, and they have shallow _____ relationships.

● *What are the most common sexual disorders?*

24. Definitions of _____ _____ are highly subjective. Many publicly disapproved sexual behaviors are acceptable in private or in some cultures.
25. Sexual deviations that often cause difficulty are called _____ (destructive deviations in sexual preferences or behavior).
26. Some of these problems include: _____ (sex with children), fetishism (sexual arousal associated with inanimate objects), _____ (viewing the genitals of others without their permission), and exhibitionism (displaying the genitals to unwilling viewers).
27. Others are: _____ fetishism (achieving sexual arousal by wearing clothing of the opposite sex), sexual sadism (deriving sexual pleasure from inflicting pain), sexual masochism (desiring pain as part of the sex act), and _____ (sexually touching or rubbing against a non-consenting person).
28. _____ ("flashers") are rarely dangerous and can best be characterized as sexually inhibited and immature.
29. The effects of child molestation vary greatly, depending on the severity of the _____ and the child's _____ to the molester.
30. Rape is primarily a violent crime of _____ rather than a sex crime.

● *What problems result when a person suffers high levels of anxiety?*

31. Anxiety disorders, _____ disorders, and _____ disorders are characterized by high levels of anxiety, rigid defense mechanisms, and self-defeating behavior patterns.
32. The term nervous _____ has no formal meaning. However, people do experience _____ disorders, in which the person is overwhelmed by ongoing life stresses.
33. Anxiety disorders include _____ anxiety disorder (chronic anxiety and worry) and _____ disorder (anxiety attacks, panic, free-floating anxiety).
34. Panic disorder may occur with or without _____ (fear of public places or leaving the home).
35. Other anxiety disorders are _____ (fear of public places, _____ situations, or leaving the home) and specific phobia (irrational fears of specific objects or situations).
36. In the anxiety disorder called _____ _____, the person fears being observed, _____, embarrassed, or humiliated by others in social situations.
37. _____-compulsive disorders, and _____ stress disorder (PTSD) or _____ stress disorder (emotional disturbances triggered by severe stress) are also classified as anxiety disorders.
38. Dissociative disorders may take the form of dissociative _____ (loss of memory and personal identity) or dissociative _____ (flight from familiar surroundings).
39. A more dramatic problem is dissociative _____ _____, in which a person develops multiple personalities.
40. _____ disorders center on physical complaints that mimic disease or disability.

41. In _____, persons think that they have specific diseases, when they are, in fact healthy.

42. In a _____ disorder, the person has numerous physical complaints. The person repeatedly seeks medical treatment for these complaints, but no organic problems can be found.

43. _____ _____ refers to discomfort for which there is no identifiable physical cause.

44. In _____ disorders, actual symptoms of disease or disability develop but their causes are actually psychological.

● *How do psychologists explain anxiety-based disorders?*

45. The _____ approach emphasizes unconscious conflicts within the personality as the cause of disabling anxiety.

46. The _____ approach emphasizes the effects of a faulty self-image.

47. The _____ approach stresses a loss of meaning in one's life.

48. The _____ approach emphasizes the effects of previous learning, particularly _____ learning.

49. Some patterns in anxiety disorders can be explained by the anxiety _____ hypothesis, which states that immediate relief from anxiety rewards _____ behaviors.

50. The _____ view of anxiety disorders states that distorted thinking causes people to magnify ordinary _____ and failures, leading to distress.

● *Is psychiatric labeling damaging?*

51. David Rosenhan's use of _____ (fake patients) to study mental hospitals suggests that problems in _____ exist and that psychiatric labeling can affect perceptions of others' behavior.

● *What role does the concept of insanity play in criminal trials?*

52. In Western law, the insanity defense evolved from the _____ rule.

53. Insanity is closely related to claims of _____ capacity (impaired ability to control actions) or claims that a person had an _____ impulse (uncontrollable urge to act).

54. Insanity is determined by courts of law, usually on the basis of testimony by _____

_____ .

55. _____ in applying the insanity defense have fueled debate about its validity.

MASTERY TEST

1. The difference between an acute stress disorder and PTSD is
   a. how long the disturbance lasts   b. the severity of the stress   c. whether the anxiety is free-floating
   d. whether *la belle indifférence* is observed

2. The majority of violent crimes are committed by people who are
   a. insane b. psychotic c. actively psychotic d. not mentally ill

3. A core feature of all abnormal behavior is that it is
   a. statistically extreme b. associated with subjective discomfort c. ultimately maladaptive
   d. marked by a loss of contact with reality

4. Expert witnesses are usually involved in judging
   a. sanity b. psychosis c. neurosis d. sexual dysfunctions

5. The descriptions "animal type," and "blood, injection, injury type" refer to
   a. common obsessions b. specific phobias c. free-floating anxieties d. hypochondriasis

6. Glove anesthesia strongly implies the existence of a _____ disorder.
   a. organic b. depersonalization c. somatization d. conversion

7. The odds that a man would commit rape are increased if he
   a. is low in sex role stereotyping b. is an exhibitionist c. is high in sex role stereotyping
   d. suffers from transvestic fetishism

8. David Rosenhan's study involving pseudo-patients demonstrated the effects of _____ on
   perceptions of normality.
   a. diagnosis and faking good b. context and labels c. the halo effect d. expert testimony and
   levels of functioning

9. Failures of socialization are closely related to which facet of abnormality?
   a. subjective discomfort b. statistical deviation c. non-conformity d. social phobia

10. Psychopathology is defined as an inability to behave in ways that
    a. foster personal well-being b. match social norms c. lead to personal achievement
    d. do not cause anxiety

11. A cold, unemotional response to stimuli that are normally very upsetting is characteristic of
    _____ personality disorder.
    a. histrionic b. paranoid c. antisocial d. schizotypal

12. Fear of using the rest room in public is
    a. a social phobia b. an acute stress disorder c. a panic disorder d. an adjustment disorder

13. The modern insanity defense descended from the
    a. Moscone rule b. MacKeachie rule of the British Parliament c. M'Naghten rule d. use of expert
    witnesses in the British Parliament

14. Child molestation would be a rare event if the sexual deviation known as _____ didn't
    occur.
    a. paraphilia b. sexual sadism c. frotteurism d. pedophilia

15. A major problem with statistical definitions of abnormality is
   a. calculating the normal curve   b. choosing dividing lines   c. that they do not apply to groups of people
   d. that they do not take norms into account

16. DSM-IV primarily describes and classifies _____ disorders.
   a. mental   b. organic   c. psychotic   d. cognitive

17. A person who is a frequent "checker" may have which disorder?
   a. agoraphobic   b. somatization   c. free-floating fugue   d. obsessive-compulsive

18. The most direct explanation for the anxiety reducing properties of self-defeating behavior is found in
   a. an overwhelmed ego   b. avoidance learning   c. the loss of meaning in one's life   d. the concept of
   existential anxiety

19. A person with a(an) _____ personality disorder might be described as "charming" by
   people who don't know the person well.
   a. avoidant   b. schizoid   c. antisocial   d. dependent

20. One of the most powerful situational contexts for judging the normality of behavior is
   a. culture   b. gender   c. statistical norms   d. private discomfort

21. A person who is manic most likely suffers from a(an) _____ disorder.
   a. anxiety   b. somatoform   c. organic   d. mood

22. Which case involved a claim of diminished capacity?
   a. Richard Chase-Vampire Defense   b. Dan White-Twinkie Defense   c. David Chapman-Beatle Defense
   d. Jeffrey Dahmer-Freezer Defense

23. A problem that may occur with or without agoraphobia is
   a. dissociative disorder   b. somatoform disorder   c. panic disorder   d. obsessive-compulsive disorder

24. Hearing voices that do not exist is an almost sure sign of a _____ disorder.
   a. psychotic   b. dissociative   c. personality   d. delusional

25. A conversion reaction is a type of _____ disorder.
   a. somatoform   b. dissociative   c. obsessive-compulsive   d. post-traumatic

26. The existence, in the past, of "disorders" such as "drapetomania" and "nymphomania" suggests that
   judging normality is greatly affected by
   a. gender   b. cultural disapproval   c. levels of functioning   d. subjective discomfort

27. Which of the following terms does NOT belong with the others?
   a. neurotic disorder   b. somatoform disorder   c. personality disorder   d. dissociative disorder

28. Threats to one's self-image are a key element in the _____ approach to understanding anxiety
   and disordered functioning.
   a. Freudian   b. humanistic   c. existential   d. behavioral

29. Which of the following is NOT classified as an anxiety disorder?
a. adjustment disorder b. panic disorder c. agoraphobia d. obsessive-compulsive disorder

30. A person with an extremely unstable self-image and erratic moods and impulses has a
_____ personality disorder.
a. antisocial b. avoidant c. narcissistic d. borderline

ANSWERS

Recite and Review

1. well-being, society
2. discomfort
3. high, low
4. norms, minimum
5. cultural
6. All
7. behavior, environment
8. mental
9. *Manual, Mental*
10. reality, social
11. brain, diseases
12. mood, drugs
13. emotion
14. anxiety, anxiety
15. disease, cause
16. personality
17. personality
18. gender, sexual
19. anxiety
20. legal, court
21. maladaptive
22. borderline, compulsive
23. conscience, emotionally
24. subjective, cultures
25. deviations
26. fetishism, exhibitionism
27. sadism, masochism
28. inhibited
29. severity
30. Rape
31. anxiety, defense
32. life stresses
33. anxiety, floating
34. public, home
35. specific

36. observed, social
37. stress, anxiety
38. memory, dissociative
39. multiple
40. disease
41. healthy
42. physical, treatment
43. physical
44. psychological
45. unconscious
46. self-image
47. meaning
48. learning, learning
49. anxiety, relief
50. thinking, magnify
51. fake, mental
52. insanity
53. capacity, impulse
54. testimony
55. validity

Relate

1. f
2. a
3. g
4. j
5. b
6. c
7. i
8. d
9. e
10. h
11. c
12. e
13. a

14. j
15. b
16. d
17. i
18. f
19. h
20. g
21. h
22. i
23. g
24. a
25. j
26. b
27. d
28. f
29. c
30. e

Check Your Memory

1. T
2. F
3. F
4. T
5. T
6. T
7. T
8. T
9. F
10. F
11. T
12. F
13. T
14. F
15. T
16. F

17. F
18. T
19. T
20. F
21. T
22. F
23. F
24. F
25. T
26. T
27. T
28. T
29. F
30. T
31. T
32. T
33. T
34. F
35. F
36. F
37. T
38. F
39. T
40. T
41. F
42. T
43. F
44. T
45. T
46. T
47. T
48. T
49. F
50. T
51. T
52. F
53. F
54. F
55. T
56. F
57. F
58. T
59. F
60. T
61. T
62. T

Final Survey and Review

1. Psychopathology
2. subjective
3. Statistical
4. Social non-conformity
5. context
6. relative
7. maladaptive
8. psychological
9. *Diagnostic, Statistical*
10. Psychotic, hallucinations
11. Organic
12. Substance related
13. Mood, affect
14. Anxiety
15. Somatoform
16. Dissociative, amnesia
17. Personality
18. identity, dysfunctions
19. neurosis
20. Insanity
21. ingrained
22. dependent, paranoid, schizotypal
23. sociopaths, interpersonal
24. sexual deviance
25. paraphilias
26. pedophilia, voyeurism
27. transvestic, frotteurism
28. Exhibitionists
29. molestation, relationship
30. aggression
31. dissociative, somatoform
32. breakdown, adjustment
33. generalized, panic
34. agoraphobia
35. agoraphobia, unfamiliar
36. social phobia, evaluated
37. Obsessive, post-traumatic, acute
38. amnesia, fugue
39. identity disorder
40. Somatoform
41. hypochondriasis
42. somatization
43. Somatoform pain
44. conversion
45. psychodynamic
46. humanistic
47. existential
48. behavioral, avoidance
49. reduction, self-defeating
50. cognitive, threats
51. pseudo-patients, diagnosis
52. M'Naghten
53. diminished, irresist
54. expert witnesses
55. Inconsistencies

Mastery Test

1. a (p. 574)
2. d (p. 565-566)
3. c (p. 561)
4. a (p. 565)
5. b (p. 573)
6. d (p. 576)
7. c (p. 570)
8. b (p. 579-580)
9. c (p. 559)
10. a (p. 559)
11. c (p. 568)
12. a (p. 573)
13. c (p. 581)
14. d (p. 569)
15. b (p. 559)
16. a (p. 562)
17. d (p. 574)
18. b (p. 577-578)
19. c (p. 567)
20. a (p. 560)
21. d (p. 562)
22. b (p. 581)
23. c (p. 572)
24. a (p. 562)
25. a (p. 575)
26. b (p. 560)
27. a (p. 565)
28. b (p. 577)
29. a (p. 572)
30. d (p. 567)

Chapter 18

Major Mental Disorders

CHAPTER OVERVIEW

Psychosis is a break in contact with reality. A brief reactive psychosis may follow extremely stressful life events. An organic psychosis is based on known injuries or diseases of the brain. Other problems of unknown origin are termed functional psychoses.

Persons suffering from delusional disorders have delusions of grandeur, persecution, infidelity, romantic attraction, or physical disease. The most common delusional disorder is paranoid psychosis.

Schizophrenia is the most prevalent form of psychosis. Four types of schizophrenia are: disorganized, catatonic, paranoid, and undifferentiated. Explanations of schizophrenia emphasize environmental stress, inherited susceptibility, and biochemical abnormalities.

Mood disorders primarily involve disturbances of emotion. Two moderate mood disorders are dysthymic disorder and cyclothymic disorder. Major mood disorders include bipolar disorders and major depressive disorder. A major mood disorder that includes psychotic symptoms is called an affective psychosis. Postpartum depression affects some women after they give birth. Seasonal affective disorder is another common form of depression. Biological, psychoanalytic, cognitive, and behavioral theories of depression have been proposed. Heredity is clearly a factor in susceptibility to mood disorders.

Five approaches to the treatment of psychosis are pharmacotherapy, electroconvulsive therapy, psychosurgery, hospitalization, and psychotherapy. Prolonged hospitalization has been discouraged by deinstitutionalization and by partial-hospitalization policies. Community mental health centers attempt to prevent mental health problems.

Suicide is statistically related to such factors as age, sex, and marital status. However, in individual cases the potential for suicide is best identified by a desire to escape, unbearable psychological pain, frustrated psychological needs, and a constriction of options. Suicide can sometimes be prevented by the efforts of family, friends, and mental health professionals.

Thomas Szasz has raised challenging questions about the nature of abnormal behavior and its relationship to personal responsibility and civil rights. Public policies concerning treatment of the chronically mentally ill continue to evolve as authorities try to strike a balance between providing help and taking away personal freedoms.

RECITE AND REVIEW

● *What are the general characteristics of psychosis?*

Recite and Review: Pages 584-588

1. Psychosis is a _____ in contact with reality.
2. Psychosis is marked by delusions, _____ (false sensations), and sensory changes.

3. Other symptoms of psychosis are disturbed emotions, disturbed communication, and
_____ disintegration.

4. A brief reactive psychosis may follow extremely _____ life events.

5. An organic psychosis is based on known injuries or _____ of the brain.

6. Problems of _____ origin are called functional psychoses.

7. Three common causes of _____ psychosis are untreated syphilis (general paresis),
poisoning, and _____ dementia (especially Alzheimer's disease).

● *How do delusional disorders differ from other forms of psychosis?*

Recite and Review: Page 588

8. A diagnosis of delusional disorder is based primarily on the presence of _____.

9. Delusions may concern grandeur, _____ (harassment or threat), infidelity,
_____ attraction, or physical disease.

10. The most common delusional disorder is paranoid psychosis. Because they often have intense and
irrational delusions of _____, paranoids may be violent if they believe they are
threatened.

● *What forms does schizophrenia take?*

Recite and Review: Pages 589-591

11. Schizophrenia is the most frequently occurring _____.

12. Schizophrenia is distinguished by a _____ between _____ and emotion, and by
delusions, hallucinations, and communication difficulties.

13. Schizophrenia should not be confused with multiple _____ disorder which is a
non-_____ dissociative disorder.

14. Schizophrenia also should not be confused with schizotypal personality disorder, which involves gradual
_____ into isolation from others and _____, apathetic behavior.

15. Disorganized schizophrenia is marked by extreme _____ disintegration and silly,
bizarre, or obscene behavior. _____ impairment is usually extreme.

16. Catatonic schizophrenia is associated with stupor, _____ (inability to speak), _____
flexibility, and odd postures. Sometimes violent and agitated behavior also occurs.

17. In paranoid schizophrenia (the most common type), outlandish delusions of grandeur and
_____ are coupled with psychotic symptoms and personality breakdown.

18. Undifferentiated schizophrenia is the term used to indicate a _____ of clear-cut patterns of
disturbance.

● *What causes schizophrenia?*

Recite and Review: Pages 591-595

19. Current explanations of schizophrenia emphasize a combination of environmental _____,
inherited susceptibility, and biochemical _____ in the body or brain.

20. A number of environmental factors appear to increase the risk of developing schizophrenia. These include viral _____ during the mother's pregnancy and _____ complications.
21. Early psychological _____ (psychological injury or shock) and a disturbed _____ environment, especially one marked by deviant communication, also increase the risk of schizophrenia.
22. Studies of _____ and other close relatives strongly support heredity as a major factor in schizophrenia.
23. Recent biochemical studies have focused on abnormalities in brain _____ substances, especially dopamine and its receptor sites.
24. Additional abnormalities in brain structure or _____ have been detected in schizophrenic brains by the use of CT scans, MRI scans, and PET scans.
25. The dominant explanation of schizophrenia is the _____-vulnerability model.

● *What are mood disorders? What causes depression?*

Recite and Review: Pages 596-599

26. Mood disorders primarily involve disturbances of mood or _____, producing manic (agitated, elated, hyperactive) or _____ (sad, apathetic, suicidal) states.
27. Long-lasting, though relatively moderate, _____ is called a dysthymic disorder.
28. Chronic, though moderate, swings in mood between _____ and _____ are called a cyclothymic disorder.
29. Reactive depressions are often triggered by _____ events; however, they are more _____ or prolonged than normal reactions to similar events.
30. Bipolar disorders are _____ _____ disorders that combine mania and depression.
31. In a bipolar I disorder the person is mostly _____, but has had at least one major depression.
32. In a bipolar II disorder the person is mostly _____, but has had at least one manic episode.
33. The problem known as major depressive disorder involves extreme sadness and despondency, but no evidence of _____.
34. When a major mood disorder is accompanied by _____ symptoms, it is called an affective psychosis.
35. Major mood disorders more often appear to be endogenous (produced from _____) rather than reactions to _____ events.
36. _____ affective disorder (SAD), which occurs during the _____ months is another common form of depression. SAD is typically treated with phototherapy.
37. Biological, psychoanalytic, cognitive, and _____ theories of depression have been proposed. Heredity is clearly a factor in susceptibility to mood disorders.

● *How are major mental disorders treated?*

Recite and Review: Pages 599-604

38. Three _____ (bodily) approaches to treatment of psychosis are pharmacotherapy (use of _____), electroconvulsive therapy (ECT) (brain shock for the treatment of depression), and psychosurgery (surgical alteration of the _____).

39. Psychotherapy is any psychological treatment for behavioral or emotional problems. _____ _____ disorders are more often treated medically, rather than with psychotherapy.
40. Pharmacotherapy is done with _____ tranquilizers (anti-anxiety drugs), antipsychotics (which reduce delusions and _____), and antidepressants (_____ elevators).
41. All psychiatric drugs involve a trade-off between _____ and benefits.
42. Hospitalization is often associated with the administration of _____ therapy, and it is also considered a form of treatment.
43. Prolonged hospitalization has been discouraged by deinstitutionalization (reduced use of commitment to treat mental disorders) and by _____-hospitalization policies.
44. Half-way _____ within the community can help people make the transition from a hospital or institution to _____ living.
45. Community mental health centers were created to help avoid or minimize

_____.

46. Community mental health centers also have as their goal the prevention of mental health problems through education, consultation, and _____ intervention.

● *Why do people commit suicide? Can suicide be prevented?*

Recite and Review: APPLICATIONS

47. _____ is statistically related to such factors as age, sex, and marital status.
48. Major risk factors for suicide include _____ or _____ abuse, a prior attempt, depression, hopelessness, antisocial behavior, suicide by relatives, shame, failure, or rejection, and the availability of a _____.
49. In individual cases the potential for suicide is best identified by a desire to _____, unbearable psychological pain, frustrated psychological needs, and a constriction of _____.
50. Suicidal _____ usually precede suicide threats, which progress to suicide attempts.
51. Suicide can often be prevented by the efforts of family, friends, and mental health professionals to establish _____ and rapport with the person, and by gaining day-by-day commitments from her or him.

● *What does it mean to be "crazy"? What should be done about it?*

Recite and Review: EXPLORATION

52. Thomas Szasz has raised challenging questions about the nature of abnormal behavior and its relationship to personal _____ and civil rights.
53. Szasz rejects the medical model of mental illness that treats emotional problems as _____ with symptoms that can be cured.
54. Public policies concerning treatment of the chronically mentally ill continue to evolve as authorities try to strike a balance between providing help and taking away personal _____.

RELATE

1. _____	delusion	a.	imaginary sensation
2. _____	hallucination	b.	lead poisoning
3. _____	flat affect	c.	mercury poisoning
4. _____	word salad	d.	Alzheimer's disease
5. _____	Mad Hatter	e.	self-importance
6. _____	mental retardation	f.	psychotic speech
7. _____	senile dementia	g.	bodily delusions
8. _____	somatic type	h.	romantic delusions
9. _____	grandiose type	i.	false belief
10. _____	erotomanic type	j.	lack of emotion

11. _____	schizotypal	a.	incoherence, bizarre thinking
12. _____	catatonic type	b.	antipsychotic drug
13. _____	paranoid type	c.	personality disorder
14. _____	disorganized type	d.	manic depression
15. _____	double-bind	e.	stuporous or agitated
16. _____	Genain	f.	depressed
17. _____	dopamine	g.	schizophrenic quads
18. _____	clozapine	h.	grandeur or persecution
19. _____	dysthymic	i.	chemical messenger
20. _____	cyclothymic	j.	deviant communication

21. _____	bipolar I	a.	antidepressant
22. _____	bipolar II	b.	brain scan
23. _____	PET	c.	antipsychotic
24. _____	lithium carbonate	d.	deep lesioning
25. _____	SAD	e.	memory loss
26. _____	Clozaril	f.	mostly manic
27. _____	tardive dyskinesia	g.	mental health staff
28. _____	psychosurgery	h.	drug side effect
29. _____	ECT	i.	mostly depressed
30. _____	paraprofessionals	j.	short days

CHECK YOUR MEMORY

Check Your Memory: Pages 584-588

1. In delusions of reference, people feel they are being controlled by others or unseen forces. T or F?
2. A person who falsely believes she has committed a sinful deed suffers from a depressive delusion. T or F?
3. The most common psychotic delusion is hearing voices. T or F?

4. Even a person who displays flat affect may continue to privately feel strong emotion. T or F?
5. Extremely psychotic behavior tends to occur in brief episodes. T or F?
6. Psychosis usually occurs without warning. T or F?
7. A brief reactive psychosis rarely lasts more than a week. T or F?
8. Severe brain injuries sometimes cause functional psychoses. T or F?
9. Children must eat leaded paint flakes before they are at risk for lead poisoning. T or F?
10. Roughly 80 percent of all cases of Alzheimer's disease are genetic. T or F?

Check Your Memory: Page 588

11. In delusional disorders, people have auditory hallucinations of grandeur or persecution. T or F?
12. Delusions of persecution are a key symptom of paranoid psychosis. T or F?
13. A person who believes that his body is diseased and rotting has a erotomanic type of delusional disorder. T or F?

Check Your Memory: Pages 589-591

14. One person out of 100 will become schizophrenic. T or F?
15. Many of the symptoms of schizophrenia are related to an impairment of selective attention. T or F?
16. Schizophrenia is the most common dissociative psychosis. T or F?
17. People with schizotypal personalities may be eccentric, but they are not psychotic. T or F?
18. Silliness, laughter, and bizarre behavior are common in disorganized schizophrenia. T or F?
19. Disorganized schizophrenia typically first appears after middle age. T or F?
20. Periods of immobility and odd posturing are characteristic of paranoid schizophrenia. T or F?
21. Catatonic schizophrenia is the most common schizophrenic disorder. T or F?
22. At various times, patients may shift from one type of schizophrenia to another. T or F?

Check Your Memory: Pages 591-595

23. Exposure to influenza during pregnancy produces children who are more likely to become schizophrenic later in life. T or F?
24. A double-bind message creates a "no-win" emotional conflict. T or F?
25. If one identical twin is schizophrenic, the other twin has a 46 percent chance of also becoming schizophrenic. T or F?
26. If both parents are schizophrenic, their child has a 46 percent chance of also becoming schizophrenic. T or F?
27. All four of the Genain sisters developed schizophrenia at about the same time. T or F?
28. Heredity is the only way to explain the simultaneous schizophrenia suffered by the Genain quads. T or F?
29. Excess amounts of the neurotransmitter substance PCP are suspected as a cause of schizophrenia. T or F?
30. The brains of schizophrenics tend to have a greater number of dopamine receptors than the brains of normal persons do. T or F?
31. The antipsychotic drug clozapine reduces the number of dopamine receptors in the brain. T or F?
32. PET scans show that the left side of the brain is overactive in schizophrenics. T or F?

Check Your Memory: Pages 596-599

33. The two most basic types of mood disorder are bipolar I and bipolar II. T or F?
34. In bipolar disorders, people experience both mania and depression. T or F?
35. If a person is moderately depressed for at least two weeks, a dysthymic disorder exists. T or F?

36. A cyclothymic disorder is characterized by moderate levels of depression and manic behavior. T or F?
37. Reactive depressions appear to be generated from within, with little connection to external events. T or F?
38. Behavioral theories of depression emphasize the concept of learned helplessness. T or F?
39. Overall, women are twice as likely as men are to become depressed. T or F?
40. SAD is most likely to occur during the winter, in countries lying near the equator. T or F?

Check Your Memory: Pages 599-604

41. Three out of 4 schizophrenics recover or improve within 10 years of being diagnosed as psychotic. T or F?
42. Major mental disorders are primarily treated with psychotherapy. T or F?
43. When used for long periods of time, tranquilizers frequently cause tardive dyskinesia. T or F?
44. Two percent of all patients taking clozaril suffer from a serious blood disease. T or F?
45. One problem in taking Prozac is that it increases the risk of suicide. T or F?
46. ECT treatments are usually given in a series of 20 to 30 sessions, occurring once a day. T or F?
47. ECT is most effective when used to treat depression. T or F?
48. The prefrontal lobotomy is the most commonly performed type of psychosurgery today. T or F?
49. Psychosurgeries performed by deep lesioning can be reversed if necessary. T or F?
50. In the approach known as partial hospitalization, patients live at home. T or F?
51. Deinstitutionalization increased the number of homeless persons living in many communities. T or F?
52. Most half-way houses are located in community mental health centers. T or F?

Check Your Memory: APPLICATIONS

53. The greatest number of suicides during a single day take place at New Year's. T or F?
54. More men than women complete suicide. T or F?
55. Suicide rates steadily decline after young adulthood. T or F?
56. Most suicides involve despair, anger, and guilt. T or F?
57. People who threaten suicide rarely actually attempt it—they're just crying wolf. T or F?
58. Only a minority of people who attempt suicide really want to die. T or F?
59. The risk of attempted suicide is high if a person has a concrete, workable plan for doing it. T or F?

Check Your Memory: EXPLORATION

60. Thomas Szasz regards mental illness as the greatest problem facing our society today. T or F?
61. Szasz estimates that 90 percent of the patients in mental hospitals are there voluntarily. T or F?
62. According to Szasz, the only legitimate reason for depriving a person of freedom is for breaking the law. T or F?
63. Recently, several states in the U.S. have made it easier to force the mentally ill into hospitals. T or F?

FINAL SURVEY AND REVIEW

● *What are the general characteristics of psychosis?*

1. _____ is a break in contact with _____.
2. Psychosis is marked by _____ (false beliefs), hallucinations, and _____ changes.

3. Other symptoms of psychosis are disturbed emotions, disturbed _____, and personality _____ .

4. A _____ _____ psychosis may follow extremely stressful life events.

5. An _____ psychosis is based on known injuries or diseases of the brain.

6. Problems of unknown origin are called _____ psychoses.

7. Three common causes of organic psychosis are untreated syphilis (general _____), poisoning, and senile _____ (especially Alzheimer's disease).

● *How do delusional disorders differ from other forms of psychosis?*

8. A _____ of _____ disorder is based primarily on the presence of delusions.

9. Delusions may concern _____ (personal importance), persecution, infidelity, romantic attraction, or physical _____ .

10. The most common delusional disorder is _____ psychosis. Because they often have intense and irrational delusions of persecution, afflicted persons may be _____ if they believe they are threatened.

● *What forms does schizophrenia take?*

11. _____ is the most frequently occurring psychosis.

12. Schizophrenia is distinguished by a split between thought and _____, and by delusions, hallucinations, and _____ difficulties.

13. Schizophrenia should not be confused with multiple personality disorder which is a non-psychotic _____ disorder.

14. Schizophrenia also should not be confused with _____ personality disorder, which involves gradual withdrawal into isolation from others and odd, _____ behavior.

15. _____ schizophrenia is marked by extreme personality _____ and silly, bizarre, or obscene behavior. Social impairment is usually extreme.

16. _____ schizophrenia is associated with stupor, mutism, waxy _____, and odd postures. Sometimes violent and agitated behavior also occurs.

17. In _____ schizophrenia (the most common type), outlandish delusions of _____ and persecution are coupled with psychotic symptoms and personality breakdown.

18. _____ schizophrenia is the term used to indicate a lack of clear-cut patterns of disturbance.

● *What causes schizophrenia?*

19. Current explanations of schizophrenia emphasize a combination of _____ stress, inherited susceptibility, and _____ abnormalities in the body or brain.

20. A number of _____ factors appear to increase the risk of developing schizophrenia. These include viral infection during the mother's pregnancy and birth complications.

21. Early _____ trauma and a disturbed family environment, especially one marked by _____ communication, also increase the risk of schizophrenia.

22. Studies of twins and other close relatives strongly support _____ as a major factor in schizophrenia.
23. Recent biochemical studies have focused on abnormalities in brain transmitter substances, especially _____ and its _____ sites.
24. Additional abnormalities in brain structure or function have been detected in schizophrenic brains by the use of _____ scans, _____ scans, and _____ scans.
25. The dominant explanation of schizophrenia is the stress-_____ model.

● *What are mood disorders? What causes depression?*

26. Mood disorders primarily involve disturbances of _____ or emotion, producing _____ (agitated, elated, hyperactive) or depressive (sad, apathetic, suicidal) states.
27. Long-lasting, though relatively moderate, depression is called a _____ disorder.
28. Chronic, though moderate, swings in mood between depression and elation are called a _____ disorder.
29. _____ depressions are often triggered by external events; however, they are more intense or prolonged than normal reactions to similar events.
30. _____ disorders are major mood disorders that combine mania and depression.
31. In a _____ _____ disorder the person is mostly manic, but has had at least one major depression.
32. In a _____ _____ disorder the person is mostly depressed, but has had at least one manic episode.
33. The problem known as _____ _____ disorder involves extreme sadness and despondency, but no evidence of mania.
34. When a major mood disorder is accompanied by psychotic symptoms, it is called an _____ _____.
35. Major mood disorders more often appear to be _____ (produced from within) rather than reactions to external events.
36. Seasonal _____ disorder (SAD), which occurs during the winter months is another common form of depression. SAD is typically treated with _____ (exposure to bright light).
37. _____, psychoanalytic, _____, and behavioral theories of depression have been proposed. Heredity is clearly a factor in susceptibility to mood disorders.

● *How are major mental disorders treated?*

38. Three somatic approaches to treatment of psychosis are _____ (use of drugs), _____ therapy (ECT), and psychosurgery.
39. _____ is any psychological treatment for behavioral or emotional problems. Major mental disorders are more often treated medically.
40. Pharmacotherapy is done with minor tranquilizers (anti-anxiety drugs), _____ (which control delusions and hallucinations), and _____ (mood elevators).
41. All psychiatric drugs involve a trade-off between risks and _____.
42. Psychiatric _____ is often associated with the administration of somatic therapy, and it is also considered a form of treatment.

43. Prolonged hospitalization has been discouraged by _____ (reduced use of commitment to treat mental disorders) and by partial-hospitalization policies.

44. _____ houses within the community can help people make the transition from a hospital or institution to independent living.

45. _____ _____ health centers were created to help avoid or minimize hospitalization.

46. These centers also have as their goal the _____ of mental health problems through education, consultation, and crisis _____.

● *Why do people commit suicide? Can suicide be prevented?*

47. Suicide is _____ related to such factors as age, sex, and marital status.

48. Major _____ _____ for suicide include drug or alcohol abuse, a prior attempt, depression, hopelessness, _____ behavior, suicide by relatives, shame, failure, or rejection, and the availability of a firearm.

49. In individual cases the potential for suicide is best identified by a desire to escape, unbearable psychological _____, _____ psychological needs, and a constriction of options.

50. Suicidal thoughts usually precede suicide _____, which progress to suicide _____.

51. Suicide can often be prevented by the efforts of family, friends, and mental health professionals to establish communication and _____ with the person, and by gaining day-by-day _____ from her or him.

● *What does it mean to be "crazy"? What should be done about it?*

52. Thomas Szasz has raised challenging questions about the nature of _____ behavior and its relationship to personal responsibility and _____ rights.

53. Szasz rejects the _____ model of mental illness that treats emotional problems as diseases with _____ that can be cured.

54. Public policies concerning treatment of the chronically _____ _____ continue to evolve as authorities try to strike a balance between providing help and taking away personal freedom.

MASTERY TEST

1. Word salad is to communication as flat affect is to
   a. emotion b. sensation c. cognition d. personality

2. A person is at greatest risk of becoming schizophrenic if he or she has
   a. schizophrenic parents b. a schizophrenic fraternal twin c. a schizophrenic mother
   d. a schizophrenic sibling

3. Deep lesioning is a form of
   a. ECT b. psychosurgery c. pharmacotherapy d. PET

4. Thomas Szasz is especially opposed to the _____ model of emotional problems.
a. moral b. criminal c. behavioral d. medical

5. All antipsychotic drugs block the action of _____ in the brain.
a. clozapine b. reserpine c. dopamine d. lithium receptors

6. Which of the following refers to a personality disorder?
a. catatonic b. schizotypal c. dysthymic d. disorganized

7. The problem that is most likely to be endogenous is
a. a major depressive disorder b. SAD c. a reactive depression d. maternal bipolar disorder

8. Partial hospitalization shares some of the same goals as
a. psychosurgery b. deinstitutionalization c. involuntary commitment d. paraprofessional staffing

9. In the stress-vulnerability model of psychosis, vulnerability is primarily attributed to
a. heredity b. exposure to influenza c. psychological trauma d. disturbed family life

10. Somatic, reference, grandeur, and influence are types of
a. hallucinations b. delusions c. schizophrenia d. personality disorders

11. Brain scans show that the brains of schizophrenics tend to display
a. smaller fissures, enlarged ventricles, overactive right brain b. enlarged fissures, shrunken ventricles, overactive right brain c. enlarged fissures, enlarged ventricles, overactive left brain d. enlarged fissures, shrunken ventricles, overactive left brain

12. A sudden psychotic break that lasts less than a month is most typical of
a. schizophrenia b. an affective psychosis c. paranoid psychosis d. a reactive psychosis

13. Phototherapy is used primarily to treat
a. postseasonal depression b. SAD c. catatonic depression d. affective psychoses

14. Which of the following is NOT characteristic of suicidal thinking?
a. desires to escape b. psychological pain c. frustrated needs d. too many options

15. An example of what is meant by deviant communication is a _____ message.
a. double-bind b. pseudo-disturbed c. bipolar d. mood-reactive

16. _____ explanations of depression emphasize repressed anger, self-blame, and self-hate.
a. Psychoanalytic b. Behavioral c. Cognitive d. Endogenous

17. Which of the following is NOT used to treat depression?
a. Prozac b. ECT c. Clozaril d. lithium chloride

18. A person who displays personality disintegration, waxy flexibility, and delusions of persecution suffers from _____ schizophrenia.
a. disorganized b. catatonic c. paranoid d. undifferentiated

19. A psychosis caused by mercury poisoning would be classified as
    a. an organic disorder   b. general paresis   c. toxic Alzheimer's disease   d. a functional disorder

20. A patient believes that she has mysterious disease that is causing her body to "rot away." What type of delusion is she suffering from?
    a. depressive   b. somatic   c. reference   d. persecution

21. Tardive dyskinesia is a potential side effect of
    a. pharmacotherapy   b. antidepressants   c. ECT   d. Prozac

22. The principal problem in paranoid psychosis is
    a. delusions   b. hallucinations   c. disturbed emotions   d. personality disintegration

23. Cyclothymic disorder is most closely related to
    a. reactive depression   b. major depressive disorder   c. bipolar disorder   d. SAD

24. A split between thought and emotion is most characteristic of
    a. bipolar disorders   b. delusional disorders   c. dysthymia   d. schizophrenia

25. Manic behavior would most often be observed in a person suffering from a
    a. bipolar I disorder   b. bipolar II disorder   c. major depression   d. reactive mood disorder

ANSWERS

Recite and Review

1. break
2. hallucinations
3. personality
4. stressful
5. diseases
6. unknown
7. organic, senile
8. delusions
9. persecution, romantic
10. persecution
11. psychosis
12. split, thought
13. personality, psychotic
14. withdrawal, odd
15. personality, Social
16. mutism, waxy
17. persecution
18. lack

19. stress, abnormalities
20. infection, birth
21. trauma, family
22. twins
23. transmitter
24. activity
25. stress
26. emotion, depressive
27. depression
28. depression, elation
29. external, intense
30. major mood
31. manic
32. depressed
33. mania
34. psychotic
35. within, external
36. Seasonal, winter
37. behavioral
38. somatic, drugs, brain

39. Major mental
40. minor, hallucinations, mood
41. risks
42. somatic
43. partial
44. houses, independent
45. hospitalization
46. crisis
47. Suicide
48. alcohol, firearm
49. escape, options
50. thoughts
51. communication
52. responsibility
53. diseases
54. freedom

Relate

1. i
2. a
3. j
4. f
5. c
6. b
7. d
8. g
9. e
10. h
11. c
12. e
13. h
14. a
15. j
16. g
17. i
18. b
19. f
20. d
21. f
22. i
23. b
24. a
25. j
26. c
27. h
28. d
29. e
30. g

Check Your Memory

1. F
2. T
3. F
4. T
5. T
6. F
7. F
8. F
9. F
10. F
11. F
12. T
13. F
14. T
15. T
16. F
17. T
18. T
19. F
20. F
21. F
22. T
23. T
24. T
25. T
26. T
27. F
28. F
29. F
30. T
31. F
32. T
33. F
34. T
35. F
36. T
37. F
38. T
39. T
40. F
41. T
42. F
43. F
44. T
45. F
46. F
47. T
48. F
49. F
50. T
51. T
52. F
53. T
54. T
55. F
56. T
57. F
58. T
59. T
60. F
61. F
62. T
63. T

Final Survey and Review

1. Psychosis, reality
2. delusions, sensory
3. communication, disintegration
4. brief reactive
5. organic
6. functional
7. paresis, dementia
8. diagnosis, delusional
9. grandeur, disease
10. paranoid, violent
11. Schizophrenia
12. emotion, communication
13. dissociative
14. schizotypal, apathetic
15. Disorganized, disintegration
16. Catatonic, flexibility
17. paranoid, grandeur
18. Undifferentiated
19. environmental, biochemical
20. environmental
21. psychological, deviant
22. heredity
23. dopamine, receptor
24. CT, MRI, PET
25. vulnerability
26. mood, manic
27. dysthymic
28. cyclothymic
29. Reactive
30. Bipolar
31. bipolar I
32. bipolar II
33. major depressive
34. affective psychosis
35. endogenous
36. affective, phototherapy
37. Biological, cognitive
38. pharmacotherapy, electroconvulsive
39. Psychotherapy
40. antipsychotics, antidepressants
41. benefits
42. hospitalization
43. deinstitutionalization
44. Half-way
45. Community mental
46. prevention, intervention
47. statistically
48. risk factors, antisocial

49. pain, frustrated
50. threats, attempts
51. rapport, commitments
52. abnormal, civil
53. medical, symptoms
54. mentally ill

Mastery Test

1. a (p. 585-586)
2. a (p. 591)
3. b (p. 602)
4. d (p. 608)
5. c (p. 594)
6. b (p. 589)
7. a (p. 597)
8. b (p. 602-603)
9. a (p. 595)
10. b (p. 585)
11. c (p. 594-595)
12. d (p. 586)
13. b (p. 598)
14. d (p. 607)
15. a (p. 591)
16. a (p. 597)
17. c (p. 601)
18. d (p. 590)
19. a (p. 586)
20. b (p. 585)
21. a (p. 601)
22. a (p. 588)
23. c (p. 596)
24. d (p. 589)
25. a (p. 596)

Chapter 19

Therapies

CHAPTER OVERVIEW

Psychotherapies may be classified as individual, group, insight, action, directive, non-directive, or supportive, and combinations of these. Primitive and superstitious approaches to mental illness have included trepanning and demonology. More humane treatment began in 1793 with the work of Philippe Pinel in Paris.

Freudian psychoanalysis seeks to release repressed thoughts and emotions from the unconscious. Short-term dynamic therapy has largely replaced traditional psychoanalysis.

Client-centered (or person-centered) therapy is a non-directive humanistic technique dedicated to creating an atmosphere of growth. Existential therapies focus on the meaning life choices. Gestalt therapy attempts to rebuild thinking, feeling, and acting into connected wholes.

Behavior therapists use behavior modification techniques such as aversion therapy, systematic desensitization, operant shaping, extinction, and token economies.

Cognitive therapists attempt to change troublesome thought patterns. In rational-emotive therapy, clients learn to recognize and challenge their own irrational beliefs.

Group therapies, such as psychodrama and family therapy, may be based on individual therapy methods or special group techniques. Sensitivity groups, encounter groups, and large-group awareness trainings also try to promote constructive changes.

All psychotherapies offer a caring relationship, emotional rapport, a protected setting, catharsis, explanations for one's problems, a new perspective, and a chance to practice new behaviors.

Cognitive and behavioral techniques such as covert sensitization, thought stopping, covert reinforcement, and desensitization can aid self-management. In most communities, competent therapists can be located through public sources or by referrals.

Many cultural barriers to effective counseling and therapy have been identified. Aware therapists are beginning to seek out the knowledge and skills needed to intervene successfully in the lives of clients from diverse cultural backgrounds.

RECITE AND REVIEW

● *How do psychotherapies differ?*

Recite and Review: Pages 612-614

1. Psychotherapy is any psychological technique used to facilitate _____ changes in a person's personality, _____, or adjustment.
2. _____ therapies seek to produce personal understanding. Action therapies try to directly change troublesome thoughts, feelings, or behaviors.
3. Directive therapists provide strong _____. Non-directive therapists assist, but do not _____ their clients.
4. Supportive therapies provide on-going support, rather than actively promoting personal _____.
5. Therapies may be conducted either individually or in groups, and they may be _____ limited (restricted to a set number of sessions).

● *How did modern therapies originate?*

Recite and Review: Pages 614-615

6. Primitive approaches to mental illness were often based on _____.
7. Trepanning involved boring a hole in the _____.
8. Demonology attributed mental disturbance to supernatural forces and prescribed _____ as the cure.
9. In some instances, the actual cause of bizarre behavior may have been ergotism or _____ fungus _____.
10. More humane treatment began in 1793 with the work of Philippe Pinel who created the first _____ _____ in Paris.

● *Is Freudian psychoanalysis still used?*

Recite and Review: Pages 615-617

11. Sigmund Freud's psychoanalysis was the first formal _____.
12. Psychoanalysis was designed to treat cases of hysteria (physical symptoms without known _____ causes).
13. Psychoanalysis seeks to release repressed thoughts, memories, and emotions from the _____ and resolve _____ conflicts.
14. The psychoanalyst uses _____ association, _____ analysis, and analysis of resistance and transference to reveal health-producing insights.
15. Some critics have argued that traditional psychoanalysis may frequently receive credit for _____ remissions of symptoms. However, psychoanalysis has been shown to be better than no treatment at all.
16. _____ dynamic therapy (which relies on psychoanalytic theory but is brief and focused) is as effective as other major therapies.

● *What are the major humanistic therapies?*

Recite and Review: Pages 618-620

17. _____ therapies try to help people live up to their potentials and to give tendencies for mental health to emerge.

18. Carl Rogers' client-centered (or _____-centered) therapy is non-directive and is dedicated to creating an atmosphere of _____.

19. In client-centered therapy, unconditional _____ regard, _____ (feeling what another is feeling), authenticity, and reflection are combined to give the client a chance to solve his or her own problems.

20. Existential therapies, such as Victor Frankl's logotherapy, focus on the end result of the _____ one makes in life.

21. Clients in existential therapy are encouraged through confrontation and encounter to exercise free _____, to take responsibility for their _____, and to find _____ in their lives.

22. Frederick Perls' Gestalt therapy emphasizes immediate _____ of thoughts and feelings.

23. The goal of Gestalt therapy is to rebuild thinking, feeling, and acting into connected _____ and to help clients break through emotional blocks.

● *What is aversion therapy?*

Recite and Review: Pages 620-622

24. Behavior therapists use various behavior modification techniques that apply _____ principles to change human behavior.

25. Classical conditioning is a basic form of _____ in which existing reflex responses are _____ with new conditioned stimuli.

26. In aversion therapy, classical conditioning is used to associate maladaptive behavior with _____ or other aversive events in order to inhibit undesirable responses.

27. To be most effective, aversive _____ must be response-contingent (closely connected with responses).

● *How is behavior therapy used to treat phobias, fears, and anxieties?*

Recite and Review: Pages 622-625

28. Classical conditioning also underlies _____ desensitization, a technique used to reduce fears, phobias, and anxieties.

29. In desensitization, gradual _____ and reciprocal inhibition break the link between fear and particular situations.

30. Typical steps in desensitization are: Construct a fear hierarchy; learn to produce total _____; and perform items on the hierarchy (from least to most disturbing).

31. Desensitization may be carried out in real settings or it may be done by vividly _____ scenes from the fear hierarchy.

32. Desensitization is also effective when it is administered vicariously; that is, when clients watch _____ perform the feared responses.

33. In a newly developed technique, virtual _____ exposure is used to present _____ stimuli to patients undergoing desensitization.

34. Another new technique called eye-movement desensitization shows promise as a treatment for traumatic _____ and _____ disorders.

● *What role does reinforcement play in behavior therapy?*

Recite and Review: Pages 625-628

35. Behavior modification also makes use of operant principles, such as positive reinforcement, non-reinforcement, extinction, punishment, shaping, stimulus _____, and _____ out.

36. Non-reward can extinguish troublesome behaviors. Often this is done by simply identifying and eliminating _____.

37. Time out is an extinction technique in which attention and approval are withheld following undesirable _____.

38. Time out can also be done by _____ a person from the setting in which misbehavior occurs, so that it will not be reinforced.

39. To apply positive reinforcement and operant shaping, symbolic rewards known as tokens are often used. Tokens allow _____ reinforcement of selected target _____.

40. Full-scale use of _____ in an institutional setting produces a token economy.

41. Toward the end of a token economy program, patients are shifted to social rewards such as recognition and _____.

● *Can therapy change thoughts and emotions?*

Recite and Review: Pages 628-629

42. Cognitive therapy emphasizes changing _____ patterns that underlie emotional or behavioral problems.

43. The goals of cognitive therapy are to correct distorted thinking and/or teach improved coping _____.

44. Aron Beck's cognitive therapy for depression corrects major distortions in thinking, including _____ perception, overgeneralization, and all-or-nothing _____.

45. In a variation of cognitive therapy called rational-emotive behavior therapy (REBT), clients learn to recognize and challenge their own irrational _____ which lead to upsetting consequences.

● *Can psychotherapy be done with groups of people?*

Recite and Review: Pages 630-633

46. Group therapy may be a simple extension of _____ methods or it may be based on techniques developed specifically for groups.

47. In psychodrama, individuals use _____ playing, _____ reversals, and the mirror technique to gain insight into incidents resembling their real-life problems.

48. In family therapy, the family group is treated as a _____ so that the entire _____ system is changed for the better.

49. Although they are not literally _____, sensitivity groups and encounter groups attempt to encourage positive personality change.
50. In recent years, commercially offered large-group awareness _____ have become popular.
51. The therapeutic benefits of large-group techniques are questionable and may reflect nothing more than a _____ placebo effect.
52. Media psychologists, such as those found on the radio are supposed to restrict themselves to _____ listeners, rather than actually doing _____.
53. Telephone therapists and cybertherapists working on the _____ may or may not be competent. Even if they are, their effectiveness may be severely limited.

● *What do various therapies have in common?*

Recite and Review: Pages 633-636

54. To alleviate personal problems, all psychotherapies offer a caring relationship and _____ rapport in a protected _____.
55. All therapies encourage catharsis and they provide explanations for the client's _____.
56. In addition, psychotherapy provides a new perspective and a chance to practice new _____.
57. Many basic _____ skills are used in therapy. These include listening actively and helping to clarify the problem.
58. Effective therapists also focus on feelings and avoid giving unwanted _____.
59. It helps to accept the person's perspective, to reflect thoughts and feelings, and to be patient during _____.
60. In counseling it is important to use _____ questions when possible and to maintain confidentiality.

● *How are behavioral principles applied to everyday problems? How would a person go about finding professional help?*

Recite and Review: APPLICATIONS

61. In covert sensitization, aversive _____ are used to discourage unwanted behavior.
62. Thought stopping uses mild _____ to prevent upsetting thoughts.
63. Covert reinforcement is a way to encourage desired _____ by mental rehearsal.
64. Desensitization pairs _____ with a hierarchy of upsetting images in order to lessen fears.
65. In most communities, a competent and reputable therapist can usually be located through public sources of information or by a _____.
66. Practical considerations such as _____ and qualifications enter into choosing a therapist. However, the therapist's personal characteristics are of equal importance.
67. Self-help groups and bibliotherapy (use of self-help _____) can sometimes add valuable support to professional treatment.

● *Do cultural differences affect counseling and psychotherapy?*

Recite and Review: EXPLORATION

68. Many _____ barriers to effective counseling and therapy exist.

69. Culturally skilled _____ have the knowledge and skills needed to intervene successfully in the lives of clients from diverse cultural backgrounds.

70. The culturally skilled counselor must be able to establish rapport with a person from a _____ cultural background and adapt traditional theories and techniques to meet the needs of clients from non-European ethnic or racial groups.

RELATE

1. _____	trepanning	a. tainted rye
2. _____	exorcism	b. old relationships
3. _____	ergotism	c. hysteria
4. _____	Pinel	d. reflection
5. _____	Freud	e. waiting list control
6. _____	dream analysis	f. client-centered
7. _____	transference	g. Bicêtre
8. _____	spontaneous remission	h. latent content
9. _____	Rogers	i. possession
10. _____	rephrasing	j. release of evil spirits

11. _____	authenticity	a. meaning
12. _____	existentialist	b. operant extinction
13. _____	logotherapy	c. no facades
14. _____	Gestalt therapy	d. thinking error
15. _____	rapid smoking	e. being in the world
16. _____	desensitization	f. token economy
17. _____	time out	g. whole experiences
18. _____	target behaviors	h. aversion therapy
19. _____	overgeneralization	i. irrational beliefs
20. _____	REBT	j. fear hierarchy

21. _____	psychodrama	a. public education
22. _____	family therapy	b. enhanced self-awareness
23. _____	sensitivity group	c. emotional release
24. _____	encounter group	d. positive imagery
25. _____	media psychologist	e. shared problems
26. _____	therapeutic alliance	f. systems approach
27. _____	catharsis	g. aversive imagery
28. _____	covert sensitization	h. role reversals
29. _____	covert reinforcement	i. caring relationship
30. _____	self-help group	j. intense interactions

CHECK YOUR MEMORY

Check Your Memory: Pages 612-614

1. A particular psychotherapy could be both insight- and action-oriented. T or F?
2. With the help of psychotherapy, chances of improvement are fairly good for phobias and low self-esteem. T or F?
3. Psychotherapy is sometimes used to encourage personal growth for people who are already functioning well. T or F?
4. Personal autonomy, a sense of identity, and feelings of personal worth are elements of mental health. T or F?

Check Your Memory: Pages 614-615

5. Trepanning was really an excuse to kill people since none of the patients survived. T or F?
6. Exorcism sometimes took the form of physical torture. T or F?
7. Trepanning was the most common treatment for ergotism. T or F?
8. Pinel was the first person to successfully treat ergotism. T or F?
9. The problem Freud called hysteria is now called a somatoform disorder. T or F?

Check Your Memory: Pages 615-617

10. During free association, patients try to remember the earliest events in their lives. T or F?
11. Freud called transference the royal road to the unconscious. T or F?
12. The manifest content of a dream is its surface or visible meaning. T or F?
13. In an analysis of resistance, the psychoanalyst tries to understand a client's resistance to forming satisfying relationships. T or F?
14. Therapists use direct interviewing as part of short-term dynamic therapy. T or F?
15. If members of a waiting list control group improve at the same rate as people in therapy, it demonstrates that the therapy is effective. T or F?

Check Your Memory: Pages 618-620

16. Through client-centered therapy, Carl Rogers sought to explore unconscious thoughts and feelings. T or F?
17. The client-centered therapist does not hesitate to react with shock, dismay, or disapproval to a client's inappropriate thoughts or feelings. T or F?
18. In a sense, the person-centered therapist acts as a psychological mirror for clients. T or F?
19. Existential therapy emphasizes our ability to freely make choices. T or F?
20. According to the existentialists, our choices must be courageous. T or F?
21. Logotherapy emphasizes the integration of fragmented experiences into connected wholes. T or F?
22. Fritz Perls was an originator of logotherapy. T or F?
23. Gestalt therapy may be done individually or in a group. T or F?
24. Gestalt therapists urge clients to intellectualize their feelings. T or F?

Check Your Memory: Pages 620-622

25. Aversion therapy is based primarily on operant conditioning. T or F?

26. For many children, the sight of a hypodermic needle becomes a conditioned stimulus for fear because it is often followed by pain. T or F?
27. Rapid smoking creates an aversion because people must hyperventilate to smoke at the prescribed rate. T or F?
28. About one half of all people who quit smoking begin again. T or F?
29. In aversion therapy for alcohol abuse, the delivery of shock must appear to be response-contingent to be most effective. T or F?
30. Poor generalization of conditioned aversions to situations outside of therapy can be problem. T or F?

Check Your Memory: Pages 622-625

31. During desensitization, the steps of a hierarchy are used to produce deep relaxation. T or F?
32. Relaxation is the key ingredient of reciprocal inhibition. T or F?
33. Clients typically begin with the most disturbing item in a desensitization hierarchy. T or F?
34. Desensitization is most effective when people are directly exposed to feared stimuli. T or F?
35. Live or filmed models are used in vicarious desensitization. T or F?
36. During eye-movement desensitization, clients concentrate on pleasant, calming images. T or F?

Check Your Memory: Pages 625-628

37. Operant punishment is basically the same thing as non-reinforcement. T or F?
38. Shaping involves reinforcing ever closer approximations to a desired response. T or F?
39. An undesirable response can be extinguished by reversing stimulus control. T or F?
40. In elementary school, misbehavior by students tends to decrease when teachers ignore it. T or F?
41. To be effective, tokens must be tangible rewards, such as slips of paper or poker chips. T or F?
42. The value of tokens is based on the fact that they can be exchanged for other reinforcers. T or F?
43. A goal of token economies is to eventually switch patients to social reinforcers.

Check Your Memory: Pages 628-629

44. Cognitive therapy is especially successful in treating depression. T or F?
45. Depressed persons tend to magnify the importance of events. T or F?
46. Cognitive therapy is as effective as drugs for treating many cases of depression. T or F?
47. Stress inoculation is a form of rational-emotive behavior therapy. T or F?
48. The A in the ABC analysis of REBT stands for "anticipation." T or F?
49. The C in the ABC analysis of REBT stands for "consequence." T or F?

Check Your Memory: Pages 630-633

50. The mirror technique is the principal method used in family therapy. T or F?
51. Family therapists try to meet with the entire family unit during each session of therapy. T or F?
52. A "trust walk" is a typical sensitivity group exercise. T or F?
53. Sensitivity groups attempt to tear down defenses and false fronts. T or F?
54. Large-group awareness training has been known to create emotional crises where none existed before. T or F?
55. The APA suggests that media psychologists should discuss only problems of a general nature. T or F?

Check Your Memory: Pages 633-636

56. Half of all people who begin psychotherapy feel better after 8 sessions. T or F?

57. Emotional rapport is a key feature of the therapeutic alliance. T or F?

58. Therapy gives clients a chance to practice new behaviors. T or F?

59. Competent counselors do not hesitate to criticize clients, place blame when it is deserved, and probe painful topics. T or F?

60. "Why don't you . . . Yes, but . . ." is a common game used to avoid taking responsibility in therapy. T or F?

61. Closed questions tend to be most helpful in counseling another person. T or F?

Check Your Memory: APPLICATIONS

62. Disgusting images are used in thought stopping. T or F?

63. To do covert sensitization, you must first learn relaxation exercises. T or F?

64. Covert reinforcement should be visualized before performing steps in a fear hierarchy. T or F?

65. The tension-release method is used to produce deep relaxation. T or F?

66. Significant changes in your work, relationships, or use of drugs or alcohol can be signs that you should seek professional help. T or F?

67. Marital problems are the most common reason for seeing a mental health professional. T or F?

68. For some problems, paraprofessional counselors and self-help groups are as effective as professional psychotherapy. T or F?

69. All major types of psychotherapy are about equally successful. T or F?

Check Your Memory: EXPLORATION

70. Cultural barriers to effective counseling include differences in language, social class, and non-verbal communication. T or F?

71. A necessary step toward becoming a culturally skilled counselor is to adopt the culture of your clients as your own. T or F?

72. Multicultural counselors must be aware of their clients' degree of acculturation. T or F?

73. Cultural barriers to successful counseling include differences in age, sexual orientation, handicaps, and religion. T or F?

FINAL SURVEY AND REVIEW

● *How do psychotherapies differ?*

1. _____ is any psychological technique used to facilitate positive changes in a person's _____, behavior, or adjustment.

2. Insight therapies seek to produce personal understanding. _____ therapies try to directly change troublesome thoughts, feelings, or behaviors.

3. _____ therapists provide strong guidance. _____ therapists assist, but do not guide their clients.

4. _____ therapies provide on-going assistance, rather than actively promoting personal change.

5. Therapies may be conducted either _____ or in _____, and they may be time _____ (restricted to a set number of sessions).

● *How did modern therapies originate?*

6. _____ approaches to mental illness were often based on superstition.

7. _____ involved boring a hole in the skull.

8. _____ attributed mental disturbance to supernatural forces and prescribed exorcism as the cure.

9. In some instances, the actual cause of bizarre behavior may have been _____, a type of _____ poisoning.

10. More humane treatment began in 1793 with the work of Philippe _____ who created the first mental hospital in _____.

● *Is Freudian psychoanalysis still used?*

11. Sigmund _____ _____ was the first formal psychotherapy.

12. Psychoanalysis was designed to treat cases of _____ (physical symptoms without known physical causes).

13. Psychoanalysis seeks to release _____ thoughts, memories, and emotions from the unconscious and resolve unconscious conflicts.

14. The psychoanalyst uses free _____, dream analysis, and analysis of _____ and transference to reveal health-producing insights.

15. Some critics have argued that traditional psychoanalysis may frequently receive credit for spontaneous _____ of symptoms. However, psychoanalysis has been shown to be better than no treatment at all.

16. Short-term _____ therapy (which relies on _____ theory but is brief and focused) is as effective as other major therapies.

● *What are the major humanistic therapies?*

17. Humanistic therapies try to help people live up to their _____ and to give tendencies for mental health to emerge.

18. Carl _____ client-centered (or person-centered) therapy is non-_____ and is dedicated to creating an atmosphere of growth.

19. In client-centered therapy, _____ positive regard, empathy, authenticity, and _____ (restating thoughts and feelings) are combined to give the client a chance to solve his or her own problems.

20. _____ therapies, such as Victor Frankl's _____, focus on the end result of the choices one makes in life.

21. Clients in existential therapy are encouraged through _____ and _____ to exercise free will, to take responsibility for their choices, and to find meaning in their lives.

22. Frederick Perls' _____ therapy emphasizes immediate awareness of thoughts and feelings.

23. The goal of Perls' approach is to rebuild thinking, feeling, and acting into connected wholes and to help clients break through _____ _____.

● *What is aversion therapy?*

24. _____ therapists use various behavior _____ techniques that apply learning principles to change human behavior.
25. _____ conditioning is a basic form of learning in which existing _____ responses are associated with new conditioned stimuli.
26. In _____ therapy, classical conditioning is used to associate maladaptive behavior with pain or other unpleasant events in order to inhibit undesirable responses.
27. To be most effective, aversive stimuli must be _____ (closely connected with responses).

● *How is behavior therapy used to treat phobias, fears, and anxieties?*

28. Classical conditioning also underlies systematic _____, a technique used to reduce fears, phobias, and anxieties.
29. In this approach, gradual adaptation and reciprocal _____ break the link between fear and particular situations.
30. Typical steps are: Construct a fear _____; learn to produce total relaxation; and perform items on the _____ (from least to most disturbing).
31. Desensitization may be carried out in real settings or it may be done by vividly imagining scenes from the _____ _____.
32. Desensitization is also effective when it is administered _____; that is, when clients watch models perform the feared responses.
33. In a newly developed technique, _____ reality _____ is used to present fear stimuli to patients undergoing desensitization.
34. Another new technique called _____ desensitization shows promise as a treatment for traumatic memories and stress disorders.

● *What role does reinforcement play in behavior therapy?*

35. Behavior modification also makes use of _____ principles, such as positive reinforcement, non-reinforcement, _____ (eliminating responses), punishment, _____ (molding responses), stimulus control, and time out.
36. _____ can extinguish troublesome behaviors. Often this is done by simply identifying and eliminating reinforcers.
37. Time out is an _____ technique in which attention and approval are withheld following undesirable responses.
38. Time out can also be done by removing a person from the _____ in which misbehavior occurs, so that it will not be _____.
39. To apply positive reinforcement and operant shaping, symbolic rewards known as _____ are often used. These allow immediate reinforcement of selected _____ behaviors.
40. Full-scale use of symbolic rewards in an institutional setting produces a _____ _____.
41. Toward the end of such programs, patients are shifted to _____ rewards such as recognition and approval.

● *Can therapy change thoughts and emotions?*

42. _____ therapy emphasizes changing thinking patterns that underlie emotional or behavioral problems.
43. Its goals are to correct distorted thinking and/or teach improved _____ skills.
44. Aron _____ therapy for depression corrects major distortions in thinking, including selective perception, _____ , and all-or-nothing thinking.
45. In a variation called _____ _____ therapy (REBT), clients learn to recognize and challenge their own irrational beliefs which lead to upsetting consequences.

● *Can psychotherapy be done with groups of people?*

46. _____ therapy may be a simple extension of individual methods or it may be based on techniques developed specifically for _____ _____.
47. In _____, individuals use role playing, role _____, and the mirror technique to gain insight into incidents resembling real-life problems.
48. In _____ therapy, the _____ group is treated as a unit so that the entire family _____ is changed for the better.
49. Although they are not literally psychotherapies, sensitivity groups and _____ groups attempt to encourage positive personality change.
50. In recent years, commercially offered large-group _____ trainings have become popular.
51. The therapeutic benefits of large-group techniques are questionable and may reflect nothing more than a therapy _____ effect.
52. _____ psychologists, such as those found on the radio are supposed to restrict themselves to educating listeners, rather than actually doing therapy.
53. Telephone therapists and _____ working on the Internet may or may not be competent. Even if they are, their effectiveness may be severely limited.

● *What do various therapies have in common?*

54. To alleviate personal problems, all psychotherapies offer a caring relationship and emotional _____ in a _____ setting.
55. All therapies encourage _____ (emotional release) and they provide explanations for the client's problems.
56. In addition, psychotherapy provides a new _____ and a chance to practice new behaviors.
57. Many basic counseling skills are used in therapy. These include listening _____ and helping to _____ the problem.
58. Effective therapists also focus on _____ and avoid giving unwanted advice.
59. It helps to accept the person's _____, to _____ thoughts and feelings, and to be patient during silences.
60. In counseling it is important to use open questions when possible and to maintain _____ .

● *How are behavioral principles applied to everyday problems?*

61. In _____ sensitization, aversive images are used to discourage unwanted behavior.
62. _____ _____ uses mild punishment to prevent upsetting thoughts.
63. Covert _____ is a way to encourage desired responses by mental rehearsal.
64. _____ pairs relaxation with a hierarchy of upsetting images in order to lessen fears.

● *How would a person go about finding professional help?*

65. In most communities, a _____ and reputable therapist can usually be located through public sources of information or by a referral.
66. Practical considerations such as cost and qualifications enter into choosing a therapist. However, the therapist's _____ _____ are of equal importance.
67. _____ groups and _____ (use of self-help books) can sometimes add valuable support to professional treatment.

● *Do cultural differences affect counseling and psychotherapy?*

68. Many cultural _____ to effective counseling and therapy exist.
69. _____ _____ counselors have the knowledge and skills needed to intervene successfully in the lives of clients from diverse cultural backgrounds.
70. The aware counselor must be able to establish _____ with a person from a different cultural background and _____ traditional theories and techniques to meet the needs of clients from non-European ethnic or racial groups.

MASTERY TEST

1. To demonstrate that spontaneous remissions are occurring, you could use a
   a. patient-defined hierarchy   b. waiting list control group   c. target behavior group
   d. short-term dynamic correlation

2. In desensitization, relaxation is induced to block fear, a process known as
   a. systematic adaptation   b. vicarious opposition   c. stimulus control   d. reciprocal inhibition

3. Role reversals and the mirror technique are methods of
   a. psychodrama   b. person-centered therapy   c. family therapy   d. short-term dynamic therapy

4. One thing that both trepanning and exorcism have in common is that both were used
   a. to treat ergotism   b. by Pinel in the Bicêtre Asylum   c. to remove spirits   d. to treat cases of hysteria

5. Unconditional positive regard is a concept particularly associated with
   a. Beck   b. Frankl   c. Perls   d. Rogers

6. Many of the claimed benefits of large-group awareness trainings appear to represent a therapy _____ effect.
   a. remission b. education c. placebo d. transference

7. Personal change is LEAST likely to be the goal of
   a. supportive therapy b. action therapy c. desensitization d. humanistic therapy

8. Which counseling behavior does not belong with the others listed here?
   a. paraphrasing b. judging c. reflecting d. active listening

9. In psychoanalysis, the process most directly opposite to free association is
   a. resistance b. transference c. symbolization d. remission

10. Identification of target behaviors is an important step in designing
    a. a desensitization hierarchy b. activating stimuli c. token economies d. encounter groups

11. A person who wants to lose weight looks at a dessert and visualizes maggots crawling all over it. The person is obviously using
    a. systematic adaptation b. covert sensitization c. stress inoculation d. systematic desensitization

12. Which of the following is NOT a humanistic therapy?
    a. client-centered b. Gestalt c. existential d. cognitive

13. Not many emergency room doctors drive without using their seatbelts. This observation helps explain the effectiveness of
    a. systematic desensitization b. aversion therapy c. covert reinforcement d. the mirror technique

14. Telephone counselors have little chance of using which element of effective psychotherapy?
    a. empathy b. non-directive reflection c. the therapeutic alliance d. accepting the person's frame of reference

15. Which of the following is a self-help technique?
    a. bibliotherapy b. vicarious desensitization c. logotherapy d. systematic adaptation

16. A good example of a non-directive insight therapy is _____ therapy.
    a. client-centered b. Gestalt c. psychoanalytic d. short-term dynamic

17. Which statement about psychotherapy is true?
    a. Most therapists are equally successful. b. Most techniques are equally successful. c. Therapists and clients need not agree about the goals of therapy. d. Effective therapists instruct their clients not to discuss their therapy with anyone else.

18. Analysis of resistances and transferences is a standard feature of
    a. client-centered therapy b. Gestalt therapy c. REBT d. psychoanalysis

19. Both classical and operant conditioning are the basis for
    a. desensitization b. token economies c. behavior therapy d. aversion therapy

20. Rational-emotive behavior therapy is best described as
a. insight, non-directive, individual   b. insight, supportive, individual   c. action, supportive, group
d. action, directive, individual

21. Emotional excitability and apparent physical disabilities are symptoms of what Freud called
a. hypochondria   b. hysteria   c. somatic transference   d. somatization

22. Identifying and removing rewards is a behavioral technique designed to bring about
a. operant shaping   b. extinction   c. respondent aversion   d. token inhibition

23. Culturally skilled counselors must be aware of their own cultural backgrounds, as well as
a. the average level of acculturation in the community   b. that of their clients   c. the importance
of maintaining confidentiality   d. the life goals of minorities

24. A behavioral therapist would treat acrophobia with
a. desensitization   b. aversion therapy   c. covert sensitization   d. logotherapy

25. Which technique most closely relates to the idea of non-directive therapy?
a. confrontation   b. dream analysis   c. role reversal   d. reflection

26. Fifty percent of psychotherapy patients say they feel better after the first _____ sessions.
a. 4   b. 8   c. 12   d. 20

27. Overgeneralization is a thinking error that contributes to
a. depression   b. somatization   c. phobias   d. emotional reprocessing

28. Death, freedom, and meaning are special concerns of
a. REBT   b. cognitive therapy   c. existential therapy   d. psychodrama

29. An intense awareness of present experience and breaking through emotional impasses is the heart of
a. action therapy   b. Gestalt therapy   c. time-limited therapy   d. REBT

30. The ABCs of REBT stand for
a. anticipation, behavior, conduct   b. action, behavior, conflict   c. activating experience,
belief, consequence   d. anticipation, belief, congruent experience

ANSWERS

Recite and Review

1. positive, behavior
2. Insight
3. guidance, guide
4. change
5. time
6. superstition
7. skull
8. exorcism
9. ergot, poisoning
10. mental hospital
11. psychotherapy
12. physical
13. unconscious, unconscious

14. free, dream
15. spontaneous
16. Short-term
17. Humanistic
18. person, growth
19. positive, empathy
20. choices
21. will, choices, meaning
22. awareness
23. wholes
24. learning
25. learning, associated
26. pain
27. stimuli
28. systematic
29. adaptation
30. relaxation
31. imagining
32. models
33. reality, fear
34. memories, stress
35. control, time
36. reinforcers
37. responses
38. removing
39. immediate, behaviors
40. tokens
41. approval
42. thinking
43. skills
44. selective, thinking
45. beliefs
46. individual
47. role, role
48. unit, family
49. psychotherapies
50. trainings
51. therapy
52. educating, therapy
53. Internet
54. emotional, setting
55. problems
56. behaviors
57. counseling
58. advice
59. silences
60. open
61. images
62. punishment
63. responses
64. relaxation
65. referral

66. cost (or fees)
67. books
68. cultural
69. counselors
70. different

Relate

1. j
2. i
3. a
4. g
5. c
6. h
7. b
8. e
9. f
10. d
11. c
12. e
13. a
14. g
15. h
16. j
17. b
18. f
19. d
20. i
21. h
22. f
23. b
24. j
25. a
26. i
27. c
28. g
29. d
30. e

Check Your Memory

1. T
2. T
3. T
4. T
5. F
6. T
7. F
8. F
9. T

10. F
11. F
12. T
13. F
14. T
15. F
16. F
17. F
18. T
19. T
20. T
21. F
22. F
23. T
24. F
25. F
26. T
27. F
28. T
29. T
30. T
31. F
32. T
33. F
34. T
35. T
36. F
37. F
38. T
39. F
40. T
41. F
42. T
43. T
44. T
45. T
46. T
47. F
48. F
49. T
50. F
51. F
52. T
53. F
54. T
55. T
56. T
57. T
58. T
59. F
60. T
61. F

62. F
63. F
64. F
65. T
66. T
67. F
68. T
69. T
70. T
71. F
72. T
73. T

Final Survey and Review

1. Psychotherapy, personality
2. Action
3. Directive, Non-directive
4. Supportive
5. individually, groups, limited
6. Primitive
7. Trepanning
8. Demonology
9. ergotism, fungus
10. Pinel, Paris
11. Freud's, psychoanalysis
12. hysteria
13. repressed
14. association, resistance
15. remissions
16. dynamic, psychoanalytic
17. potentials
18. Rogers', directive
19. unconditional, reflection
20. Existential, logotherapy
21. confrontation, encounter
22. Gestalt
23. emotional blocks
24. Behavior, modification
25. Classical, reflex
26. aversion
27. response-contingent
28. desensitization
29. inhibition
30. hierarchy, hierarchy
31. fear hierarchy
32. vicariously
33. virtual, exposure
34. eye-movement
35. operant, extinction, shaping
36. Non-reward (or non-reinforcement)
37. extinction
38. setting, reinforced
39. tokens, target
40. token economy
41. social
42. Cognitive
43. coping
44. Beck's, overgeneralization
45. rational-emotive behavior
46. Group, groups
47. psychodrama, reversals
48. family, family, system
49. encounter
50. awareness
51. placebo
52. Media
53. cybertherapists
54. rapport, protected
55. catharsis
56. perspective
57. actively, clarify
58. feelings
59. perspective, reflect
60. confidentiality
61. covert
62. Thought stopping
63. reinforcement
64. Desensitization
65. competent
66. personal characteristics
67. Self-help, bibliotherapy
68. barriers
69. Culturally skilled
70. rapport, adapt

Mastery Test

1. b (p. 617)
2. d (p. 623)
3. a (p. 630)
4. c (p. 614)
5. d (p. 618)
6. c (p. 631)
7. a (p. 614)
8. b (p. 635)
9. a (p. 615-616)
10. c (p. 627)
11. b (p. 637-638)
12. d (p. 618-619)
13. b (p. 621)
14. c (p. 632)
15. a (p. 641)
16. a (p. 618, 634)
17. b (p. 642)
18. d (p. 616)
19. c (p. 620)
20. d (p. 629, 634)
21. b (p. 615)
22. b (p. 626)
23. b (p. 643-644)
24. a (p. 623)
25. d (p. 618)
26. b (p. 633)
27. a (p. 628)
28. c (p. 619)
29. b (p. 619)
30. c (p. 629)

Chapter 20

Social Behavior

CHAPTER OVERVIEW

Social psychology is the study of individual behavior in social situations. Social roles, status, group structure, norms, and group cohesiveness influence interpersonal behavior.

Attribution theory summarizes how we make inferences about behavior. The fundamental attributional error is to ascribe the actions of others to internal causes, while attributing our own behavior to external causes.

The need to affiliate is related to needs for approval, support, friendship, information, and desires to reduce anxiety or uncertainty. Social comparison theory holds that we affiliate to evaluate our actions, feelings, and abilities. Interpersonal attraction is increased by physical proximity, frequent contact, physical attractiveness, competence, and similarity. Self-disclosure, which follows a reciprocity norm, occurs more when two people like one another. According to social exchange theory, we tend to maintain relationships that are profitable. Romantic love can be distinguished from liking by the use of attitude scales. Adult love relationships tend to mirror patterns of emotional attachment observed in infancy and early childhood. Evolutionary psychology attributes human mating patterns to the reproductive challenges faced by men and women since the dawn of time.

Social influence refers to alterations in behavior brought about by the behavior of others. Examples are conformity, groupthink, and obedience to authority. Social influence is also related to five types of social power: reward power, coercive power, legitimate power, referent power, and expert power. Compliance with direct requests is another means by which behavior is influenced.

Self-assertion, as opposed to aggression, involves clearly stating one's wants and needs to others. Learning to be assertive is accomplished by role-playing, rehearsing assertive actions, overlearning, and use of specific techniques, such as the "broken record."

A social trap is a social situation in which immediately rewarded actions have undesired effects in the long run.

RECITE AND REVIEW

● *How does group membership affect individual behavior?*

Recite and Review: Pages 647-650

1. Social psychology studies how individuals behave, think, and feel in _____ situations.

2. Culture provides a broad social context for our behavior. One's position in _____ defines a variety of roles to be played.

3. _____ _____, which may be achieved or ascribed, are particular behavior patterns associated with social positions.

4. When two or more _____ roles are held, role conflict may occur.

5. The Stanford _____ experiment showed that destructive roles may override individual motives for behavior.

6. Positions within _____ typically carry higher or lower levels of status. High status is associated with special privileges and respect.

7. Group structure refers to the organization of _____, communication pathways, and power within a group.

8. Group cohesiveness is basically the degree of _____ among group members.

9. Norms are _____ of conduct enforced (formally or informally) by _____.

10. The autokinetic effect (the illusion of _____ in a stationary light in a darkened room) has been used to demonstrate that norms rapidly form even in _____ groups.

● *What unspoken rules govern the use of personal space?*

Recite and Review: Pages 650-651

11. The study of _____ _____ is called proxemics.

12. Four basic spatial zones around each person's body are intimate distance (0-18 inches), _____ distance (1.5-4 feet), _____ distance (4-12 feet), and public distance (12 feet or more).

13. Norms for the use of personal space vary considerably in various _____.

● *How do we perceive the motives of others, and the causes of our own behavior?*

Recite and Review: Pages 652-654

14. Attribution theory is concerned with how we make inferences about the _____ of behavior.

15. Behavior can be attributed to internal _____ or external _____.

16. To infer _____ we take into account the _____, the object of the action, and the setting in which the action occurs.

17. The _____ of behavior on different occasions and its distinctiveness (whether it occurs only in certain circumstances) affect the attributions we make.

18. Situational demands tend to cause us to discount _____ causes as explanations of someone's behavior.

19. Consensus in behavior (in which many people act alike) implies that their behavior has an _____ cause.

20. The fundamental attributional _____ is to ascribe the actions of others to _____ causes, while attributing your own behavior to _____ causes.

21. Self-handicapping involves arranging excuses for poor _____ as a way to protect your self-image or self-esteem.

● *Why do people affiliate?*

Recite and Review: Pages 654-655

22. The need to affiliate is tied to needs for _____, support, friendship, and

_____.

23. Additionally, research indicates that we sometimes affiliate to _____ anxiety and uncertainty.

24. Social comparison theory holds that we affiliate to _____ our actions, feelings, and abilities.

25. Social _____ are also made for purposes of self-protection and self-enhancement.

26. Downward _____ are sometimes used to make us feel better when faced with a threat. Upward _____ may be used for self-improvement.

● *What factors influence interpersonal attraction?*

Recite and Review: Pages 655-661

27. Interpersonal attraction is increased by physical proximity (_____) and frequent

_____.

28. Initial acquaintance and _____ are influenced by physical attractiveness (beauty), competence (high ability), and _____ (being alike).

29. A large degree of _____ on many dimensions is characteristic of _____ selection, a pattern called homogamy.

30. Self-disclosure (_____ oneself to others) occurs to a greater degree if two people like one another.

31. Self-disclosure follows a reciprocity _____: Low levels of self-disclosure are met with low levels in return, whereas moderate self-disclosure elicits more personal replies.

32. Overdisclosure tends to inhibit _____ by others.

33. According to social exchange theory, we tend to maintain relationships that are profitable; that is, those for which perceived _____ exceed perceived _____.

34. Romantic love can be distinguished from liking by the use of attitude scales. Dating couples _____ and _____ their partners but only _____ their friends.

35. Romantic love is also associated with greater _____ absorption between people.

36. Adult _____ relationships tend to mirror patterns of emotional attachment observed in infancy and early childhood.

37. _____, avoidant, and ambivalent patterns can be defined on the basis of how a person approaches romantic and affectionate relationships with others.

38. Evolutionary psychology attributes human _____ patterns to the differing reproductive challenges faced by men and women since the dawn of time.

● *What have social psychologists learned about conformity, social power, obedience, and compliance?*

Recite and Review: Pages 662-670

39. Social influence refers to alterations in _____ brought about by the behavior of _____.

40. Conformity to group pressure is a familiar example of social influence. Virtually everyone _____ to a variety of broad social and cultural _____.

41. Conformity pressures also exist within small _____. The famous Asch experiments demonstrated that various _____ sanctions encourage conformity.

42. Groupthink refers to compulsive conformity in group _____ _____. Victims of groupthink seek to maintain each other's approval, even at the cost of critical thinking.

43. Social influence is also related to five types of _____ _____: reward power, coercive power, legitimate power, referent power, and expert power.

44. Obedience to _____ has been investigated in a variety of experiments, particularly those by Stanley Milgram.

45. _____ in Milgram's studies decreased when the victim was in the same room, when the victim and subject were face to face, when the authority figure was absent, and when others refused to obey.

46. Compliance with direct _____ by a person who has little or no social _____ is another means by which behavior is influenced.

47. Three strategies for inducing compliance are the _____-in-the-door technique, the door-in-the-_____ approach, and the low-ball technique.

48. Recent research suggests that in addition to excessive obedience to _____, many people show a surprising passive compliance to unreasonable _____.

● *How does self-assertion differ from aggression?*

Recite and Review: APPLICATIONS

49. Self-assertion involves clearly stating one's _____ and _____ to others.
50. Aggression expresses one's feelings and desires, but it _____ others.
51. Non-assertive behavior is self-_____ and inhibited.
52. Learning to be _____ is accomplished by role-playing and rehearsing assertive actions.
53. Self-assertion is also aided by overlearning (practice that _____ after initial mastery of a skill) and use of specific techniques, such as the "broken record" (_____ a request until it is acknowledged).

● *What is a social trap?*

Recite and Review: EXPLORATION

54. A social trap is a social situation in which immediately rewarded actions have _____ effects in the long run.
55. One prominent social trap occurs when limited public _____ are overused, a problem called the tragedy of the commons.

RELATE

1. _____   culture   a. privilege and importance
2. _____   ascribed role   b. rule or standard
3. _____   achieved role   c. 0-18 inches
4. _____   status   d. way of life
5. _____   cohesiveness   e. self-moving
6. _____   norm   f. 12 feet plus
7. _____   autokinetic   g. use of space
8. _____   proxemics   h. 1.5-4 feet
9. _____   intimate distance   i. assigned role
10. _____   personal distance   j. 4-12 feet
11. _____   social distance   k. degree of attraction
12. _____   public distance   l. voluntary role

13. _____   attribution   a. relating self to others
14. _____   self-handicapping   b. honest expression
15. _____   need to affiliate   c. following authority
16. _____   social comparison   d. generalized impression
17. _____   social exchange   e. yielding to requests
18. _____   halo effect   f. rewards and punishments
19. _____   conformity   g. delayed harm
20. _____   group sanctions   h. desire to associate
21. _____   obedience   i. matching behavior
22. _____   compliance   j. impairing performance
23. _____   assertiveness   k. rewards minus costs
24. _____   social trap   l. social inference

CHECK YOUR MEMORY

Check Your Memory: Pages 647-650

1. The average number of first-name acquaintance links needed to connect two widely separated strangers is about 70 people. T or F?
2. Language and marriage customs are elements of culture. T or F?
3. *Son, husband,* and *teacher* are achieved roles. T or F?
4. The Stanford prison experiment investigated the impact of the roles "prisoner" and "guard." T or F?
5. Persons of higher status are more likely to touch persons of lower status than the reverse. T or F?
6. Women are more likely to touch men than men are to touch women. T or F?
7. A group could have a high degree of structure but low cohesiveness. T or F?
8. The more trash that is visible in public places, the more likely people are to litter. T or F?
9. An autokinetic light appears to move about the same distance for everyone who observes it. T or F?

Check Your Memory: Pages 650-651

10. Most people show signs of discomfort when someone else enters their personal space without permission. T or F?

11. The Dutch sit closer together when talking than the English do. T or F?

12. Social distance basically keeps people within arm's reach. T or F?

13. Formal interactions tend to take place in the 4 to 12 foot range. T or F?

Check Your Memory: Pages 652-654

14. The deliberateness of another person's behavior affects the attributions we make about it. T or F?

15. If someone always salts her food before eating, it implies that her behavior has an external cause. T or F?

16. Situational demands lead us to discount claims that a person's behavior is externally caused. T or F?

17. A strong consensus in the behavior of many people implies that their behavior is externally caused. T or F?

18. Getting drunk is a common form of self-handicapping. T or F?

19. Attributing the actions of others to external causes is the most common attributional error. T or F?

20. Good performances by women are more often attributed to luck than skill. T or F?

Check Your Memory: Pages 654-655

21. The need to affiliate is a basic human characteristic. T or F?

22. People who are frightened prefer to be with others who are in similar circumstances. T or F?

23. Social comparisons are used to confirm objective evaluations and measurements. T or F?

24. Useful social comparisons are usually made with persons similar to ourselves. T or F?

25. Some social comparisons are made for self-protection. T or F?

26. Downward social comparisons are typically made for self-improvement. T or F?

Check Your Memory: Pages 655-661

27. Nearness has a powerful impact on forming friendships. T or F?

28. Physical proximity leads us to think of people as competent, and therefore worth knowing. T or F?

29. The halo effect is the tendency to generalize a positive or negative first impression to other personal characteristics. T or F?

30. Physical attractiveness is closely associated with intelligence, talents, and abilities. T or F?

31. Physical attractiveness has more influence on women's fates than men's. T or F?

32. The risk of divorce is higher than average for couples who have large differences in age and education. T or F?

33. In choosing mates, women rank physical attractiveness as the most important feature. T or F?

34. Self-disclosure is a major step toward friendship. T or F?

35. Overdisclosure tends to elicit maximum self-disclosure from others. T or F?

36. Male friendships tend to be activity-based; women's friendships tend to be based on shared feelings and confidences. T or F?

37. The personal standard used to judge the acceptability of a social exchange is called the comparison level. T or F?

38. The statement, "I find it easy to ignore _____'s faults" is an item on the Liking Scale. T or F?

39. People with an avoidant attachment style tend to form relationships that are marked by mixed emotions. T or F?

40. Where their mates are concerned, men tend to be more jealous over a loss of emotional commitment than they are over sexual infidelities. T or F?

Check Your Memory: Pages 662-670

41. Conformity situations occur when a person becomes aware of differences between his or her own behavior and that of a group. T or F?

42. Most subjects in the Asch conformity experiments suspected that they were being deceived in some way. T or F?

43. Seventy-five percent of Asch's subjects yielded to the group at least once. T or F?

44. People who are anxious are more likely to conform to group pressure. T or F?

45. Groupthink is more likely to occur when people emphasize the task at hand, rather than the bonds between group members. T or F?

46. Rejection, ridicule, and disapproval are group norms that tend to enforce conformity. T or F?

47. A unanimous majority of 3 is more powerful than a majority of 8 with 1 person dissenting. T or F?

48. If you identify with a particular person, that person has referent power with respect to your behavior. T or F?

49. Milgram's famous shock experiment was done to study compliance and conformity. T or F?

50. Over half of Milgram's "teachers" went all the way to the maximum shock level. T or F?

51. Being face-to-face with the "learner" had no effect on the number of subjects who obeyed in the Milgram experiments. T or F?

52. People are less likely to obey an unjust authority if they have seen others disobey. T or F?

53. The foot-in-the-door effect is a way to gain compliance from another person. T or F?

54. The low-ball technique involves changing the terms that a person has agreed to, so that they are less desirable from the person's point of view. T or F?

Check Your Memory: APPLICATIONS

55. Many people have difficulty asserting themselves because they have learned to be obedient and "good." T or F?

56. Self-assertion involves the rights to request, reject, and retaliate. T or F?

57. Aggression does not take into account the rights of others. T or F?

58. Overlearning tends to lead to aggressive responses. T or F?

59. In order to be assertive, you should never admit that you were wrong. T or F?

60. If someone insults you, an assertive response should include getting the person to accept responsibility for his or her aggression. T or F?

Check Your Memory: EXPLORATION

61. Panic during a theater fire is an example of a social trap. T or F?

62. In social traps, behavior that seems to make sense from an individual point of view ends up doing harm to the group. T or F?

63. Underuse of natural resources is called the tragedy of the commodities. T or F?

64. In a social trap, people are more likely to restrain their own behavior if they believe others will too. T or F?

FINAL SURVEY AND REVIEW

● *How does group membership affect individual behavior?*

1. _____ _____ studies how individuals behave, think, and feel in social situations.

2. _____ provides a broad social context for our behavior. One's position in groups defines a variety of _____ to be played.

3. Social roles, which may be _____ or _____, are particular behavior patterns associated with social positions.

4. When two or more contradictory roles are held, role _____ may occur.

5. The _____ prison experiment showed that destructive _____ may override individual motives for behavior.

6. Positions within groups typically carry higher or lower levels of _____. _____ _____ is associated with special privileges and respect.

7. Group _____ refers to the organization of roles, _____ pathways, and power within a group.

8. Group _____ is basically the degree of attraction among group members.

9. _____ are standards of conduct enforced (formally or informally) by groups.

10. The _____ effect (the illusion of movement in a _____ light in a darkened room) has been used to demonstrate that _____ rapidly form even in temporary groups.

● *What unspoken rules govern the use of personal space?*

11. The study of personal space is called _____.

12. Four basic spatial zones around each person's body are _____ distance (0-18 inches), personal distance (1.5-4 feet), social distance (4-12 feet), and _____ distance (12 feet or more).

13. _____ for the use of personal space vary considerably in various cultures.

● *How do we perceive the motives of others, and the causes of our own behavior?*

14. _____ theory is concerned with how we make inferences about the causes of behavior.

15. Behavior can be attributed to _____ causes or _____ causes.

16. To infer causes we take into account the actor, the _____ of the action, and the _____ in which the action occurs.

17. The consistency of behavior on different occasions and its _____ (whether it occurs only in certain circumstances) affect the attributions we make.

18. _____ _____ demands tend to cause us to _____ (downgrade) internal causes as explanations of someone's behavior.

19. _____ in behavior (in which many people act alike) implies that their behavior has an external cause.

20. The _____ _____ error is to ascribe the actions of others to internal causes, while attributing your own behavior to external causes.

21. _____ involves arranging excuses for poor performance as a way to protect your self-image or self-esteem.

● *Why do people affiliate?*

22. The _____ to _____ is tied to additional needs for approval, support, friendship, and information.

23. Additionally, research indicates that we sometimes affiliate to reduce _____ and uncertainty.

24. Social _____ theory holds that we affiliate to evaluate our actions, feelings, and abilities.

25. Social comparisons are also made for purposes of self-_____ and self-enhancement.

26. _____ comparisons are sometimes used to make us feel better when faced with a threat. _____ comparisons may be used for self-improvement.

● *What factors influence interpersonal attraction?*

27. Interpersonal attraction is increased by physical _____ (nearness) and frequent contact.

28. Initial acquaintance and attraction are influenced by _____ attractiveness (beauty), _____ (high ability), and similarity.

29. A large degree of similarity on many dimensions is characteristic of mate selection, a pattern called _____.

30. _____ (revealing oneself to others) occurs to a greater degree if two people like one another.

31. Self-disclosure follows a _____ norm: Low levels of self-disclosure are met with low levels in return, whereas moderate self-disclosure elicits more personal replies.

32. _____ (excessive) tends to inhibit self-disclosure by others.

33. According to social _____ theory, we tend to maintain relationships that are _____; that is, those for which perceived rewards exceed perceived costs.

34. Romantic love can be distinguished from liking by the use of _____ _____. Dating couples love and like their partners but only like their friends.

35. Romantic love is also associated with greater mutual _____ between people.

36. Adult love relationships tend to mirror patterns of emotional _____ observed in infancy and early childhood.

37. Secure, _____ (non-committal), and _____ (conflicted) patterns can be defined on the basis of how a person approaches romantic and affectionate relationships with others.

38. _____ psychology attributes human mating patterns to the differing _____ challenges faced by men and women since the dawn of time.

● *What have social psychologists learned about conformity, social power, obedience, and compliance?*

39. _____ _____ refers to alterations in behavior brought about by the behavior of others.

40. _____ to group pressure is a familiar example of social influence. Virtually everyone conforms to a variety of broad social and _____ norms.

41. Conformity pressures also exist within small groups. The famous _____ experiments demonstrated that various group _____ encourage conformity.

42. _____ refers to compulsive conformity in group decision making. Its victims seek to maintain each other's _____, even at the cost of critical thinking.

43. Social influence is also related to five types of social power: _____ power, _____ power (based on an ability to punish), legitimate power, referent power, and expert power.

44. _____ to authority has been investigated in a variety of experiments, particularly those by Stanley _____.

45. Obedience in his studies _____ when the victim was in the same room, when the victim and subject were face to face, when the _____ figure was absent, and when others refused to obey.

46. _____ with direct requests by a person who has little or no social power is another means by which behavior is influenced.

47. Three strategies for getting people to comply are the foot-in-the-_____ technique, the _____-in-the-face approach, and the _____ technique.

48. Recent research suggests that in addition to excessive obedience to authority, many people show a surprising _____ compliance to unreasonable requests.

⬤ *How does self-assertion differ from aggression?*

49. _____ involves clearly stating one's wants and needs to others.

50. _____ expresses one's feelings and desires, but it hurts others.

51. _____ behavior is self-denying and inhibited.

52. Learning to be assertive is accomplished by _____ and rehearsing assertive actions.

53. Self-assertion is also aided by _____ (practice that continues after initial mastery of a skill) and use of specific techniques, such as the _____ _____ (repeating a request until it is acknowledged).

⬤ *What is a social trap?*

54. A social trap is a social situation in which _____ _____ actions have undesired effects in the long run.

55. One prominent social trap occurs when limited public resources are _____, a problem called the _____ of the _____.

MASTERY TEST

1. Homogamy is directly related to which element of interpersonal attraction?
   a. competence b. similarity c. beauty d. proximity

2. Being an agent of an accepted social order is the basis for _____ power.
   a. coercive b. legitimate c. referent d. compliant

3. Suspicion and reduced attraction are associated with
   a. reciprocity b. self-disclosure c. competence and proximity d. overdisclosure

4. We expect people to be respectful and polite at funerals because of
   a. situational demands b. the door-in-the-face effect c. attributional discounting d. self-handicapping

5. Conflicting feelings of anger, affection, doubt, and attraction are characteristic of what attachment style?
   a. avoidant b. ambivalent c. compliant d. kinetic

6. Which of the following is an assertiveness technique?
   a. foot-in-the-door b. calm absorption c. door-in-the-face d. broken record

7. Using social comparison for self-protection typically involves
   a. external attributions b. comparisons with group norms c. downward comparisons
   d. comparison with a person of higher ability

8. "President of the United States" is
   a. an ascribed role b. an achieved role c. an structural norm d. a cohesive role

9. Where attribution is concerned, wants, needs, motives, or personal characteristics are perceived as
   a. external causes b. situational attributions c. discounted causes d. internal causes

10. Asch is to _____ experiments as Milgram is to _____ experiments.
   a. compliance, assertion b. conformity, obedience c. autokinetic, social power
   d. groupthink, authority

11. Social psychology is the scientific study of how people
   a. behave in the presence of others b. form into groups and organizations c. form and maintain interpersonal relationships d. make inferences about the behavior of others

12. "A person who first agrees with a small request is later more likely to comply with a larger demand." This summarizes the
   a. low-ball technique b. set-the-hook technique c. door-in-the-face effect d. foot-in-the-door effect

13. Large desks in business offices almost ensure that interactions with others take place at
   a. ascribed distance b. social distance c. personal distance d. public distance

14. Comparison level is an important concept in
   a. social comparison theory b. social exchange theory c. evolutionary psychology
   d. social compliance theory

15. The _____ is a classic social trap.
   a. error of misattribution b. compulsion for unanimity c. tragedy of the commons
   d. downward comparison dilemma

16. Group structure involves all but one of the following elements. Which does NOT belong?
   a. roles b. communication pathways c. allocation of power d. social comparisons

17. A "guard" in the Stanford prison experiment who discovers that one of the "prisoners" is a friend would very likely experience
    a. role conflict   b. a change in status   c. groupthink   d. a shift to coercive power

18. Groupthink is a type of _____ that applies to decision making in groups.
    a. conformity   b. social comparison   c. social power   d. obedience

19. If procrastinating on school assignments helps protect your self-image, you have used procrastination as a type of
    a. double standard   b. attributional error   c. self-handicapping   d. situational demand

20. When two people view an autokinetic light at the same time, their estimates of movement
    a. polarize   b. normalize   c. cohere   d. converge

21. In Milgram's studies, the smallest percentage of subjects followed orders when
    a. the teacher and learner were in the same room   b. the teacher received orders by phone   c. the teacher and learner were face to face   d. the experiment was conducted off campus

22. The most basic attributional error is to attribute the behavior of others to _____ causes, while attributing one's own behavior to _____ causes.
    a. inconsistent, consistent   b. internal, external   c. random, distinctive   d. situational, personal

23. In an experiment, most women waiting to receive a shock preferred to wait with others who
    a. were about to be shocked   b. did not share their fears   c. were trained to calm them
    d. had been shocked the day before

24. Evolutionary theories attribute mate selection, in part, to the _____ of past generations.
    a. food-gathering habits   b. tribal customs   c. maternal instincts   d. reproductive success

25. The "what is beautiful is good" stereotype typically does NOT include the assumption that physically attractive people are more
    a. likable   b. intelligent   c. honest   d. mentally healthy

ANSWERS

Recite and Review

1. social	7. roles	15. causes, causes
2. groups	8. attraction	16. causes, actor
3. Social roles	9. standards, groups	17. consistency
4. contradictory	10. movement, temporary	18. internal
5. prison	11. personal space	19. external
6. groups	12. personal, social	20. error, internal, external
	13. cultures	21. performance
	14. causes	22. approval, information

23. reduce
24. evaluate
25. comparisons
26. comparisons, comparisons
27. nearness, contact
28. attraction, similarity
29. similarity, mate
30. revealing
31. norm
32. self-disclosure
33. rewards, costs
34. like, love, like
35. mutual
36. love
37. Secure
38. mating
39. behavior, others
40. conforms, norms
41. groups, group
42. decision making
43. social power
44. authority
45. Obedience
46. requests, power
47. foot, face
48. authority, requests
49. wants, needs
50. hurts
51. denying
52. assertive
53. continues, repeating
54. undesired
55. resources

Relate

1. d
2. i
3. l
4. a
5. k
6. b
7. e
8. g
9. c
10. h
11. j
12. f
13. l
14. j
15. h

16. a
17. k
18. d
19. i
20. f
21. c
22. e
23. b
24. g

Check Your Memory

1. F
2. T
3. F
4. T
5. T
6. F
7. T
8. T
9. F
10. T
11. F
12. F
13. F
14. F
15. F
16. F
17. T
18. T
19. F
20. T
21. T
22. T
23. F
24. T
25. T
26. F
27. T
28. F
29. T
30. F
31. T
32. T
33. F
34. T
35. F
36. T
37. T
38. F
39. F

40. F
41. T
42. F
43. T
44. T
45. F
46. F
47. T
48. T
49. F
50. T
51. F
52. T
53. T
54. T
55. T
56. F
57. T
58. F
59. F
60. T
61. T
62. T
63. F
64. T

Final Survey and Review

1. Social psychology
2. Culture, roles
3. achieved, ascribed
4. conflict
5. Stanford, roles
6. status, High status
7. structure, communication
8. cohesiveness
9. Norms
10. autokinetic, stationary, norms
11. proxemics
12. intimate, public
13. Norms
14. Attribution
15. internal, external
16. object, setting
17. distinctiveness
18. Situational, discount
19. Consensus
20. fundamental attributional
21. Self-handicapping
22. need, affiliate

23. anxiety
24. comparison
25. protection
26. Downward, Upward
27. proximity
28. physical, competence
29. homogamy
30. Self-disclosure
31. reciprocity
32. Overdisclosure
33. exchange, profitable
34. attitude scales
35. absorption
36. attachment
37. avoidant, ambivalent
38. Evolutionary, reproductive
39. Social influence
40. Conformity, cultural
41. Asch, sanctions
42. Groupthink, approval
43. reward, coercive
44. Obedience, Milgram
45. decreased, authority
46. Compliance
47. door, door, low-ball
48. passive
49. Self-assertion
50. Aggression
51. Non-assertive
52. role-playing
53. overlearning, "broken record"
54. immediately rewarded
55. overused, tragedy, commons

14. b (p. 659)
15. c (p. 673)
16. d (p. 649)
17. a (p. 648)
18. a (p. 663)
19. c (p. 653)
20. d (p. 650)
21. b (p. 667)
22. b (p. 653)
23. a (p. 655)
24. d (p. 660-661)
25. c (p. 656)

Mastery Test

1. b (p. 657)
2. b (p. 665)
3. d (p. 658)
4. a (p. 652)
5. b (p. 660)
6. d (p. 672)
7. c (p. 655)
8. b (p. 648)
9. d (p. 652)
10. b (p. 663, 665)
11. a (p. 647)
12. d (p. 668)
13. b (p. 651)

Chapter 21

Attitudes, Culture, and Human Relations

CHAPTER OVERVIEW

Attitudes have a belief component, an emotional component, and an action component. Attitudes may be formed by direct contact, interaction with others, child-rearing, group pressures, peer group influences, the mass media, and chance conditioning. Attitudes are measured by open-ended interviews, social distance scales, and attitude scales. Attitude change is related to reference group membership, to deliberate persuasion, and to personal experiences. Effective persuasion occurs when characteristics of the communicator, the message, and the audience are well matched. Cognitive dissonance theory explains how attitudes are maintained and changed. Brainwashing is forced attitude change. Many cults recruit new members with high-pressure techniques similar to brainwashing.

Prejudice is a negative attitude held toward out-group members. Prejudice can be attributed to scapegoating, personal prejudice, group norms, and authoritarian personality traits. Intergroup conflict leads to hostility and stereotyping. Status inequalities tend to build prejudices. Equal-status contact and superordinate goals tend to reduce these problems.

Ethologists blame aggression on instincts. Biological explanations emphasize brain mechanisms and physical factors. Aggression tends to follow frustration, especially when aggression cues are present. Social learning theory relates aggressive behavior to the influence of aggressive models.

Four decision points that must be passed before we give help to others are: noticing, defining an emergency, taking responsibility, and selecting a course of action. Helping is less likely at each point when other potential helpers are present. Giving help tends to encourage others to help too.

Multiculturalism is an attempt to give equal status to different ethnic, racial, and cultural groups. Cultural awareness is a key element in promoting greater social harmony.

Sociobiology attempts to explain human social behavior by relating it to natural selection and human evolution.

RECITE AND REVIEW

● *What are attitudes? How are they acquired?*

Recite and Review: Pages 676-679

1. Attitudes are learned tendencies to respond in a _____ or _____ way.

2. Attitudes are made up of a belief component, an emotional component, and an _____ component.

3. Attitudes may be formed by _____ contact, interaction with others, the effects of _____-rearing practices, and social pressures from group membership.

4. Peer group influences, the mass _____, and _____ conditioning (accidental learning) also appear to be important in attitude formation.

5. The _____ consequences of actions, how we think others will _____ our actions, and habits all influence whether attitudes are converted to actions.

6. Attitudes held with conviction are most likely to be _____ in behavior.

● *How are attitudes measured and changed?*

Recite and Review: Pages 679-680

7. One way of measuring attitudes is the open-ended _____, in which a person freely states his or her views.

8. A social distance scale is a rating of the degree of _____ a person would be willing to have with a member of another _____.

9. Attitude scales are a collection of statements with which people express _____ or _____.

10. People tend to change their attitudes to match those of their reference group (a group the person _____ with and refers to for guidance).

● *Under what conditions is persuasion most effective?*

Recite and Review: Page 680-681

11. Effective persuasion occurs when characteristics of the communicator, the _____, and the audience are well matched.

12. In general, a likable and believable communicator who repeats a credible message that arouses _____ in the audience and states clear-cut _____ will be persuasive.

13. Consumer psychologists study consumer behaviors such as selecting brands, _____, and deciding to _____.

14. Consumer psychologists often do marketing research, which is a type of public opinion _____ to aid the promotion of various products.

● *What is cognitive dissonance? What does it have to do with attitudes and behavior?*

Recite and Review: Pages 681-683

15. Significant personal experiences (which may be engineered through role-playing) tend to _____ attitudes.

16. One reason for this is that maintaining and changing attitudes is closely related to needs for _____ in thoughts and actions. Cognitive dissonance theory explains the dynamics of such needs.

17. Cognitive dissonance occurs when there is a _____ between thoughts or between thoughts and actions.
18. The amount of reward or justification (reasons) for one's actions influences whether _____ occurs.
19. We are motivated to _____ dissonance when it occurs, often by changing beliefs or attitudes.

● *Is brainwashing actually possible? How are people converted to cult membership?*

Recite and Review: Pages 683-685

20. Brainwashing is a form of _____ attitude change. It depends on control of the target person's total environment.
21. Three steps in brainwashing are unfreezing (loosening) old attitudes and beliefs, _____, and refreezing (rewarding and strengthening) new attitudes and beliefs.
22. Many cults recruit new members with high-pressure indoctrination techniques resembling _____.

23. Cults attempt to catch people when they are vulnerable. Then they combine isolation, displays of _____, discipline and rituals, intimidation, and escalating commitment to bring about _____.

● *What causes prejudice and intergroup conflict? What can be done about these problems?*

Recite and Review: Pages 685-691

24. Prejudice is a _____ attitude held toward members of various out-groups.
25. Racism, ageism, and sexism are specific types of prejudice based on race, age, and _____.
26. One theory attributes prejudice to scapegoating, which is a type of displaced _____.

27. A second account says that prejudices may be held for personal reasons such as direct threats to a person's well being (personal prejudice) or simply through adherence to group _____ (group prejudice).
28. Prejudiced individuals tend to have an authoritarian or dogmatic _____, characterized by rigidity, inhibition, intolerance, and _____-simplification.
29. Authoritarians tend to be very ethnocentric (they use their own _____ as a basis for judging all others).
30. Intergroup _____ gives rise to hostility and the formation of social stereotypes (over-simplified images of members of various groups).
31. Symbolic prejudice, or prejudice expressed in _____ ways, is common today.
32. _____ inequalities (differences in power, prestige, or privileges) tend to build prejudices.
33. Equal-status contact (social interaction on an equal footing) tends to _____ prejudice.
34. Superordinate _____ (those that rise above all others) usually reduce intergroup conflict.
35. On a small scale, jigsaw _____ (which encourage cooperation through _____ interdependence) have been shown to be an effective way of combating prejudice.

● *How do psychologists explain human aggression?*

Recite and Review: Pages 692-697

36. Ethologists explain aggression as a natural expression of inherited _____.
37. Biological explanations emphasize brain mechanisms and physical factors that _____ the threshold (trigger point) for aggression.
38. According to the frustration-_____ hypothesis, frustration and _____ are closely linked.
39. Frustration is only one of many aversive _____ that can arouse a person and make aggression more likely. Aggression is especially likely to occur when _____ cues (stimuli associated with aggression) are present.
40. Social learning theory has focused attention on the role of aggressive _____ in the development of aggressive behavior.
41. Aggressive _____ on television encourage aggression because they desensitize (lower the sensitivity of) _____ to violence and disinhibit (remove restraints against) aggressive impulses.

● *Why are bystanders so often unwilling to help in an emergency?*

Recite and Review: Pages 697-699

42. Prosocial behavior is _____, constructive, or altruistic toward others.
43. Bystander apathy is the unwillingness of bystanders to offer _____ to others during emergencies.
44. Four decision points that must be passed before a person gives help are: _____, defining an emergency, taking responsibility, and selecting a course of action.
45. Helping is _____ likely at each point when other potential helpers are present.
46. Helping is encouraged by general arousal, empathic _____, being in a good mood, low effort or _____, and perceived similarity between the victim and the helper.

● *What can be done to lower prejudice and promote social harmony?*

Recite and Review: APPLICATIONS

47. Multiculturalism is an attempt to give _____ status to different ethnic, racial, and cultural groups.
48. Greater tolerance can be encouraged by neutralizing stereotypes with individuating information (which helps see others as _____).
49. Tolerance comes from looking for commonalties with others and by avoiding the effects of just-world _____, self-fulfilling prophecies, and _____ competition.
50. _____ awareness is a key element in promoting greater social harmony.

● *How does the theory of sociobiology try to explain social behavior?*

Recite and Review: EXPLORATION

51. Sociobiology attempts to explain human social behavior by relating it to natural selection and human _____.
52. Sociobiology relies heavily on the idea of biological determinism (belief that behavior is controlled by _____ processes.)

RELATE

1. _____	Mrs. Keech	a.	belief plus strong emotion
2. _____	misdirected letter	b.	standard for comparison
3. _____	mean world	c.	unequal treatment
4. _____	conviction	d.	doomsday group
5. _____	social distance	e.	thought reform
6. _____	reference group	f.	aggression target
7. _____	dissonance	g.	uncomfortable clash
8. _____	brainwashing	h.	attitude-behavior test
9. _____	discrimination	i.	allowed contact
10. _____	scapegoat	j.	television perspective

11. _____	authoritarianism	a.	modern bias
12. _____	ethnocentric	b.	above all others
13. _____	dogmatism	c.	F scale
14. _____	stereotype	d.	instincts
15. _____	symbolic prejudice	e.	group-centered
16. _____	superordinate	f.	altruistic
17. _____	ethology	g.	aggression cue
18. _____	weapons effect	h.	group rivalry
19. _____	prosocial	i.	unwarranted certainty
20. _____	social competition	j.	simplified image

CHECK YOUR MEMORY

Check Your Memory: Pages 676-679

1. Attitudes predict and direct future actions. T or F?

2. The misdirected letter technique was used to measure the belief component of attitudes toward the Irish. T or F?

3. What you think about the object of an attitude makes up its belief component. T or F?

4. If both parents belong to the same political party, their child probably will too. T or F?

5. A person who deviates from the majority opinion in a group tends to be excluded from conversation. T or F?

6. Heavy TV viewers feel safer than average because they spend so much time in security at home. T or F?

7. The combination of music and antisocial behavior in rock videos can make antisocial behavior seem more acceptable. T or F?

8. An attitude held with conviction is more likely to be acted upon. T or F?

Check Your Memory: Pages 679-680

9. In an open-ended interview, people respond to a series of statements for and against a particular issue. T or F?

10. A social distance scale is used to measure attitudes toward members of various social groups. T or F?

11. Five-point rating scales are frequently used in open-ended attitude interviews. T or F?

12. Our attitudes are more likely to match those held by members of our reference groups than our membership groups. T or F?

Check Your Memory: Page 680-681

13. Persuasion refers to a deliberate attempt to change a person's reference groups. T or F?

14. Persuasion is less effective if the message appeals to the emotions. T or F?

15. For a poorly informed audience, persuasion is more effective if only one side of the argument is presented. T or F?

16. A persuasive message should not be repeated; doing so just weakens its impact. T or F?

Check Your Memory: Pages 681-683

17. Emotional experiences can alter attitudes, even if the experience is created by role-playing. T or F?

18. Acting contrary to one's attitudes or self-image causes cognitive dissonance. T or F?

19. Public commitment to an attitude or belief makes it more difficult to change. T or F?

20. Romantic couples reduce the dissonance caused by their partner's faults by ignoring them. T or F?

21. The greater the reward or justification for acting contrary to one's beliefs, the greater the cognitive dissonance felt. T or F?

22. Dissonance is especially likely to be felt when a person causes an undesired event to occur. T or F?

Check Your Memory: Pages 683-685

23. Roughly 16 percent of American POWs in the Korean war signed false confessions. T or F?

24. True brainwashing requires a captive audience. T or F?

25. In brainwashing, the target person is housed with other people who hold the same attitudes and beliefs that he or she does. T or F?

26. In most cases, the effects of brainwashing are very resistant to further change. T or F?

27. A cult is a group in which the belief system is more important than the leader who espouses it. T or F?

28. Cults play on emotions and discourage critical thinking. T or F?

29. Cult members are typically isolated from former reference groups. T or F?

Check Your Memory: Pages 685-691

30. Sexism is a type of prejudice. T or F?

31. Scapegoating is a prime example of discrimination. T or F?

32. A person who views members of another group as competitors for jobs displays group prejudice. T or F?

33. Authoritarian persons tend to be prejudiced against all out-groups. T or F?

34. The *F* in F scale stands for fanatic. T or F?

35. An authoritarian would agree that people can be divided into the weak and the strong. T or F?

36. Dogmatic personalities are found at both ends of the political spectrum. T or F?

37. Social stereotypes can be positive as well as negative. T or F?

38. People who feel they are being evaluated in terms of a stereotype tend to become anxious, which can lower their performance and seemingly confirm the stereotype. T or F?

39. Symbolic prejudice is the most obvious and socially unacceptable form of bigotry. T or F?

40. Images of national enemies tend to humanize the inhabitants of other countries, making them seem less threatening. T or F?

41. The key to creating prejudice in Jane Elliot's experiment was her use of scapegoating to cause group conflict. T or F?
42. Equal-status contact tends to reduce prejudice and stereotypes. T or F?
43. Superordinate groups help people of opposing groups to see themselves as members of a single larger group. T or F?
44. The term nuclear winter refers to widespread crop failures following the Chernobyl Nuclear Power Plant disaster. T or F?

Check Your Memory: Pages 692-697

45. Over 75 percent of all married persons physically attack their spouses at one time or another. T or F?
46. Ethologists argue that humans learn to be aggressive by observing aggressive behavior in lower animals. T or F?
47. Specific areas of the brain are capable of initiating or ending aggression. T or F?
48. Intoxication tends to raise the threshold for aggression, making it more likely. T or F?
49. Higher levels of the hormone testosterone are associated with more aggressive behavior by both men and women. T or F?
50. The frustration-aggression hypothesis says that being aggressive is frustrating. T or F?
51. People exposed to aversive stimuli tend to become less sensitive to aggression cues. T or F?
52. Murders are less likely to occur in homes where guns are kept. T or F?
53. Social learning theorists assume that instinctive patterns of human aggression are modified by learning. T or F?
54. The erotic content of pornography is usually more damaging than the aggressive content. T or F?
55. Aggressive crimes in TV dramas occur at a much higher rate than they do in real life. T or F?
56. Preferring violent TV programs at age 8 predicts higher levels of violent behavior at age 19. T or F?
57. Prosocial TV programs have little effect on viewer behavior. T or F?
58. An important element of anger control is looking at upsetting situations as problems to be solved. T or F?

Check Your Memory: Pages 697-699

59. In the Kitty Genovese murder, no one called the police until after the attack was over. T or F?
60. In an emergency, the more potential helpers present, the more likely a person is to get help. T or F?
61. The first step in giving help is to define the situation as an emergency. T or F?
62. Emotional arousal, especially empathic arousal, lowers the likelihood that one person will help another. T or F?
63. You are more likely to help a person who seems similar to yourself. T or F?
64. In many emergency situations it can be more effective to shout "Fire!" rather than "Help!" T or F?

Check Your Memory: APPLICATIONS

65. Multiculturalism is an attempt to blend multiple ethnic backgrounds into one universal culture. T or F?
66. The emotional component of prejudicial attitudes may remain even after a person intellectually renounces prejudice. T or F?
67. Both prejudiced and non-prejudiced people are equally aware of social stereotypes. T or F?
68. Individuating information forces us to focus mainly on the labels attached to a person. T or F?
69. People who hold just-world beliefs assume that people generally get what they deserve. T or F?
70. Every major ethnic group rates itself better than other groups. T or F?

Check Your Memory: EXPLORATION

71. Sociobiologists believe that human social behavior is shaped by the process of evolution. T or F?
72. Sociobiology explains altruistic suicide as an action that may help close kin survive. T or F?
73. Sociobiologists assume that species with highly evolved brains and high intelligence do not need any genetically programmed social behaviors to survive. T or F?

FINAL SURVEY AND REVIEW

● *What are attitudes? How are they acquired?*

1. Attitudes are _____ _____ to respond in a positive or negative way.
2. Attitudes are made up of a _____ component, an _____ component, and an action component.
3. Attitudes may be formed by direct _____, interaction with others, the effects of child-rearing practices, and social pressures from _____ _____ .
4. _____ group influences, the mass media, and chance _____ (accidental learning) also appear to be important in attitude formation.
5. The immediate _____ of actions, how we think others will evaluate our actions, and _____ all influence whether attitudes are converted to actions.
6. Attitudes held with _____ are most likely to be expressed in behavior.

● *How are attitudes measured and changed?*

7. One way of measuring attitudes is the _____ interview, in which a person freely states his or her views.
8. A _____ _____ scale is a rating of the degree of contact a person would be willing to have with a member of another group.
9. _____ _____ are a collection of statements with which people express agreement or disagreement.
10. People tend to change their attitudes to match those of their _____ group (a group the person identifies with and refers to for guidance).

● *Under what conditions is persuasion most effective?*

11. Effective persuasion occurs when characteristics of the _____, the message, and the _____ are well matched.
12. In general, a likable and believable _____ who repeats a credible message that arouses emotion in the _____ and states clear-cut conclusions will be persuasive.
13. _____ psychologists study behaviors such as selecting _____, shopping, and deciding to purchase.
14. They often do _____ _____, which is a type of public opinion polling to aid the promotion of various products.

● *What is cognitive dissonance? What does it have to do with attitudes and behavior?*

15. Significant personal experiences (which may be engineered through _____) tend to change attitudes.
16. One reason for this is that maintaining and changing attitudes is closely related to needs for consistency in thoughts and actions. Cognitive _____ theory explains the dynamics of such needs.
17. Cognitive _____ occurs when there is a clash between _____ or between thoughts and actions.
18. The amount of _____ or _____ (reasons) for one's actions influences whether dissonance occurs.
19. We are motivated to reduce dissonance when it occurs, often by changing _____ or _____, rather than behavior.

● *Is brainwashing actually possible? How are people converted to cult membership?*

20. Brainwashing is a form of forced attitude change. It depends on _____ of the target person's total _____.
21. Three steps in brainwashing are _____ (loosening) old attitudes and beliefs, change, and _____ (rewarding and strengthening) new attitudes and beliefs.
22. Many cults recruit new members with high-pressure _____ techniques resembling brainwashing.
23. Cults attempt to catch people when they are vulnerable. Then they combine isolation, displays of affection, discipline and _____, intimidation, and escalating _____ to bring about conversion.

● *What causes prejudice and intergroup conflict? What can be done about these problems?*

24. Prejudice is a negative attitude held toward members of various _____.
25. _____, _____, and _____ are specific types of prejudice based on race, age, and gender.
26. One theory attributes prejudice to _____, which is a type of _____ aggression.
27. A second account says that prejudices may be held for personal reasons such as direct threats to a person's well being (_____ prejudice) or simply through adherence to group norms (_____ prejudice).
28. Prejudiced individuals tend to have an _____ or _____ personality, characterized by rigidity, inhibition, intolerance, and over-simplification.
29. Authoritarians tend to be very _____ (they use their own group as a basis for judging all others).
30. Intergroup conflict gives rise to hostility and the formation of _____ _____ (over-simplified images of members of various groups).
31. _____ prejudice, or prejudice expressed in disguised ways, is common today.
32. Status _____ (differences in power, prestige, or privileges) tend to build prejudices.
33. _____ contact (social interaction on an equal footing) tends to reduce prejudice.
34. _____ goals (those that rise above all others) usually reduce intergroup conflict.

35. On a small scale, _____ classrooms (which encourage cooperation through mutual _____) have been shown to be an effective way of combating prejudice.

● *How do psychologists explain human aggression?*

36. _____ explain aggression as a natural expression of inherited instincts.
37. Biological explanations emphasize brain mechanisms and physical factors that lower the _____ (trigger point) for aggression.
38. According to the _____-aggression hypothesis, _____ and aggression are closely linked.
39. Frustration is only one of many _____ stimuli that can arouse a person and make aggression more likely. Aggression is especially likely to occur when aggression _____ (stimuli associated with aggression) are present.
40. _____ _____ theory has focused attention on the role of aggressive models in the development of aggressive behavior.
41. Aggressive models on television encourage aggression because they _____ (lower the sensitivity of) viewers to violence and _____ (remove restraints against) aggressive impulses.

● *Why are bystanders so often unwilling to help in an emergency?*

42. Prosocial behavior is helpful, constructive, or _____ toward others.
43. Bystander _____ is the unwillingness of bystanders to offer help to others during emergencies.
44. Four decision points that must be passed before a person gives help are: noticing, defining an _____, taking _____, and selecting a course of action.
45. Helping is less likely at each point when other _____ _____ are present.
46. Helping is encouraged by general arousal, _____ arousal, being in a good mood, low effort or risk, and perceived _____ between the victim and the helper.

● *What can be done to lower prejudice and promote social harmony?*

47. _____ is an attempt to give equal status to different ethnic, racial, and cultural groups.
48. Greater tolerance can be encouraged by neutralizing stereotypes with _____ information (which helps see others as individuals).
49. Tolerance comes from looking for commonalties with others and by avoiding the effects of _____ beliefs, _____ prophecies, and social competition.
50. Cultural _____ is a key element in promoting greater social harmony.

● *How does the theory of sociobiology try to explain social behavior?*

51. _____ attempts to explain human social behavior by relating it to natural _____ and human evolution.

52. Sociobiology relies heavily on the idea of biological _____ (belief that behavior is controlled by biological processes.)

MASTERY TEST

1. The weapons effect refers to the fact that weapons can serve as aggression
  a. thresholds b. cues c. models d. inhibitors

2. The Seekers' renewed conviction and interest in persuading others after the world failed to end can be explained by the
  a. social competition hypothesis b. frustration-persuasion hypothesis c. group's just-world beliefs
  d. theory of cognitive dissonance

3. One thing that REDUCES the chances that a bystander will give help in an emergency is
  a. heightened arousal b. empathic arousal c. others who could help d. similarity to the victim

4. The misdirected letter technique is a way to demonstrate the _____ component of an attitude.
  a. emotional b. belief c. action d. reactive

5. One consequence of seeing aggression portrayed on TV is a loss of emotional response, called
  a. disinhibition b. disassociation c. deconditioning d. desensitization

6. If you are speaking to a well-informed audience, it is important to _____ if you want to persuade them.
  a. repeat your message b. give both sides of the argument c. be likable d. appeal to their emotions

7. Which view of human aggression is most directly opposed to that of the ethologists?
  a. social learning b. brain mechanisms c. sociobiological d. innate releaser

8. Development of a mean world view is usually associated with which source of attitudes?
  a. child rearing b. mass media c. chance conditioning d. group membership

9. Research suggests that the most damaging element of pornography is the
  a. erotic content b. nudity c. aggressive content d. impersonality

10. Creating superordinate goals is an important way to
  a. reduce group conflict b. break the frustration-aggression link c. promote bystander intervention
  d. reverse self-fulfilling prophecies

11. Children who learn good manners by watching television demonstrate that TV can promote
  a. disinhibition b. prosocial behavior c. deconditioning d. superordinate behavior

12. A person who is dogmatic and politically conservative would be most likely to score high on the
  a. R Scale b. Individuation Inventory c. Social Competition Scale d. F Scale

13. A major problem with the ethological view of human aggression is that
    a. labeling a behavior does not explain it   b. aversive stimuli alter the threshold for aggression
    c. it assumes that aggression begets aggression   d. it assumes that aggression is related to
    biological processes

14. The Bennington College study showed that attitudes are not affected very much by
    a. membership groups   b. child-rearing   c. reference groups   d. chance conditioning

15. Students who were paid to lie about a boring task experienced the most dissonance and changed their
    ratings the most when they were
    a. paid $1   b. paid $10   c. paid $20   d. asked to help lure other students into the experiment

16. A key element in the effectiveness of jigsaw classrooms is
    a. deindividuation   b. the promotion of self-fulfilling prophecies   c. mutual interdependence
    d. selecting competent student leaders

17. A good antidote for social stereotyping is
    a. adopting just-world beliefs   b. creating self-fulfilling prophecies   c. accepting status inequalities
    d. seeking individuating information

18. A learned tendency to respond to people and objects in positive or negative ways. This defines a(an)
    a. opinion   b. belief   c. attitude   d. social distance scale

19. An important difference between brainwashing and other types of persuasion is that brainwashing
    a. requires a captive audience   b. is almost always permanent   c. changes actions, not attitudes
    and beliefs   d. is reversed during the refreezing phase

20. The effects of frustration on aggression are most like the effects of _____ on aggression.
    a. social learning   b. prosocial models   c. defining an emergency   d. aversive stimuli

21. Sociobiologists argue that many basic patterns of social behavior ultimately help us to
    a. inhibit natural instincts for aggression   b. survive and reproduce   c. benefit from culture
    d. make full use of our potential for learning

22. A negative attitude toward eggplant would be best explained by _____ if you were ill the first
    time you tried it.
    a. chance conditioning   b. attitudinal freezing   c. scapegoating   d. dogmatic association

23. The top three categories on which social stereotypes are based are
    a. employment, age, race   b. age, race, income   c. race, national origin, income   d. gender, age, race

24. Status inequalities are to _____ as equal-status contact is to _____.
    a. dependence, independence   b. discrimination, stereotyping   c. prejudice, tolerance
    d. aggression, individuation

25. Your actions are most likely to agree with one of your attitudes when
    a. the actions reverse an old habit   b. the attitude is held with conviction   c. you know that others disagree with your position   d. you score high on an attitude scale

26. Conversion to membership in a cult usually involves
    a. depression, disorientation, and intimidation   b. a series of emotional disturbances similar to post-traumatic stress   c. loyalty tests and unfreezing   d. a progression from small to large commitments

27. If it is easier for Anglo Americans to get automobile insurance than it is for African Americans, then African Americans have experienced
    a. discrimination   b. scapegoating   c. ethnocentrism   d. personal prejudice

28. The presence of other potential helpers reduces the likelihood that a bystander will offer help in an emergency during which decision point?
    a. all of the decision points   b. noticing   c. defining an emergency   d. taking responsibility

29. You mark a 5-point scale after reading a series of statements on the issue of rent control. Obviously you are completing an
    a. attitude differential   b. attitude scale   c. R scale   d. attitudinal distance test

30. Racism expressed in a disguised form, so that it appears to be socially acceptable, is called
    _____ prejudice.
    a. secondary   b. subjective   c. silent   d. symbolic

ANSWERS

Recite and Review

1. positive, negative
2. action
3. direct, child
4. media, chance
5. immediate, evaluate
6. expressed
7. interview
8. contact, group
9. agreement, disagreement
10. identifies
11. message
12. emotion, conclusions
13. shopping, purchase
14. polling
15. change
16. consistency
17. clash
18. dissonance
19. reduce
20. forced
21. changing
22. brainwashing
23. affection, conversion
24. negative
25. gender (or sex)
26. aggression
27. norms
28. personality, over
29. group
30. conflict
31. disguised
32. Status
33. reduce
34. goals
35. classrooms, mutual
36. instincts
37. lower
38. aggression, aggression
39. stimuli, aggression
40. models
41. models, viewers
42. helpful
43. help
44. noticing
45. less
46. arousal, risk
47. equal
48. individuals
49. beliefs, social
50. Cultural
51. evolution
52. biological

Relate

1. d
2. h
3. j
4. a
5. i
6. b
7. g
8. e
9. c
10. f
11. c
12. e
13. i
14. j
15. a
16. b
17. d
18. g
19. f
20. h

Check Your Memory

1. T
2. F
3. T
4. T
5. T
6. F
7. T
8. T
9. F
10. T
11. F
12. T
13. F
14. F
15. T
16. F
17. T
18. T
19. T
20. F
21. F
22. T
23. T
24. T
25. F
26. F
27. F
28. T
29. T
30. T
31. F
32. F
33. T
34. F
35. T
36. T
37. T
38. T
39. F
40. F
41. F
42. T
43. T
44. F
45. F
46. F
47. T
48. F
49. T
50. F
51. F
52. F
53. F
54. F
55. T
56. T
57. F
58. T
59. T
60. F
61. F
62. F
63. T
64. T
65. F
66. T
67. T
68. F
69. T
70. T
71. T
72. T
73. F

Final Survey and Review

1. learned tendencies
2. belief, emotional
3. contact, group membership
4. Peer, conditioning
5. consequences, habits
6. conviction
7. open-ended
8. social distance
9. Attitude scales
10. reference
11. communicator, audience
12. communicator, audience
13. Consumer, brands
14. marketing research
15. role-playing
16. dissonance
17. dissonance, thoughts
18. reward, justification
19. beliefs, attitudes
20. control, environment
21. unfreezing, refreezing
22. indoctrination
23. rituals, commitment
24. out-groups
25. Racism, ageism, sexism
26. scapegoating, displaced
27. personal, group
28. authoritarian, dogmatic
29. ethnocentric
30. social stereotypes
31. Symbolic
32. inequalities
33. Equal-status
34. Superordinate
35. jigsaw, interdependence
36. Ethologists
37. threshold
38. frustration, frustration
39. aversive, cues
40. Social learning
41. desensitize, disinhibit
42. altruistic
43. apathy
44. emergency, responsibility
45. potential helpers
46. empathic, similarity
47. Multiculturalism
48. individuating
49. just-world, self-fulfilling
50. awareness
51. Sociobiology, selection
52. determinism

Mastery Test

 1. b (p. 693-694)
 2. d (p. 682)
 3. c (p. 697)
 4. c (p. 677)
 5. d (p. 695)
 6. b (p. 681)
 7. a (p. 692, 694)
 8. b (p. 678-679)
 9. c (p. 694)
10. a (p. 690)
11. b (p. 696)
12. d (p. 686)
13. a (p. 692)
14. a (p. 680)
15. a (p. 682)
16. c (p. 691)
17. d (p. 700)
18. c (p. 677)
19. a (p. 684)
20. d (p. 693)
21. b (p. 702-703)
22. a (p. 679)
23. d (p. 687)
24. c (p. 690)
25. b (p. 679)
26. d (p. 685)
27. a (p. 686)
28. a (p. 697)
29. b (p. 679)
30. d (p. 689)

Chapter 22

Applied Psychology

CHAPTER OVERVIEW

Applied psychologists attempt to solve practical problems. Some major applied specialties are: clinical and counseling, industrial/organizational, environmental, educational, legal, and sports psychology.

    Industrial/organizational psychologists are interested in the problems people face at work. They specialize in personnel psychology and human relations at work. Personnel psychologists try to match people with jobs by combining job analysis with various tests and selection procedures. Two basic approaches to business and industrial management are scientific management and human relations approaches.

    Environmental psychologists study the effects of behavioral settings, physical or social environments, and human territoriality, among many other major topics. Over-population is a major world problem, often reflected at an individual level in crowding. Environmental psychologists are solving many practical problems--from noise pollution to architectural design.

    Educational psychologists seek to understand how people learn and teachers instruct. They are particularly interested in teaching styles and teaching strategies.

    The psychology of law includes courtroom behavior and other topics that pertain to the legal system. Psychologists serve various consulting and counseling roles in legal, law enforcement, and criminal justice settings.

    Sports psychologists seek to enhance sports performance and the benefits of sports participation. A careful task analysis of sports skills is a major tool for improving coaching and performance. The psychological dimension contributes greatly to peak performance.

    Communication at work can be improved by following a few simple guidelines for effective speaking and listening.

    Space psychologists study the behavioral challenges that accompany space flight, space habitats, and life in restricted environments.

RECITE AND REVIEW

● *How is psychology applied in business and industry?*

Recite and Review: Pages 706-712

1. Applied psychology refers to the use of psychological principles and research methods to solve
_____ _____.

2. Major applied specialties include clinical and _____ psychology.

3. Other applied areas are related to business, such as _____/organizational psychology.

4. Psychology is also applied to problems that arise in the environment, in education, in law, and in _____.

5. Industrial/organizational psychologists are interested in the problems people face at _____ and within organizations.

6. Typically they specialize in personnel psychology and human _____ at work.

7. Personnel psychologists try to match people with _____ by combining _____ analysis with a variety of selection procedures.

8. To effectively match people with jobs, it is important to identify critical incidents (situations with which _____ employees must be able to cope).

9. Personnel selection is often based on gathering biodata (detailed _____ information about an applicant).

10. The traditional _____ interview is still widely used to select people for jobs. However, interviewers must be aware of the halo effect and other sources of _____.

11. Standardized psychological _____, such as vocational interest inventories, aptitude tests, and multi-media _____ tests, are mainstays of personnel selection.

12. In the assessment center approach, in-depth _____ of job candidates are done by observing them in simulated _____ situations.

13. Two popular assessment center techniques are the in-basket test, and leaderless _____ discussions.

14. Two basic approaches to business and industrial management are scientific management (Theory ___) and human relations approaches (Theory ___).

15. Theory ___ is most concerned with work efficiency (productivity), whereas, Theory ___ emphasizes psychological efficiency (good human relations).

16. Two common Theory ___ methods are participative management and _____ by objectives.

17. Recently, many companies have given employees more autonomy and responsibility by creating self-managed _____.

18. Below the management level, employees may be encouraged to become more involved in their work by participating in _____ circles.

19. Job satisfaction is related to _____, and it usually affects absenteeism, morale, employee turnover, and other factors that affect overall business efficiency.

20. Job satisfaction is usually enhanced by _____ ___ oriented job enrichment.

● *What have psychologists learned about the effects of our physical and social environments?*

Recite and Review: Pages 713-720

21. Environmental psychologists are interested in the effects of behavioral _____, physical or _____ environments, and human territoriality, among many other major topics.

22. Territorial behavior involves defining a space as one's own, frequently by placing _____ markers (signals of ownership) in it.

23. Over-population is a major world problem, often reflected at an individual level in _____.

24. Animal experiments indicate that excessive crowding can be unhealthy and lead to _____ and pathological behaviors.

25. However, human research shows that psychological feelings of _____ do not always correspond to density (the number of people in a given space).

26. One major consequence of _____ is attentional overload (stress caused when too many demands are placed on a person's attention).

27. Toxic or poisoned environments, pollution, excess consumption of natural resources, and other types of environmental _____ pose serious threats to future _____.

28. In many cases, solutions to environmental problems are the result of doing a careful _____ assessment (an analysis of the effects environments have on behavior).

29. Architectural psychology is the study of the effects _____ have on behavior and the design of _____ using _____ principles.

30. Recycling can be encouraged by monetary _____, removing barriers, persuasion, obtaining public commitment, _____ setting, and giving feedback.

● *How has psychology improved education?*

Recite and Review: Pages 720-721

31. Educational psychologists seek to understand how people _____ and teachers _____.

32. An effective teaching strategy involves _____ preparation, stimulus presentation, the learner's _____, reinforcement, evaluation of the learner' progress, and periodic review.

33. They are particularly interested in teaching styles, such as direct instruction (_____ and demonstrations) and open teaching (active student-teacher _____).

● *What does psychology reveal about juries and court verdicts?*

Recite and Review: Pages 721-723

34. The psychology of law includes studies of courtroom behavior and other topics that pertain to the _____ system.

35. Studies of mock juries (_____ juries) show that jury decisions are often far from _____.

36. Psychologists are sometimes involved in jury _____. Demographic information, a community survey, non-verbal behavior, and looking for authoritarian _____ traits may be used to select jurors.

● *Can psychology enhance athletic performance?*

Recite and Review: Pages 723-726

37. Sports psychologists seek to enhance sports performance and the benefits of sports _____.

38. A careful task analysis breaks _____ _____ into their subparts.

39. Motor skills are the core of many sports performances. Motor skills are non-verbal _____ chains assembled into a smooth sequence.

40. Motor skills are guided by internal _____ plans or models called motor programs.

41. _____ performances are associated with the flow experience, an unusual mental state.

42. Top athletes typically _____ their arousal level so that it is appropriate for the task.. They also focus _____ on the task and mentally rehearse it beforehand.

43. Most top athletes use various self-regulation strategies to _____ their performances and make necessary adjustments.

● *What can be done to improve communication at work?*

Recite and Review: APPLICATIONS

44. To improve communication at work you should state your message _____ and precisely.
45. Try to avoid overuse of obscure vocabulary, jargon, _____, and loaded words.
46. Learn and use people's _____. Be polite, but not servile.
47. Be expressive when you _____. Pay attention to non-verbal cues and the messages they send.
48. To be a good listener, you should _____ pay attention.
49. Try to identify the speaker's purpose and core _____.
50. Suspend evaluation while listening but check your _____ frequently and note non-verbal information.

● *How is psychology being applied in space missions?*

Recite and Review: EXPLORATION

51. Space psychologists study the many behavioral challenges that accompany space flight and life in restricted _____.
52. Space habitats (living areas) must be designed with special attention to environmental stressors, such as noise, control of the environment, _____ cycles, and _____ restriction.
53. Psychological issues, such as _____ isolation, _____ resolution, privacy, cultural differences, and maintaining mental health are equally important.

RELATE

1. _____	community psychology	a.	simulated trial
2. _____	I-O psychology	b.	mental health
3. _____	flexitime	c.	communication barrier
4. _____	biodata	d.	vocational interests
5. _____	mock jury	e.	essential work problem
6. _____	feedback	f.	variable schedule
7. _____	jargon	g.	work efficiency
8. _____	critical incident	h.	personal history
9. _____	Kuder	i.	information about effects
10. _____	in-basket test	j.	work and organizations
11. _____	Theory X	k.	psychological efficiency
12. _____	Theory Y	l.	typical work problems

13. _____	quality circle	a. persons in area
14. _____	territorial marker	b. better for thinking
15. _____	density	c. better for facts
16. _____	noise pollution	d. movement plan
17. _____	cognitive map	e. flow
18. _____	direct instruction	f. strong emotional meaning
19. _____	open teaching	g. ownership signal
20. _____	School of the Future	h. discussion group
21. _____	loaded word	i. micro-society
22. _____	motor program	j. full service institution
23. _____	peak performance	k. mental area plan
24. _____	space habitat	l. intrusive sounds

CHECK YOUR MEMORY

Check Your Memory: Pages 706-712

1. Applied psychology can be defined as the use of learning principles to change undesirable human behavior. T or F?

2. Psychological research has shown that the best fire alarm is a recorded voice. T or F?

3. During a fire in a high-rise building, you should use the elevators, rather than the stairwell, so that you can leave as quickly as possible. T or F?

4. Personnel psychology is a specialty of I-O psychologists. T or F?

5. The basic idea of flexitime is that employees can work as many or as few hours a week as they choose. T or F?

6. One way of doing a job analysis is to interview expert workers. T or F?

7. Critical incidents are serious employee mistakes identified by doing a job analysis. T or F?

8. Use of biodata is based on the idea that past behavior predicts future behavior. T or F?

9. Because of their many shortcomings, personal interviews are fading from use as a way of selecting job applicants. T or F?

10. The halo effect is a major problem in aptitude testing. T or F?

11. Excessive self-promotion tends to lower the ratings candidates receive in job interviews. T or F

12. "I would prefer to read a good book," is the kind of statement typically found on aptitude tests. T or F?

13. Multi-media computerized tests seek to present realistic work situations to job candidates. T or F?

14. Leaderless quality circles are a typical task applicants face in assessment centers. T or F?

15. Theory X assumes that workers enjoy autonomy and accept responsibility. T or F?

16. The main benefit of a Theory X management style is a high level of psychological efficiency among workers. T or F?

17. Participative management aims to make work a cooperative effort. T or F?

18. Quality circles are typically allowed to choose their own methods of achieving results as long as the group is effective. T or F?

19. Job satisfaction comes from a good fit between work and a person's interests, needs, and abilities. T or F?
20. Job enrichment involves assigning workers a large number of new tasks. T or F?

Check Your Memory: Pages 713-720

21. A study of the pace of life found that the three fastest cities in the U.S. are Boston, New York, and Los Angeles. T or F?
22. Environmental psychologists study physical environments rather than social environments. T or F?
23. A dance is a behavioral setting. T or F?
24. Saving a place at a theater is a type of territorial behavior. T or F?
25. Burglars tend to choose houses to break into that have visible territorial markers. T or F?
26. World population doubled between 1950 and 1987. T or F?
27. In Calhoun's study of overcrowding in a rat colony, food and water rapidly ran out as the population increased. T or F?
28. High densities invariably lead to subjective feelings of crowding. T or F?
29. Stress is most likely to result when crowding causes a loss of control over a person's immediate social environment. T or F?
30. People suffering from attentional overload tend to ignore non-essential events and their social contacts are superficial. T or F?
31. Exposure to toxic hazards increases the risk of mental disease, as well as physical problems. T or F?
32. Long-corridor dormitories reduce feelings of crowding and encourage friendships. T or F?
33. Providing feedback about energy consumption tends to promote conservation of resources. T or F?
34. Direct monetary rewards have little or no effect on whether or not people recycle. T or F?

Check Your Memory: Pages 720-721

35. Reinforcement, evaluation, and spaced review are elements of a teaching strategy. T or F?
36. Students of direct instruction do a little better on achievement tests than students of open teaching do. T or F?
37. Students of open instruction tend to be better at thinking and problem solving than students of direct instruction. T or F?
38. One feature of the School of the Future was that children were evaluated and sent to appropriate agencies around the community for help. T or F?
39. The School of the Future model is based on a very high level of teacher, parent, and community involvement in children's education and welfare. T or F?

Check Your Memory: Pages 721-723

40. In court, attractive defendants are less likely to be found guilty than unattractive persons. T or F?
41. Jurors are supposed to take into account the severity of the punishment that a defendant faces, but many don't. T or F?
42. Scientific jury selection is only used in laboratory studies—the practice isn't allowed in real jury trials. T or F?
43. Demographic information consists of the most prominent personality traits a person displays. T or F?
44. All members of a death-qualified jury must be opposed to the death penalty. T or F?

Check Your Memory: Pages 723-726

45. Peak performances in sports require both mental and physical training. T or F?
46. Distance running tends to reduce anxiety, tension, and depression. T or F?
47. The most accurate marksmen are those who learn to pull the trigger just as their heart beats. T or F?
48. Motor programs adapt complex movements to changing conditions. T or F?
49. Verbal rules add little to learning a sports skill; you should concentrate on lifelike practice. T or F?
50. To enhance motor skill learning, feedback should call attention to correct responses. T or F?
51. Mental practice refines motor programs. T or F?
52. The top athletes in most sports are the ones who have learned how to force the flow experience to occur. T or F?
53. Better athletes often use imagery, relaxation techniques, and fixed routines to control their arousal levels. T or F?

Check Your Memory: APPLICATIONS

54. Effective communication addresses the who, what, when, where, how, and why of events. T or F?
55. Ambiguous messages are desirable because they leave others room to disagree. T or F?
56. Jargon is an acceptable means of communication as long as you are sure that listeners are familiar with it. T or F?
57. True politeness puts others at ease. T or F?
58. To add credibility to your message, you should learn to speak very slowly and deliberately. T or F?
59. Arriving late for meetings is a form of communication. T or F?
60. To be a good listener, learn to evaluate each sentence as it is completed. T or F?
61. Good listening improves communication as much as effective speaking does. T or F?

Check Your Memory: EXPLORATION

62. Many of the social and psychological problems of space flight can be prevented by carefully selecting astronauts before they leave Earth. T or F?
63. In space, astronauts have no preference for rooms with an obvious top or bottom. T or F?
64. Sleep cycles are best allowed to run freely in space since there are no real light and dark cycles. T or F?
65. The need for privacy in space habitats can be met, in part, by defining private territories for each astronaut. T or F?
66. Most people in restricted environments prefer games and other interactive pastimes as a way to break the monotony. T or F?
67. In the specialized environment of a space station, differences in culture no longer seem important. T or F?
68. Fifteen percent of space inhabitants are expected to experience a serious psychological disturbance. T or F?
69. Most major problems facing the world day are behavioral. T or F?

FINAL SURVEY AND REVIEW

● *How is psychology applied in business and industry?*

1. Applied psychology refers to the use of psychological _____ and _____ methods to solve practical problems.

2. Major applied specialties include _____ and counseling psychology.

3. Other applied areas are related to business, such as industrial/_____ psychology.

4. Psychology is also applied to problems that arise in the natural and social _____, in _____, in law, and in sports.

5. _____ psychologists are interested in the problems people face at work and within organizations.

6. Typically they specialize in _____ psychology (testing, selecting, and promoting employees) and human relations at work.

7. _____ psychologists try to match people with jobs by combining job _____ with a variety of selection procedures.

8. To effectively match people with jobs, it is important to identify _____ incidents (situations with which competent employees must be able to cope).

9. Personnel selection is often based on gathering _____ (detailed biographical information about an applicant).

10. The traditional personal _____ is still widely used to select people for jobs. However, interviewers must be aware of the _____ effect and other sources of bias.

11. Standardized psychological tests, such as _____ interest inventories, _____ tests, and multi-media computerized tests, are mainstays of personnel selection.

12. In the _____ _____ approach, in-depth evaluations of job candidates are done by observing them in simulated work situations.

13. Two popular assessment center techniques are the in-_____ test, and _____ group discussions.

14. Two basic approaches to business and industrial management are _____ management (Theory X) and _____ _____ approaches (Theory Y).

15. Theory X is most concerned with work _____ (productivity), whereas, Theory Y emphasizes _____ efficiency (good human relations).

16. Two common Theory Y methods are _____ management and management by _____.

17. Recently, many companies have given employees more autonomy and responsibility by creating _____ teams.

18. Below the management level, employees may be encouraged to become more involved in their work by participating in _____ _____.

19. Job _____ is related to productivity, and it usually affects absenteeism, _____, employee turnover, and other factors that affect overall business efficiency.

20. Comfort with one's work is usually enhanced by Theory Y-oriented job _____.

● *What have psychologists learned about the effects of our physical and social environments?*

21. _____ psychologists are interested in the effects of _____ settings, physical or social environments, and human territoriality, among many other major topics.

22. Territorial behavior involves defining a space as one's own, frequently by placing territorial _____ (signals of ownership) in it.

23. _____ is a major world problem, often reflected at an individual level in crowding.

24. Animal experiments indicate that excessive _____ can be unhealthy and lead to abnormal and pathological behaviors.

25. However, human research shows that psychological feelings of crowding do not always correspond to _____ (the number of people in a given space).

26. One major consequence of crowding is _____ _____ (stress caused when too many demands are placed on a person's attention).

27. Toxic or poisoned environments, _____, excess consumption of natural _____, and other types of environmental damage pose serious threats to future generations.

28. In many cases, solutions to environmental problems are the result of doing a careful environmental _____ (an analysis of the effects environments have on behavior).

29. _____ psychology is the study of the effects buildings have on behavior and the design of buildings using psychological principles.

30. Recycling can be encouraged by _____ rewards, removing barriers, persuasion, obtaining public _____, goal setting, and giving feedback.

● *How has psychology improved education?*

31. _____ psychologists seek to understand how people learn and teachers instruct.

32. An effective teaching _____ involves learner preparation, stimulus presentation, the learner's response, _____, evaluation of the learner's progress, and periodic _____.

33. They are particularly interested in teaching styles, such as _____ _____ (lecture and demonstrations) and _____ teaching (active student-teacher _____).

● *What does psychology reveal about juries and court verdicts?*

34. The psychology of _____ includes studies of courtroom behavior and other topics that pertain to the legal system.

35. Studies of _____ juries (simulated juries) show that jury decisions are often far from objective.

36. Psychologists are sometimes involved in jury selection. _____ information (population data), a community survey, non-verbal behavior, and looking for _____ personality traits may be used to select jurors.

● *Can psychology enhance athletic performance?*

37. Sports psychologists seek to enhance sports _____ and the benefits of sports participation.

38. A careful _____ _____ breaks sports skills into their subparts.

39. _____ skills are the core of many sports performances. Such skills are non-_____ response _____ assembled into a smooth sequence.

40. Motor skills are guided by internal mental plans or models called _____ _____.

41. Peak performances are associated with the _____ experience, an unusual _____ state.

42. Top athletes typically adjust their _____ level so that it is appropriate for the task.. They also focus attention on the task and mentally _____ it beforehand.

43. Most top athletes use various _____ strategies to evaluate their performances and make necessary adjustments.

● *What can be done to improve communication at work?*

44. To improve communication at work you should state your _____ clearly and precisely.

45. Try to avoid overuse of obscure _____, _____ (inside lingo), slang, and loaded words.

46. Learn and use people's names. Be _____, but not servile.

47. Be _____ when you speak. Pay attention to _____ cues and the messages they send.

48. To be a good _____, you should actively _____ _____.

49. Try to identify the speaker's _____ and core message.

50. Suspend _____ while listening but check your understanding frequently and note non-verbal information.

● *How is psychology being applied in space missions?*

51. _____ psychologists study the many behavioral challenges that accompany space flight and life in _____ environments.

52. Space _____ (living areas) must be designed with special attention to environmental _____, such as noise, control of the environment, sleep cycles, and sensory restriction.

53. Psychological issues, such as social _____, conflict _____, privacy, cultural _____, and maintaining mental health are equally important.

MASTERY TEST

1. Praise and feedback make up what part of a teaching strategy?
   a. learner preparation   b. stimulus presentation   c. reinforcement   d. review

2. Which is POOR advice for learning motor skills?
   a. Observe a skilled model.   b. Learn only non-verbal information.   c. Get feedback.
   d. Avoid learning artificial parts of a task.

3. Which of the following would be a question for applied psychology?
   a. How does conditioning occur?   b. How can eyewitness memory be improved?   c. What are the most basic personality traits?   d. Do athletes have unusual personality profiles?

4. Signs are placed on a recycling container each week showing how many aluminum cans were deposited during the previous week. This practice dramatically increases recycling, showing the benefits of using _____ to promote recycling.
   a. feedback   b. public commitment   c. consumer symbolization   d. persuasion

5. Psychological efficiency is promoted by
   a. scientific management   b. Theory Y   c. time-and-motion studies   d. progressive pay schedules

6. In court, being attractive does NOT help a defendant avoid being found guilty when
    a. a majority of jurors are also attractive   b. the defendant is a man   c. the defendant is over age 30
    d. being attractive helped the person commit a crime

7. The best antidote for social isolation on extended space missions is expected to be
    a. defining private social territories for crew members   b. coordinated sleep schedules   c. radio contact
    with Earth   d. making conflict resolution teams part of all missions

8. Which of the following is NOT a specialty of I-O psychologists?
    a. personnel psychology   b. theories of management   c. human relations   d. architectural psychology

9. Dividing long-corridor dormitories into smaller living areas
    a. makes residents feel more crowded, not less   b. decreases social contacts   c. increases energy
    consumption   d. decreases stress

10. You leave a book on a table in the library to save your place. The book is a territorial
    a. display   b. marker   c. strategy   d. control

11. When professional golfer Jack Nicklaus talks about "watching a movie" in his head before each shot, he is
    referring to the value of _____ for enhancing sports performance.
    a. mental rehearsal   b. self-regulation   c. skilled modeling   d. task analysis

12. What cognitive maps, behavioral settings, and crowding have in common is that all
    a. are studied by community psychologists   b. produce attentional overload   c. are studied by
    environmental psychologists   d. are characteristics of Type A cities

13. Potentials for learning the skills used in various occupations are measured by
    a. interest tests   b. aptitude tests   c. in-basket tests   d. cognitive mapping

14. To encourage creative thinking by students, a teacher would be wise to use
    a. direct instruction   b. demonstrations as well as lectures   c. open teaching   d. spaced review

15. A good job analysis should identify
    a. critical incidents   b. compatible controls   c. motor programs   d. essential biodata

16. High _____ is experienced as crowding when it leads to a loss of _____ one's
    immediate environment.
    a. overload, attention to   b. density, control over   c. stimulation, interest in   d. arousal, contact with

17. Studies of flexitime would most likely be done by a _____ psychologist.
    a. community   b. environmental   c. I-O   d. consumer

18. The halo effect is a problem in
    a. collecting biodata   b. scoring interest inventories   c. conducting interviews   d. aptitude testing

19. Mental practice is one way to improve
    a. motor programs   b. the flow experience   c. the accuracy of cognitive maps   d. job satisfaction

20. Joan has been given a specific sales total to meet for the month, suggesting that she works for a company that uses
a. quality circles   b. job enrichment   c. flexi-quotas   d. management by objectives

21. Which of the following is NOT recommended for people who want to be effective listeners in the workplace?
a. Identify the speaker's purpose.   b. Evaluate as you listen.   c. Check your understanding.
d. Attend to non-verbal messages.

22. Planning, control, and orderliness are typical of _____ management.
a. Theory X   b. participative   c. Theory Y   d. enriched

23. A psychologist who checks demographic information, does a community survey, and looks for authoritarian traits is most likely
a. a personnel psychologist   b. doing a community mental health assessment   c. a consumer welfare advocate   d. a legal consultant

24. A very important element of job enrichment is
a. switching to indirect feedback   b. increasing worker knowledge   c. use of bonuses and pay incentives
d. providing closer supervision and guidance

ANSWERS

Recite and Review

1. practical problems
2. counseling
3. industrial
4. sports
5. work
6. relations
7. jobs, job
8. competent
9. biographical
10. personal, bias
11. tests, computerized
12. evaluations, work
13. group
14. X, Y
15. X, Y
16. Y, management
17. teams
18. quality
19. productivity
20. Theory Y
21. settings, social
22. territorial
23. crowding
24. abnormal
25. crowding
26. crowding
27. damage, generations
28. environmental
29. buildings, buildings, behavioral
30. rewards, goal
31. learn, instruct
32. learner, response
33. lecture, discussion
34. legal
35. simulated, objective
36. selection, personality
37. participation
38. sports skills
39. response
40. mental
41. Peak
42. adjust, attention
43. evaluate
44. clearly
45. slang
46. names
47. speak
48. actively
49. message
50. understanding
51. environments
52. sleep, sensory
53. social, conflict

Relate

1. b
2. j
3. f
4. h
5. a
6. i

7. c
8. e
9. d
10. l
11. g
12. k
13. h
14. g
15. a
16. l
17. k
18. c
19. b
20. j
21. f
22. d
23. e
24. i

Check Your Memory

1. F
2. T
3. F
4. T
5. F
6. T
7. F
8. T
9. F
10. F
11. T
12. F
13. T
14. F
15. F
16. F
17. T
18. F
19. T
20. F
21. F
22. F
23. F
24. T
25. F
26. T
27. F
28. F
29. T

30. T
31. T
32. F
33. T
34. F
35. T
36. T
37. T
38. F
39. T
40. T
41. F
42. F
43. F
44. F
45. T
46. T
47. F
48. T
49. F
50. T
51. T
52. F
53. T
54. T
55. F
56. T
57. T
58. F
59. T
60. F
61. T
62. T
63. F
64. F
65. T
66. F
67. F
68. F
69. T

Final Survey and Review

1. principles, research
2. clinical, community
3. organizational
4. environment, education
5. Industrial/organizational
6. personnel
7. Personnel, analysis

8. critical
9. biodata
10. interview, halo
11. vocational, aptitude,
12. assessment center
13. basket, leaderless
14. scientific, human relations
15. efficiency, psychological
16. participative, objectives
17. self-managed
18. quality circles
19. satisfaction, morale
20. enrichment
21. Environmental, behavioral
22. markers
23. Over-population
24. crowding
25. density
26. attentional overload
27. pollution, resources
28. assessment
29. Architectural
30. monetary, commitment
31. Educational
32. strategy, reinforcement, review
33. direct instruction, open, discussion
34. law
35. mock
36. Demographic, authoritarian
37. performance
38. task analysis
39. Motor, verbal, chains
40. motor programs
41. flow, mental
42. arousal, rehearse
43. self-regulation
44. message
45. vocabulary, jargon
46. polite
47. expressive, non-verbal
48. listener, pay attention
49. purpose
50. evaluation
51. Space, restricted
52. habitats, stressors
53. isolation, resolution, differences

Mastery Test

1. c (p. 721)
2. b (p. 725)
3. b (p. 706)
4. a (p. 719)
5. b (p. 710)
6. d (p. 722)
7. c (p. 731)
8. d (p. 707)
9. d (p. 717-718)
10. b (p. 713)
11. a (p. 726)
12. c (p. 713-714, 717)
13. b (p. 709)
14. c (p. 721)
15. a (p. 708)
16. b (p. 715)
17. c (p. 707)
18. c (p. 708)
19. a (p. 725)
20. d (p. 711)
21. b (p. 728)
22. a (p. 710)
23. d (p. 722-723)
24. b (p. 712)

Appendix A

Statistics

OVERVIEW

Descriptive statistics are used to summarize data. Inferential statistics are used to make decisions and generalizations or to draw conclusions. Graphical statistics, such as histograms and frequency polygons, provide pictures (graphs) of groups of numbers. Measures of central tendency, such as the mean, median, and mode, supply a number describing an "average" or "typical" score in a group of scores. The range and standard deviation are measures of variability, or how spread out scores are. Standard scores (z-scores) combine the mean and standard deviation in a way that tells how far above or below the mean a particular score lies. The normal curve is a bell-shaped distribution of scores that has useful and well known properties.

While psychologists are ultimately interested in entire populations, they must usually observe only a representative sample. Nevertheless, it is possible to tell if the results of an experiment are statistically significant (unlikely to be due to chance alone).

When measurements, scores, or observations come in pairs, it is possible to determine if they are correlated. The correlation coefficient tells if the relationship between two measures is positive or negative and how strong it is. While correlations are quite useful, correlation does not demonstrate causation.

RECITE AND REVIEW

Recite and Review: Pages A1-A10

1. Descriptive statistics are used to _____ data. Inferential statistics are used to make decisions and generalizations or to draw _____.

2. Three basic types of _____ statistics are graphical statistics, measures of central tendency, and measures of variability.

3. A frequency distribution organizes data by breaking an entire range of scores into _____ of equal size. Then, the number of scores falling in each _____ is recorded.

4. Graphical statistics provide _____ (graphs) of collections of numbers.

5. A histogram is drawn by placing _____ intervals on the abscissa (_____ line) and frequencies on the ordinate (_____ line) of a graph.

6. Next, vertical bars are drawn for each class interval, with the _____ of the bars being determined by the number of scores in each class.

7. A frequency polygon (line graph) results when points are plotted at the _____ of each class interval and connected by lines.

8. Measures of central tendency are numbers describing an "_____" or "typical" score in a group of scores.

9. The mean is calculated by _____ all the scores for a group and then dividing by the total number of scores.

10. The median is found by arranging scores from the highest to the lowest and then selecting the _____ score.

11. The mode is the _____ _____ occurring score in a group of scores.

12. Measures of variability tell how varied or widely _____ scores are.

13. The range is the _____ score minus the _____ score.

14. The standard deviation is calculated by finding the difference between each score and the _____. These differences are then _____. Then the squared deviations are totaled and their mean is found.

15. Standard scores (___-scores) are found by subtracting the _____ from a score. The resulting number is then divided by the standard deviation.

16. Standard scores tell how far above or below the _____ a particular score lies.

17. When they are collected from large groups of people, many psychological measures form a normal _____.

18. In a normal curve, 68 percent of all scores fall between plus and minus 1 standard deviations from the _____.

19. Ninety-five percent of all cases fall between plus and minus ___ standard deviations from the mean.

20. Ninety-nine percent of all cases fall between plus and minus ___ standard deviations from the mean.

21. The _____ _____ of subjects, objects, or events of interest in a scientific investigation is called a population.

22. When an entire population cannot be observed, a sample (smaller cross section) of the _____ is selected.

23. Samples must be representative (they must truly reflect the characteristics of the _____).

24. _____ drawn from representative samples are assumed to apply to the entire population.

25. Tests of statistical significance tell how often the results of an experiment could have occurred by _____ alone.

26. An experimental result that could have occurred only 5 times out of 100 (or less) by chance alone is considered _____.

27. When measurements, scores, variables, or observations come in pairs, it is possible to determine if they are correlated (varying together in an _____ fashion).

28. The coefficient of correlation tells if the relationship between two measures is _____ or _____ and how strong it is.

29. While correlations are quite useful, correlation does not _____ causation.

RELATE

1. _____	frequency distribution	a.	z-score
2. _____	histogram	b.	subset
3. _____	mean	c.	model distribution
4. _____	range	d.	graphed correlation
5. _____	standard deviation	e.	randomly selected
6. _____	standard score	f.	correlation coefficient
7. _____	normal curve	g.	no relationship
8. _____	population	h.	central tendency
9. _____	sample	i.	grouped scores
10. _____	representative	j.	entire set
11. _____	zero correlation	k.	percent of variance
12. _____	scatter diagram	l.	average squared difference
13. _____	Pearson *r*	m.	picture of frequencies
14. _____	*r* squared	n.	spread of scores

CHECK YOUR MEMORY

Check Your Memory: Pages A1-A10

1. Descriptive statistics extract and summarize information. T or F?
2. Inferential statistics are used to make pictures (graphs) out of data. T or F?
3. Measures of variability are descriptive statistics. T or F?
4. A frequency distribution is made by recording the most frequently occurring score. T or F?
5. A frequency polygon is a graphical representation of a frequency distribution. T or F?
6. On a graph, the ordinate is the line that shows the frequency of scores at the center of each class interval. T or F?
7. The mean, median, and mode are all averages. T or F?
8. The median is the most frequently occurring score in a group of scores. T or F?
9. To find the mode, you would have to know how many people obtained each possible score. T or F?
10. The standard deviations can be different in two groups of scores even if their means are the same. T or F?
11. To find the range, you would have to know what the highest and lowest scores are. T or F?
12. To find a z-score you must know the median and the standard deviation. T or F?
13. a z-score of 1 means that a person scored exactly at the mean. T or F?
14. The majority of scores are found near the middle of a normal curve. T or F?
15. Fifty percent of all scores are found below the mean in a normal curve. T or F?
16. Psychologists prefer to study entire populations whenever it is practical to do so. T or F?
17. Random selection of subjects usually makes a sample representative. T or F?
18. A result that could have occurred by chance alone 25 times out of 100 is considered statistically significant. T or F?
19. A probability of .05 or less is statistically significant. T or F?
20. A scatter diagram is a plot of two sets of unrelated measurements on the same graph. T or F?

21. In a positive relationship, increases in measure X are matched by increases in measure Y. T or F?
22. A correlation coefficient of .100 indicates a perfect positive relationship. T or F?
23. The Pearson r ranges from −.100 to +.100. T or F?
24. Correlations allow psychologists to make predictions. T or F?
25. Two correlated measures may be related through the influence of a third variable. T or F?
26. Correlation proves that one variable causes another if the correlation coefficient is significant. T or F?

FINAL SURVEY AND REVIEW

1. _____ statistics are used to summarize data. _____ statistics are used to make decisions and generalizations or to draw conclusions.
2. Three basic types of descriptive statistics are graphical statistics, measures of _____ tendency, and measures of _____.
3. A _____ _____ organizes data by breaking an entire range of scores into classes of equal size. Then, the number of scores falling in each class is recorded.
4. _____ statistics provide pictures of collections of numbers.
5. A _____ is drawn by placing class intervals on the _____ (horizontal line) and frequencies on the _____ (vertical line) of a graph.
6. Next, vertical bars are drawn for each _____ _____, with the height of the bars being determined by the number of scores in each class.
7. A _____ _____ (line graph) results when points are plotted at the center of each class interval and connected by lines.
8. Measures of _____ _____ are numbers describing an "average" or "typical" score in a group of scores.
9. The _____ is calculated by adding all the scores for a group and then _____ by the total number of scores.
10. The _____ is found by arranging scores from the highest to the lowest and then selecting the middle score.
11. The _____ is the most frequently occurring score in a group of scores.
12. Measures of _____ tell how varied or widely spread scores are.
13. The _____ is the highest score minus the lowest score.
14. The _____ _____ is calculated by finding the difference between each score and the mean. These differences are then squared. Then the squared deviations are totaled and their mean is found.
15. _____ scores (z-scores) are found by subtracting the mean from a score. The resulting number is then divided by the _____ _____.
16. _____ tell how far above or below the mean a particular score lies.
17. When they are collected from large groups of people, many psychological measures form a _____ curve.
18. In such curves, _____ percent of all scores fall between plus and minus 1 standard deviations from the mean.
19. _____ percent of all cases fall between plus and minus 2 standard deviations from the mean.

20. _____ percent of all cases fall between plus and minus 3 standard deviations from the mean.

21. The entire set of subjects, objects, or events of interest in a scientific investigation is called a _____.

22. When an entire set cannot be observed, a _____ (smaller cross section) is selected.

23. Samples must be _____ (they must truly reflect the characteristics of the population).

24. Conclusions drawn from _____ _____ are assumed to apply to the entire population.

25. Tests of statistical _____ tell how often the results of an experiment could have occurred by chance alone.

26. An experimental result that could have occurred only ___ times out of _____ (or less) by chance alone is considered significant.

27. When measurements, scores, variables, or observations come in pairs, it is possible to determine if they are _____ (varying together in an orderly fashion).

28. The _____ of correlation tells if the relationship between two measures is positive or negative and how _____ it is.

29. While correlations are quite useful, correlation does not demonstrate _____.

MASTERY TEST

1. _____ statistics are especially valuable for decision making and drawing conclusions.
   a. graphical b. descriptive c. inferential d. significant

2. Measures of central tendency are _____ statistics.
   a. graphical b. descriptive c. inferential d. significant

3. Sorting scores into classes is a necessary step in creating a
   a. frequency distribution b. correlation c. scatter diagram d. variability plot

4. Vertical bars are used to indicate frequencies in a
   a. frequency polygon b. scatter diagram c. normal distribution d. histogram

5. Which is NOT a measure of central tendency?
   a. mean b. midst c. mode d. median

6. A group of scores must be arranged from the lowest to the highest in order to find the
   a. mean b. midst c. mode d. median

7. The _____ is sensitive to extremely high or low scores in a distribution.
   a. mean b. midst c. mode d. median

8. Which is a measure of variability?
   a. Pearson r b. z-score c. midst d. range

9. What two statistics are needed to calculate a standard score?
   a. range and midst b. mean and standard deviation c. range and mode
   d. standard deviation and z-score

10. If the mean on a test is 90, and the standard deviation is 10, a person with a z-score of -1 scored _____ on the test.
    a. 70   b. 80   c. 100   d. 110

11. The largest percentage of scores fall between _____ SD in a normal curve.
    a. 0 and +1   b. +1 and −1   c. +2 and +3   d. −3 and −2

12. What percent of all cases are found between +3 SD and −3 SD in a normal curve?
    a. 50   b. 86   c. 95   d. 99

13. An effective way to make sure that a sample is representative is to
    a. use random selection b. calculate the correlation coefficient c. make sure that the standard deviation is low d. use a scatter diagram

14. Results of an experiment that have a chance probability of _____ are usually regarded as statistically significant.
    a. .5   b. .05   c. 1.5   d. 1.05

15. A good way to visualize a correlation is to plot a
    a. frequency histogram b. polygon coefficient c. scatter diagram d. normal ordinate

16. When measure X gets larger, measure Y gets smaller in a
    a. zero correlation b. positive relationship c. variable relationship d. negative relationship

17. When plotted as a graph, a zero correlation forms a cluster of points in the shape of a
    a. diagonal oval to the right b. diagonal oval to the left c. horizontal line d. circle

18. The largest possible correlation coefficient is
    a. 1   b. .001   c. 100   d. 10

19. To find the percent of variance in one measure accounted for by knowing another measure you should square the
    a. mean b. z-score c. Pearson *r* d. standard deviation

20. Correlations do not demonstrate whether
    a. a relationship is positive or negative b. a cause-and-effect connection exists c. knowing one measure allows prediction of another d. two events are really co-relating

ANSWERS

Recite and Review

1. summarize, conclusions
2. descriptive
3. classes, class
4. pictures
5. class, horizontal, vertical
6. height
7. center
8. average
9. adding
10. middle
11. most frequently
12. spread
13. highest, lowest
14. mean, squared
15. z, mean
16. mean
17. curve
18. mean
19. 2
20. 3
21. entire set
22. population
23. population
24. Conclusions
25. chance
26. significant
27. orderly
28. positive, negative
29. demonstrate

Relate

1. i
2. m
3. h
4. n
5. l
6. a
7. c
8. j
9. b
10. e
11. g
12. d
13. f
14. k

Check Your Memory

1. T
2. F
3. T
4. F
5. T
6. F
7. T
8. F
9. T
10. T
11. T
12. F
13. F
14. T
15. T
16. T
17. T
18. F
19. T
20. F
21. T
22. F
23. F
24. T
25. T
26. F

Final Survey and Review

1. Descriptive, Inferential
2. central, variability
3. frequency distribution
4. Graphical
5. histogram, abscissa, ordinate
6. class interval
7. frequency polygon
8. central tendency
9. mean, dividing
10. median
11. mode
12. variability
13. range
14. standard deviation
15. Standard, standard deviation
16. Z-scores (or standard scores)
17. normal
18. 68
19. Ninety-five
20. Ninety-nine
21. population
22. sample
23. representative
24. representative samples
25. significance
26. 5, 100
27. correlated
28. coefficient, strong
29. causation

Mastery Test

1. c (p. A1, A7)
2. b (p. A1)
3. a (p. A1)
4. d (p. A1)
5. b (p. A2, A3)
6. d (p. A2)
7. a (p. A2)
8. d (p. A4)
9. b (p. A5)
10. b (p. A5)
11. b (p. A6)
12. d (p. A6)
13. a (p. A7)
14. b (p. A7)
15. c (p. A7)
16. d (p. A7)
17. d (p. A8)
18. a (p. A8)
19. c (p. A8)
20. b (p. A8)

Appendix B

Using Electronic Media in Psychology

OVERVIEW

Gathering information in psychology is no longer restricted to books, journals, and other print materials. An immense amount of information is now stored, transmitted, and made available electronically. The Internet allows computers all over the globe to interconnect and exchange information through the telephone system. Online databases, in particular, contain a wealth of information that can be searched and transferred to a personal computer by modem. Many of these databases specialize in particular types of information. An example is PsycINFO, the premier source of scientific information in psychology. Other databases have been stored on compact discs (CD-ROMs). This makes them portable and useable on any computer with the appropriate software.

In order to use the Internet you must know how to locate various sites, services, electronic addresses, and bulletin boards. It is also valuable to learn how to use indexes, gophers, and various search engines to find information. Boolean logic can be used to define searches (that is, to broaden or narrow searches) conducted in either online databases or compact discs.

Multimedia CD-ROMS are the newest electronic resource in psychology. Such CDs typically contain text, art, photographs, animations, film clips, audio clips, and interactive exercises. The visual impact and interactive qualities of CDs make them an excellent way to explore psychology and learn its concepts.

RECITE AND REVIEW

Recite and Review: Pages B1-B7

1. The Internet is an electronic network that enables _____ to communicate directly with each other through the _____ system.

2. A subpart of the _____ called the World Wide Web is a system of information "sites" or "_____" that can be accessed from personal computers.

3. You can view a web site by using a personal computer with a _____ and a software browser. A browser allows you to see text, images, sounds, movies, and other information contained on a web _____.

4. Many web pages also have links to other web sites. These connections allow users to jump around the _____ to find additional information.

5. A gopher is a system for organizing information on the Internet, usually in the form of simple lists, called _____.

6. Internet _____ Transfer Protocol (FTP) sites contain information "files" that can be copied from one _____ to another.

7. The _____ _____ Information Server (WAIS) searches through the text of entire documents.

8. Usenet groups are electronic "_____ boards" that allow discussion of a variety of topics through _____ (electronic mail).

9. On the Internet, the _____ of each site is known as a URL. URL stands for Uniform Resource Locator. A URL really is nothing more than an electronic _____.

10. _____ engines are software programs that allow you to find specific topics in a larger body of information.

11. Boolean _____ is a system that combines the operators AND, OR, and _____ to make searches narrower or broader.

12. Using the AND operator helps to limit the scope of a search, making it _____.

13. Using the OR instruction _____ a search.

14. The Boolean logic operator NOT _____ the scope of a search by excluding certain topics.

15. PsycINFO is a major online _____ that provides summaries and references to the scientific and literature in psychology.

16. To search electronic databases it is necessary to identify keywords, terms, or topics that may be _____ within the database. This process can be aided by using the *Thesaurus of Psychological* _____ *Terms*.

17. Medline is the primary online database for _____ and biogenetic information.

18. ERIC (Educational Resources _____ _____) is a national clearinghouse that provides information and services on education-related issues.

19. Rather than being stored on _____ at remote locations, CD-ROM databases are stored on compact discs.

20. The American Psychiatric Electronic _____ (APEL) CD contains the complete text, including graphics, of ten psychiatric _____, fifteen psychiatric textbooks, and the American Psychiatric Association's Practice Guidelines.

21. PsycLIT and ClinPSYC are computerized CD-ROM _____ produced by the American _____ Association.

22. ClinPSYC is a collection of information related to abnormal and _____ psychology.

23. A special quality of multimedia CD-ROMs is their capacity to provide interactive _____ experiences.

Relate

1. _____	Veronica	a.	transferable files
2. _____	FTP site	b.	search logic
3. _____	WAIS	c.	Medline
4. _____	http	d.	psychiatric information
5. _____	Boolean operator	e.	multimedia CD
6. _____	PsycINFO	f.	CD-ROM database
7. _____	PsycLIT	g.	gopher software
8. _____	Grateful Med	h.	web address
9. _____	APEL	i.	online database
10. _____	PsychNow!	j.	document searching

CHECK YOUR MEMORY

Check Your Memory: Pages B1-B7

1. The *World Wide Web* allows people in different locations to rapidly exchange information. T or F?
2. Each web site is a collection of information stored on a large central computer in New York that is linked to the World Wide Web. T or F?
3. The software used by gophers to search the Internet is called Veronica. T or F?
4. Archie is the name of software designed to explore FTP sites. T or F?
5. Archie searches for words found in the file names of FTP sites. T or F?
6. Archie and Veronica primarily search through the contents of individual files rather than menus and file names. T or F?
7. Most college and university libraries provide computer terminals that can be used to search electronic databases and sometimes even the Internet. T or F?
8. Commercial online services, such as CompuServe or America Online provide Internet access at relatively low cost. T or F?
9. The URL for a World Wide Web page begins with the prefix *ftp.* T or F?
10. The last part of a URL gives the directory where a file can be found on a remote computer, and the name of the file. T or F?
11. Veronica, Archie, and the Internet are search engines. T or F?
12. Boolean logic is a system developed in the 19th century by English mathematician George Boole. T or F?
13. Searching for the keywords "depression" and "stress" will identify a wider range of information than searching for either "depression" or "stress." T or F?
14. PsycINFO is a popular psychology web site. T or F?
15. PsycINFO provides online access to 100 electronic books about psychology. T or F?
16. PsycINFO also covers work from related fields, such as psychiatry, education, medicine, and social work. T or F?
17. The CD-ROM version of PsycINFO is called PsycLIT. T or F?
18. To reach PsycINFO on the Internet, you must go through a "gateway" such as CompuServe or other Internet providers. T or F?

19. It is almost always worthwhile to target searches in electronic databases as precisely as possible. T or F?
20. The *Metathesaurus* helps Medline users change common terms into the exact medical terms found in the database. T or F?
21. One disadvantage of CD-ROM databases is that users are restricted to using menus, the database itself cannot be searched using keywords. T or F?
22. PsycLIT is stored on two compact discs covering different time periods. T or F?
23. An electronic booklet describing how to search PsycLIT and ClinPSYC is available on the Internet. T or F?

FINAL SURVEY AND REVIEW

1. The _____ is an electronic _____ that enables computers to communicate directly with each other through the phone system.
2. A subpart of the Internet called the _____ _____ _____ is a system of information "sites" or "pages" that can be accessed through the Internet.
3. You can view a web site by using a personal computer with a modem and a software _____.
A _____ allows you to see text, images, sounds, movies, and other information contained on a web page.
4. Many web pages also have _____ to other web sites. These connections allow users to jump around the Internet to find additional information.
5. A _____ is a system for organizing information on the Internet, usually in the form of simple lists, called menus.
6. Internet File _____ _____ (FTP) sites contain information "files" that can be copied from one computer to another.
7. The Wide Area _____ _____ (WAIS) searches through the text of entire documents.
8. _____ groups are electronic "bulletin boards" that allow discussion of a variety of topics through e-mail (electronic mail).
9. On the Internet, the location of each site is known as a URL. URL stands for _____ _____ _____. A URL really is nothing more than an electronic address.
10. Search _____ are software programs that allow you to find specific topics in a larger body of information.
11. _____ logic is a system that combines the _____ AND, OR, and NOT to make searches narrower or broader.
12. Using the _____ operator helps to limit the scope of a search.
13. Using the _____ instruction widens a search.
14. The Boolean logic operator _____ limits the scope of a search by excluding certain topics.
15. _____ is a major online database that provides summaries and references to the scientific and literature in psychology.
16. To search electronic databases it is necessary to identify _____, terms, or topics that may be indexed within the database. This process can be aided by using the _____ *of Psychological Index Terms.*
17. _____ is the primary online database for medical and biogenetic information.
18. ERIC (_____ _____ Information Center) is a national clearinghouse that provides information and services on education-related issues.

19. Rather than being stored on computers at remote locations, _____ databases are stored on compact discs.

20. The American _____ _____ Library (APEL) CD contains the complete text, including graphics, of ten psychiatric journals, fifteen psychiatric textbooks, and the American Psychiatric Association's Practice Guidelines.

21. _____ and ClinPSYC are computerized CD-ROM databases produced by the American Psychological Association.

22. ClinPSYC is a collection of information related to _____ and _____ psychology.

23. A special quality of _____ CD-ROMs is their capacity to provide _____ learning experiences.

Mastery Test

1. Which of the following is a URL?
   a. *ftp*   b. *http*   c. *gopher*   d. all of the preceding

2. Gopher computers use software called _____ to search the Internet.
   a. WAIS   b. Veronica   c. FTP   d. PsychNow!

3. Which of the following is designed to search through large numbers of documents, extracting only items of interest to a researcher?
   a. WAIS   b. Veronica   c. Usenet   d. PsychNow!

4. Bulletin boards and e-mail are particularly associated with
   a. WAIS   b. APEL   c. Usenet groups   d. The Integrator

5. You would need access to a computer with a compact disc player to make use of
   a. ERIC   b. WAIS   c. Grateful Med   d. PsychLIT

6. Which two operators limit or narrow the scope of a search?
   a. AND, OR   b. AND, NOT   c. OR, NOT   d. OR, ADD

7. Which of the following must you access online?
   a. PsycINFO   b. APEL   c. PsychLIT   d. ClinPSYC

8. "Pages" that contain text, images, sounds, and other types of information, and that have *http* addresses are found on
   a. gophers   b. the Wide Area Information Server   c. the PsycLIT database
   d. the World Wide Web

9. Educational materials and information are a specialty of
   a. ERIC   b. WAIS   c. APEL   d. Archie

10. Which of the following is a multimedia CD-ROM?
   a. ClinPSYC   b. PsychNow!   c. Medline   d. the *Thesearus*

ANSWERS

Recite and Review

1. computers, phone
2. Internet, pages
3. modem, page
4. Internet
5. menus
6. File, computer
7. Wide Area
8. bulletin, e-mail
9. location, address
10. Search
11. logic, NOT
12. narrower
13. widens
14. limits
15. database
16. indexed, *Index*
17. medical
18. Information Center
19. computers
20. Library, journals
21. databases, Psychological
22. clinical
23. learning

Relate

1. g
2. a
3. j
4. h
5. b
6. i
7. f
8. c
9. d
10. e

Check Your Memory

1. T
2. F
3. T
4. T

5. T
6. F
7. T
8. T
9. F
10. T
11. F
12. T
13. F
14. F
15. F
16. T
17. T
18. T
19. T
20. T
21. F
22. T
23. T

Final Survey and Review

1. Internet, network
2. World Wide Web
3. browser, browser
4. links
5. gopher
6. Transfer Protocol
7. Information Server
8. Usenet
9. Uniform Resource Locator
10. engines
11. Boolean, operators
12. AND
13. OR
14. NOT
15. PsycINFO
16. keywords, *Thesaurus*
17. Medline
18. Educational Resource
19. CD-ROM
20. Psychiatric Electronic
21. PsycLIT
22. abnormal, clinical
23. multimedia, interactive

Mastery Test

1. d (p. B3)
2. b (p. B1)
3. a (p. B2)
4. c (p. B2)
5. d (p. B5)
6. b (p. B3)
7. a (p. B3)
8. d (p. B1)
9. a (p. B5)
10. b (p. B6)